THE QUEST FOR PEACE

The Authors

J. Pérez de Cuéllar
D. Senghaas
A. Eskola
C. J. Greenhouse
K. E. Boulding
F. M. Hinsley
R. Väyrynen
A. Chubaryan
B. Marushkin
E. B. Haas
J. Delbrück
Y. Sakamoto
A. Rapoport
K. W. Deutsch
N. Choucri
Robert C. North
C. Schmidt
R. J. Johnston
J. O'Loughlin
P. J. Taylor
G. D. Deshingkar
J. A. Silva Michelena
Soedjatmoko
N. Young
E. Boulding
J. Galtung

THE QUEST FOR PEACE

Transcending Collective Violence and War
among
Societies, Cultures and States

Edited by
Raimo Väyrynen
in collaboration with
Dieter Senghaas and Christian Schmidt
ISSC Issue Group on Peace

Foreword by
Javier Pérez de Cuéllar

International Social Science Council

⑨ SAGE Publications

© International Social Science Council 1987
First published 1987

Sage Publications Ltd   SAGE Publications Inc
28 Banner Street   275 South Beverly Drive
London EC1Y 8QE   Beverly Hills, California 90212

SAGE Publications India Pvt Ltd   SAGE Publications Inc
C–236 Defence Colony   2111 West Hillcrest Street
New Delhi 110 024   Newbury Park, California 91320

British Library Cataloguing in Publication Data

The Quest for peace : transcending
  collective violence and war among
  societies, cultures and states.
  1. War   2. Peace
  I. Väyrynen, Raimo   II. Senghaas, Dieter
  III. Schmidt, Christian   IV. International
  Social Science Council
  327.1   JX1952

  ISBN 0–8039–8034–5
  ISBN 0–8039–8035–3 Pbk

Library of Congress catalog card number 87–061114

Typeset by System 4 Associates, Gerrards Cross,
Buckinghamshire
Printed in Great Britain by
J. W. Arrowsmith Ltd, Bristol

Contents

Notes on the Authors

E. Boulding is Emeritus Professor at Dartmouth College.

K. E. Boulding is Distinguished Professor of Economics, Emeritus, at the University of Colorado at Boulder.

N. Choucri is Professor of Political Science at the Massachusetts Institute of Technology and Associate Director of the Technology Development Programme at MIT.

A. Chubaryan is head of the department of modern history of West European countries of the Institute of General History, USSR Academy of Sciences.

J. Delbrück is President of the Christian Albrechts University of Kiel and Director of the Institute of International Law at Kiel University.

G. D. Deshingkar is Senior Fellow at the Centre for the Study of Developing Societies in Delhi and Programme Coordinator of the UNU Peace and Global Transformation.

K. W. Deutsch is Professor Emeritus, Harvard University.

A. Eskola is Professor of Social Psychology at the University of Tampere and Research Professor at the Academy of Finland.

J. Galtung is University Professor, University of Hawaii, Honolulu.

C. J. Greenhouse is Associate Professor of Anthropology at Cornell University.

E. B. Haas is Robson Research Professor of Government at the University of California, Berkeley.

F. H. Hinsley is Professor of St John's College, Cambridge, UK.

R. J. Johnston is Professor of Geography at the University of Sheffield.

B. Marushkin is head of the research group on peace and war of the Institute of General History, USSR Academy of Science.

Robert C. North is Emeritus Professor Political Science at Stanford University.

J. O'Loughlin is Associate Professor Geography at the University of Illinois at Urbana-Champaign.

Javier Pérez de Cuéllar is Secretary-General of the United Nations.

A. Rapoport is Professor of Peace Studies at the University of Toronto.

Y. Sakamoto is Professor of International Politics at the University of Tokyo.

C. Schmidt is Professor of Economics at the University of Paris-IX-Dauphine and President of the International Defence Economic Association.

D. Senghaas is Professor of Social Science at the University of Bremen.

J. A. Silva Michelena is Professor and Latin American Coordinator of the UNU Peace and Global Transformation Programme at the Central University of Venezuela.

Soedjatmoko is Rector of the United Nations University.

P. J. Taylor is Senior Lecturer in Geography at the University of Newcastle upon Tyne.

R. Väyrynen is Professor of International Relations at the University of Helsinki and Chairman of the ISSC Issue Group on Peace.

N. Young is Cooley Professor of Peace Studies at Colgate University, New York.

Foreword – Javier Pérez de Cuéllar, Secretary-General of the United Nations

Peace is a basic notion but its connotations and requirements in concrete situations constitute a complex subject. These can be analysed with clarity through a joint approach by scholars from the various social science disciplines. The International Social Science Council (ISSC) provides opportunities to scholars in the relevant fields to exchange ideas and collaborate in serious reflection on the issues faced in the task of preserving and enhancing world peace. *The Quest for Peace*, prepared by the Council in commemoration of the International Year of Peace, is a result of one of its commendable initiatives.

The United Nations was created out of a commitment to maintain international peace and security on durable foundations. We have seen this commitment reaffirmed by its members in their proclamation of 1986 as the International Year of Peace. To promote a better understanding of the necessities of peace, projects were launched during the Year by governments, organs and agencies of the United Nations system, non-governmental organizations and academic institutions. *The Quest for Peace* provides valuable insights about the direction that needs to be given to the continuing effort for peace.

The scholars who have contributed to this work have sought to synthesize elements and trends which are crucial from the viewpoint of not only social scientists but of every individual committed to a life of peace. There are no simple formulas; peace-building is a long and arduous task. Through concerted effort, however, and with a vision of the future which incorporates the lessons of the past, the prospects of peace can certainly be brightened.

In expressing my appreciation to the Council, I voice the hope that its work will stimulate further efforts by all concerned to overcome the difficulties of peace-building and to realize its potential as we approach the end of this historically most important century.

Javier Pérez de Cuéllar

Preface

The International Social Science Council

Peace and conflict are by their very nature social phenomena which appear in widely diverse contexts – within and between individuals, social groups and organizations, nation-states and in the world-system. Their causes and consequences are of a very heterogeneous nature. The contribution of several disciplines is needed to capture pertinent aspects of peace and conflict and to explain and understand them.

By calling on the co-operation of its member associations, which cover practically all the fields of social sciences, the ISSC has aimed to develop a transdisciplinary perspective to these phenomena. Only by systematic co-operation between economists, anthropologists, psychologists, sociologists and political scientists can the multifaceted and complex appearance of peace and conflict issues be better understood.

Following the recommendations of its Scientific Activities Committee, the Executive Committee of the ISSC at its 52nd session, which took place in Paris on 14–15 June 1984, decided to establish an Issue Group on Peace. Professor Raimo Väyrynen (representative of the International Peace Research Association on the Scientific Activities Committee) agreed to serve as chairman of the group.

In establishing this Issue Group on Peace, the ISSC also intended to contribute to the preparation and implementation of the UN International Year of Peace.

The first meeting of the Issue Group on Peace took place in Paris at Unesco House on 19–20 September 1984. Twelve ISSC member associations had appointed a representative to the Issue Group. In addition, the International Studies Association, the Academy of Sciences of the USSR, the UN Department for Disarmament Affairs, the Faculdad Latino Americana de Ciencias Sociales, the European Coordination Centre for Research and Documentation in the Social Sciences (Vienna Centre), the Centre interdisciplinaire de recherches sur la paix et d'études stratégiques (CIRPES) and the Centre d'études sociologiques were represented. Professor Raimo Väyrynen, convener of the Issue Group, chaired the meeting.

The Issue Group focused on the following three areas: relevant activities of member associations in the field of peace and conflict, opportunities to promote their mutual co-operation in this particular field and the preparation of a major book on war and its consequences in human communities.

The Issue Group unanimously agreed to start preparing a high-level, transdisciplinary study of warfare as a human institution which would

examine the causes and consequences of large-scale violence at different
social levels ranging from human consciousness to the global system. The
title of the proposed book was to be *The Quest for Peace: Transcending Collective
Violence and War among Societies, Cultures and States*.

The United Nations University, which was represented at the Issue
Group meeting by its Vice-Rector Professor K. Mushakoji, agreed to
co-operate with the ISSC in the preparation of the book by suggesting
potential contributors from Third World countries and commissioning
their papers.

Professors R. Väyrynen, D. Senghaas (representing the International
Political Science Association) and C. Schmidt (representing the Inter-
national Economic Association) were appointed as the Editorial
Committee.

Through intensive exchanges with invited contributors and thanks to
the continuous work of the Editorial Committee and the constructive
co-operation of all, the ISSC now has the pleasure of presenting the book.
It is hoped that readers will find in *The Quest for Peace* a comprehensive
presentation of advanced knowledge from different disciplines concerning
the problems of war and peace. The intention is to provide both
theoretically and substantively informed perspectives of the roots,
manifestations and consequences of collective violence in human institutions. It is also hoped that the book will contribute ideas and patterns
of action on how wars and collective violence could be transcended in
different cultural contexts, thus combining theoretical, empirical and
action-oriented approaches. It should be understood that the book brings
together authors from many different disciplines, schools of thought and
geographical regions.

The ISSC would like to thank most warmly those who took part in
this endeavour, particularly the Editorial Committee and the authors
whose contributions reflect their respective views.

The ISSC also wishes to express its gratitude to the United Nations
for the interest manifested in the preparation of the book, to the UN
University for its support and co-operation, and to Unesco for facilitating
the establishment of the ISSC Issue Group on Peace and other related
ISSC activities in the field of peace; the research leading to this publication
was in part financed by Unesco.

PART I

Theoretical Introduction

1

Transcending Collective Violence,
the Civilizing Process and
the Peace Problem

Dieter Senghaas

The transcending of collective violence will be a major task for mankind
if mankind is to survive. A failure in this respect will make many other
human endeavours fairly meaningless. Mankind, however, has never
been a coherent political entity. It neither disposes of a political order
of its own, nor does it possess a collective self-awareness, although the
latter seems to have gradually emerged at least with respect to most urgent
global problems. Transcending collective violence, therefore, remains in
the present world a context-specific problem, reflecting the political and
socio-economic heterogeneity of international society. There are some
small areas of relatively 'stable peace'; there are other areas where the
propensity to use force as a political means will probably increase; and
there are vast 'grey' areas where neither stable nor unstable peace exists
and where the prospects for peace are, to say the least, ambiguous. But
for everybody on the globe the probability of a holocaust by nuclear war,
crippling or even eliminating most of mankind, remains the most serious
and ominous danger of the present and of the foreseeable future.

Transcending collective violence and peace are, to some extent,
synonymous concepts. Peace, however, has to be defined more broadly
as a political *modus vivendi*, characterized both by the absence of direct
violence and by an increasing degree of political liberty and social justice.
Both in modern and in modernizing societies such a broad definition
is essential since according to all historical and present experience within
such societies the absence of direct violence cannot be maintained without
sustained efforts in the realization of liberty and justice. If such political
efforts are lacking, or remain insufficient, the use of direct violence is
likely to re-emerge. Only when political and social orders are considered
as fairly legitimate, do people, in general, abstain from the resort to open
violence; and only under such conditions do they accept common rules
for the peaceful processing of political conflicts. Peace in this sense is
to be understood as a civilizational achievement which is extremely
difficult to attain.

In the course of modern history the peace problem was intrinsically
linked to the nation-state formation process. Since the nation-state has

become the spatial and social unit underlying political life throughout the world, four major historical trends are still noteworthy in this context:

1. Power monopolization at ever higher social levels

In the early history of most present societies the use of violence was considered natural and legitimate. Violence was a simple means in the struggle for survival and an instrument in endless political conflicts. Belligerency was built into the political situation; it was structurally endemic, dominated by zero-sum logic, particularly in the classic case of European feudalism.

As a result of such competitive drop-out contests, more and more power centres were gradually eliminated. Over centuries, this process, replete with minor and major wars and violence, led to the emergence of internally consolidated nation-states. The development was well described by the classic authors of social science, particularly by Weber, when he characterized the modern territorial state, the final product of this secular political process, as the only remaining political entity to dispose of 'a monopoly of the legitimate use of force'.

At least in highly developed societies this monopolization of the use of violence is taken for granted in everyday life. But still some centuries ago even people in the old European nation-states that Weber had in mind in his treatise would not have understood his formula: there was no consolidated state, neither was there a monopoly of violence. Feuds were waged by expediency, depending on the economic situation and on the whims and will of power-holders. And most people, living in spatially and mentally confined localities, probably considered such a situation as an inescapable fate.

The uncontested state monopoly of violence, and even more so the rule of law, were relatively late political achievements in the history of modern states. It took centuries until the use of violence became an exclusive prerogative of the state, and it took even longer until the activities of the state became limited by law at least with respect to internal affairs and embryonically in international relations. As a result individuals of whatever class, status and social group were deprived of their individual right to resort to the use of violence. Although restricted to internal affairs and for a long time biased in favour of privileged classes, this process was one major contribution to the transcending of collective violence in modern times.

2. Emerging socio-economic interdependencies caused by the development of modern national economies

Modern economies, particularly market economies, are characterized by a self-extending division of labour leading to ever expanding macro-economic circuits. Compared with small-scale subsistence economies, these modern economies are extremely impersonal and abstract entities built upon innumerable interlinkages and interdependencies. Their operation depends upon a high degree of self-control by individuals, social groups and institutions. Self-control presupposed reliable constraints on affect-led behaviour. Thus, under the conditions of self-differentiating societies, the use of violence tends to be mitigated in the long run. There seems to be a direct correlation between the degree of their complexity and the dysfunctionality of physical, not necessarily structural, violence.

The power-monopoly process and the spreading of the market economy were systematically interrelated: both are based on competitive behaviour. Moreover, growing market economies needed expanding as well as legally and institutionally consolidated domains within which they could operate unimpeded. In turn, the emerging dominant political powers were dependent on the new surplus potential of the market economy as a dynamically growing tax base. Tapping this resource, such powers succeeded in extending and entrenching their political position.

3. The erosion of power monopolies by democratization
In functionally differentiated societies (*and only there*) monopolization processes on top reliably provoke at the bottom the persistent demand for participation. There are many examples – the history of capital–labour relations is a case in point. The more people have become deprived of their means of production – as they are in modern economies to a large extent – the more they have tried to organize themselves politically to fight for a fairer share of the economic product and for their legitimate political rights. In general, democratizing or socializing political monopolies has always been an extremely painful political conflict, in its early phases widely interspersed with acts of violence. Where democratization succeeded, multiple institutionalized forms of conflict articulation, conflict management and conflict resolution became a differentiated basis for the processing of correspondingly more complex political conflicts. State bureaucrats in state-socialist societies in which the degree of monopolization of the political and economic powers is historically unprecedented will still face such a challenge of democratization in the future as recent events in such societies have demonstrated.

4. Imposed self-control or affect-control
Power monopolization and the integration of people into wide-ranging impersonal economic circuits do not leave the psychology of individuals unaffected. There is a symbiotic interrelation between these processes on the one side and the degree of affect-control imposed upon individuals by such political and social circumstances on the other side. This is the result of unplanned social change at the macro-level of the political and social order.

At a very late stage of this development, Freud's theory of culture shed some light into the interrelation between the restructuring of the macro-level of state, society and economy, and the restructuring of the micro-level of the individual psyche. Being exposed to, and socialized into, modern societies, individuals ('the ego') are forced to skilfully steer between the drives and the needs of the individual ('the pleasure principle') and the constraints of reality ('the reality principle'). The status quo between the individual and the society and within the individual arising from such conflicts necessarily remains fragile since there is no natural equilibrium between the two principles. Regression from already reached levels of self-control to a predominantly affect-led behaviour remains an ever-present danger, as is demonstrated in this century by inherently irrational political movements on a mass scale (like Nazism in Germany). But, in general, regression on a massive scale has not occurred too often – a phenomenon which may reflect, besides moral inhibitions, the considerable dysfunctionality of violence in modern societies.

Violence consciously initiated by individuals and social groups re-emerges only under conditions of a growing inauthenticity of the political and social order, for example, if there develops an increasing discrepancy between new social needs and the malperformance of an unresponsive political system. The state monopoly of violence is, then, challenged by new social forces, and in the extreme case time becomes ripe for revolution. But even then the early reconstitution of a newly legitimized state monopoly of violence becomes a prerequisite for the political self-steering of the new political order and for the viability of individuals within a new social context. What for a short time is considered functional, soon becomes dysfunctional again.

The logic of these development processes was extremely dialectical. Power monopolization led both to the pacification of societies, states and individuals, *and* to the exacerbation of power contests at ever higher social levels, finally reaching the world level. The open use of direct violence within societies seems to become exceptional in the long run, but even as these societies have developed, international society has remained potentially anarchical. The expansion of modern economies in terms of a widening division of labour and of growing factor productivities led to functional and institutional networks at the national, and increasingly at the international, level. But at the same time, more efficient economies became the basis for a more efficient production of more sophisticated weaponry from low-calibre weapons to nuclear arsenals. But this development has, in turn, resulted in a political situation where no rational use of force among the major contestants, at least with respect to nuclear, chemical and the most advanced conventional weapons, can be imagined any more. The unprecedented destructive potential of such weapons has, more than anything else, contributed to their gradual political delegitimization. But in general there seems to develop a connection between the quest for peace and the quest for further democratization and social justice, pretty much along the lines as originally prognosticated in typically liberal theories.

The operation of the monopoly mechanism consisting in self-extending processes of power centralization and concentration did not end at the frontiers of the classic nation-state. Even when nation-states were not yet fully consolidated internally, the monopolization process began to take effect at the international level, in international politics. And today, the essence of international politics is still, rightly or wrongly, understood by many as a continuation of a secular power conflict. In fact, from the seventeenth to the twentieth century various schemes and policies aimed at the balancing of power among nations have been theoretically conceptualized and some of them have even been tested in practice. They were considered as means of containing the threat of one nation, or of an alliance of nations, becoming a hegemonical power, e.g. a world-power monopolist. Actually, the major modern wars, at least the Napoleonic wars, and the First and Second World Wars were manifestations of such contests on a world scale. After the Second World War the global context culminated in the bipolarity between the United States and the Soviet Union, incorporating an international conflict formation which had dominated the world political structure for some two or three decades and which is still, at least in its military dimension, dominating international politics. There are good reasons to assume that only the threat of a catastrophic nuclear war has prevented this most recent drop-out contest to become an open and disastrous military conflict. This persistent threat has forced the two contesting powers to adopt a competitive yet peaceful coexistence. Explicitly or implicitly, it has been considered by both powers as a continuation of the political and ideological contest without resorting to open military violence at least in their bilateral relations. However, the Clausewitzian revival of nuclear-war winning strategies, which have been formulated since the middle of the 1950s, clearly demonstrates the persistence of the class monopoly mechanism regardless of its obvious illusionary implications in present international politics, particularly in the military field. To use arms control as a means of steering the arms race in mutual agreement upwards, not downwards, as has been the case within the last thirty years, is another illustration for such persistence. The same is true of the rhetoric about the political aspirations of major powers to be the first in the world or to operate in international politics from an unambiguous position of strength.

But if the world is no longer ready to accept one nation as a hegemonical power, perhaps because of the existence of nuclear weapons and as a result of far-reaching changes in international society, what then are the prospects for the future development of global society and for peace?

According to present evidence the contest between the two major powers, the United States and the Soviet Union, which contains the most serious danger for mankind, will most likely continue as if there could be a final political victory of one over the other in some meaningful sense. The present probability of a voluntary mutual accommodation is very low since there are still too many factors and forces which keep this contest alive. The logic of the situation is now not very different from the drop-out contests on a smaller scale some decades and centuries ago – pretentious rival ideologies; political, economic and social interests geared to the continuation of the contest; and psychological needs in search of self-confirmation. Such forces operate at the highest level, the world-wide contest, as they have operated in modern history at lower levels. The differences between the past and the present experience are not too conspicuous; they lie in particular in the far more potentially catastrophic consequences of the present world contest. The probability of these factors and forces receding – of self-correction – is very small. At present the prospects for a self-encapsulation of this international conflict formation are no better than they were when such a self-encapsulation was suggested some two decades ago as a desirable and likely way out.

What are, then, the prospects for deep changes in the East–West conflict as a result of structural changes in the wider environment of the two major contestants?

Some hope exists in this respect. For years there have been clear signs of a gradual erosion of the spheres of influence of the two major powers, the United States and the Soviet Union. Among nations belonging to the West, Japan in particular, but also Western Europe, have succeeded – without a political programme and simply driven by the imperatives of successful capitalist competition – in undermining the once predominant post-Second World War economic position of the United States. Such a shift in the economic position leading to a relative decline of the hegemonical power and to upward mobility in the world-economy of new powers has been a regular feature in modern times, at least among capitalist economies. At present, it is not yet quite clear what the future political configuration among these nations will be. In particular, it is an open question whether the relations between the United States, Japan and Western Europe – the OECD economies – will remain relatively open and fairly balanced, or whether the present multipolar intra-capitalist configuration will be replaced by a more unipolar order. However, a continuation of present trends towards an even further multi-polarization seems likely.

Within her own sphere of influence, the Soviet Union has particularly been challenged in Eastern Europe and by other communist states like China. This challenge is probably more fundamental than the conflict arising from shifting power structures and economic changes within the West, since it affects the ideological premise of state-socialist societies. But there is a further reason. State-socialist societies have been structurally far more rigid than market societies. Already seventy-five years ago Weber noted the unprecedented degree of monopolization of power in state-socialist societies, reflecting an extreme centralization of politics and economics, respectively, and the merging of the political and economic spheres. Adjusting to growing social complexities and new social needs is, therefore, far more difficult in such societies than in the less centralized. This complexity, however, continues to grow as a result of state-induced development and as a structural consequence of social mobilization derived from development efforts. It is, by now, quite clear that a flexible political adaptation to continually changing socio-economic conditions is an inescapable prerequisite for further socialist growth and development. As in Western development, democratization would be a contribution to the solution of the problem, but the broadening of political and social participation seems to be as difficult to achieve in this context as it used to be in the century-long historical experiences of Western societies.

The real challenges with long-term political implications for the present world powers have developed from changes in the social structure of international society in general. This structure is undergoing a fundamental change, and the total picture of international society – Third World countries included – is already very different from what it used to be thirty to fifty years ago. Over the decades the share of the world population able to read and write has steadily grown. With very few exceptions most of mankind will soon live in urban settings. Today in 50 percent of Third World countries peasants are a minority of the total labour force. Notwithstanding the serious problems in the industrialization processes within most Third World countries, industrialization will continue with its own impetus. People who are now able to read and write, who are no longer peasants, no longer isolated and trapped in subsistence economies and who live in urban agglomerations and are dependent on employment opportunities outside their own household economy, sooner or later become politically self-conscious and gradually able to organize their self-perceived interests, politicizing their social, economic and cultural needs.

Such structural changes have been the basis for the spread of nationalism in the world. As in the past, nationalism at present emerges from rapidly changing yet unconsolidated and conflict-loaded social conditions as they have spread all over the Third World in recent decades. There has been enough economic growth to induce further social mobilization, but for well-known reasons not many development efforts will be success stories in the short term so that more and more political and social orders will prove unviable.

This is the social context within which in the Third World multiple kinds of *coup d'états*, civil wars, conventional wars and arms races will take place, whether they are supported from the exterior or not. And in such a political context major powers have tended to intervene openly or clandestinely in the political affairs of other nations. However, nationalism emerging from social mobilization and politicization counteracts the hegemonic aspirations of major powers. These powers have the potential for unprecedented destruction. In this sense, they appear to be omnipotent. But the actual political use-value of their destructive potential is relatively small. And there seem to be diminishing and increasingly counter-productive returns from the actual use of military potential by major powers – a phenomenon deeply reflecting the growing self-assertiveness and autonomy of more and more societies in the world. This is one of the most important political developments within the present international society, although, as a rule, it does not yet emerge from the political and socio-economic viability of internally consolidated new societies and states, but simply from their growing unmanageability from the exterior and sometimes even from the interior. It is this chaos-power which works against the self-defined imperatives of major powers and which will increasingly contribute to undermine their geopolitical aspirations.

This does not mean that there will be an end to geopolitics in the immediate future. There will probably be a short-lived era of reasserted geopolitics based in the world-wide competitive interests of both major powers. The prospects for its success have, however, already considerably diminished, but this political context will still be a breeding ground for many types of interventionist and violent conflicts. In some sense these will, however, be hopeless running fights against an inescapable trend in modern history. Yet fights in retreat are still fights, and this will give no consolidation to their victims.

Are there positive prospects for transcending collective violence in international society as a result of increasing interdependencies?

International or world society has not yet reached a development stage (and it will not reach such a stage in the immediate future) where interdependencies are numerous, dense and balanced enough to mitigate potentially violent conflicts. Overall, there seems to be no clear correlation between growing interdependencies and the occurrence of violent conflicts in international relations. But this correlation looks different if it is disaggregated with respect to specific contexts.

Positive interdependencies have grown in some areas, for example, among the highly industrialized Western countries. Their major conflicts of interest are usually solved without any resort to the open use of force. In the past three decades these countries have become more and more 'trading states'. Although it should not be assumed that the use of force can be totally excluded, there are relatively good prospects for stable peace in this area.

Between the two major powers in the present world mainly negative interdependencies have been created. This is demonstrated by the ongoing qualitative and quantitative arms race between the United States and the Soviet Union. Whether this context will remain self-contained by mutual deterrence is an open question which is hotly debated by the proponents of deterrence and the representatives of the peace movement. Nevertheless, positive transactions in terms of trade and communication between the members of the two major alliances are of some use in stabilizing the present political situation, but they are still extremely limited and, because of systemic differences, they cannot be extended much further.

Interdependencies between developed and developing countries are usually asymmetrical. This reflects the well-known *dependencia* situation:

linkages are unbalanced, the power differentials remain considerable, and in most cases the welfare gap has even increased. Prospects for the evolution of fairly symmetrical relations are limited mostly to a few newly industrializing countries, particularly in the Far East.

Finally, most states and societies in the present world still do not and will not interact with each other to any considerable degree. This fact reflects the unsystemic character of large segments of international society, at least its relatively loose structure.

Thus, a picture of international society is quite multifaceted, corresponding to its considerable heterogeneity. The changes of transcending collective violence are quite different in its different contexts. In each of them specific issues predominate: political *integration* among Western countries; *détente* and *co-operation* between East and West; *development* in North–South relations; and *co-operation* or *collective self-reliance* within the South.

In none of these contexts do present developments look promising. Political integration has been stagnating for years, which is deeply disappointing (probably more so than is justified) to the proponents of 'functionalism'. The détente process has experienced a serious setback. There is even the danger of a second cold war between East and West. In development policy, there have been so many failures that even remarkable successes like the steady increase of life-expectancy, the spread of education, health and sanitary facilities, have remained underrated. But in most cases other elementary aims of development policy like the creation of viable national economies have persistently been missed. And most attempts to get Third World countries together in order to promote collective self-reliance got stuck during their first steps.

By way of conclusion three further observations may be added:

1. In some sense the present contest between the two world powers and their military alliances should be understood as a logical extrapolation of one typical feature of modern, particularly of European, history: as a further stage in a secular series of power conflicts beginning at least one millennium ago and operating at ever higher levels. Perhaps the bipolar confrontation between the United States and the Soviet Union will be the last contest, either because the world will be blown up or because both contenders will remain rational enough to curtail their aspirations and to accommodate each other in time. But there is another possibility: the present international conflict formation may be superseded by fresh power constellations, now still unimaginable, but not totally unlikely within the next fifty years or so, comprising new major states like Japan, Brazil and China. At least it may be wise to assume that the logic of the past will not simply and totally end with the political confrontation of the two present world powers.

What will happen will depend very much on the members of international society below the top level, particularly on their readiness or unwillingness to function as patient political playgrounds for the proxy contests of powers with hegemonical aspirations. The more countries resist such a definition of their role, the less chance there will be for major powers to fight out their contests outside their bilateral relations.

In general, one of the promising development trends within the present international society consists in the prospect that considerable parts of the globe have already become, and more will become, inhospitable arenas for the hegemonic conflicts of major powers. In international politics this will lead to a situation fundamentally different compared with 100 or even 50 years ago when major powers could still pursue their imperialist policies in foreign continents according to their own discretion and with relatively low costs.

2. For good or bad, the logic of the history of the modern European nation-state will repeat itself in most societies outside the present Western and Eastern developed world. There will be a comparable insistence on the political sovereignty of individual nation-states. Dominant political forces in new societies will pursue policies to overcome internal ethnic and linguistic cleavages by strategies of nation-wide assimilation and amalgamation, and state bureaucracies will emerge as institutions with entrenched political self-interests. But there are also major differences: in the classic nation-states of the West development went, at least to some degree, from the bottom up: from small-scale power conflicts to the formation of a central state authority; from competitive capitalism to organized capitalism; from regional to national economies; and from national economies to the world-economy. Development proceeded step by step, gradually integrating originally incoherent territorial areas into coherent societies. A comparable development could not have taken place in Third World countries because of colonial and imperialist penetration which, in particular, contributed to the formation of structurally heterogeneous economies and societies, and in the extreme cases to the split of dependent countries into a monocultural enclave and a traditional sector. This colonial heritage is still to be felt in most developing societies and it has made development an extremely difficult, though not impossible, political task, as quite different experiences show. However, one can take it for granted that under such conditions the conflict potential of development processes will be far greater than in the European experience. The probability of direct violence will therefore be very high. And one must face the problem that violence will be a persistent social phenomenon in these countries until they reach internal viability by socio-economic coherence and by a political balance between new state authorities (mostly the state bureaucracies) and political as well as social participation, e.g. democratization. Taking a broad range of historical and contemporary experiences into consideration, one must assume that such a goal cannot be reached within a short time, and even underlying a long-term perspective such a goal will be reached only if development policy meets the challenge of the most serious problems of Third World countries adequately. Only then will there be a change that the most serious potential for violence will be eliminated, and that political conflicts will be mitigated by means of accepted and legitimized institutional procedures.

3. As argued at the beginning, the civilizing process contributing to the transcending of violence has been the result of long-term changes in the political structure and in the socio-economic basis of societies and individuals. But in the course of time cultural changes have become more and more important, contributing to the moral illegitimization of violence, or at least to the casuistic specification of instances when the use of force is still considered to be legitimate within societies as well as among them. In this respect international law has made great progress in this century.

Moreover, the danger of an all-out nuclear war has sensitized a wider public and also many academic disciplines. In some of them serious efforts to analyse contemporary war and peace problems have been made recently for the first time.

The search for alternative modes of conflict management and conflict resolution has also become a legitimate academic undertaking, and some alternatives have even become the basis for powerful political programmes.

These new concepts will have to be turned into dependable practical imperatives if mankind is to survive by overcoming the logic of potentially violent power contests. Whether mankind will become civilized is the most existential question of the present and the future. The difficulty of the task can be seen in everyday life, from very close by to the most distant international arenas.

References

Amin, Samir (1979) *Classe et nation dans l'histoire et la crise contemporaine*. Paris: Les Editions de Minuit.

Aron, Raymond (1962) *Paix et guerre entre les nations*. Paris: Calmann-Lévy.

Bartlett, C. J. (1984) *The Global Conflict 1880–1970. The International Rivalry of the Great Powers*. London, New York: Longman.

Beer, Francis A. (1981) *Peace Against War. The Ecology of International Violence*. San Francisco: W. H. Freeman.

Braudel, Fernand (1985) *La dynamique du capitalisme*. Paris: Les Editions Arthaud.

Bull, Hedley (1977) *The Anarchical Society. A Study of Order in World Politics*. Basingstoke: Macmillan Education.

Bull, Hedley and Watson, Adam (eds) (1984) *The Expansion of International Society*. Oxford: Clarendon Press.

Buzan, Barry (1983) *People, States and Fear. The National Security Problem in International Relations*. Sussex: Wheatsheaf Books.

Craig, Gordon A. and George, Alexander L. (1983) *Force and Statecraft. Diplomatic Problems of Our Time*. New York and Oxford: Oxford University Press.

Czempiel, Ernst Otto (1986) *Friedensstrategien*. Paderborn: Schoeningh Verlag.

Dehio, Ludwig (1948) *Gleichgewicht oder Hegemonie. Betrachtungen über ein Grundproblem der neueren Staatengeschichte*. Krefeld: Scherpe Verlag.

Deutsch, Karl, W. (1966) *Nationalism and Social Communication. An Inquiry into the Foundations of Nationality*. Cambridge and London: MIT Press.

Deutsch, Karl W. and Senghaas, Dieter (1971) 'A Framework for a Theory of War and Peace', in Albert Lepawsky, Edward H. Buehrig and Harold D. Lasswell (eds), *The Search for World Order. Studies by Students and Colleagues of Quincy Wright*, pp. 23–46. New York: Appleton-Century-Crofts.

Deutsch, Karl, W. and Senghaas, Dieter (1973) 'The Steps to War: A Survey of System Levels, Decision Stages, and Research Results', in *Sage International Yearbook of Foreign Policy Studies*, Vol. 1, pp. 275–329. Beverly Hills and London: Sage Publications.

Deutsch, Karl W. and Senghaas, Dieter (1975) 'The Fragile Sanity of States: A Theoretical Analysis', in Martin Kilson (ed.) *New States in the Modern World*, pp. 200–44. Cambridge and London: Havard University Press.

Deutsch, Karl W. et al. (1968) *Political Community and the North Atlantic Area. International Organization in the Light of Historical Experience*. Princeton: Princeton University Press.

Elias, Norbert (1982) *The Civilizing Process*, Vol. 2: *State Formation and Civilization*. Oxford: Basil Blackwell.

Elias, Norbert (1985) *Humana Conditio*. Frankfurt: Suhrkamp Verlag.

Etzioni, Amitai (1968) *The Active Society. A Theory of Societal and Political Processes*. New York: Free Press.

Falk, Richard A. (1971) *This Endangered Planet. Prospects and Proposals for Human Survival*. New York: Random House.

Falk, Richard A. (1975) *A Study of Future Worlds*. New York: Free Press.

Falk, Richard A. and Kim, Samuel S. (eds) (1980) *The War System: An Interdisciplinary Approach*. Boulder: Westview Press.

Falk, Richard A., Kim, Samuel S. and Mendlovitz, Saul H. (eds) (1982) *Toward a Just World Order*. Boulder: Westview Press.

Freud, Sigmund (1949) *Civilization and Its Discontent*. London: Hogarth Press.

Galtung, Johan (1980) *The True Worlds. A Transnational Perspective*. New York: Free Press.

Gantzel, Klaus Jürgen (1972) *System und Akteur. Beiträge zur vergleichenden Kriegsursachenforschung*. Düsseldorf: Bertelsmann Universitatsverlag.

Gantzel, Klaus Jürgen and Meyer-Stamer, Jörg (eds) (1986) *Die Kriege nach dem Zweiten Weltkrieg bis 1984. Daten und erste Analysen*. München, Köln, London: Weltforum Verlag.

Giddens, Anthony (1985) *The Nation-State and Violence*. Vol. 2 of *A Contemporary Critique of Historical Materialism*. Cambridge: Polity Press.

Gilpin, Robert (1981) *War and Change in World Politics*. Cambridge: Cambridge University Press.

Hall, John A. (1985) *Powers and Liberties. The Causes and Consequences of the Rise of the West*. Harmondsworth: Penguin Books.

Hinsley F. H. (1967) *Power and the Pursuit of Peace. Theory and Practice in the History of Relations Between States*. Cambridge: Cambridge University Press.

Hintze, Otto (1964) *Soziologie und Geschichte. Gesammelte Abhandlungen zur Soziologie, Politik und Theorie der Geschichte*. Göttingen: Vandenhoeck & Ruprecht.

Horvat, Branko (1982) *The Political Economy of Socialism. A Marxist Social Theory*. Armonk, NY: M. E. Sharpe.

Howard, Michael (1976) *War in European History*. Oxford, New York, London: Oxford University Press.

Jaguaribe, Helio (1985) *El nuevo escenario internacional*. Mexico: Fondo de Cultura Económica.

Jones, E. L. (1981) *The European Miracle, Environments, Economies and Geopolitics in the History of Europe and Asia*. Cambridge: Cambridge University Press.

Keohane, Robert O. (1984) *After Hegemony. Cooperation and Discord in the World Political Economy*. Princeton: Princeton University Press.

Krasner, Stephen D. (1985) *Structural Conflict. The World Against Global Liberalism*. Berkeley, Los Angeles, London: University of California Press.

Krippendorff, Ekkehart (1985) *Krieg und Staat. Die historische Logik politischer Unvernunft*. Frankfurt: Suhrkamp Verlag.

Levi, Werner (1981) *The Coming End of War*. Beverly Hills, London: Sage Publications.

Link, Werner (1984) *The East–West Conflict. The Organisation of International Relations in the 20th Century*. Leamington Spa, Dover: Berg Publishers.

McNeill, William H. (1982) *The Pursuit of Power*. Chicago: University of Chicago Press.

Nef, John U. (1950) *Western Civilization Since the Renaissance. Peace, War, Industry and the Arts*. New York, Evanston: Harper and Row.

Nove, Alec (1983) *The Economics of Feasible Socialism*. London: George Allen and Unwin.

Parker, Geoffrey (1985) *Western Geopolitical Thought in the Twentieth Century*. London, Sydney: Croom Helm.

Predöhl, Andreas (1971) *Aussenwirtschaft*. Göttingen: Vandenhoeck & Ruprecht.

Rosencrance, Richard (1985) *The Rise of the Trading State. Commerce and Conquest in the Modern World*. New York: Basic Books.

Senghaas, Dieter (1974) 'Towards an Analysis of Threat Policy in International Relations', in *German Political Studies*, Vol. 1, pp. 59–103. Beverly Hills, London: Sage Publications.

Senghaas, Dieter (1985) *The European Experience. A Historical Critique of Development Theory*. Leamington Spa, Dover: Berg Publishers.

Small, Melvin and Singer, David J. (1982) *Resort to Arms. International and Civil Wars, 1816–1980*. Beverly Hills, London, New Delhi: Sage Publications.

Smith, Tony (1981) *The Pattern of Imperialism. The United States, Great Britain, and the Late-Industrializing World Since 1815*. Cambridge: Cambridge University Press.

Taylor, Peter J. (1985) *Political Geography: World-Economy, Nation-State and Locality*. London: Longman.

Thompson, William R. (ed.) (1983) *Contending Approaches to World System Analysis*. Beverly Hills, London, New Delhi: Sage Publications.

Tilly, Charles (ed.) (1975) *The Formation of National States in Western Europe*. Princeton: Princeton University Press.

Toynbee, Arnold J. (1950) *War and Civilisation*. Selected by Albert V. Fowler from *A Study of History*. London: Oxford University Press.

Triepel, Heinrich (1974) *Die Hegemonie. Ein Buch von führenden Staaten*. Aalen: Scienta Verlag.

Wallensteen, Peter (1973) *Structure and War. On International Relations 1920–1968*. Stockholm: Rabén & Slögren.

Wallerstein, Immanuel (1984) *The Politics of the World-Economy. The States, the Movements, and the Civilizations*. Cambridge: Cambridge University Press.

Weber, Max (1956) *Soziologie. Weltgeschichtliche Analysen. Politik*. Stuttgart: Alfred Kröner Verlag.

Wittfogel, Karl A. (1957) *Oriental Despotism. A Comparative Study of Total Power*. New Haven, London: Yale University Press.

Wright, Quincy (1965) *A Study of War*. Chicago, London: University of Chicago Press.

PART II

Violence, Human Consciousness and Social Evolution

2

Human Consciousness
and Violence

Antti Eskola

Animal aggression and human violence

It has often been assumed that the roots of war and collective violence
lie somewhere in the biological mechanisms that animals and man have
in common. The favourite explanation has been some sort of a 'destructive
instinct', which Sigmund Freud dealt with in his famous letter to Albert
Einstein in 1932 (Freud, 1959); or 'a genetic commitment to territory',
which has also been proposed as a major cause of war (e.g. Ardrey, 1966).
But what does modern scientific psychology have to say about these
genetic explanations?

In their textbook of general psychology, Brown and Herrnstein (1975)
discuss aggression under an interesting heading: 'Aggression: from the
Albino Mouse to the American Soldier'. This, for the social psychologist
concerned with the interrelationships of aggression, human violence and
war, immediately invites two critical questions. First, is it possible to
uncover the true essence of human violence by studies of the aggressiveness of albino mice, or do these two phenomena have so little in common
that they should be dealt with separately? Second, is it possible to say
anything relevant about the nature of war on the basis of studies concerning characteristics of individuals, or is war a sociological phenomenon
that cannot be explained by individual behaviour? Shouldn't it be obvious
that there are two important things that distinguish the American soldier
from the albino mouse: he is a human being and a soldier.

It soon becomes clear, however, that Brown and Herrnstein are not
ignorant of the differences between aggressive behaviour and social action,
or the differences between animal and man. They reserve the word
'aggression' for reference to attack on conspecifics and thus exclude from
the concept activities such as predation, shooting grouse for food or sport,
bug extermination, or slaughtering animals as a vocation. Omitting to
say anything about war as employed by man, they point out that in
animal fighting, behaviour is quite different when directed against a
conspecific from when it is directed against another species: 'Giraffes use
their relatively harmless short horns against one another [Eibl-Eibesfeldt,
1970], but their sharp hooves on predators. Rattlesnakes rear up and
hit each other with their heads until one of them tires'. . .; they bite you
and me. Oryx antelope do not use their sharp horns against one another

but rather bump heads, avoiding the easy, probably lethal stab into the exposed side; but when the antagonist is a lion, they try to use the horns to stab' (Brown and Herrnstein, 1975: 211).

We could imagine that human beings also have a non-lethal weapon of their own: words. It is useless to try and catch a rabbit or stop a charging rhinoceros by the power of words, but words are a good weapon for subjecting another person and for hurting his feelings; not, however, for killing him. So inference from animal to human behaviour would suggest that words are the weapon people use in fights against each other, whilst shotguns and the like would be kept only for hunting. However, this is not how it goes; the deadliest weapons of human invention are used precisely for fighting other people. In this chapter we shall try to find out why, as far as aggression is concerned, animal behaviour does *not* predict the action of humans.

Brown and Herrnstein are also convinced in the end that there is no direct connection between aggressive mice and fighting soldiers, nor indeed do they make any attempt in their chapter on aggression to explain the causation of war. They only use the research results on the American soldier in the Second World War for discussing what is known as relative deprivation and how it affects dissatisfaction (as well as aggressiveness). Kirsti Lagerspetz (1982), a Finnish psychologist and expert in breeding aggressive and non-aggressive mouse generations, is also unwilling to draw direct conclusions concerning human violence and warfare on the basis of her animal experiments. When the emotional aspect of aggression is taken into account, she says, it becomes evident that war does not always involve aggression – far from it. The reasons why weapons are produced and used in international conflicts are to be found somewhere else than in aggression.

Consciousness and human activity

So what is it that makes human violence against other humans different from the intraspecific aggression of animals? What, more generally, distinguishes man from inanimate nature, a plant, and from an animal?

In an attempt to answer this question, Schumacher (1977: 15–25) calls the inanimate matter or 'the mineral level' m, and the plant level $m + x$. The x that is added represents the mysterious and multidimensional factor that is called life. Moving up from plant to animal, there is another addition of powers, which Schumacher refers to by y: consciousness. And finally when we move from animal to man, z is included: consciousness recoiling upon itself. So according to Schumacher it is possible to recognize consciousness in animals, but 'self-awareness' only in man $(m + x + y + z)$. However, it is easy to see that these cannot be the only differences between animal and plant, or man and animal. For example, a plant is characterized by more or less stationary existence; it has to obtain its food from where it stands, and it is dependent on the humidity, light and heat of its habitat. Animals have organs of locomotion and can thus move around in search of food, but at the same time they can also make better use of their environment. So while the plant is totally dependent on its habitat, the animal is to some extent a subject of its own life.

Human subjects enjoy even greater independence of their immediate environment than animals, and they are also better equipped to control their own life. A human being is also a personality with a complex motivational structure and many attachments to other people through a highly developed language. Thus people can avail themselves of the experience of earlier generations and of the various tools they have developed, which importantly adds to their independence of biological heritage. Schumacher's formula $(m + x + y + z)$ actually gives an erroneous picture of man because the appearance of factor z in evolution brings about changes at the preceding level $(m + x + y)$. When man acquired reliable fire-making techniques, learned how to build huts and to make clothes, he could move into colder climates without having to wait for nature to develop a thick hair and layer of fat to provide him with protection from the cold. Brown and Herrnstein (1975: 174) write that 'Mankind's genius for social innovation cushions us from the press of evolution, at least in comparison with creatures whose only defence against extinction is biological'. They add that 'Our species is unlikely to grow wings, now that it has airplanes, helicopters, and spaceships'.[1]

In short, animals are guided by instincts, humans by consciousness. Very little of what people do, whether good or bad, is automatic 'behaviour', or direct instinctual response to stimuli. The most important part of what they do is social activity mediated by consciousness; activity that is distinguished by meaning, which it obtains from the actor's relationships with other human individuals and which can be given verbal expression. Part of this meaningful social activity is automatic in the sense that it is not continuously reflected upon; but if problems emerge in the flow of activity, it can without delay be taken under conscious reflection (cf. Uznadze, 1966: 109–19). Also, part of this activity is of a kind where the motives are not always clear to the actor himself. This area is a particular concern of psychoanalysis.

Normally, however, people reminisce about the past, analyse the present, make plans for the future. In doing so they use thought categories and mental representations – which with lesser or greater accuracy can be expressed in verbal form – selected from among the immense reserves of culture largely on the basis of their relationships with other individuals. They may develop these representations according to their specific needs, and new useful forms that are given in this process to the representations are deposited back into the reserves for future use. It is clear that under-lying all this is a biological basis, but because human activity cannot be reduced to this basis, the psychologist concerned with human activity can bracket this off (cf. Davidson, 1980: 259); this irreducibility also applies to violence (see Chorover, 1980).

It is useful to illustrate these concepts by looking at Frankl's account of his survival in a Nazi concentration camp. When interned to Auschwitz, Frankl was dispossessed of a manuscript that was ready for publication. He believes that his deep ambition to rewrite the manuscript actually helped him survive: he kept working at it every day, little by little, and thus found a meaning to his life. Just any kind of 'behaviour' would hardly have helped. If the sentries had made him scribble nonsensical words on pieces of paper and then destroy them, he might not have survived; on the contrary, this is one of the many methods of breaking a prisoner mentally. It is crucial for survival that activity has some meaning ('writing a book'), which it obtains from the relationship with other human individuals (such as the prospective readers of the book or the scientific community). What is noteworthy here is that by his imagination man can create things that then have a profound influence in his life. Ernst Bloch (1980) includes this idea in his philosophy with the concept 'not-yet', referring to something that 'as yet is unsure and unsolved, but for this reason is not out of the world'; just like the book that for Frankl was only a distant dream, but which still had a great impact on his life.[2]

All that has been said above is also relevant with regard to violence. For instance, it may well apply to humans also that it is difficult to kill a member of the same species. However, by active mental work it is possible to overcome the weakened instinctive barrier: it is easy to imagine that killing is done for the universal cause of putting an end to all wars, or to building a just and free world. Likewise, people can imagine that the 'enemy' belongs to a completely different species – and thus that killing is not actually violence directed against someone of the same species. For example, by adopting the name of wolf, a clan could express its unity: all clan members are alike, but differ from other clans like wolves differ from foxes or moose. Tribal wars were waged as if they were between species rather than within a species. Modern war-propaganda works in precisely the same way in trying to support individual imagination and to make it easier to use violence.

Violence in society and in individual consciousness

An historical overview

Man is a product of the process of biological evolution; but his development is still continuing as an historical evolution. Even during the comparatively short period of time from the Middle Ages till today, there have been important changes in the role of conscious deliberation in human behaviour, as well as in the forms of violence that man uses against other men.

Violence, aggression and sexual cruelty were everyday events in medieval Europe. Anything that belonged to the enemy would be destroyed, tortured or ravished, but at the same time being caught by the enemy often meant a slow, painful death (Elias 1982: 236–7). People enjoyed watching a living creature suffer; for example, in sixteenth-century Paris it was one of the festive pleasures of Midsummer Day to burn alive a dozen or two cats (Elias 1978: 203). Children watched their parents have sex, and one of their amusements was to watch public executions. On the other hand, children often fell victim to adult violence or sexual desires. Indeed, deMause (1974) characterizes the whole history of childhood as a nightmare from which we have only recently begun to wake. Given the statistics and horrifying reports that Masson (1984) cites in evidence of the cruelty that children in many places were exposed to as late as the nineteenth century, it is easy to agree with deMause.

Medieval man also tended to express his emotions more openly than we are prone to do. For example, people wept more easily than we do, both in happiness and in sorrow, says Le Roy Ladurie (1978: 139) in his study describing a small fourteenth-century mountain village in France. Renvall's (1949) study of trial records from sixteenth-century Finland show that people would also often get violent with no warning at all. The inner world responsible for putting a curb on responses, Renvall says, was still relatively undeveloped in sixteenth-century man. His responses were based on immediate observations, and if there were sudden changes in the environment, his response would be sudden too. In the words of the extensive English summary in Renvall's book:

> Finnish 16th century man was not an independent individual, but a member of a community, very closely tied to his social environment. His life in general was for the most part the spontaneous community life of relatively primit've man...One of the things that linked 16th century man with his environm nt was his highly emotional, *affective attitude*. He was never just an onlooker; he took up an emotional attitude towards everything that entered the sphere of his observations. He was specially sensitive to things that had a disturbing effect on his activities and aspirations. The equilibrium of his mind, supposing a mental state like that existed, was easily disturbed; his weak power of reflection went to the winds and affective indignation took hold of him...On the other hand, 16th century man was bound by strong ties to the world around him because of the fact that *he lived mainly in the world of his perceptions*. His own inner world, the world of his thoughts, had very little self-sufficiency in comparison with his perceptions of the outer world. Consequently, he was far more a part of the field formed by himself and his environment than a separate individual, acting according to the requirements of his own mental world. (Renvall, 1949: 201–1, original emphasis)

An important historical process which brought on changes in forms of violence was the concentration of power, first to a few princes more powerful than others and later to the modern state, which according to Max Weber's (1958: 78) well-known definition '(successfully) claims the monopoly of the legitimate use of physical force within a given territory'. Along with this process, a new culture began to develop in courts, so that noblemen were sometimes seen as a completely new sanguine type of personality. Behind all of this, important changes were taking place in the economy: industrial labour and its capitalist form of organization emerged in a process that extended over hundreds of years and that proceeded at a different pace and assumed different forms in different countries. Capitalism presupposes free labour-power; it pulls people away from their established living conditions and touches off a cultural development that begins to shape a new kind of man. The pace of work is no longer determined by nature but by abstract work-time as measured by the clock. A work discipline develops that requires putting a curb on immediate impulses. The affectual action of medieval man, in particular sexual and aggressive outbursts, are suppressed and replaced by rational calculation required by the capitalist economic system. All this calls for new verbal representations: words such as 'responsibility' or 'self-discipline' come into everyday usage – and actually come to influence the way in which people perceive and act.

Violence, repression and anxiety
Sigmund Freud's theorizing in the late 1920s about the emergence of a new kind of man who learns to repress his violent impulses opens interesting perspectives to the study of human consciousness and violence. Freud (1959) refers not to capitalism, but to 'civilization' or 'culture' as responsible for shaping the human being. However, this is not at variance with Marx's analysis of capitalism; Marx (1973: 409) was well aware of 'the great civilizing effect of capital'. The underlying economic factors will emerge when we ask why 'culture' starts to function in the way that Freud described it.

   Freud's theory is actually an attempt to explain the anxiety of modern man. He starts from the assumption that people inherently pursue happiness and satisfaction, but in doing so meet with several obstacles and sources of distress. Culture is one of the means with which we may try to remove these obstacles. It is a means by which people try to control nature, one source of suffering and distress; and to control the nature of man himself, another source of suffering. The drives that are disciplined most are sexuality and aggressiveness. The individual agrees to these restrictions, for in return he can expect security and welfare; but the price he has to pay is growing anxiety. 'In fact, primitive man was better off in knowing no restrictions to instinct', Freud (1961: 115) writes; 'civilized man has exchanged a portion of his possibilities of happiness for a portion of security'.

   This was probably true in the days that Freud did his analysis. Individuals and states knew that by refraining from violence they would earn security – even though this has not stopped two world wars from breaking out. However, as far as the promise is concerned, there have been important changes since Freud's day. The rewards are much more uncertain now, and the very same civilization that was to give us security as long as we comply with its demands has turned into a serious threat to our life. There are three kinds of threats that today trouble people, all of

which originate in man-made systems rather than those created by nature.
˧First, there is nuclear war, other nuclear catastrophes, or international
terrorism, which threaten our everyday life from the outside by a sudden
and surprising disturbance. Second, people are very much concerned
about technological change, pollution, additives in their food, etc., threats
that are slowly creeping into our everyday life and contaminating it from
within. And third, fearing that the economic and other expanding systems
we have built have just about exhausted their growth potentials, people
are asking themselves: what is going to happen when the growth we are
so used to is gone? (Eskola, 1984)

From the anxiety point of view this implies a crucial change. Anxiety
is no longer caused merely by having to give up this or that for 'a portion
of security'; there is also growing anxiety and fear that we can no longer
trust these promises of security, happiness and well-being. Not so long
ago for most people in Western Europe 'not-yet' was something that
aroused hope: not-yet equality, economic democracy, just society...,
but it was worth while pursuing these goals and accepting the restrictions
even at the cost of anxiety. Now 'not-yet' is something that causes fear:
not-yet nuclear war, not-yet dead forests.... And although these things
are 'not-yet', they are still not 'out of the world', but give rise to a kind
of anxiety that differs from the one Freud described.

One possible consequence of this is a revival of forms of violence which
we thought belonged to the past. The new generation for whom the future
seems to contain only uncertainty and threatening visions whatever it
does, no doubt has great difficulties in motivating itself for self-control.
It is also surrounded by violence, although it is less naked than the
violence of the Middle Ages. The mechanisms of repression that Freud
described have only meant that violence has assumed new forms. It is
no longer as overt and as immediate as it used to be, but to an ever
greater extent it is *mediated by economic and technical systems*. Although
children can no longer watch criminals being tortured in public, the scenes
they get to see where commercial videofilms are readily available are at
least as horrifying.

Forms of rational activity

How is it possible that end-results differ from intentions?
From a certain point of view, it must also be counted as violence that
our economic systems are causing the death of vast numbers of people
through starvation even though the earth provides enough food for
everyone; or that our technological systems are responsible for the illness
and premature death of more people than we dare admit to. And if our
weapon systems in the end lead to the extermination of mankind, this
will in a sense be the ultimate example of collective violence.

To what extent are these highly developed economic and technological
systems autonomous, independent of people's will and consciousness? The

motive force of the capitalist economic system is the pursuit of growth and expansion. But what happens when growth reaches its limits? Is the inevitable outcome a violent political conflict by which room is made for more economic expansion? What if the most dangerous threat is not the 'logic of capitalism', but 'the logic of exterminism' based on the arms race (see Thompson, 1980)? We must leave these questions at this point to be dealt with in the other chapters of this book by experts in economy, politics, technology and military science. However, the more general question as to whether man-made systems can really do things that people do not want them to do deserves the psychologist's attention. If these systems produce violence even against people's conscious will, is it possible to detect some kind of psychological factors that explain this phenomenon?

The problem is by no means a new one. In the nineteenth century Friedrich Engels illustrated the problem in several writings by ecological examples. The people who once cut down large areas of forest land for cultivation could not suspect that they were going to be responsible for the waste of those lands. The end-result was something that these people had neither intended nor expected, Engels (1940) writes. The ongoing arms race is just as good an example. It seems that nobody really wants a global nuclear war, but only peace and security. Nevertheless, every arms acquisition, while advocated by reference to security interests, actually causes growing fear that we are one step closer to a nuclear war. On the other hand, in some cases the opposite happens when people wish to take advantage of each other and they only succeed in doing something good. Liberalists have traditionally believed in these 'good mechanisms'. A common good is brought about by 'an invisible hand' at a moment when the actor is pursuing purely egoistic goals. 'I have never known much good done by those who affected to trade for the public good', Adam Smith wrote (1963: 181).

When intentions are good and outcomes bad and vice versa, it seems as if the human individual is not born to be a rational actor. Should we assume that there is some kind of an 'instinct' that makes people destroy their good (or bad) intentions? From a scientific point of view, such explanations are not satisfactory because it is more or less impossible either to refute them or to prove them. What we would need to find is something in the structure of action that would lead to 'irrationality' when people themselves act rationally.

As a matter of fact there is an explanatory theory of the latter kind. One of the most important findings in the history of social sciences is the detection of a mechanism that shows how rational decisions may lead to an irrational end-result. The finding was made and described in the early 1950s; in literature this description is usually referred to by the name 'Prisoner's Dilemma' (see Rapaport, 1982). Different variants of the same mechanism have also been called 'social traps' (Platt, 1973) or 'the commons problem' (Edney, 1980). However, what all of these cases represent is what Olson (1980) calls *the logic of collective action*.

People's acts usually form a network of interdependencies so that what the individual actor eventually gets depends not only on what he decides to do, but also on what other people do. In this sense action is collective. This is the situation that has been described in the Prisoner's Dilemma. It is no doubt familiar to all social scientists, but the story should be told to every citizen at school: the story where two prisoners, A and B, suspected of having committed a crime together, are put into separate cells. The district attorney, trying to get the men to confess, lays down the following alternatives to each prisoner separately: if they both do not confess, they will be booked on a minor charge and each will get a one-year sentence. If both confess, they will be prosecuted, but the district attorney will recommend less than the most severe sentence: both will get five years. If one confesses and the other does not, then the one who confesses will receive lenient treatment for turning state's evidence and get six months while the other will get the maximum penalty of ten years. The sentences of both men depend on what the other does.

In such situations actors rarely know what their counterpart will do; this is the case here too. However, prisoner A wants to make a rational decision irrespective of what B does. So he reasons that is B does not confess, he will do best to confess, because he will get off with just six months instead of a year. But it is wisest to confess even if B confesses too, because in this case he will get five instead of ten years. Rational reasoning will lead B to precisely the same conclusion. So while both A and B act rationally, the outcome is not the best possible: they both get five years, whereas they could have got off with one year each.

The problem was of course partly that both had to make their decisions alone, without knowing the intentions of the other. So let us assume that the prisoners are allowed to discuss with each other and agree on both not confessing. After they have come to an agreement, the men return to their cells and continue rational deliberation. Naturally, both are tempted to go back on their word: they are more than well aware that the one who betrays the agreement while the other keeps it will get a six-month sentence instead of one year. And that is not all. Both realize that the temptation is the same for the other one. So in both there is now the fear of being betrayed, which develops into horror when the prisoner realizes that if he still keeps to the agreement, the outcome will be the worst possible: he will get ten years. So despite the agreement, both prisoners hurry to confess – and again they fail to achieve the best possible common solution.[3]

From *Zweckrationalität* to *Wertrationalität*

The Prisoner's Dilemma makes it perfectly plain that there is no need for assumptions of 'subconscious needs', 'instincts', or 'genes' that make people destroy their good and rational intentions. In this case 'irrationality' indeed follows precisely from rational inference plus a given reward structure. Nor is it necessary to assume that the devil himself whispered to the prisoner, 'why not betray your mate?', or that there is an 'Oedipus complex' which explains the prisoner's fear of being betrayed; because both the temptation and the fear arise out of rational inference and a given structure of action.

Most importantly, however, they arise out of a very specific historically developed form of thought which we are used to calling 'rational'. Max Weber had a more accurate concept for it, *zweckrational*. Action falls under this category 'when the end, the means and the secondary results are all rationally taken into account and weighed' (Weber, 1947: 117). But what would happen if we told our story of the prisoners to the boy who in Andersen's fairy tale cried, 'But the emperor wears no clothes'? We might have to confess that there is little left of our problem if he said: 'But you *have* to confess if you've committed a crime!' Or: 'if you've made an agreement, then *of course* you have to keep to it!' For *him*, this would be consistent and rational. In other words, he would believe in some sort of an absolute value, like in truth or keeping your word, and in this case rationality would be weighing and choosing means on the basis of how well they lead to the realization of these values. Weber (1947: 115) referred to this kind of action by the concept *wertrational*, typical of which is 'a conscious belief in the absolute value of some ethical, aesthetic, religious, or other form of behaviour, entirely for its own sake and independently of any prospects of external success'.

In the nuclear era it would be in the interest of the whole world to stop the spreading of nuclear arms and never to use these weapons; as a matter of fact it would be wisest simply to get rid of them. The Prisoner's Dilemma shows why it is so difficult to do this, even if we wanted to. Even if individual actors were well aware of what their common interests are, and even if they were rational actors, this does *not* mean that they would act in accordance with their common interest, says Olson; 'Indeed, unless the number of individuals in a group is quite small, or unless there is coercion or some other special device to make individuals act in their common interest, *rational, self-interested individuals will not act to achieve their common or group interest*' (Olson, 1980: 1–2, original emphasis).

But what would happen if action were not controlled by *Zweckrationalität* but by *Wertrationalität*? Surely belief in ethical, religious or some other absolute values is a 'special device' that could make individuals act in their common interest? and if going to war is understood as the common interest of the nation, then *Wertrationalität* becomes coupled to the service of war. But replacing *zweckrational* action by a kind of *Wertrationalität* would also seem to be necessary when pursuing peace. In this case, however, it would be necessary to enlarge the concept of 'common interest', or as Deutsch (1983) says, 'the old notion of "national security" must be replaced by the new notion of "mutual security"'. Everything that can be characterized as *wertrational* action based on the absolute value of mutual security can also be regarded as action that promotes peace in the world.

But is there any hope that the action of the individuals and peoples of the world will develop in this direction? Perhaps there is, for two reasons.

First, what we now call rational action is not something that belongs to 'human nature'. It is one historical form of action that has evolved to meet the requirements of a certain kind of society. In past times action, in Weber's (1947: 115–16) terms, was largely 'traditional' and 'affectual', but in the same way as *zweckrational* action once replaced these forms, action in the future may well become more of a *wertrational* kind – depending on how we develop our societies in other respects.

Second, the utter absurdity of warfare is now, in the nuclear era, much clearer to us than ever. It is not possible to 'win' a nuclear war in the sense that wars were won in the past; 'civil defence' no longer means what it used to; and the same applies to 'reconstruction' after war. Marx (1973: 104) argues that the true essence of a phenomenon cannot be grasped until the phenomenon has matured into its full complexity. Thus, it was possible to see the true nature of work only 'in the midst of the richest possible concrete development' of real kinds of labour. We are now in the midst of the richest possible concrete development' of real kinds of labour. We are now in the midst of the richest possible concrete development of real kinds of war. This, hopefully, will at last force its way into our consciousness and provide a basis for value-rational action that is the only real lesson of war: that peace is absolutely necessary.[4]

Acknowledgement

This chapter was written as a part of research project 12/111 funded by the Academy of Finland. I wish to thank my research assistant David Kivinen for his valuable contribution in preparing it.

Notes

1. However, we may soon be witnessing radical changes in this respect as a consequence of the rapid development of gene technology; one day, we may fancy, it may be able to create a bird-like human who can fly without the aid of aircraft and helicopters.

2. This is related to the question of how different positive or negative things that are possible but not very probable influence our action (see Eskola, 1985).

3. In the continuous interaction of everyday life, the egoistic individuals do not always defect. Co-operation can emerge when individuals have a sufficiently large chance to meet again so that they have a stake in their future interaction (Axelrod, 1984).

4. I have dealt with some ways in which psychologists can promote this cognitive process in three papers prepared for the following scientific congresses: (1) VII Meeting of Psychologists from the Danubian Countries, Symposium of the Psychological Problems of Peace, Varna, September 1985 ('Social Psychology for Peace: Some Research Proposals'); (2) Ninth Annual Scientific Meeting of the International Society of Political Psychology, Amsterdam, June–July 1986 ('Can Social Psychology Contribute to Peace-making and Peacebuilding?'); (3) European Psychologists for Peace, Helsinki, August 1986. For offprints, please write to Professor Antti Eskola, University of Tampere, PO Box 607, SF-33101 Tampere, Finland.

References

Ardrey, Robert (1966) *The Territorial Imperative*. New York: Atheneum.

Axelrod, Robert (1984) *The Evolution of Cooperation*. New York: Basic Books.

Bloch, Ernst (1980) *Abschied von der Utopie?* Frankfurt am Main: Suhrkamp.

Brown, Roger and Herrnstein, Richard J. (1975) *Psychology*. London: Methuen.

Chorover, Stephan L. (1980) 'Violence: a Localizable Problem?', in Elliot S. Valenstein (ed.) *The Psychosurgery Debate*. San Francisco: Freeman.

Davidson, Donald (1980) *Essays on Actions and Events*. Oxford: Clarendon Press.

deMause, Lloyd (ed.) (1974) *The History of Childhood*. London: Souvenir.

Deutsch, Morton (1983) 'The Prevention of World War III: a Psychological Perspective', *Political Psychology* 4, 1: 3–31.

Edney, Julian J. (1980) 'The Commons Problem. Alternative Perspectives', *American Psychologist* 35 (2): 131–50.

Eibl-Eibesfeldt, Irenaus (1970) *Ethology, The Biology of Behaviour*. New York: Holt, Rinehart and Winston.

Elias, Norbert (1978) *The Civilizing Process*, Vol. 1: *The History of Manners*. Oxford: Basil Blackwell.

Elias, Norbert (1982) *The Civilizing Process*, Vol. 2: *State Formation and Civilization*. Oxford: Basil Blackwell.

Engels, Frederick (1940) *The Dialectics of Nature*. New York: International Publishers.

Eskola, Antti (1984) 'Psychology in the 1990's: Trends, Threats and Challenges', in Kirsti M. J. Lagerspetz and Pekka Niemi (eds) *Psychology in the 1990's*. Amsterdam: Elsevier.

Eskola, Antti (1985) 'Mass Media and Consciousness: Social Psychological Perspectives', *The Nordicom Review* 2.

Frankl, Victor E. (1963) *Man's Search for Meaning*. New York: Simon and Schuster.

Freud, Sigmund (1959) 'Why War?' in *Collected Papers*, Vol. 5. New York: Basic Books.

Freud, Sigmund (1961) *Civilization and its Discontents*, in *The Standard Edition of the Complete Psychological Works of Sigmund Freud*, Vol. XXI. London: Hogarth Press.

Lagerspetz, Kirsti (1982) 'Are Wars Caused by Human Aggression?', *Adult Education in Finland* 19 (1): 21–9.

Le Roy Ladurie, Emmanuel (1978). *Montaillou. Cathars and Catholics in a French Village*. Harmondsworth: Penguin Books.

Marx, Karl (1973) *Grundrisse. Foundations of the Critique of Political Economy (Rough Draft)*. Harmondsworth: Penguin Books.

Masson, Jeffrey Moussaieff (1984) *The Assault on Truth. Freud's Suppression of the Seduction Theory*. New York: Farrar, Straus and Giroux.

Olson, Mancur (1980) *The Logic of Collective Action. Public Goods and the Theory of Groups*. 8th printing. Cambridge: Harvard University Press.

Platt, John (1973) 'Social Traps', *American Psychologist* 28 (8): 641–51.

Rapoport, Anatol (1982) 'Prisoner's Dilemma – Recollections and Observations', in Brian Barry and Russel Hardin (eds) *Rational Man and Irrational Society? An Introduction and Sourcebook*. Beverly Hills: Sage publications.

Renvall, Pentti (1949) *Suomalainen 1500–luvun ihminen oikeuskatsomustensa valossa*. Annales Universitatis Turkuensis, Series B, Tom. XXXIII.

Schumacher, Fritz (1977) *A Guide for the Perplexed*. New York: Harper and Row.

Smith, Adam (1963) *The Works of Adam Smith*, Vol. III (reprint of the edition 1811–12). Aalen: Otto Zeller.

Thompson, E. P. (1980) 'Notes on Exterminism, the Last Stage of Civilization', *New Left Review* 121.

Uznadze, Dmitrii N. (1966) *The Psychology of Set*. New York: Consultants Bureau.

Weber, Max (1947) *The Theory of Social and Economic Organization.* New York: Oxford
   University Press.
Weber, Max (1958) 'Politics as a Vocation', in Hans H. Gerth and C. Wright Mills (eds)
   From Max Weber: Essays in Sociology. New York: Oxford University Press.

3

Cultural Perspectives on War

Carol J. Greenhouse

The problem

At the end of *Patterns of Culture*, now an anthropological classic, Ruth Benedict (1937: 278) looked forward to the new day that would result when the disciplined relativism of anthropology's cultural approach to the diversity of human experience would be a common mode of thought. Written on the eve of the Second World War, her words still carry a haunting challenge to anthropologists to assess both what their work has contributed to the understanding of the human condition as it bears on world peace, and how that understanding might be made accessible to the public at large. In this chapter, my aims are to review anthropological literature written in English and published since 1975 on the topic of warfare, and, in my conclusion, to point to the implication of that literature for anthropological and non-anthropological audiences.[1] Since the readers of this volume are particularly concerned with the social sciences, I emphasize the cultural and social anthropological literature. Archaeological data provide insight into the ancient roots of war's social forms (e.g. Goldberg and Findlow, 1984), but, for the most part, I focus on contemporary people. Finally, since I draw only on the anthropological literature which centres on collective, organized violence, this chapter does not explore relevant issues in the related realms of inter-personal violence, violence among non-human primates, psychological orientations towards violence, or (for another example) violence in art and popular culture (but see Nettleship et al., 1975 for a comprehensive anthology).

The literature in anthropology is highly diverse, both because the societies anthropologists study are themselves diverse, and because scholars take what are in some cases fundamentally different approaches to the task of understanding them. Ethnographic debates – such as the ones that centre on the Yanomamo of the Amazon or the New Guinea highlanders – raise deeper questions whose central issues are far from resolution. These questions pervade the anthropological literature on war, both implicitly and explicitly: is human aggression innate? Are the causes of war in nature or in culture? Are the causes of war internal or external to society? The orientation of the literature suggests strongly that war is a cultural phenomenon, that is, that its roots are in the human mind, not in our genes.

Violence and warfare as cultural concepts

The anthropological literature makes very clear the difficulties of setting definitional boundaries around such concepts as warfare, violence, aggression and even disputing, to take just a few of what might be many examples. The difficulties are twofold. First, these terms express cultural categories. That is, the ideas and actions that we (writers and readers of English) symbolize with these words have meanings which are themselves embedded in our particular cultural understandings. While the Yanomamo, or the Mae Enga, might engage in activity that looks to us like warfare, we must preserve some of our enquiry for the question of how their activities are understood by them. Warfare, in other words, in not only a 'what' and a 'when', it is also a 'how' and a 'why'. This point might be made of ethnographic writing in general, as Geertz (1973: 20) makes clear:

> There are three characteristics of ethnographic description: it is interpretive; what it is interpretive of is the flow of social discourse; and the interpreting involved consists of trying to rescue the 'said' of such discourse from its perishing occasions and fix it in perusable terms.

In other words, *causes* ultimately elude ethnographers; it is the *meanings* of experience that comprise our subject. The importance of this point for our purposes will emerge again later, as we turn to the problem of how to generalize from the case studies reviewed below.

The second sort of difficulty in defining our terms in advance is that – even as cultural categories – violence and warfare are not phenomena *sui generis*; they occur as part of many kinds of social relationships and cultural forms: exchange (Brown, 1979; Isaac, 1983), productive intensification (Price, 1984), ritual (Schieffelin, 1976), administration (Podolefsky, 1984; Schmink, 1982), sorcery (Chanock, 1985; Simmons, 1980), even myth (Gewertz, 1978; Helm and Gillespie, 1981). In some cases, these are structural alternatives to war; in others, activities such as feasting and trading constitute a counterpoint to organized armed conflict that together form the larger rhythm of a people's social life. For this reason, by no means can it be said as a general proposition that violence signals the breakdown of social order. When violence occurs, it is not necessarily the only or dominant mode of dealing with the conflict at hand, but is part of a wider context. Anthropologists emphasize the comparative, contextual aspects of war for this reason.

To put all of this another way, war has both social and cultural dimensions that affect the comparability of war processes.[2] The distinction between culture and society points to the disjunctions between 'the tone and feeling of life as it is experienced and expressed by the actors' on the one hand and 'social causes and effects, whether these are perceived by the actors. . . or not' on the other (Strathern, 1984: 2–3). As Strathern (1984: 107) concludes in his study of recent cultural and social change in two highland communities in Papua New Guinea, 'conceptually material and cultural factors can indeed be distinguished, but...the question of dominance or determination between them cannot be settled'. He makes the point about the specific changes he observed in the region, but in spite of his own demurrer, it has more general validity.

The concept of culture is the heart of anthropology's contribution to the understanding of war. Culture is not itself 'caused' or 'determined' except by its own logic and meaning, that is, it is self-validating. The premise that culture is self-validating has a long tradition in anthropological thought. The implication of this premise is that the roots of social action are not only anchored in the material world, but also reach into the realm of values, preferences and givens that constitute the cultural domain. Anthropological writing on war has tended to emphasize the material (if not always the materialist) perspective; indeed, much current research searches for the causes of war in various forms of social and material contingency. An emergent line of enquiry begins with an altogether different proposition, that war exists to justify itself. LaFontaine's (1977: 434) discussion of initiation rites provides an analogy: the rites are concerned primarily with the 'transfer and vindication of traditional knowledge' and they 'create occasions in which traditional wisdom is communicated, tested and vindicated as the source of the power of rights'. LaFontaine comes to this conclusion not by asking what ritual is, nor what its functions are, but by asking how people think about ritual.

If we, in turn, adopt a cultural perspective in order to ask how people who practise war think about war, questions shift from the causes of war to the meaning of war. Even if we were to focus on causes, we could not escape the interpretive questions of meaning, since cause is, itself, a cultural concept. LaFontaine (1977: 433) writes: 'The determination of what constitutes a cause...appears to vary cross-culturally and can be assigned to...the legitimation of belief, the basic assumptions which justify knowledge.' In other words, the concept of cause reflects culture's inner logic; thus, a comparison of causes (e.g. of war) would necessarily lead to a comparison of concepts of causation.[3] My point here is not that war is ritual (Kurtz, 1981, argues convincingly that it is not), but that war can be studied as a self-validating expression of culture, as ritual is. To put this more concretely, we can better account for the variation in the comparative literature by shifting from the functional questions of what causes war, and what war accomplishes materially or politically, to the contextual and interpretative question of how people think about war.[4]

In any event, there is no single 'because' of war; in multiple ways, war entails the transfer of important cultural knowledge concerning identity, opposition, causation, and ultimate meanings. This is as true of nation-states as it is of the social groups anthropologists conventionally study. In the nuclear age, it is useful to remember that war results from careful calculation and planning. Popular mobilizations for war draw on anger and hate, perhaps, but war between nations is born in the cool chambers of diplomats and politicians. It is this observation that drives home the importance of understanding the tolerance and preference for war – i.e. the cultural meaning of war – in modern life.

With this point in mind, let us now turn to current anthropological literature on war. The chapter has three parts. In the first part, I review anthropologists' explanations of war. In the second, discussion turns to the consequences of war. In the third, I point to new questions and new developments in the field.

Explanations of war

To the extent that anthropologists attempt to account for war, they tend to focus on sources of competition and/or collective political action. In this section, I consider first the competitive approaches, and then the political.

War as competition

Among the causes anthropologists attribute to war in tribal and national contexts is the organized pursuit of some prized or scarce material good. This approach has a long genealogy in anthropological thinking and there are many examples in reports of current research. For example, among the Chambri of East Sepik Province (Papua New Guinea), warfare developed when traditional hierarchies in marketing relations were challenged (Gewertz, 1978). In this area, where subsistence depended on barter of sago and fish, successful barter for sago depended on a hierarchy of sago producers. When this hierarchy was effectively challenged by competitors, 'the marketing system could no longer operate. It would frequently be replaced by symmetrical competitive exchange which frequently, in the Middle Sepik, develops into warfare' (Gewertz, 1978: 580). In the recent past, the Chambri wiped out two neighbouring groups. To discover the meaning of these events to the Chambri themselves, Gewertz explored the Chambri 'myth of blood-men', and collected narratives from informants.

A second example of competitive warfare comes from the New World. The Aztec 'flowery war', which began in 1450 and continued until it was absorbed by the process of the Spanish conquest (Isaac, 1983: 416), has been variously interpreted by Harner (1977), Hicks (1979) and Isaac (1983). Isaac's position is that the Aztec triple alliance (Tenochtitlán, Tetzcoco and Tlacopan) had multiple aims in maintaining a protracted state of war against Tlaxcala, Huexotinco and Cholula. Commoners participated in the war inspired by the hope of material gains from the capture of enemy soldiers and booty. Elites sought political conquest out of 'geopolitical, administrative, and sumptuary concerns' (Isaac, 1983: 428). Montezuma II offered religious explanations for warfare, which Isaac dismisses as 'rationalizations' (1983: 428). Harner and Hicks do not disagree on these points, but offer additional explanations, ranging from alleged cannibalism among what Harner (1977) proposes were protein-deficient Aztecs, to Hicks's (1979) point that the Aztec empire required not captives, but a training ground for the military.

A third example comes from the tribes along the northwest coast of North America in the early nineteenth century, where indigenous people engaged in war for the capture of slaves, who were later exchanged or sold for goods. Slaves and fortune were the result of war, but the motives for war included 'revenge, territorial expansion and plunder' (Mitchell, 1984: 39, 42).

These examples help to contextualize a long-standing interpretive debate between two major theorists over the causes of war among the Yanomamo of Brazil. Marvin Harris (1984) has argued that Yanomamo warfare results from their need for protein. Harris (1984: 187–9) argues that 'progressive deterioration in the cost–benefit ratio of protein capture' leads to the persistent intermittent warfare in which the Yanomamo engage with neighbouring groups. Against critics, such as Gross (1975), who find that the forest remains an abundant reserve of animal and vegetable protein, Harris (1984: 189) responds that the Yanomamo are not starving in any clinical sense, but a cultural sense in that they do not have enough of the sorts of proteins they prefer.[5] Harris's approach differs from that of Napoleon Chagnon, whose research among the Yanomamo leads him to conclude that the Yanomamo fight over a wide range of causes, generally under the rubric of sovereignty and specifically over women (Chagnon, 1968: 118–37). Over the past twenty years, Chagnon's writings and films of the Yanomamo have connected various aspects of their kinship and alliances to biological and evolutionary requirements (most fully in Chagnon and Irons, 1979). Both Harris and Chagnon relate the Yanomamo patterns of aggression to competition generated by biological needs (food or women), but, it should be stressed, neither proposes that aggression itself is biologically determined.

Anthropologists concerned with human relations to the natural environment divide over the question of the extent to which war is a response to shifting ecology and/or demography. On the one hand, Dirks (1980: 26–31), for example, charts the responses of social groups to prolonged food shortages and famine. While the sort of violent confrontations Harris proposes for the Yanomamo can occur under conditions of starvation, they are accompanied by the concomitant breakdown of internal social ties, as well. This level of conflict has not occurred among the Yanomamo. Dirks finds that perceived food shortage tends, instead, to elicit positive responses, for example increased reciprocity and heightened intensity of activity to obtain food, thus confirming Saffirio and Scaglion's (1982) finding that Yanomamo adapt well to changing ecological environments. From another perspective, Dyson-Hudson and Smith (1978) review three case studies (of the Northern Ojibwa, and Basin-Plateau Indians and the Karimojong) to support their conclusion that the costs of defending (or extending) territory by means of armed conflict mean that territorial wars tend to occur under conditions of predictable affluence, not shortage, as

Harris proposes. When food supplies are scarce or unpredictable, the more efficient response to aggression is strategic withdrawal to another range. As Dyson-Hudson and Smith also acknowledge, where territoriality – which implies a commitment to defence – occurs, it is a social response that has developed over the course of human experience. Peterson (1975: 63) suggests that if territoriality is an evolved response, it has evolved not only in the course of humankind's biological evolution, but also social evolution. Thus, what a population knows about its environment, and how it acts on that knowledge, is, he argues, a complex interplay of biological *and* social forces.[6]

On the other hand, Ferguson's (1984: 2) edited volume on war pursues the following theme: 'The occurrence and form of war are intimately related to processes of material production and other exigencies of survival.' The ten papers in the volume relate the natural environment to its 'correlates' in economic, social, political and military organization. The gist of contributors' arguments, which are based on rich ethnographic and historical data, is perhaps most succinctly stated by Balée (in Ferguson, 1984: 241), that wars 'ensure the well-being of the living'. His point concerns sixteenth-century warfare among indigenous Brazilian populations, but it aptly summarizes the volume's recurring theme. Thus, war is related, by these authors, albeit in differing ways, to scarce resources, population pressure or commerce.

It is worth noting that neither side of the current materialist arguments on warfare supports the proposition that warfare among human populations is due to innate aggression. Once again, we come back to the point that for anthropologists, war is, broadly speaking, a cultural phenomenon (see also Gewertz, 1978: 581).

War as politics

Explanations of war that centre on shortages of land, wealth or food locate the source of war outside of the population that is the subject of study: war is a response to some externally induced stimulus. Such arguments can be contrasted with another set of explanations, which focus instead on cultural or social factors intrinsic to local situations. I call these explanations 'political' in that they stress the adversarial structure of war, but locate the sources of competition in social organization rather than in the material objects of competition. Political factors most extensively discussed by anthropologists are vengeance and protest. I consider these in turn.

The term 'vengeance' is not meaningful in itself, but refers to a logic of social identity that calls for reciprocal responses to offences. Vengeance, or retaliation, for physical acts of violence, insult, theft and so on, is a major theme of the ethnography of conflict and conflict resolution in the highlands of New Guinea (Koch, 1974; Schieffelin, 1976; Strathern, 1984: 48–9); it is also reported elsewhere in Melanesia (Brown, 1979: 721), among the Yanomamo (Chagnon, 1968; Lizot, 1977: 515) and among Arab Muslims (Kressel, 1981). The New Guinea literature is now quite extensive (see Gordon and Meggitt, 1985, and Strathern, 1984, for current bibliographies). I can do no more here than simply refer to it in the most general way. Especially interesting and problematic in the region is the re-emergence of violent feuding, or warfare, among western highland groups who had been 'pacified' for thirty or forty years before.

Strathern (1984) considers this issue from the perspective of recent regional history and socio-cultural change, and Gordon and Meggitt from the perspective of the relationship between criminal behaviour and the structure of state authority. The New Guinea material raises two exceptionally interesting questions of interest to non-specialist readers. The first is, what role does the state have to play in the mediation of inter-personal and intergroup differences at the local level? Second, what is the nature of the logic of violence that it continues to be an attractive remedial option even when non-violent alternatives are available? These questions have specific answers in the New Guinea highlands, for which I refer readers to the work of Gordon and Meggitt (1985). Some brief and more general discussion is in order here.

One dimension of the question of why violence persists in the highlands is the relationship of violent remedies to alternative dispute–resolution processes. Koch's (1974) ethnographic work in Jalémó (Irian Jaya) suggested that the pattern of rapid escalation in cases of conflict there was due to the lack of available third parties to mediate differences. Specifically, villages were so pervaded by cross-cutting social bonds that potential third parties were readily compromised by their conflicting loyalties to one side or the other. Men's houses provided some exception to this general rule, and Koch concluded that the Jalé do not prefer violent remedies, but have no alternatives to violence. Violence is also positively sanctioned by beliefs concerning the ghosts of the dead (see also Heider, 1976: 191, and Strathern, 1984: 48–9).

Even where courts are accessible to highlanders, they have not proved to be adequate forums, in part because the nature of imposed social and cultural change in the highlands region has transformed the social fabric in multiple negative ways that create new social tensions. The implications of this aspect of the New Guinea case for the world at large are intriguing. Barkun (1968) suggested that international relations are analogous to 'primitive law' situations in which no jural institutions are available to mediate disputes. The New Guinea experience confirms the importance of third parties in the preservation of peace, but it also seems to urge caution on those who assume that the creation of centralized jural institutions alone can accomplish a cultural transformation from violent to verbal disputing.

The second point in the New Guinea material that raises considerable interest more generally is the question of the nature of the logic of retaliation. LaFontaine's discussion of the cultural relativities implicit in the concept of causation is helpful, as here again the keynote must be caution in assuming a priori the logic and significance of a retaliatory response. Schieffelin (1976: 92–5, 135–6) develops most fully the differences between Kaluli (Papua New Guinea) ideas about vengeance and those of the Western readers he assumes his book addresses. The Kaluli cite a myth that suggests that the origin of diverse life forms in the natural and social environment began in a 'splitting of house' among cosmic ancestors; this original differentiation provides them with an analogy for contemporary divisions over disputed issues. The Kaluli strive to behave in a way that avoids others' anger; at the same time, violence is understood as an expressive venting of rage, not (as Schieffelin claims for the West) as a punitive action. In fact, he observed that expressions of anger are carefully modulated according to the relationship involved (1976: 135–6). Further, Kaluli construct their ideas of the universe in a way that obviates the delineation of sequences of events; thus, what Westerners perceive as pendulum swings of retribution are understood otherwise by the actors themselves. Writing of the Chambri, also in the New Guinea highlands, Gewertz (1984: 619) notes that indigenous concepts of person do not centre on the individual, but on his or her relationships: '[The] individual has no significant reality, and hence no power, apart from his or her relationships'. These ethnographic findings suggest (among other things) that cultural differences restrict analogies between the dispute practices of small-scale societies and nation-states.

While vengeance and protest might be impossible to distinguish on the ground, anthropologists use the terms differently. In practice, the term 'vengeance' applies to violence among equals. 'Protest' applies to violent responses of subordinated groups against the persons or groups who dominate them. Thus, Burnham and Christensen (1983) analyse the Karnu rebellion of 1928 in east-central Cameroon and western Central African Republic as protest. Cooke and Doornbos (1982) interpret the protest songs of the Rwenzururu movement in western Uganda in this century. Rosen (1983) examines West African feminist protests. Simmons's (1980: 447) analysis of Badyaranke (Senegal) sorcery identifies it as a response among peasants to their conflicts with the state. Stoler's (1985) study of the perceptions of protest in colonial Sumatra charts the changing interpretations of local protest by planters and agents of the state over time. Moss (1979) examines banditry as protest, and explores the transformations in the understood meanings of the term 'banditry' in Sardinia since the last century.

In another vein, Johnson (1981) offers a reinterpretation of ethnography that he concludes misrepresents the significance of warfare. The case he reopens is that of the Nuer (Sudan), known through the work of Evans-Pritchard and others as aggressive and belligerent. Johnson explains the stereotype as deriving from specific European interests in the Nuer region, and goes on to suggest that Nuer violence was rather selective, aimed at 'colonial invaders' (1981: 522) as a violent protest. Johnson's study indicates the necessity of contextualizing anthropological explanation in the specifics of regional and local history.

Finally, analyses which stress the importance of social forces in bringing about warfare include important studies which explain violence as the result of intolerable pressures brought on local populations by regional or national developments. Schmink (1982) examines epochs of violence in Amazonia and Paraná and in the Santa Catarina states of Brazil respectively. Podolefsky (1984), working in New Guinea, attributes the re-emergence of violence to the inadequacy of the local law-enforcement agents and the negative social transformations they introduced to the highlands. Stone (1983) compares frontier violence among miners and whalemen in the nineteenth-century Yukon, and finds that violence prevailed among whalers due to the overcentralization of authority in the whaling captains.

Schmink's study of protracted land conflicts in the Brazilian Amazon raises important comparative issues in her explicit rejection of the hypothesis, sometimes raised in the New Guinea case (e.g. by Koch, 1974), that violence is the result of the absence of viable jural alternatives at the local level (Schmink, 1982: 352): 'land conflicts are not the result of distance from moderating influences of the state but rather the outcome of contradictory elements in government policy that have brought fundamentally distinct groups into repeated confrontations over land on the frontier'. The confrontations between peasants and capitalists are, in Schmink's view, unlikely to be resolved by those parties who are directly involved, but instead (if at all) by the political and administrative process at the national level (Schmink, 1982: 355). While she is concerned only with the particular difficulties of the Amazon region, her conclusion would seem to be in increasing relevance everywhere in the contemporary world. Wolf's volume on peasant wars in this century explores in depth six cases of rebellion that he ascribes to the 'large-scale cultural encounter' between capitalist and non-capitalist peripheries (Wolf, 1969: 278).

Consequences and functions of warfare and collective violence

Anthropological explanations of war tend to examine the resources over which people are presumed to fight – women, protein, land or power. In some cases, the fruits of war are taken as the motivations for war; however, this assumption is problematic. Perhaps paradoxically, anthropologists have been more concerned to study the causes of war than the consequences of war. None of the anthropological works cited in the previous section take as a central theme the costs of war to the people who engage in it.

Dyson-Hudson and Smith (1978: 21) refer in passing to the fact that territorial defence is expensive. Heider (1976: 197) notes that Grand Valley Dani (Irian Jaya) resist the intense expenditure of energy and life that Western readers expect from war situations. Dani warfare – which generally lasts no more than a day of fighting with spears – is largely spectatorship (Heider, 1976: 197): '[Most] significant in this context is the marked absence of aggression, hatred for the enemy, or even much at all in the way of sustained excitement.' Perhaps it is only in the West where, since the French invented general conscription in 1793, men are taken involuntarily from their private lives and thrust into the theatre of war, that the question of costs insists itself as a question separate from the causes of war.

Similarly, few of the anthropological writers whose work is cited above consider the related question of how warfare might have been avoided in the specific situations they studied. Gordon and Meggitt (1985) and Strathern (1984) address this question more or less directly, as do Koch (1974), Podolefsky (1984) and Stone (1983). Of these writers, only Stone did not work in the New Guinea highlands; thus, it is perhaps not surprising that there is a general consensus among these analysts, to the effect that the lack of adequate authority at the local level was a factor in recurring violence. Their individual interpretations of what 'adequate' might mean certainly differ, and Strathern's analysis is particularly detailed on this point.

On the other hand, anthropological research points to, or implies, positive functions of warfare that merit mention here. The implication of the materialist arguments is that warfare limits overexploitation of scarce and valued resources. This is, for example, one aspect of Gross's (1975) discussion of the relative abundance of protein supplies in the Amazon region. A related argument would be that of Rappaport (1968: 114–17) that warfare allows for a reduction in population density by extending the victors' land base, and that this has positive effects, at least for the conquerors.

War has other distributive and organizational consequences as well. War has been shown to result in a restructuring of social relations, directly or indirectly. Cooke and Doornbos (1982) indicate that some positive changes resulted from the violence characterized as the Rwenzururu movement in the Kingdom of Toro (western Uganda), in terms of reduced discrimination against ethnic minorities. The Chambri preserved important asymmetries in their social structure by means of war (Gewertz, 1978). In assessing the consequences of war in statements such as these, the difference between winners' and losers' perspectives is especially clear.

Most generally, war can be said to reinforce a population's sense of identity. Ethnographic illustration can be found in Chagnon (1968) on the Yanomamo, Helm and Gillespie (1981) on the Dogrib (Canada) and, more generally, in the New Guinea ethnography. Binns (1979) offers a detailed study of the nationalistic themes in Soviet public ceremonies, including displays of weapons. Much earlier, Warner (1962) analysed the American ritual of Memorial Day in national and cultural terms.

The ethnology of war: new themes and questions

My purpose has been to recreate for readers some of the intellectual issues anthropologists grapple with in their attempts to understand war. A review of this sort can only begin to sketch out the range of variation anthropologists report. Indeed, the high degree of variation in the 'logics' of war that anthropologists describe is an important theme.

In some areas, and for some analysts, war is of primary importance (e.g. Chagnon, 1968); for others, it is relatively unimportant (e.g. Heider, 1976). Most of the violence recorded here is not technologically sophisticated; generally, weaponry is not detailed, but it appears that where warfare is most studied by anthropologists, the people involved use clubs, spears or bow and arrow. This is not to say that even highly localized warfare, or warfare in non-industrial societies, cannot exact high tolls; Siegel (1977) reports that the Contestado rebellion (Brazil) took over three thousand lives, and Gewertz (1978) states that the Chambri were able to wipe out two neighbouring villages.

The most general summary of the literature is that the particular historical, cultural and social contexts out of which violence emerges are highly variable. This observation suggests some themes that go beyond the immediate causes and consequences of war. Taken together, the literature reviewed here illuminates a pair of related issues.

Social change as a factor in the emergence of war
Ethnographic studies suggest that certain types of change can exacerbate patterns of violence. Specifically, centralization of the services of the state can add to the risk of violence in two ways. First, as states grow stronger, indigenous political structures lose their autonomy or collapse altogether. A recurrent theme in anthropological writing on these regions is the relationship between 'modernization' on the one hand, and the costs of modernization in peripheral areas on the other. Dennis (1976), for example, charts the mutually reinforcing relationship between government encroachment in the rural areas around Oaxaca, Mexico, and the rise of local violence there. Violent feuding in the Oaxaca highlands provides a pretext for government intervention; Dennis find that the principal beneficiaries of violence in the area are lawyers and government agents. Second, a closely related point is the extent to which national development generates new problems at the local level that indigenous political structures may be ill-equipped to handle. Chanock (1985) points to economic and political problems of this kind in Africa, as does Harris (1984) concerning the exploitation of natural resources in the Amazon region. Several writers on the New Guinea highlands make the same point concerning a wide array of social and cultural factors (Gordon and Meggitt, 1985; Podolefsky 1984; Strathern 1984).

Institutional alternatives to war
The second point that emerges from the literature cited above is the positive role to be played by political or legal structures capable of absorbing conflict. I word this statement in this tentative way because the ethnographic and historical record to date is not entirely encouraging.

Some institutional alternatives are well documented; foremost among them is law and its role as one element of wider systems of social control. Koch (1974) suggests that need for a jural authority at the local level; this would be the place to introduce a discussion of the relationship between law and violence if this chapter were of somewhat larger scope.[7]

The literature also suggests the extent to which alternatives to violence need not be jural in nature. Brown's analysis of the relationship between Polopa (Melanesia) feasting and warfare indicates that these two sets of activities shared important structural features, which Brown examines in detail. While the heart of Brown's article lies elsewhere, he makes the point in passing that warfare no longer occurs (although fears of sorcery do), but that feasting remains important (Brown, 1979: 721–9). Podolefsky (1984) and Gewertz (1978) suggest the extent to which trade absorbs political relations which, in the New Guinea highlands, are otherwise capable of becoming violent. In each of these situations, there would be no alternative to violence without the presence of ongoing reciprocal interaction on a variety of bases.

These points about the relevance of change and institutional contexts stand as an interpretive summary of current anthropological literature on war. Now we can no longer postpone the central question of what this literature can contribute to our understanding of war and the prospects of peace at the international level.[8] From an anthropological perspective, this is a comparative problem, that is, one that requires us to draw connections between the violent situations discussed above and larger international development. If we attempt to draw such connections at the level of the *causes* of war, we can only end in a serious muddle. Such a project would involve somehow reducing the variation cited throughout this chapter. We would also have to sort out the multiple cultural meanings of causation and resolve the debates outlined above. Such a task is neither feasible nor, I would suggest, desirable. Instead, lines of comparison await at the point where this chapter began: at the cultural preference for war, not only in the small-scale situations mentioned here, but also among large, modern nations. To put this another way, the most immediate cause of war is human choice-making, and so it is in the realm of preferences, values and understandings that anthropologists have something to add to the public discussions of war and peace.

The possibility of armed conflict has been embedded in the social and cultural experience of humankind at least since the palaeolithic era, when the spear and spear-thrower were developed, presumably for the purposes of hunting game. What does this mean for the future? It certainly does not mean that human societies are in some sense 'programmed' for war, nor does it mean that the history of human progress tells Hobbes's grim story after all. We do know that war is an aspect of many cultural ideologies, but we also know that ideologies – that is, people's statements about their beliefs – are flexible idioms that express selectively the cultural propositions that are capable of life in human minds. This is cause for hope, since cultural analysis suggests that the causes of war lie not in the land, nor in some implacable demand for blood or honour, nor in human genes, but in imaginations that tolerate both the image and the reality of wholesale violence, at least for the moment.

Notes

1. I want to express sincere thanks to the following people, for their critical readings of earlier versions of this chapter: Mary LeCron Foster, Barbara Jo Lantz, Robert A. Rubinstein, Raimo Väyrynen, and especially Peter Worsley. I am grateful to Drs Foster and Rubinstein for sharing the page proofs of *Peace and War*, cited in the text, and to Dr David Riches for sharing the unpublished report of the Economic and Social Research Council (ESRC) conference cited in note 8.

2. The term 'process' in this context comes from Ferguson's (1984) introduction to his edited volume, *Warfare, Culture and Environment*.

3. This is, indeed, what anthropologists such as Schieffelin (1976) attempt; it is also the direction taken by Gewertz (1984), Heider (1976), Lizot (1977), Lutz (1982), Moss (1979) and Stoler (1985).

4. Some anthropologists do ask how war is understood by its participants, e.g. Brown (1979), Gewertz (1978), Heider (1976), Schieffelin (1976) and Strathern (1984).

5. The question of whether hunting-gathering groups, such as the Yanomamo, go to war for food has aroused considerable debate. At issue is the response a population makes or is likely to make to situations of increasing scarcity, or, as Harris would have it, diminished choices. Saffirio and Scaglion (1982) compared Yanomamo villages, at varying distances from a highway, and found that the acculturated villagers near the highway had better yields from more efficient hunting than the unacculturated villagers to whom they were compared. The explanation Saffirio and Scaglion offer is that the villagers near the highway, aware of the scarcities there, walk further into the forest than the more remote villagers who continue to hunt in familiar home ranges. This is an interesting finding because it suggests that Yanomamo do precisely what Harris says they will not do, and that is 'walk longer distances' (Harris, 1984: 187–9) for protein. Lizot makes the strongest case against an earlier version of Harris's argument, on nutritional, environmental and cultural grounds. First, he argues that the Yanomamo rely primarily on a variety of vegetable proteins sufficiently available in their annual growth cycle (Lizot, 1977: 505). Second, he argues that the Yanomamo economy is 'in harmony' with their natural environment (1977: 515). Finally, he agrees with Chagnon that the Yanomamo offer their own ideology of conquest and capture of women as an explanation for their aggression, but adds, 'the ideology of a people is one thing, the deeper, underlying motivations for action another. The Yanomamo make war to punish insults, avenge deaths, and fulfil kinship obligations' (1977: 515).

6. Indeed, the search for food may have provided the initial impulse for the rational, purposive thinking that characterizes *homo sapiens* (Wilson, 1977).

7. Legal development is not without risks. As later writers on the New Guinea highlands (where Koch worked) have demonstrated, the introduction of jural authority can generate, as well as resolve, local problems.

8. I do not mean to suggest that anthropologists have not considered this question, only that it has not yet been considered in this chapter. Indeed, Nettleship et al.'s (1975) edited volume reflects the contributions of scholars at the ninth Congress of the International Union of Anthropological and Ethnological Sciences (IUAES). Foster and Rubinstein's (1986) volume offers papers from the eleventh IUAES Congress. The Nettleship et al. volume and the Foster and Rubinstein volume are very wide ranging. I suggest that readers

interested in an efficient survey of anthropological treatments of war, violence and aggression begin with these two works. An earlier volume, edited by Fried et al. (1968) offers a broad range of anthropological papers on war; these works were presented to a plenary session of the American Anthropological Association in 1967 as a response to the involvement of the United States in Vietnam. A recent ESRC conference on Violence as a Social Institution was held at the University of St Andrews in Scotland.

References

Baker, Paul R. (1984) 'The Adaptive Limits of Human Populations', *Man* (new series) 19(1): 1–14.

Barkun, Michael (1968) *Law Without Sanctions*. New Haven: Yale University Press.

Benedict, Ruth (1937) *Patterns of Culture*. Boston: Houghton Mifflin.

Binns, Christopher, A. P. (1979) 'The Changing Face of Power: Revolution and Accommodation in the Development of the Soviet Ceremonial System', Part I. *Man* (n.s.) 14(4): 585–606; Part II. *Man* (n.s.) 15(1): 170–87.

Brown, D. J. J. (1979) 'The Structuring of Polopa Feasting and Warfare', *Man* (n.s.) 14(4): 712–33.

Burnham, Philip and Christensen, Thomas (1983) 'Karnu's Message and the "War of the Hoe Handle": Interpreting a Central African Resistance Movement', *Africa* 53(4): 3–22.

Chagnon, Napoleon A. (1968) *Yanomamo: The Fierce People*. New York: Holt, Rinehart and Winston.

Chagnon, Napoleon A. and Irons William (eds) (1979) *Evolutionary Biology and Human Social Behaviour: An Anthropological Perspective*. North Scituate, MA: Duxbury Press.

Chanock, Martin (1985) *Law, Custom and Social Order: The Colonial Experience in Malawi and Zambia*. Cambridge: Cambridge University Press.

Cooke, Peter and Doornbos, Martin, (1982) 'Rwenzururu Protest Songs', *Africa* 52(1): 37–60.

Dennis, Philip A. (1976) 'The Uses of Inter-Village Feuding', *Anthropological Quarterly* 49(3): 174–84.

Dirks, Robert (1980) 'Social Responses During Severe Food Shortages and Famine', *Current Anthropology* 21(1): 21–44.

Dyson-Hudson, Rada and Alden Smith, Eric (1978) 'Human Territoriality: An Ecological Assessment', *American Anthropologist* 80(1): 21–41.

Ember, Melvin (1974) 'Warfare, Sex Ratio and Polygyny', *Ethnology* 13(2): 197–206.

Ferguson, R. Brian (ed.) (1984) *Warfare, Culture and Environment*. Orlando: Academic Press.

Foster, Mary LeCron and Rubinstein, Robert A. (eds) (1986) *Peace and War: Cross-Cultural Perspectives*. New Brunswick: Transaction Books.

Fried, Morton, Harris, Marvin and Murphy, Robert (1968) *War: The Anthropology of Armed Conflict and Aggression*. Garden City, NJ: Natural History Press.

Fukui, Katsuyoshi and Turton, David (eds) (1979) *Warfare Among East African Herders*. National Museum of Ethnology, Osaka. Senri Ethnological Studies, No. 3.

Geertz, Clifford (1973) *The Interpretation of Cultures*. New York: Basic Books.

Gewertz, Deborah (1978) 'The Myth of Blood-Men: an Explanation of Chambri Warfare', *Journal of Anthropological Research* 34(4): 577–88.

Gewertz, Deborah (1984) 'The Tchambuli View of Persons: a Critique of Individualism in the Works of Mead and Chodorow', *American Anthropologist* 86(3): 615–29.

Goldberg, Neil J. and Findlow, Frank J. (1984) 'A Quantitative Analysis of Roman Military Operations in Britain, Circa A.D. 43 to 68', in Ferguson (1984): 359–85.

Gordon, Robert J. and Meggitt, Mervyn J. (1985) *Law and Order in the New Guinea Highlands: Encounters with Enga*. Hanover, NH, London: University Press of New England.

Gross, Daniel R. (1975) 'Protein Capture and Cultural Development in the Amazon Basin', *American Anthropologist* 77(3): 526–49.

Harner, Michael (1977) 'The Ecological Basis for Aztec Sacrifice', *American Ethnologist* 4(1): 117–35.

Harris, Marvin (1984) 'Animal Capture and Yanomamo Warfare: Retrospect and New Evidence', *Journal of Anthropological Research* 40(1): 183–201.

Heider, Karl G. (1976) 'Dani Sexuality: A Low Energy System', *Man* (n.s.) 11(1): 188–201.

Helm, June and Gillespie, Beryl G. (1981) 'Dogrib Oral Tradition as History: War and Peace in the 1820s', *Journal of Anthropological Research* 37(1): 8–27.

Hicks, Frederic (1979) '"Flowery War" in Aztec History', *American Ethnologist* 6(1): 87–92.

Isaac, Barry L. (1983) 'The Aztec "Flowery War": A Geopolitical Explanation', *Journal of Anthropological Research* 39(4): 415–32.

Johnson, Douglas H. (1981) 'The Fighting Nuer: Primary Sources and the Origins of a Stereotype', *Africa* 51(1): 508–27.

Koch, Klaus-Friedrich (1974) *War and Peace in Jalémó*. Cambridge: Harvard University Press.

Kressel, Gideon M. (1981) 'Sororicide/Filiacide: Homicide for Family Honour', *Current Anthropology* 22(2): 141–58.

Kurtz, Donald V. (1981) '*War as a rite de passage*', *Reviews in Anthropology* 8(1): 59–68.

LaFontaine, Jean (1977) 'The Power of Rights', *Man* (n.s.) 12(3/4): 421–37.

Lizot, J. (1977) 'Population, Resources and Warfare Among the Yanomamo', *Man* (n.s.) 12(3/4): 497–517.

Lutz, Catherine (1982) 'The Domain of Emotion Words on Ifaluk', *American Ethnologist* 9(1): 113–28.

Mitchell, Donald (1984) 'Predatory Warfare, Social Status, and the North Pacific Slave Trade', *Ethnology* 23(1): 39–48.

Moss, David (1979) 'Bandits and Boundaries in Sardinia', *Man* (n.s.) 14(3): 477–96.

Nettleship, Martin A., Givens, R. Dale and Nettleship, Anderson (1975) *War, Its Causes and Correlates*. The Hague: Mouton.

Peterson, Nicholas (1975) 'Hunter-Gatherer Territoriality: the Perspective from Australia', *American Anthropologist* 77(1): 53–68.

Podolefsky, Aaron (1984) 'Contemporary Warfare in New Guinea Highlands', *Ethnology* 23(2): 73–88.

Price, Barbara (1984) 'Competition, Productive Intensification and Ranked Society: Speculations from Evolutionary Theory', in Ferguson (1984): 209–40.

Rappaport, Roy A. (1968) *Pigs for the Ancestors*. New Haven: Yale University Press.

Rosen, David M. (1983) 'The Peasant Context of Feminist Revolt in West Africa', *Anthropological Quarterly* 56(1): 35–43.

Saffirio, Giovanni and Scaglion, Richard (1982) 'Hunting Efficiency in Acculturated and Unacculturated Yanomamo Villages', *Journal of Anthropological Research* 38(3): 315–327.

Schieffelin, Edward L. (1976) *The Sorrow of the Lonely and Burning of the Dancers*. New York: St Martin's Press.

Schmink, Marianne (1982) 'Land Conflicts in Amazonia', *American Ethnologist* 9(2): 341–57.

Siegel, Bernard J. (1977) 'The Contestado Rebellion, 1912–1916: a Case Study in Brazilian Messianism and Regional Dynamics', *Journal of Anthropological Research* 33(2): 202–13.

Simmons, William S. (1980) 'Powerlessness, Exploitation and the Soul-Eating Witch: an Analysis of Badyaranke Witchcraft', *American Ethnologist* 7(3): 447–65.

Stoler, Ann (1985) 'Perceptions of Protest: Defining the Dangerous in Colonial Sumatra', *American Ethnologist* 12(4): 642–58.

Stone, Thomas (1983) 'Atomistic Order and Frontier Violence: Miners and Whalemen in the Nineteenth Century', *Ethnology* 22(4): 327–40.

Strathern, Andrew (1984) *A Line of Power*. London: Tavistock.

Warner, W. Lloyd (1962) *American Life, Dream and Reality*. Chicago: University of Chicago Press.

Wilson, Peter J. (1977) '*la pensée alimentaire*: the Evolutionary Context of Rational Objective Thought', *Man* (n.s.) 12(2): 320–35.

Wolf, Eric R. (1969) *Peasant Wars of the Twentieth Century*. New York: Harper and Row.

4

Peace and the Evolutionary Process

Kenneth E. Boulding

The patterns of evolution
In the widest sense, evolution is simply the history of the universe from the 'big bang' on. This history, however, includes three rather different patterns. The first is physical-chemical evolution, which produces the elements, the stars, the compounds, eventually producing DNA and life. With DNA, planet earth takes on a new pattern of biological evolution. This eventually produces the human race, which again sets off a new pattern of societal evolution. Both biological and societal evolution have many patterns in common. A basic concept is that of the ecosystem, which is a system of the interaction of a considerable number of species or populations. Living species, like bacteria, insects, mammals, and humans, consist of populations or sets of individual members of different ages. Each member originates either in a divided cell or in a fertilized egg containing genetic information or 'know-how', which enables it to capture energy to transport and transform selected materials into the form of the phenotype, which grows, ages and eventually dies. The population of a species grows if births exceed deaths, declines if deaths exceed births, or remains stationary if births and deaths are equal. There are complex interactions among the populations in an ecosystem. There is, for instance, a food chain in which the outputs in the shape of bodily growth or excrement of one species become the inputs of another. For the ecosystem to persist indefinitely these have to form a cycle, like the nitrogen cycle, the carbon cycle, the phosphorus cycle, and so on. These cycles require a throughput of energy which in biological species comes mainly from the sun. There are some examples of species using the output of energy from the earth, for instance, in hot springs, on land, or even in the deep oceans.

The interrelations among the species in an ecosystem are quite complex. Three major relationships can be distinguished: co-operative, in which an increase in the population of either of two species will increase the population of the other; competitive, in which an increase in the population of either of two species diminishes the population of the other; and predative – if A eats B, an increase in A diminishes B, an increase in B increases A. This relationship is often surprisingly stable and leads to the survival both of the predator and the prey. Two species competing for the same food supply, such as lions and tigers, will be competitive.

Two species each of which increases the food supply of the other, like sheep and dung beetles, are co-operative. Two species in which one eats the other are predative.

'Struggle' as a poor strategy for survival

The metaphors used by Herbert Spencer and Darwin contributed, unfortunately, to the misunderstanding of the evolutionary process. The 'survival of the fittest' is a rather meaningless tautology. If we ask 'fit what for?', it means simply fit to survive. It signifies little more than the survival of the surviving, which does not tell us very much. The 'struggle for existence' is also a very poor metaphor. Struggle in the sense of conscious conflict is very rare in the biosphere. Competition is usually unconscious. Struggle and conscious conflict appear in sexual selection, where the males fight for the females, but this often leads to the extinction of the species, as the traits which enable males to win their fights are not necessarily those which lead to the survival of the species.

There are innumerable strategies for survival, only very few of which involve overt conflict. The sloth survives by being lazy and therefore having a very small throughput of energy. Some species survive by individualism, some by community, in herds. Some survive by being visible, some by being invisible. The critical concept here is that of the niche, which is an equilibrium population of the species in which births equal deaths. If this is positive, the species will survive if it exists. If the population is below the equilibrium level, things will be easy: food will be plentiful, the species as prey will be hard to find, births will exceed deaths and population will grow. Above the equilibrium population, things will be hard: food will be scarcer, predators will be more effective, deaths will exceed births and the population will decline. A good metaphor is 'the survival of the fitting', that is, the species that fits into a niche in the ecosystem. There are innumerable ways of doing this. There are niches for both the lion and the lamb. The ecosystem is a home for both. Some species survive by having high birth and death rates, some by having low birth and death rates, and every variation in between.

On the whole, biological evolution is a process in which strictly dialectical processes, in which there is conscious struggle and in which something wins and something loses, are of very minor significance. Competition indeed is very important. But competition is not the same as conflict. Success in competition on the whole comes from outproducing, outbreeding, outgrowing other species, not by beating them down. There is virtually no analogy to war in biological evolution. There are occasionally some analogies to theft, like the cuckoo that lays its eggs in other birds' nests. The predator may be a little red in tooth and claw, but even the predator helps its prey to survive as a species and prevents it from suffering possible Malthusian catastrophe.

There is indeed a role in evolution for catastrophe, though it is not wholly clear what it is. Each geographical age seems to end in a catastrophe with the widespread extinction of existing species, which then opens up a lot of new niches for other species, often of a more complex nature. Humans probably would not be here today if it had not been for some catastrophe that exterminated the dinosaurs and opened up the niches for larger animals, to the mammals. Many of these catastrophes seem to have been external to the system, like the asteroid that is credited with exterminating the dinosaurs, though there is some doubt about this. It is not inconceivable that an evolutionary system could create an internal catastrophe through the breakdown of food chains and cycles, the using up of ultimately limited resources, or the development of predative efficiency, to the point where the predators eat all the prey and then die out themselves. The record of evolutionary catastrophe, however, is so fragmentary that we really do not know very much about it.

Societal evolution
Societal evolution, which begins with the human race, although there are traces of it earlier, arises from the extraordinary capacity of the human race for knowledge and know-what, that is, images in the mind which correspond to structures in the real world, out of which comes continually increasing know-how in the production of human artefacts. There are now far more species of human artefacts than there are biological species, and societal evolution can be thought of mainly as the evolution of these artefacts. There are roughly three kinds of human artefacts: things, from flint knives to the space shuttle; organizations, from the hunting band to the Catholic Church, the national state, the corporation, and the United Nations – and we should not forget the family, which still survives. The third human artefact is people themselves. Each of us is a combination of a biological artefact from a fertilized egg and a human artefact in terms of language, custom, behaviour, occupation, and so on.

Human artefacts like automobiles are 'born' when they are produced. They may even exhibit growth, although this is rarer than in biological artefacts, and they will eventually age, decay and die. The production of human artefacts does not essentially differ from the processes by which biological artefacts, that is, living creatures, are created. Both of them start off with some form of genetic factor or know-how. This has to be able to capture energy in suitable forms to transport and transform selected materials of the proper kind into the structure of the artefact. Human artefacts differ from biological artefacts mainly because their genetic structure is not contained in the artefacts themselves. The know-how which produces an automobile is not contained in the automobile itself in the way that the know-how that produces the horse is contained in the genes of the stallion and the mare. Human artefacts are multi-parental. Their genetic structures have to be found in human knowledge, in computers, in libraries, plans, blueprints, and so on, but this genetic structure still has to have control over energy and materials if the product of the know-how is to be realized. Production is always the transformation of the genotype into the phenotype. Besides energy and materials, it also requires space and time. These, however, are limiting factors. They may prevent the emergence of the phenotype if they are not there in the right kind of quantities, but they cannot themselves create it.

Organizations based on threat, exchange and integrative relations

The production of organizations in large numbers of different kinds is almost unique to the human race. Prehuman organizations like beehives, beaver dams, and so on, are mainly biogenetic in origin. Things like wolf packs, caribou herds, and so on, and even more baboon groups, presage human organization. Human organization grows mainly out of the capacity for language and communication and the human capacity for knowledge and very complex images of the world. Organizations (in which we should also include informal groups, reference groups as the line between an organization and a group is not very clear) arise out of relationships both among individuals and groups which are virtually peculiar to the human race. Three such relationships may be identified, which can be described as threat, exchange or integrative relationships. These are not wholly unknown in the prehuman biosphere – mating, the family, child-rearing and even something like organized defence against predators, warning calls, and so on, are precursors of these human relationships at a very simple level.

Threat systems develop when one person or group says to another, 'You do something I want or I will do something you don't want'. What happens then depends on the reaction of the threatened party, which can be submission, as in slavery; defiance, as in tax refusal or rebellion; counter-threat ('you do something nasty to me and I'll do something nasty to you!'), which may lead to deterrence; threat reduction, like armour plate and city walls; or flight, getting out of range of the threatener, which has also been very important in human history. War is primarily a product of the threat system, especially organized threat systems, particularly where the reaction is counter-threat. It is the ability of humans to communicate threats, which create these threat systems, and the very limited ability to communicate threat on the part of prehuman animals that makes war a peculiarly human institution.

The exchange relationship begins when A says to B, 'You do something I want and I'll do something you want.' This may involve the exchange of human artefacts, though it has larger aspects in terms of reciprocity. The perception of terms of reciprocity is a very fundamental human motivator. How much do I get per unit of what I give? This is a function of the price system in terms of commodities, that is, the ratios of exchange. The concept can also be broadened to include status, legitimacy, services, and so on, as in the family, the group or the organization. If one member of such a group perceives a situation as one in which that member is giving a great deal and is not getting very much, that it has poor terms of reciprocity, the group relationship is endangered and may end in divorce in the case of the family, quitting or being fired in the case of the firm, emigrating or rebelling in the case of the nation, and so on.

The integrative relationship is a little harder to capture in systematic form. In some sense, however, it dominates all the others, as neither threat nor exchange can develop very far without some sort of legitimacy and acceptance into a group. Integrative power arises when someone says, 'You do something because of what you are and what I am', and these identities are mutually recognized. The complex interactions among threat, exchange and integrative systems, and all human institutions and organizations, involve all three in different proportions. The stock market is high on exchange, but it has an underlying legal threat system and requires integrative structures of trust and courtesy. Armed forces are strong on threat, but rely on their integrative structure with the state and the tax system for most of their exchange capacity and, of course, on markets for things they buy. The church and the family are strong on integrative structures, but also have an underlying background of threat and exchange.

Inclusive peace defined as 'not war'

Where, then, does war and peace fit into this larger evolutionary pattern? Peace is a word of many meanings and qualities. There is the peace of the grave, peace of mind, the *Pax Romana*, the peace that passeth understanding, and so on. The simplest and largest concept is that peace is that part of activity, particularly human activity, which is not war. This might be called 'inclusive peace', and it is a very important concept. Inclusive peace, of course, can have different qualities. There may be an imposed peace, imposed by a threat system to which there is no counter-threat, which most people would regard as rather low quality. It may be an unjust peace, a situation in which there is no war, but in which many people feel that their terms of reciprocity are very poor, in which there is inequality, poverty, exploitation, and so on. It will help perhaps if we think of the division of total human activity into various sections, as shown in Figure 1. Thus, the line AF represents the total of human activity, which can be divided into non-conflict (AC) and conflict (CF). Non-conflict in turn can be divided into productive activity (AB) and neutral activity (BC). Total activity (AF) can also be divided into war (EF) and inclusive peace (AE), which may further be divided into just or good peace (AD) and unjust or bad peace (DE). Conflict is divided into war (EF) and peaceful conflict (CE), which is part of inclusive peace. Inclusive peace, therefore, includes such things as ploughing, sowing, reaping, growing things, making things, eating and drinking, having fun, music and dancing, learning and studying, teaching, having peaceful conflicts according to law, mediation and conciliation, and so on. Some peaceful conflicts may be productive, some may be unproductive. All these categories overlap somewhat and are hard to reduce to a linear field.

FIGURE 1
A taxonomy of peace

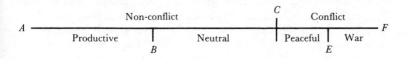

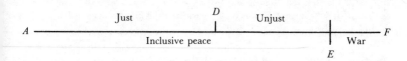

Looked at as an evolutionary-ecological system, it is clear that throughout human history there have been niches both for non-conflictual activities of many kinds and for conflict, and for peace of many kinds and for war. The critical question is, what creates these niches and what determines their size? This is by no means an easy question to answer.

War and peace as proportions of human activity

An important preliminary question, to which only very rough answers can be given in the present state of human knowledge, is that of the size of these various niches as a proportion of total human activity, and the question as to what has been happening to these various niches over time. We do know something about the division of gross national product or, what would be a better measure of the total size of the economy, the gross capacity product, that is, what the gross national product would have been if the unemployed had been producing, into activities devoted to war and those not devoted to war. In the United States, the proportion of the gross capacity product in the war industry has varied from less than 1 percent in the early 1930s to 42 percent in the Second World War, 14 percent in the Korean War, to about 7 percent today. Figures on the proportion of the total labour-force in the military show similar fluctuations, though it is hard to separate the labour-force in the whole war industry, that is, employed by firms which supply things to the military. For the world as a whole, it is doubtful whether the war industry has more than 7 to 10 percent of the world product. It is something like 15 percent in the Soviet Union, 25 or 30 percent in Israel. It is pretty high in some Arab countries, but these have very small populations. For the Third World, it tends to be in the order of 3 or 4 percent; 10 percent would be a fairly high estimate. To get the proportion devoted to conflict, we would want to add to this the legal industry, strikes (usually less than 1 percent of the total product), politicians, time spent in personal feuds and domestic conflict. It would be surprising, however, if the aggregate of human activity devoted to conflict were more than about 15 percent, leaving about 85 percent for non-conflictual and perhaps 90 percent for non-war activity. Figures of this kind do not go back much before the twentieth century. Adam Smith in 1776 remarked, however, that 'not more than one hundredth part of the inhabitants of any country can be employed as soldiers, without ruin to the country which pays the expence of their service' (Smith, 1937: 657–8). War figures prominently in written and oral history because it is so dramatic and visible, but over time it is doubtful whether it has averaged more than 5 or at most 10 percent of human activity.

War and peace as proportions of the arts

An interesting indicator in this field would be the arts. No one, as far as I know, has ever done a survey of this, though it would be quite feasible. Drama relies heavily on conflict, for this is what the plots of most plays, operas and novels are about. Actual violence, however, is concentrated heavily in detective stories. Even in Tolstoy's *War and Peace* most of the scenes are rather peaceful. In Jane Austen's novels, the most violent episode is where the heroine sprains her ankle, and these were written during the Napoleonic Wars! Even in the novel and drama, however, much of the interest lies in the resolution of conflict, the 'they lived happily ever after' syndrome. In Shakespeare's tragedies the contending parties wear themselves out or kill each other off and at the end of the play MacDuff or Fortinbras takes over and peace of some sort is restored.

When it comes to the visual arts, the 15-percent figure for conflict may well hold. Most landscape painting and portraiture is peaceful. One thinks of Vermeer, Canaletto, Constable and the Hudson Valley School. Scenes of violence are surprisingly rare. Battles seem to be poor subjects for great art. There is, of course, *Guernica*, but even most of Picasso's work is very peaceful, as is that of the Impressionists. Even Van Gogh's paintings portray inner conflict of the artist rather than scenes of violence. Television may be something of an exception. Violence on television is a perennial complaint. This may be due to its very volume. Television is the paradise of the bad artist, for whom the portrayal of violence is an easy way out, but it takes a really good artist, dramatist or novelist to portray the peaceful 85 percent in an interesting way. When it comes to music there is very little conflict, and what there is is resolved in harmony. Harmony, after all, is the business of music, with a few modern exceptions. In poetry, while dramatic poetry, like Homer and *Paradise Lost*, is about conflict and war, the great volume of lyric poetry reflects peace, of which the Japanese haiku are a wonderful example. Even in the arts, therefore, peace is much more important than historians have usually made it out to be.

Peace as characterizing economic life
When it comes to economic life, peace is overwhelmingly important. It is the industry of peace that makes war possible. Armies must be fed, clothed and transported. War on the whole is impoverishing. It diverts resources into destruction that could be used for production. The heightening of human experience which it represents may create inventions useful for peaceful pursuits which would otherwise not have been made, but even here the record is very dubious. Spill-overs are seldom very nourishing. We might have had nuclear energy and computers a little later if it had not been for the Second World War, but even here the war industry was a diversion. The light-water reactor, which essentially came out of the war industry, has been an economic disaster, and the high-tech machine-tool industry is not much better (Dumas, 1982). Swords make very poor ploughshares when they are of the wrong kind of steel.

The technology of war, especially of weaponry, and the technology of peace and economic development do come out of the same process of human learning and the development of know-how, that is, social mutation. But the technology of peace has been overwhelmingly more important. The invention of agriculture, of weaving and pottery, the domestication of more animals, the rise of commerce and finance, the development of transportation, owed very little to war. The warrior takes the inventions of peace and uses them for destruction, but rarely produces inventions of his own. It is the exchange system, not the threat system, that produces the division of labour, as Adam Smith saw so well, that increases human know-how, that creates enrichment. War impoverishes, trade enriches. The asymmetry between war and peace is reflected in the proposition that war would be impossible without the arts of peace. Peace would be entirely possible without the arts of war.

War and the integrative system
We see the same asymmetry in the relation between war and the threat system and the integrative system. War is the product, through not a necessary and inevitable product of the division of the human race into integrative groups, like nations or sometimes churches. It finds a niche

when individuals have strong integrative relationships with individuals in the same group and very weak or even negative integrative relationships with individuals in other groups. Just how these groups are created is something of a mystery. Religions originate in charismatic individuals who create an integrative structure around them that other individuals are moved to join and become part of. Nation-states are much more accidental. They are often relics of past empires, though war is sometimes important in their origins, like the United States. Many nations, however, have originated by the peaceful break-up of empire, like most of the African states. The evidence is very strong that empire is an economic burden on the imperial power, that it rewards only a very small proportion of its citizens and has a negative impact on the rest. It is not surprising, therefore, that empires are unstable. They may be created by war, as they usually are, but their disintegration to a considerable extent comes about by processes which are essentially peaceful and economic. They also dissolve because of problems with the integrative system – empires that are too large and diverse fail to become an integrated unit to which people wish to belong. The optimum size of the political unit, like the national state, may actually be quite small. Large and heterogeneous societies have great difficulty governing themselves.

War is sometimes defended on the thesis that an external war creates internal unity within a nation. The evidence for this, however, is very dubious. The feeling that Germany was surrounded by enemies may have helped to elect Hitler. The hostility of the United States has certainly unified a very heterogeneous Soviet Union, which would probably be much happier and richer if it broke up into its constituent nations. But the exceptions to this rule are also very numerous. The Vietnam War certainly disunified the United States, as the Afghan War is probably doing to the Soviet Union.

The costs of victory and the pay-offs of defeat
An aspect of the problem which has been somewhat neglected by historians is the impact of victory or defeat in war on the overall culture and economy of nations. It is nearly always just assumed that the victory is beneficial to the victor. On the other hand, the evidence against this is very strong. We see this in the economies of various nations. The Spanish victories which created the great Spanish Empire debilitated Spain both economically and culturally. The results are still noticeable today. Spain did not participate in the rise of science and the Industrial Revolution. If one asks who won the Second World War economically, the answer is fairly clear. It was Japan and Germany, who were defeated. They got rid of their military and were able to devote all their resources to getting rich. Sweden, defeated by Napoleon, entered on a course of economic development which transformed it, certainly between 1860 and, say, 1960, from one of the poorest countries in Europe to one of the

richest. Again, it abstained from being a great power and devoted most of its resources to getting rich.

No principle in a pattern as complex as human history is ever universal. Certainly Carthage took a long time to recover from its defeat by Rome, although the Roman ruins in Tunisia certainly suggest that economically the region did fairly well. The Turkish Empire was stagnant economically for many centuries, both for the Turks and for their subjects.

The cultural impacts of military defeat are even more striking than the economic impacts. It was after the defeat of France by Germany in the eighteenth century that Paris became the cultural capital of the world, with the Impressionists, Debussy, Delibes and the great upsurge of French literature, while Berlin stagnated culturally. It was after 1919 that Berlin became a great cultural capital, producing modern architecture, the Bauhaus, several schools of painting, an upsurge of literature, and so on, all of which were stopped by Hitler in 1932. Many other examples could be given.

War has to be treated as an ecological, not as an economic phenomenon. Its organizational embodiment is in what I have called 'unilateral national defence organizations', like the United States Department of Defense and its equivalent in other countries. To these we have to add unofficial military organizations, the so-called terrorists, a terrorist being essentially a soldier without a government, though terrorists usually want a government to give them legitimacy, as the Declaration of Independence gave legitimacy to the 'terrorists' of the American Revolution. As Stouffer's study of the American soldier indicated (Stouffer, 1950), integrative structures are strongest at the level of the small group. Soldiers die for their buddies rather than for any cause. There is some evidence of co-operative behaviour between small groups of opposing armies to reduce fatalities and damage, usually much opposed by the officers. This is something that usually does not get into the historical record.

We have to think of unilateral national defence organizations as ecologically co-operative with each other. They are usually competitive with their own civilian populations. The common phenomenon of the arms race is a good example of this, where the individual search for security creates insecurity for all. It is a fundamental principle of the threat system that deterrence can only be stable in the short run. If it were really stable, it would cease to deter. Historically, virtually all systems of deterrence have broken down into war unless there has been some external shift in the parameters of the system. War, then, has to be seen essentially as a self-justifying phenomenon arising out of a weakness in integrative systems. It has very little to do with the patterns of economic or cultural conflict.

A question of great interest here is the ecological difference between war and policing. Police are different from soldiers, even though they are part of the threat system, mainly because what they hope to restrain by threat – and to punish if it is not restrained – is crime, committed mainly by individuals or small groups who are still perceived as part of the larger society. Hence there are some integrative bonds between the police and criminals which are not supposed to exist between soldiers on opposite sides of a war. There is, however, something of a spectrum between policing and war. There are times when the police behave almost as if they were at war, like the Philadelphia bombings of 1985. There are times when wars are officially justified as policing operations. Even though the police and the military occupy niches essentially created by government, they do have subtle but important differences. The police are more 'economic'. There is some cost-benefit analysis involved in them, even though it may not always work very well. Cost-benefit analysis is essentially alien to military organizations and operations, perhaps because there are values involved which are regarded as absolute, such as national sovereignty. When we get to a situation like the present, however, in which in a nuclear age national sovereignty can only be preserved by creating a positive probability of national destruction, the absence of cost-benefit analysis in the military becomes very threatening.

The rise of stable peace

What, then, are the evolutionary hopes for peace, at least for the continued expansion of the proportion of human activity devoted to peace and a diminution of that portion devoted to war? The profound technical changes in both the peace segment of human activity and the war segment, in the twentieth century especially, have created a situation in which war is increasingly seen as a threat to the very existence of the human race and the legitimacy of war, therefore, is being seriously eroded, especially in the temperate zone, the so-called First and Second Worlds. There are many indicators which suggest that the evolutionary process, if it does not destroy us first, will produce a war-less world, though by exactly what institutions is by no means clear. One very important indicator is the growth of the areas of stable peace in the world, that is, groups of nations which have no plans whatever to go to war with each other. I have argued that stable peace probably began in Scandinavia after the Napoleonic Wars between Sweden and Denmark, spread to North America about 1870, to Western Europe, Japan, Australia and New Zealand after the Second World War (Boulding, 1978). Now we have a great triangle of stable peace, stretching roughly from Australia to Japan, across North America, to Finland, with about eighteen countries which have no plans whatever to go to war with each other. This has happened without much planning or even understanding, just by the development of mutual taboos on boundary change.

The critical question at the moment is how to expand this area to include the Soviet Union and the communist countries, and then how to expand it to include the rest of the world. Economic interdependence assists this process, as this increases the costs and diminishes the benefits of war, and some kind of cost-benefit analysis may be penetrating the military culture. There are striking parallels to this movement in the collapse of the feudal system after the rise of effective cannon and gunpowder, which made both the feudal castle and the walled city indefensible. This led very rapidly to the rise of national states and the abolition of feudal warfare. We see the same phenomenon in Japan, with the rise of the *shogunate* and the taming of the *daimyo*, the feudal barons. The evolutionary model, therefore, at least gives hope, even though it is profoundly indeterministic and still leaves the future highly uncertain.

References

Boulding, Kenneth E. (1978) *Stable Peace*. Austin: University of Texas Press.

Dumas, Lloyd J. (ed.) (1982) *The Political Economy of Arms Reduction: Reversing Economic Decay*. Boulder: Westview Press.

Smith, Adam (1937) *The Wealth of Nations*. Modern Library Edition. New York: Random House.

Stouffer, Samuel A., et al. (1950) *The American Soldier: Studies in Social Psychology in World War II*. Princeton: Princeton University Press.

PART III

War and Peace in the International System

5

Peace and War in Modern Times

F. H. Hinsley

In the history of relations between the world's leading states certain
features stand out prominently since the end of the eighteenth century.
One is that infrequent wars have alternated with long periods of peace.
From the 1760s to the 1790s these states were at peace; from the 1790s
to 1815 they were at war; from 1815 to 1854, peace; 1854 to 1871 war;
1871 to 1914, peace; 1914 to 1918, war; 1918 to 1939, peace; 1939 to
1945, war; and since 1945 another forty years of peace already. Just as
prominent is the fact that each of these infrequent wars has been more
demanding and devastating for all participants, more nearly total, than
that which preceded it. In these respects, as also in a third on which I
shall enlarge later on, international conduct in the past 200 years has
differed from international conduct in all earlier times.

In earlier times it is not too much to say that international conduct
everywhere conformed to patterns of conflict characteristic of primitive
societies. Either war and peace were not sharply differentiated – public
war, private war, rebellion and crime being barely distinguishable in the
absence of adequate public authority – or, if public war was a distinct
and organized activity, it was indulged in with such regularity, not to
say seasonally, and was conducted on such a restricted scale, without
escalation, that it remained a natural activity.

Most of us have some knowledge of the primitive pattern; in some
parts of the world it still operates today. And most of us are familiar
with the chief characteristics of the modern pattern. What we perhaps
find difficult to grasp is that even in Europe, in conditions that had
become far from primitive in other respects, conflict conformed to the
norms of primitive societies until so comparatively recently as 200 years
ago. During the whole of the seventeenth century, however, there were
only seven years in which none of the European states was at war. In
the first two-thirds of the eighteenth century some or other of the
European states were at war during two out of every three years; and
of the individual states the United Kingdom, which was not abnormally
belligerent, was at war for nearly two-and-a-half years out of every five.
As for the scale of warfare, its very frequency indicates how restricted
it continued to be, what lack of intensity still marked its conduct, and
there is no lack of detailed evidence to that effect.

When we ask why this situation gave way to the modern one, and why it did so when it did, we should bear in mind that for a long time after the end of the eighteenth century the transition was confined to the relations between the more developed states and societies. A condition of affairs evocative of the primitive one was not abnormal throughout the nineteenth century for such parts of the world as escaped Europe's control or were failing to share in Europe's advance, and in some areas it is not abnormal to this day. For the different experience of the developed states, on the other hand, the phenomenon of Europe's advance provides a sufficient, if also the obvious, answer to our question. In the last resort it was as a result of the subjection of societies and states to the process of modernization or industrialization – a process based since the eighteenth century to an ever-increasing extent on science and technology – that international conduct acquired the characteristics in relation to peace and war that have distinguished it in modern times. In particular, it was because that process had so great an impact on the destructiveness of weapons, on the structure of societies and on the capacities and concerns of governments that between the industrializing societies – if only between them – the modern pattern of peace and war came into being.

The continuing and accelerating increase in the deadliness of weapons began only in the eighteenth century. By the middle of the nineteenth century it had already advanced so far as to ensure of itself that war would be fought at a higher level of violence each time it recurred. Nor is that all. In the 1860s the fear that this would be so produced the first attempts by states to place international restrictions on the development and use of new weapons; and we need not doubt that although all such attempts have been ineffective, the first of them marks the point at which anxiety about the weapons revolution began to contribute to that other feature of the modern system – the alternation of bouts of war with long periods of peace – by making states more hesitant to fight each other.

By the same date the huge power of technology to transform the nature of society had begun to create out of rural, provincialized communities societies that were much more integrated, more centralized, more nationalized than ever before. One important consequence of this was that the leading states abandoned long-service professional armies and replaced them with national conscription. By 1900 this change was reinforcing the weapons revolution by making it still more certain that any future war would be more nearly total than any previous conflict; and in 1914 it was to be confirmed that the greatly increased integration, articulation and regulation of the European societies had made the exhaustion of the enemy's national resources, and of his national will to fight on, the inescapable objective in war, the only war aim for the great powers, even as the weapons revolution had erected mechanical and mass attrition, on a dreadful scale, into the centrepiece of battle. But the greater integration of societies had been accompanied, in the wake of the same industrializing process, by their greater material sophistication. Ever since the beginning of the Industrial Revolution, and at an ever-increasing rate, the range of a society's forms of enterprise, and of its means of maintaining and multiplying power and wealth, had been widening and becoming more complex, and by the 1860s the days – no, the centuries – were fast receding when land had been the main source of wealth and when, next only to marrying it, conquest had been the most cost-effective way of acquiring it. Industrialization was presenting fast-developing societies with opportunities for advancement and satisfaction other than war at the same time as it was increasing the inescapable destructiveness and risk of war. In this way, by producing a changing balance of calculation, it explains why wars between these societies were now separated by long periods of peace as well as why their wars were always increasing in scale.

This was all the more the case because industrialization, by exerting a profound impact on the character and capacity of government, was creating state structures which could calculate with some consistency, and channels through which their conclusions could be imposed. Until the eighteenth century, war was an undertaking for which, like agriculture then or manufacturing now, large sections of society were naturally organized. It was also an activity on which, appearances notwithstanding, societies embarked with scant regard for the wishes or the warnings of governments. Indeed, communications remained so negligible, and state apparatuses so weak, that it may be questioned whether rulers did more than merely reflect and channel the social consensus that pressed for war until men were tired or satisfied enough to press for peace. But from the end of the eighteenth century the impact of science and technology was producing ever more powerful and regulatory governments. And if this accentuated the ability of societies that were in any case more integrated to sustain prolonged and systematic warfare, it also enabled their governments – governments which were being forced to take more and more account of the growing burden of being prepared for war and of the growing risks involved in increasingly destructive war – to impose restraints. It thus redoubled the impetus of those other developments which were ensuring that, if peace between the leading states continued to break down, it did so only at long intervals.

It will not have escaped notice that this outcome might look less significant if we summed it up, as we equally accurately can do, as one by which, if only at long intervals, war between these states continued to break out. And I will not conceal that many historians of the detailed behaviour of the modern international system, and especially of those international crises from which war ensued, as in 1914 and 1939, would opt for this other way of stating the matter – would argue that this vast change in the context in which conflict took place produced merely an alteration in the rhythm of conflict and not any change in its fundamental dynamics.

Nor will I deny that they have a point. No one who has studied the crises of 1914 and 1939 will question that the government decisions preceding the outbreak of war were accompanied by great disarray in the government machines, or that the source of the disarray was anguish – was regret that it was necessary to take the decisions. There is no doubt that the governments were, as never before, reluctant to fight each other. But there is equally no doubt that they believed that the decisions they took were necessary and justified. At any rate until 1945, for all their increasing reluctance to fight each other, governments would not or could not in the last resort relinquish a basic right. This right, which was established long before the eighteenth century and which had since been consolidated – freed from external moral and theological sources of restraint – by the rise of the modern state and the advance of the industrializing process, was the *ius ad bellum*: the legal right of the state to go to war for any reason whatever – indeed, for no reason at all – to preserve the security or advance the interests of its society. All states conceded that any state invoking this right acquired the privileges of belligerency, and these privileges included the legal right to the spoils of war. The right to challenge the status quo was matched by the right to change it by holding on to conquests.

It may be that states clung to this right only because it corresponded to their duty to their societies; but cling to it they did. And in view of their tenacious retention of it in changing circumstances, it may well be thought that it is indeed the case that, at least until our own day, industrialization was affecting only the context and the tactics of conflict. It is at this point, however, that a third outstanding feature of the behaviour of states in modern times must be brought into the account. At the end of every war since the end of the eighteenth century, as had never been the case before, and at the time of every serious threat of war after the middle of the nineteenth century, the leading states made a concerted effort, each one more radical than the last, to reconstruct the international system on lines that would enable them, or so they believed, to avoid a further war.

These successive efforts to reform produced, after 1815, the Concert of Europe, a system under which states agreed for the first time in history, as a means of enabling them to behave towards one another with restraint and to make sparing use of their right to go to war, to meet in conference at regular intervals in time of peace. Then at the Paris Peace Congress in 1856 following the Crimean War, and again at two conferences at The Hague in 1899 and 1907 when the Concert system was breaking down in the aftermath of a period of war between 1854 and 1871, they considered for the first time the practicality of introducing legal rules that would require them to submit their disputes to arbitration. They found it was not practicable, or that they could not agree that it was practicable, thus to tamper with their absolute right to go to war; and they confined themselves to setting up an arbitration procedure to which resort was voluntary. But in 1918, at the end of the First World War, the leading states, or at least some of the victors among them, at last accepted the discipline of compulsory arbitration or compulsory conciliation of their disputes by signing the Covenant of the League of Nations.

It is evident that it was with reluctance that the signatories of the Covenant so far limited their right to go to war. The text of the Covenant rested on a series of compromises between their conviction that it was imperative to limit that right and their feeling that it was unwise or impossible to do so; and the most important of those compromises was enshrined in the League's conception of the moratorium, a period of delay during which it was illegal for a state to go to war while obligatory pacific settlement was attempted, but after the expiry of which war was as legal as ever. But the compromises of the Covenant point up the significance of the next round of experiment in revising the international system – that on which states embarked in 1928, when the League was breaking down, but did not complete until the Second World War was coming to an end. It produced in 1928 the Kellogg pact whereby some states renounced for the first time in history the right to go to war. In 1945 it produced not only reliance on that renunciation to vindicate the insistence of the War Crimes Tribunals that aggressive war was already a crime, but also, with the establishment of the United Nations, a reaffirmation of the renunciation.

The UN, like the League, was set up to enable the states to avoid further war; but it completed a process of reaction against, of revulsion from, the compromises of the Covenant in two significant respects. In its procedure for enforcing the pacific settlement of disputes, the Covenant had placed great emphasis on the distinction between war in legal and war in illegal circumstances – on the differences between just and unjust war. The Charter of the United Nations placed the emphasis on the importance of avoiding all war at almost all costs, and instead of imposing legal rules and automatic sanctions upon member states the UN required the member states to impose a new standard of conduct upon themselves by resolving that the renunciation of the right to war should be a condition of membership of the new organization.

It is not difficult to account for these differences between the League and the United Nations. The UN was set up by states which could not fail to know that since 1919 – indeed, in the few years since 1939 – the impact of industrialization on the scale of weapons, the structure of society and the capacity of government had had more effect than in the whole of previous history in raising the potential destructiveness of war and reducing its potential utility for the more advanced societies. Nor need we doubt that it is on this account that, although the renunciation of the right to war constitutes a greater limitation on the freedom of states than any that was created by the Covenant, states have not subsequently disowned the United Nations in the way they disowned the League of Nations by deserting it.

It may be felt that this last fact is no great testimony to the view that in 1945 the states achieved a great advance – so dismal has been the performance of the UN since it was established. Moreover, the renunciation of the right to war is qualified – it is subject to the right of self-defence and is waived when states are carrying out the instructions of the Security Council – and states have easily exploited these loopholes. No state now has a war office, but all retain the department and call it the ministry of defence. No state now declares war when it uses force in contravention of its pledge; if a state cannot plead self-defence or UN instructions for using force, it either resorts to it without admitting that it is doing so or it justifies its action by claiming, often with the approval of self-interested members of the General Assembly, that it is acting as the UN would act if the Security Council were not stalled – by helping a legitimate government against rebellion, for example, or helping rebels to advance an indubitably moral cause. But these subterfuges confirm rather than weaken the argument that at the end of the Second World War the states completed a monumental revision of the international system. They are subterfuges to which states descend in order to remain within the letter of a new rule of conduct and you do not make efforts to appear to conform to a rule which you do not accept. We must not forget, moreover, the difference between rules of conduct and the laws of nature. You do not make a rule to the effect that water must not flow uphill; but man-made law would not be law – indeed, it would not be made – unless it could be broken or bent. It lays down rules but does not ensure that they will be observed. What came about with the acceptance of the abolition of the right of the state to go to war was the completion of a shift of norms; and involving, as it did, the recognition that war had ceased to be a legalized or sanctified form of force, it constituted a greater displacement of assumptions about relations between states than any that has taken place in history.

If a shift is so fundamental we may be sure of two things. It will have been a long time in preparation. And once it has been made, and if it is consolidated, it will have multiple and far-reaching repercussions. In the case of this shift I have already argued that it was being prepared throughout the history of the modern international system. Indeed, its completion was nothing less than the logical outcome of those developments, and of those responses to developments, which explain the history of that system and account for its distinctive features. But is it possible to claim that the shift has as yet produced any noticeable repercussions? I believe it is. There is much evidence to suggest that other displacements of belief, subsidiary to and consequential upon the first, have been taking place in recent years.

Most prominently – and this should cause no surprise since Marxism-Leninism is the most rigorous and self-conscious of all modern ideologies – the evidence is to be found in the steps that have been taken to adjust the doctrines of Marxism-Leninism. The central tenet of Marxism-

Leninism relating to the issue of peace and war used to be the doctrine that war is enevitable between socialist and capitalist societies. But in 1956, at the Twentieth Congress of the Communist Party of the Soviet Union, it was formally cancelled. No less important, another doctrine was made central in its place – the doctrine of peaceful coexistence which insists that the rivalry which is inevitable between societies with different structures and ideologies, but is supposedly inevitable only between such societies, must for ever be kept short of war by the states.

At the time, and for years afterwards, the capitalist societies regarded this change as constituting no more than a dangerous tactical twist in the Bolshevik offensive, one that was designed to lull them into a false sense of security while Stalin's successors rescued Russia from Stalin's excesses and prepared to return to the true Bolshevik path. Even now, this suspicion is not wholly stilled. Nor is it wholly unjustified, given that the Soviets have used the new doctrine to justify the continuation of an ideological offensive in conditions of political detente. But this residue of distrust is of little significance compared with the fact that since the 1960s capitalist states have embraced the Marxist-Leninist new-model doctrine of peaceful coexistence for themselves, and made it their own overriding doctrine in the field of relations between states. Nor does China any longer remain outside the consensus. For the first time since the Bolshevik Revolution of 1917, communism and capitalism, East and West, now subscribe to the same basic view that war between the great states is outmoded and must be avoided.

We may be sure from what we know of the rigidity of the Marxist-Leninist laboratory of thought that the belief in the inevitability of war was not abandoned lightly by the Soviet authorities. Many considerations must have contributed to bring about the adjustment, not least the need to come to terms with the advocacy of peaceful coexistence by the non-aligned states of the Third World. But those considerations will also have included the need to come to terms with the consequences of the ongoing revolution in the scale and destructiveness of weapons – a problem to which we may be sure that, though we have few details about it, the response of the Soviet authorities was not greatly different from that of the Western nuclear powers.

For the Western powers the problem became acute in the early 1950s when sophisticated nuclear weapons were superseding the atomic bomb, the missile was superseding the bomber, the submarine was emerging as the perfect moving missile-platform – and when the West's monopoly of these advantages was being shattered by developments in Soviet Russia. From the outset until the middle of the 1960s the response of the West was, as all the literature on strategic studies proclaimed, to seek to reintegrate strategy with policy – to restore to diplomacy the flexibility and the range of options that the latest developments were taking away from it. Not surprisingly, and the less so in that these years were years of cold war, this amounted to an effort to develop strategies and weapons by which, if diplomacy failed, the West could preserve the options of threatening war and of going to war with other nuclear states in the last resort. Techniques of crisis management, theories for the control of escalation, strategies of flexible response, the development of tactical or little nuclear weapons – these suggestions were all advanced in the hope that, by enabling nuclear states to evade the ineluctable outcome of nuclear deadlock, the strategy of 'the great deterrent', they would preserve the possibility of limited war.

If we read these elaborations today we bring away one unmistakable impression. They possess all the cogency, all the intellectual rigour and all the irrelevance of the scholastic writings of the Middle Ages. And whence their irrelevance? The answer lies partly in the recognition that they did not pause to ask whether, if disciplines designed to avoid total war were accepted by one nuclear state, they would be accepted by another, or whether, if such disciplines were accepted by all nuclear states before the outbreak of hostilities, they would be observed by all after hostilities had broken out. But it lies mainly in the fact that since the mid-1960s the response of Western states and strategic thinkers to the continuing increase in the sophistication and deadliness of weapons has undergone a fundamental change.

Their reasoning since then has been that should provocation lead to war between the world's most developed states – or should miscalculation do so – there is no reasonable hope of avoiding massive nuclear exchanges and no possibility of providing civil defence against them; that if it is thus imperative to avoid war, then, far from trying to avoid dependence on the great deterrent of mutually assured destruction, it is imperative to ensure against provocation and miscalculation by seeing to it that all nuclear states shall be able to rely on deterring each other; and that they will be deterred by the risk of massive retaliation if all possess a retaliatory nuclear armoury that is invulnerable to a nuclear first attack. They have concluded – to put this message in other words – that whereas the chief purpose of military establishments has hitherto been to fight wars, from now on their sole logical purpose lies in their power to avert war, and that the advance of technology has at last made it possible for them to fulfil it.

It is possible to grant the significance of these developments and yet remain apprehensive lest they prove to be reversible. The initiative which produced the establishment of the League of Nations was significant but the League was ineffective and short-lived. It was already a feature of the modern international system before 1945 that its leading states contrived to enjoy long periods of peace; and the fear that the present period of peace between the leading states will break down in its turn is understandable at a time when the world-economy is again in serious disarray, détente is again under strain and some siren voices, however few, are again proclaiming that the threat of mutual destruction can be averted by further advances in technology or that war between nuclear states would not in the event be so total and so devastating as common sense persuades us to believe. There is much force in this scepticism; it would be unwise to insist that the developments which have imposed discipline on states to an unprecedented extent in the past forty years will never cease to restrain them. But two points may be made on the other side.

In the first place, it is not only understandable – it will also be beneficial – if we all remain always anxious lest the conditions on which the balance of terror rests be overlooked and the discipline it has created be allowed to be relaxed.

In the second place, it becomes increasingly unlikely that the conjunction of considerations and circumstances in which the break-down of discipline proved fatal to the international system in 1914 and again in 1939 will ever be repeated.

Of these two statements, the second may seem to be hopelessly nationalistic or hopelessly optimistic. But it does not rest only on the fact that states no longer believe that they have a legal right to go to war. It is also supported by the immense significance this change of outlook derives from what we know about the causes of war in modern times.

There is general acceptance that two different kinds of enquiry exist here – that there is a distinction not only between the occasion and the causes of the wars, but also between the causes of the wars and the circumstances in which they broke out, and that this second distinction is that between the framework set by the given conditions in which states were pursuing their policies and, on the other hand, the policies the states were pursuing. But because it is difficult to keep these fields apart – because it is impossible to deny that policies are influenced by the conditions – we generally end up by blurring the lines between them.

What is to be concluded, for example, from the following comparison between the two world wars of the twentieth century? There is widespread agreement that, from the point of view of the policies that were being pursued by Germany, there was an essential difference between the causes of these two wars. Hundreds of books have been written in the attempt to establish what were the policies of the major powers in the years before 1914, to lay bare the motives which underlay those policies, and to discover whether some, if any, of these policies were more responsible than others for the outbreak of the First World War. The debate has gone on because a degree of ambiguity, of uncertainty of goal and intention, was actually involved in the German policies of the time. We are almost free of this problem, on the other hand, in connection with the war which broke out in 1939. Historians are, rightly, nearly unanimous that, in this field of policy, the causes of the Second World War were the personality and the aims of Adolf Hitler. They may dispute as to whether Hitler's policies were more pathological than Machiavellian or more Machiavellian than pathological. They may be puzzled to know what were his long-term intentions in seeking war, which should not surprise us since, beyond a certain point, he was puzzled himself. But on this, at least, they mostly see eye to eye: on this level, at any rate, it was Hitler's aggressiveness that caused the war.

From these considerations we can deduce, if we wish, that Hitler was more ruthless and blatant in his aggressiveness than the government of Kaiser Wilhelm because he was more at the mercy of the given conditions than were his predecessors; and we can point to the intervening degradation of Germany, on the one hand, and to the increased instability of the international system, on the other, as constituting limitations and pressures that were far greater for him than any that had existed for them. Equally plausibly, however, we can conclude that, if they were more tentative and irresolute than he, it was because he was *less* in the grip of the given conditions – aware of them, but plainly and deliberately out to exploit them in a fashion that was untypical of most of the men who were influential in Germany before 1914 as also of most of the governments of his own time. At bottom, indeed, these rival deductions underlie the two schools of thought which have emerged in the controversy about the origins of the Second World War. Although even A. J. P. Taylor admits that Hitler's appetite was greater than normal and that he 'may have projected a great war all along', Taylor still adopts the first of these positions (Taylor, 1961: 106, 279). His starting point is that Hitler was at work in a profoundly disturbed and, for him, distinctly advantageous situation and that, really, when you come to think about it, he did nothing which any other government would not have been tempted or impelled to do if it had been similarly placed. The majority of students of the matter cling to the second position when they argue that it was Hitler's abnormal aggressiveness, mainly, which caused the war. But few of even those who conclude that Hitler's policies were the main cause of the war maintain that these policies were the sole cause of it. Both schools assume, in other words, that the causes of war must be sought both on the level of the policies of governments and in the framework of given conditions in which those policies were formulated.

There is something fundamentally unsatisfactory about this situation. It is worth asking, accordingly, whether we ought to go on making this assumption. And this is all the more the case in that, apart from the unsatisfactory situation which has just been outlined, there are several other grounds for abandoning it. It may be suggested, indeed, that we would make a positive advance in understanding, at least in relation to these most recent wars, if we would distinguish more rigorously than we do between the causes of war and the given conditions in which war has broken out, would insist on confining the causes wholly to the aims and the policies of the powers and would regard all other considerations as constituting only the given conditions in which the powers had to conduct themselves. To adopt this position would be tantamount to deciding that the given conditions must be seen as being a challenge thrown down to governments – a set of circumstances and problems which it was their task to surmount without the resort to war – and that these wars were the outcome of their refusal or their failure to meet the challenge.

To turn to the further arguments in favour of taking this position, the first is suggested by the thought that it is extremely difficult to find any period of time in the recent history of this wicked world in which the given conditions were not such as to make war possible or even quite likely to break out – supposing that governments had been disposed to indulge in it or, even, had not been on their guard against it. In the generation which ended in 1914 and in the generation between 1918 and 1939, there would have been an earlier war or more frequent general wars if states had not been bent on, and successful in, avoiding war – just as there would already have been general war again since 1945 if states had not resumed this salutary effort. It is almost a precondition of balanced judgement about the outbreaks of war, in modern history at least, that we should study not only the outbreaks but also those many occasions on which war might have, but did not, come.

If we push this thought a little further we come across another argument in favour of adopting the position I have advocated. Just as it takes two to make a love affair or a marriage but only one to start a fight, so – the international system being what it is – the politics and actions of a single government could still leave other governments with no alternative to war. That governments which have thus bowed to the unavoidable have done so with great reluctance is only what we should expect, even if it is a consideration which has not always been allowed due weight by students of the Triple Entente before 1914 or of the appeasement policies of the Western powers before 1939. But indecision on the ultimate issue of peace or war has been just as marked a feature in the conduct of even restless, thrusting governments during these years. The policies of the Kaiser's government present us with what is almost a problem in psychology because, while they were fundamentally aggressive, they were also, on this account, notably hesitant. Nobody will understand Hitler who fails to recognize that his tendency to shrink from a general war whenever he came up to the post was as pronounced as his determination to have war when he was brooding between the crises he engineered. One sign that he was more aggressive than his predecessors, indeed, is to be found in the fact that he engineered these crises not merely in the hope that other powers would yield, but also because he loathed his own vacillation on the ultimate issue – as a means of cutting off his own retreat.

This underlying truth about the behaviour of the more organized governments during the past hundred years has been given insufficient attention by students of the causes of recent wars. Hence, in part, the current disposition of a few German historians, in reaction against the previous inability of most German historians to admit that their country's government bore any but the slightest indirect responsibility for the First World War, to go unnecessarily far to the opposite extreme by urging that the German government deliberately exploited the Sarajevo crisis with the settled intention of bringing about a general war. Hence, again, the oversimplified assumption that Hitler possessed from the outset a cut-and-dried programme of expansion and conquest by means of war – an oversimplification against which A. J. P. Taylor has properly protested. Hence, on the other hand, the persistence with which other historians neglect altogether the detailed study of the aims and policy of governments and confine their search for the causes of the two world wars wholly to the given conditions.

The upholders of this extreme position maintain that the wars were the outcome of the capitalist system or of imperialism or of nationalism or of the regrettable existence of the independent sovereign state. Their conviction is that all governments are always and equally malign – or at least that all governments are malign except those of Marxist-Leninist states whose principles will not tolerate imperialist activity and other foreign excess – because they are all the victims of 'the system'. They believe that war has been the result of the system and will remain unavoidable until the system – the structure of given conditions – is destroyed.

But what is to be thought of an argument which maintains that capitalist states have been bent on or unable to escape war, from the fact of being capitalist states, when the evidence of international history is to the effect that it was from about the time that states became capitalist that they began to be able to avoid war, and began actually to avoid it? When almost continuous war was the inevitable concomitant – to use something like Marxist language – of the fuedal and bourgeois-liberal stages, it cannot be very helpful to assert that less frequent war has been the inevitable concomitant of the capitalist stage, and we are entitled to question whether even this claim can be true. What, again, is to be thought of the belief that during all these stages war has been the unavoid-able consequence of the very existence of the state? This may seem to be less easy to dismiss than the Marxist doctrine, if only because it is more generalized. Certainly, it is impossible to dismiss it solely on the ground that war has become less frequent as states have become more efficient. War itself has become more efficient, more devastating, in the course of this same process; and as a result, even if the existence of the state were the sufficient cause of war, the state would have needed recurring periods of peace for the recuperation of its powers. If this belief is to be thoroughly discredited we need some demonstration that it is not the existence of states that has been the cause of wars but the way in which states have behaved, and that there has been nothing inevitable about their behaviour.

We may find such a demonstration, I believe, by making a comparison between the two world wars of the kind that is rarely undertaken. If we return to the distinction between the policies pursued by states and what I have called the given conditions in which policies are formulated and applied, we can say that the given conditions in which the two wars occurred – what others term the underlying or the contributory causes of the wars – were totally unlike. Here are some of the obvious differences, with some equally obvious comments on them.

The First World War broke out at a time when governments, like peoples, had little or no inkling of the vast increase in the potential destructiveness of warfare that had been taking place since the 1860s. The war of 1939 broke out when, on the contrary, men were, if anything, too much obsessed with the fearful consequences of total war on account of their experience of trench warfare in the earlier conflict and because of the development of the bomber. Historians have concluded from the first of these facts that the persistence of an antiquated, not to say a primitive approach to the fighting of a war was a secondary or a contributory or even a profound cause of the war of 1914. What are we to conclude from the second? How do we explain the fact that in every country in 1939, not excepting Germany, the onset of war was a source of dread if not, as was in some places the case, of panic? We can conclude if we wish that ignorance of the horrors of war and obsession with its horrors equally contributed to bring war about. But would it not be more reasonable to conclude that men's assumptions and reactions on this score were irrelevant to the causes of war on each occasion?

War broke out in 1914 after years of armaments rivalry. It broke out in 1939 when all the major states, not excepting Germany, were unprepared for a major war from this point of view. It has often been urged that the armaments race was itself a profound or a secondary cause of the First World War. Was the military unpreparedness of the powers equally a profound or a secondary cause of the Second World War? Or would it be wiser to conclude that the armaments situation, as such, had nothing to do with the case on either occasion?

It used to be a widespread conviction, again, that the war of 1914 was caused by the alliance system that had grown up between the great powers. In Great Britain between the two wars, as always in the United States until after the Second World War, it was almost an article of faith that alliances themselves breed war. Using this kind of argument, however, we can equally plausibly contend that the war of 1939 was caused by the absence of alliances. For it is another serious difference between the two pre-war periods that no firm alliance existed before the Second World War. On Hitler's side it is true that there was the Rome–Berlin–Tokyo axis. But this was not an alliance to engage in war together, either defensively or offensively, and neither Italy nor Japan made her entry into the war until Germany had made her major wartime gains. The one alliance which helped Hitler to make these gains was the

Russo-German Pact of August 1939; but this was entered into not only at the eleventh hour but also because war was imminent. The onset of war created the Russo-German Pact, not the pact the onset of war. Among Hitler's future enemies no commitments in effect existed – not even of the informal kind that had been established between France and Great Britain and Great Britain and Russia before 1914 – between France, Great Britain, the United States and Russia. None of the alliances made by France against the German danger – neither those with the small Eastern European states nor that with Russian of 1935 – withstood the deterioration of the international situation after 1936. They were no more influential in bringing about that deterioration or in increasing Hitler's restlessness than they were in making resistance to Hitler effective. The same may be said of the one important engagement which Great Britain accepted in these years. Whatever may be thought of the argument that the Anglo-Polish alliance of 1939 was unwise in that it forced Hitler to act, there can be no question that it was forced upon the British government by Hitler's policy and that it contributed in no way to the deterioration of the pre-war situation.

If we are to persist in the belief that alliances were an underlying or a contributory cause of the First World War, then we have no alternative but to argue that the absence of alliances was an underlying or a contributory cause of the second – that conditions of affairs which were in this respect wholly different equally helped to cause war. Nor is this rigid alternative logically escapable if we turn our attention to what might be deduced from a wider or more general divergence between the character of the two pre-war periods – a divergence to which these more detailed differences have already pointed.

War broke out in 1914 when flexibility and room for manoeuvre between the great powers had been reduced, over a period of years, to negligible proportions. So much was it the case that war occurred in conditions of international deadlock, with all the powers insisting on at least maintaining every inch of acquired position, that it has often been concluded that it broke out as a result of the deadlock, which made every move a fateful move. But war broke out in 1939 when the international instability, though no less acute, was such as left enormous room for manoeuvre between the powers. To illustrate the extent of this difference we have only to compare the pre-war crises in the two cases. In every crisis between 1905 and 1914 the outcome of immense effort, of most intricate diplomacy, not to say duplicity, was infinitesimal concrete gain. Of each of the crises that preceded the war of 1939 the astonishing features were the size and importance of Hitler's, as of Italy's and Japan's, acquisitions – in China, Abyssinia, the Rhineland, Austria, Czechoslovakia – and the ease with which they were obtained.

This is not the place for an explanation of this difference. It is sufficient to say that if anything is clear about the pre-1939 situation it is that it was extremely favourable to the rectification of old grievances, not to speak of the assertion of new strength, without a general war – as some Germans, from Stresemann in the 1920s to German generals in the 1930s, clearly recognized. Yet a general war arose in this fluid condition of unbalance as, previously, a general war had arisen in the opposite condition of rigid deadlock. Once again, either we must conclude that fluidity was a cause of war in the one case, as deadlock was a cause of war in the previous case, or we ought to abandon an approach which looks for the causes of these wars, in any useful sense of the word, in this field. We must either insist that varying kinds of international disturbance, like different attitudes to war, different armaments situations, alliances and the absence of alliances, being equally consequences of the existence of the state, are equally liable to constitute the causes of war. Or we should abandon the notion that the existence of the state and the nature of the given conditions have any useful bearing on the causes of war.

In the first of these approaches there is nothing inherently absurd. It commits us to the belief that widely variable, not to say opposite, conditions may cause war, but the logical mind need have no difficulty in believing that. The trouble with it is that it has shortcomings in other directions. A. J. P. Taylor was searching for these when he said that it explains everything – and explains nothing (Taylor, 1961: 102). But he did not go far enough. It would be nearer the mark to say that this approach has two serious weaknesses. The first emerges if we apply it to the whole of international history: it explains everything up to the eighteenth century and nothing that has occurred in the past hundred years. The second emerges when we apply it to the past hundred years, and more particularly to the period which suffered from two world wars. It is this: while we may logically assume that highly different given conditions may cause war, we know as a matter of fact that highly dangerous given conditions have not invariably had this outcome.

For one central feature of the history of relations and of war between states, if I am right in my understanding of it, is that up to the eighteenth century, by the limitations of their nature, and the nature of their limitations, states were entirely at the mercy of circumstances, so that frequent warfare between them was as near as makes no matter inevitable. And another feature of that history, no less pronounced, is that by about a century ago states – at least the more powerful and advanced among them – had so far altered in themselves and in their relation to the given conditions that war has since occurred only when their ability to control these conditions had been abandoned. If war was inevitable before that time we cannot say that war has been inevitable in the same sense since. We can say of the past hundred years, if we wish, that while no particular war was inevitable, it remained inevitable that war would recur from time to time – that while it was enough for only one state to abandon peace, it remained inevitable that the ability to avoid war would now and again be abandoned by one or another state. If we say this, however, we shall be wise to confine the causes of war to the reasons why this ability was abandoned and to expect to find those reasons sufficiently revealed by an investigation of the aims and the policies of states.

What then emerges from a study of the policies of states since 1945? Not from those of all states, for so many of them are new and peripheral to the international system, but from those of the more advanced states which have developed the system, what emerges is further evidence that the system has begun to undergo a change no less momentous than that which was completed at the beginning of the nineteenth century. And it has begun to do so – there is here a true, a historical relationship between given conditions and policies – because a cumulative transformation in the circumstances of these states is beginning to bring about a transformation in the nature of the states themselves, and thus in their perception of their aims.

It is not only the case that, with the continued advance of those processes which have for so long increased the unavoidable scale of warfare, they have brought themselves to relinquish the right to war. In the wake of those processes, which increasingly eliminate war between themselves as a credible means of action, they have begun to measure their power and interests by new criteria and, as well as wishing to avoid war, they have ceased to doubt their ability to avoid it.

This transformation is more nearly complete in some directions than it is in others. If it is not yet at all affecting relations between the world's new states, its influence on the relations between the superpowers, though already profound, is not yet as easily detected as is its impact on those between the states of Western Europe. In that area, which as recently as fifty years ago housed most of the world's great powers and was the cockpit for the world's great wars, the years since 1945 have seen the evolution of the European Economic Community (EEC) and the organizations associated with it, now generally called the European Community. Had the movement which produced the Community replaced independent states with a United States of Western Europe, as its authors intended, it would be of little interest to the historian of international relations, as distinct from the student of the origins of new states. As it is, by bringing about a new association between six – now twelve – separate sovereign states, it has established between them a system of international relations which in its actual operation is fundamentally different from any earlier system. The rivalries between these states are no less continuous than they were when the states were less closely associated, and they are no less intense. In some respects, indeed, they are more so, or at least more openly so; but this is because they are predicated on and controlled by the axiom that they will not be settled by resort to force and war.

It is not to be expected that such an association, which with all its institutions is the specialized product of particular historical experiences, will be brought about between the superpowers. But it is not too much to say that they are moving towards the acceptance of this axiom at a slower pace and in their own way under the banner of peaceful co-existence. Peaceful coexistence is the term applied to the strange condition in which their real conflicts are already conducted with immense discretion even if they are still conducted with immense suspicion and to the accompaniment of the open insult and the public abuse of an ideological struggle. Their ideological struggle is the substitute, however, for war between states which are coming to terms with the fact that war has ceased to be one of their options. It should not be overlooked, moreover, that the ideological divide is steadily narrowing. Already it is really no wider than that which separated the advocates and the opponents of the Holy Alliance in the early years of the Concert system after 1815; and just as that gave way to the final establishment of the Concert of Europe in the 1830s, so we may soon see the great powers establishing another Concert – one for the world, and one which is based, as the European one was not, on the renunciation of the right to go to war.

Reference

Taylor, A. J. P. (1961) *The Origins of the Second World War*. London: Hamish Hamilton.

6

Global Power Dynamics and Collective Violence

Raimo Väyrynen

Introduction

The relationship between power dynamics and collective violence is a central nexus in international relations. Power is inherent in any political relationship. To be effective, power must be based on the consent of people, i.e. it must be legitimate. Violence can never be legitimate, though as an instrument, it may serve a variety of political purposes. Lack of legitimacy means that violence cannot reproduce power, but may destroy it if used to promote illegitimate objectives. In Hannah Arendt's (1969: 49–56) words 'power is the essence of government', while violence is instrumental and hence 'always stands in need of guidance and justification through the end it pursues'. In her analysis 'power and violence are opposites; where one rules absolutely, the other is absent'. Power is thus defined positively as a human ability to act collectively for positive ends. Power, in other words, is viewed as competence, non-violent in the first place, but which may also imply violence as a subordinated instrument for political goals. The definition of power as competence endows it with an emancipatory dimension in contradistinction to its conceptualization as control over human communities and their material bases.

In political realism power is usually equated with military power or force, including both the resort to armed coercion and its threat. Force is the final argument in international relations, used when other means fail. That is why no sharp distinction is drawn between power and violence. They are not qualitatively different, violence being regarded as an extension of military power. Power is almost exclusively viewed as control over the will and behaviour of other states. The primacy of power or force in turn is intimately associated with the problem of order in international relations. 'The prerequisite of order among autonomous states is that force be restrained by countervailing force within a balance (or equilibrium) of power' (Jervis, 1985). Such a balance of forces can be attained by different versions of traditional balance-of-power policies, by collective security or by a balance of terror, i.e. nuclear deterrence. They all aim at meeting the same two principal objectives: the continued independence of nation-states and restraint on major powers. In the approach of political realism to international relations, deterrence is characterized as 'a basis of order' (see Osgood and Tucker, 1967: 96–120).

The equation of power with control, dominance and order is sharply rejected by Berenice A. Carroll (1972: 587–616) who observes that such an approach leads 'only into tautologies, blind alleys, and futile exercises'. She urges the redefinition of power as competence because power as control is a building block of the international system of violence and injustice. By rejecting the cults of power and order, according to Carroll, the world can be transformed in a more peaceful direction. She lists nine types of power of the allegedly powerless, ranging from inertial and innovative to expressive and collective powers. A common denominator of them all is competence, the ability to accomplish positive things as alternatives to the use and the threat of use of force.

There are, in other words, two traditions to comprehending power. The tradition of power politics considers power and violence complementary to each other, while the critical tradition regards them as opposites. According to the former tradition power (and force) is a means of maintaining order in international relations, while the critical perspective aims rather at mobilizing alternative sources of power to break down such a hierarchical order. Power politics and peace research, representing the critical tradition, are hence dialectically related both in discourse and substance. Practically all the theories of power transitions and other versions of international power dynamics have opted for the definition of power as the ability to control and maintain or impose order. In what follows I will attempt to review some of the major theories dealing with international power dynamics and its connections with collective violence. In addition, I will try to evaluate these theories briefly in the light of the two traditions referred to above.

Dimensions of power dynamics

The picture of the world embedded in theories of international power dynamics is, almost by definition, top-heavy. The dominant powers, their challengers and the mutual relations between these two groups of countries crucially affect the course of international relations. Circumstances prevailing at the core are the pivot of history. This perspective is especially pronounced in Modelski's theory of world leadership which is defined by the capacity for global reach, i.e. by a major ocean-going navy. Such a global enterprise presupposes political stability at home and, in particular, sufficient economic resources. Once a power has achieved world leadership it has the task, dictated by self-interest, to facilitate global trade and other interactions and to assure order in international relations. World leadership thus provides an ordering principle and leads Modelski to reject both the conceptions of international anarchy and hegemony. Leadership creates a structure in part based on a division of labour; in the economic sphere this is manifested by the differentiation between producers and consumers and in the military sphere by the existence of land powers which are different from the leading sea powers.[1]

World leadership is 'a massive project of political investment' which is gradually eroded by the deconcentration of international economic power and by the political delegitimation of challengers. The weakness of international political institutions and cultural constraints increase the likelihood of global wars. Such wars – there have been five since the sixteenth century – give rise to a new basic cycle of world leadership (Modelski, 1978, 1983). An important observation in the long-cycle theory is that challengers of a world power have invariably failed owing to the inability of continental states to acquire military capabilities of global reach, because of insufficient resource bases and political miscalculations. Instead, a new world power has had a maritime orientation in its external economic and military relations (e.g. Thompson, 1983a).

Modelski does not consider international anarchy as a structural constant, but rather ponders on how and under what conditions international order is procured. What is amazing to him is 'the degree of structure created by leadership' (Modelski, 1983: 121). With that conclusion the supporters of the long-cycle theory come close to the conception of hegemonic stability, though they deny the existence of hegemonies in the Wallersteinian sense. The erosion of such stability leads to global contradictions, upheavals and, ultimately, to world wars. Robert Gilpin subscribes to a similar conceptualization of international change. Every international system allows a measure of incremental change. The uneven growth of economic resources, however, leads to the redistribution of power and to pressures to reorder the governance of the system. A rising power attempts to change the rules of this governance and the patterns of territorial control which the dominant power finds increasingly costly and difficult to defend. The efforts of the dominant power to bring resources and costs of commitments into balance usually fail. The ensuing dilemmas of power and governance are ultimately resolved by a hegemonic war which is waged by unlimited means in a direct contest between the forces of the status quo and those of challenge. As the previous hegemony is, by definition, defeated in a hegemonic war, its most important consequence is that 'it changes the system in accordance with the new international distribution of power; it brings about a reordering of the basic components of the system' (Gilpin, 1981: 186–210 and *passim*).

Modelski and Gilpin consider both causes and consequences of global wars in a dynamic structural framework in which the distribution of power is decisive. They also conclude that wars lead to the emergence of a new global or hegemonic leadership. This does not necessarily need to be the case, though. Robert Jervis (1985: 58–79) has shown that a global war may be followed by a concert of major powers which sooner or later – and in the twentieth century sooner rather than later – develops into a balance-of-power system. Related observations lead Jack S. Levy (1985: 361–5) to define general wars somewhat independently of hegemonic succession. In Levy's definition, a general war is 'one in which the decisive victory of at least one side is both a reasonable possibility and one that would likely result in the leadership or dominance by a single state over the system – or at least in the overthrow of an existing leadership or hegemony'.

The Modelskian long-cycle theory has been criticized primarily because of its self-contained character; the long cycle of global leadership is explained by the internal dynamics of the international political system without really considering its relationship with other international systems. The focus on global maritime reach neglects the impact of continental powers on the international order and leads to the erroneous identification of Portugal as the world leader in the sixteenth century (Zolberg, 1983: 275–84). There are, to my mind, two major problems with the long-cycle theory. First, it does not include any exogenous variables by which the dynamics of international change can be measured. Gilpin's theory is, on the other hand, informed by a Schumpeterian perspective and hence perceives economic and military innovations as major exogenous factors producing differential rates of economic growth (Gilpin, 1981: 55–70). Another problem in the long-cycle theory is its near total neglect of the role of peripheries, both as objects and subjects of the global leadership cycle. Gilpin does not explore the role of peripheries in any systematic fashion either, although he recognizes the possibility that the diffusion of technology from the dominant power or a shift in the locus of innovation may push a peripheral power to a growth career (Gilpin, 1981: 180–1). Such a caveat is, however, insufficient in a world-system in which pressures towards peripheralization are immanent, and associative development strategies tend at least to deprive peripheral countries of any real possibility for upward economic and political mobility (Senghaas, 1982: 26–54).

The focus on global or hegemonic wars, while justified in the analysis of systemic dynamics, means that the bulk of collective international violence remains unaccounted for. Global wars occur approximately once in a century. Meanwhile such major wars as the Crimean War, the Franco-Prussian War of 1870–1, the Russo-Japanese War of 1904–5, the Russian Civil War, the Korean War and the Vietnam War, not to speak of several bloody civil wars, are pushed beyond the explanatory realm of theory (for lists of general wars excluding those mentioned above, see Levy, 1985: 372–3). Clearly, theories of global or hegemonic wars can make only a limited contribution to the study of collective violence as a more comprehensive phenomenon in international relations.[2]

The peripheries and their war experience must be integrated more systematically into theoretically relevant points of departure. Power transitions and other forms of power dynamics are a genuine reality in discontinuous regions of the Third World. Thanks to the peripherality and discontinuity of these regions, however, their power dynamics and collective violence may not affect the global power structure. This does not make their analysis less important, even in a global perspective. By also incorporating major regional wars into studies of global collective violence, a methodological problem could further be resolved. The number of general wars studied is very small, rendering various globalist theories almost untestable. As a result, the debates between the upholders of various macro-theories boil down to an argument between believers and non-believers (cf. Zolberg, 1983: 284–5).

The world-system analysis, as developed by Immanuel Wallerstein, subscribes most strongly to the globalist dogma. At the same time, however, it explicitly recognizes core–periphery structures and associated economic processes. They are, in fact, considered as structural constants of the world-system within which individual states move upward and downward. In the tradition of world-system analysis the competitive cycles at the core are correlated with the structure of core–periphery relations (see e.g. Wallerstein, 1974).

Concentration of the productive advantage at the core, which ultimately leads to hegemony, is associated with a multilateral structure of economic exchange, while deconcentration at the core tends to lead to more politically regulated economic relations. In that sense the world-system analysis adopts a more comprehensive theoretical perspective than the other approaches outlined here, which, however, is not matched by focus on the role of force and warfare in this system. They are explored primarily from the core perspective, though armed coercion associated with the subordination of peripheries and their resistance is occasionally addressed.

In the world-system analysis hegemony is primarily an economic phenomenon in which predominance in agriculture, industry, commerce and finance in world markets are simultaneously combined. This definition emphasizes the primacy of the economic or materialist logic of the world-system analysis which has been repeatedly criticized for failure to provide autonomous explanations of politico-strategic factors and of the international systems of states (see e.g. Zolberg, 1981; Skocpol, 1979: 22–4). Due to the primacy of the materialist logic of the world-system, the intra-core struggles for hegemony are determined, in the first place, by economic efficacy and expansionism. These struggles are accompanied by long and destructive land-centred wars between the rivals at the core (Wallerstein, 1984: 39–43). Such large-scale resort to international violence has the function of reorganizing production relations on a world scale so that the accumulation process and the internationalization of capitalist production can continue. Accumulation and violent political reorganization do not precede each other, being 'truly interdependent processes' (Chase-Dunn, 1981: 23). This in fact confirms that, if a global war occurs, the political structure of the world no longer corresponds to the needs of global capital accumulation. The ensuing break has to be resolved by the reorganization at the core and may require a global war.

Though the terminology differs, this conclusion comes close to that proposed by Gilpin. Such similarity, crystallized in the discrepancy between economic and military power structures as a cause of global wars, becomes even clearer in a later observation by Chase-Dunn and Sokolovsky (1983: 363–5) that 'world wars may be used to facilitate the upward and downward mobility of individual states and the creation of a new structure of power that more accurately reflects the strengths and weaknesses of key actors'.[3] In his critical remarks Thompson (1983a: 351–2) agrees with the world-system approach that global wars have been a part of the reorganization of intra-core relations, and indeed attributes to them an even more central role. He is less certain, though, about the real impact of global wars on the reorganization of core–periphery relations. Thompson also points out that, in reality, the challenger never succeeds in becoming the new hegemonic power. It has been defeated in the global war and the new hegemony has risen out of the ranks of the victorious coalition. Chase-Dunn (1981: 37–41) tries to meet this point at two different levels. First, transnational structures associated with the capitalist commodity economy are strong enough to tip the balance in favour of preserving the state system against efforts to set up an empire. Second, this is in part due to the inability of a challenger to 'gain sufficient support from other core allies' which expect the capitalist world economy to provide more benefits to them than a world empire.

The failure of a military-industrial challenge does not discredit the theory of hegemonic competition and warfare as such. Such wars occur, as a rule, between the declining world power and the rising challenger. The probability of war between these adversaries increases if the rate of power transition is rapid (see Organski, 1964: 299–338; Organski and Kugler, 1980: 13–63). These observations can be reconciled with the suggestion of Doran and Parsons (1980) that each major power historically undergoes a rising and declining cycle of relative power and that the magnitude, severity and duration of war tend to be greatest at the inflection points of the cycle. Aside from a technical critique concerning the selection of indicators, two major issues can be raised in evaluating the significance of the theory of a relative power cycle (cf. Thompson, 1983b: 153–9). The first issue addresses the problem of context. In the formulation of Doran and Parsons (1980: 949–51), established foreign-policy roles are under pressure at the inflection points: 'the changes occurring at critical points have an abrupt and unsettling effect on a nation's self-image and foreign policy perspective'. In fact these unsettling effects are a key to explain the decisions of such nations to go to war.

The explanations may, however, turn out to be deficient unless the context in which decisions are made is considered in a more comprehensive manner. That is why the further development of Doran's theory appears to require a number of comparative case studies which would penetrate the domestic contexts of war decisions in different nations and at different critical points. The assessment of relative capabilities connects the power cycle to the international system, but this association should probably be converted from technicality to substance. This may be one reason why Doran (1983: 165–82) has made a systematic effort to integrate the state perspective with the systemic perspective. As a result he concludes that state and system interact horizontally in a balance of power and vertically in the impact of national cycles on the systemic structure. Radical changes in that structure are constrained by the demand of the balance of power and its preservation.

Economic transitions and wars

Too strong an emphasis on structural power dynamics as a cause of global wars excludes other potential explanatory variables, such as long economic cycles. Long waves of economic development, in particular the Kontratieff cycles, have been extensively studied by economists during the current period of stagnant economic growth. The results have been somewhat confusing. It seems fair to conclude from the discussion that there are long-term periodizations in the economic growth of the capitalist world, that these are not entirely regular or symmetrical and that such cycles are more manifest in prices than in production (see e.g. van Duijn, 1983; Beenstock, 1983: 137–59). These caveats in the conclusion should not, however, discourage efforts to establish empirical and theoretical relationships between economic transitions and major-power wars. It is useful to remember that economic transitions do not need to be cyclical in the sense of fixed periodizations or repeat themselves along uniform patterns. Economic transitions, in other words, may be based on phases of irregular duration and be unique in character. Empirical descriptions of the modes of economic transitions are certainly useful, but only theoretical explications of their causes can make such transitions really relevant to research on collective violence and its occurrence (see Kleinknecht, 1981: 107–12).

The complexity of international relations makes it too easy simply to correlate economic transitions and war indicators with each other. There are several types of intervening variables, for example, which mediate between economics and warfare. Some of these, such as the nature of military technology, may themselves be results of economic and technological transitions. Such intervening variables are part of the materialist logic of the world-system. Another category includes exogenous intervening variables, primarily from the realm of state-system or political logic. Military alliances and other systems of management in international relations are examples of intermediate causes which are theoretically independent of economic transitions (see Väyrynen, 1983a: 402–6). All in all, the relationships between economic transitions and warfare must be placed into a comprehensive theoretical framework to facilitate the interpretation of empirical observations.

Most of the empirical investigations on the relationships between Kontratieff's long cycles and major-power wars conclude that warfare is more frequent during the upswing phases. Rapid expansion of economic resources and accompanying political ambitions thus seem to contribute to the outbreak of major-power wars (Thompson and Zuk, 1982: 622–4;

Väyrynen, 1983a: 407–12). Goldstein (1985) in an important effort to clarify the economic cycle warfare nexus concludes that there are no significant differences in the number and duration of wars in the upswing and downswing periods of Kontratieff cycles, but that during the upswings wars are much bigger in terms of battle deaths. He observes, furthermore, that only wars between great powers correlate with the economic phases. The tendency of escalating war cycles to occur during the upswing years holds without exception until 1918, but partially breaks down subsequently. This is interpreted in different ways depending on whether war or economic dynamics is regarded as the central element in the scheme. Goldstein (1985) tends to give priority to wars rather than to economic factors.

A contending view argues, more on theoretical than on empirical grounds, that economic downswings are more conducive to major wars because of the strains they impose on the political structure of the world-system. Bergesen (1985: 325–30) stresses that 'the movement from economic downturn to upturn involves the use of coercion, force and struggle which are the by-products of struggles not only between capital and labor, but between states too'. A major war occurring during the downturn establishes the new hegemony which, by restructuring inter-national relations, gives the capitalist world economy fresh opportunities to expand (see also Senghaas 1983: 119–24). In fact the expansiveness of capitalism is a common denominator of these two contradictory sets of findings. The upswing interpretation presupposes that expansiveness itself is an important cause for major wars, as well as of great-power interventions into the peripheries (see Väyrynen, 1983a: 410–12), while the downswing interpretation stresses rather the need to remove the political obstacles to the expansion of capital. In terms of research strategy this means that intervening variables, such as military alliances and offensive/defensive mixes of military technologies, can more sensibly be inserted into the upswing interpretation. In such an interpretation the intervening variables can identify mechanisms which either accelerate or decelerate the march towards the outbreak of a major war. In the downswing interpretation such mechanisms are often overlooked by the functional explanation stressing the 'needs' of the capitalist world-system.

Bergesen's point is significant, though, in that it draws attention to the transitional processes in economic cycles. In fact it may be more useful to explore the turning points rather than the economic phases or trends. The international system is under more severe stress in periods of transition. It is an open question whether the upper or the lower turning point in an economic cycle is more conducive to war. Screpanti's (1984) somewhat casual observations hint that both domestic anti-systemic insurgencies and major interstate wars tend to cluster around transitions from upswing to downswing phases. This is at least in partial agreement with the upswing interpretation and with theories stressing perceived stagnation and deprivation, based on social comparisons, as causes of collective violence.

As pointed out above, the problem of economic transitions should be seen in a broader perspective than that provided by Kontratieff's cycles. Without attempting any extensive survey of transition theories, Marxist and non-Marxist, one many refer to Angus Maddison's periodization of the phases of capitalist development. He concludes, on the basis of an empirical exercise, that four such phases can be distinguished: *1870–1913* (which can be extended as far back as 1820), *1913–50*, *1950–73*, and *1973* onwards. He admits that the fourth phase, from 1973 onwards, is the most controversial (Maddison, 1982: 85–95; for an essentially similar phasing after 1873, see Beaud, 1981). Maddison does not specify the reason why the transitions occur; he only points out that 'the move from one phase to another is caused by system-shocks'. The economic causes of transitions are, in Maddison's view (1982: 85) predictable, but 'the timing of the change is usually governed by exogenous and accidental events which are not predictable'.

It is beyond our scope here as to provide any conclusive evidence on the role of major wars in the turning points of these phases of capitalist development. Quite evidently, though, each of these phases (with the exception of the most recent) were preceded by, or coincided with, peaks in the long cycles of international war (see Goldstein, 1985: 430). This observation is consonant with the suggestion that major wars are 'system-shocks' which expedite the transition of capitalist development from one phase to another. This argument certainly presupposes that the Franco-Prussian War of 1870–1 and preceding German confrontations in the 1860s with Austria-Hungary and Denmark significantly affected capitalist development in Europe. This is probably true, even though the significance of the military factor should not be overemphasized. The political and military resurgence of Prussia/Germany was rather part of the rapid economic and technological growth it underwent in the upswing years of the 1850s and 1860s. The military factor cannot be easily isolated from this development because political and military power was, from this era onwards, increasingly based on industrial potential.

Transition to a possible new phase in the early 1970s remains problematic in this analysis as well. There are two ways of looking at the role of war in recent capitalist development. Either one can resort to the argument that in the nuclear age wars between major powers have, rationally speaking, become impossible or one can consider the Vietnam War as a 'system-shock'. The latter perspective is not entirely unconvincing if one remembers the range of influences, many of them deep and enduring, of that war on the world economy through changes in the international economic position of the United States. The Vietnam War was also interwoven with the shift of the centre of the world capitalism from Europe and the Atlantic area to the Pacific basin (cf. Goldstein, 1985: 432–3).

Economics and politics

Recent academic discussions on international relations theory have been replete with arguments about whether processes in the global system are steered by 'one logic or two'. Neoclassical theories in economics and political realism in political science have both opted for the single-logic solution. It is also inherent in the Wallersteinian world-system analysis, though the argument is much more complex than in either neoclassical or realist theories. Alternatively, several political scientists have suggested that there are, after all, two theoretically and analytically distinct approaches to the analysis of the global system. They are called, for example, the 'military-political world' and the 'trading world' (Rosecrance, 1986) or 'political' and 'material' approaches (Rapkin, 1983). The argument is basically theoretical, because hardly anybody denies the empirical interdependencies between these two 'logics' or 'approaches'.

This debate is not without significance for the discussion of wars and collective violence, either. Theories of hegemonic struggles between industrial powers and of economic transitions may lead to a mechanistic world-view in which wars are seen as consequences of underlying struc-tural dynamics, hence neglecting political decisions and social forces. Any structural theory of war should, in other words, accommodate both state formations and structures in its explanatory scheme. The integration of state structures into the analysis also helps to solve at least a portion of the riddle concerning the relationship between economics and politics. The bulk of this debate has explored ways and degrees to which political and economic logics in the world-system condition each other. Only passing attention has been paid to the internal structure of states struggling with each other and simultaneously facing the capitalist world economy (see e.g. Chase-Dunn, 1981; Thompson, 1983a; Chase-Dunn and Sokolovsky, 1983). This discussion has not been unimportant, but it has unnecessarily narrowed the problematic. The duel is not between the primacy of economic and political logics; it is rather between particular and comprehensive efforts to account for reality.

The roots of the debate lie in the extensive criticism directed against Wallerstein's (1974) 'systematic neglect of political structures and pro-cesses'. Especially objectionable was the all-too direct correlation he proposed between the strength of state machinery and the state's position in the core–periphery structure (see Zolberg, 1981). The ensuing debate was amplified by the diffusion of the world-system analysis, on the one hand, and the resurgence of political realism and its stress on the autonomous sphere of state action on the other. In his subsequent publica-tions Wallerstein (1980) has considered the role of state formations in the historical development of capitalism much more thoroughly. Hence at least part of the objections raised against the world-system theory are no longer relevant. This does not mean, though, that differences in perspec-tives are now totally reconciled. The ultimate bone of contention – that is, whether economics and politics are analytically separate or inter-dependent elements of the global capitalist logic – still remains (see e.g. Garst, 1985). An interesting solution to this dilemma has been developed by Richard K. Ashley (1983) who, after rejecting the primacy of economics, claims that the statist perspective is unable to 'reflect upon or to check economic processes' and hence subordinates politics to economic logic. Ashley speaks for a political logic which comes close to defining power as competence instead of control over outcomes. This emerges from his observation that 'the logic of politics is an intrinsically dialectic logic, at once depending upon, anticipating, and calling into question the dominant social order' (Ashley, 1983: 478; see also Alker, 1981). This means, in short, that dominant structures and ideas have their counter-structures and counter-ideas contending with each other in international relations, lending them an inherently dynamic and open-ended character.

The dialectical foundations of war and peace can hardly be understood without dealing with state structures. Obviously a state's strength cannot be derived only from its position in the world capitalist structure. The state-formation process, including the search for security and protection, has been the history of monopolizing violence and using it to extract resources needed for the 'domestic' strengthening and 'external' warfare. The process has been conditioned by the global economy, but can hardly be reduced to its needs (see e.g. Tilly, 1985). The secular trend of the state's growing monopoly of force has contributed to the increase of inter-state wars. The pivotal importance of industrialization in the national military capacity, for instance, escalated the destructiveness of wars by the nineteenth century and hence enhanced the fear of their consequences. The centralization, rationalization and, finally, expansion of military force were all intimately connected with the institutionalization of the nation-state system. Historically, this produced longer periods of peace than ever, but at the same time more destructive global wars if they broke out (see Hinsley, 1973: 85–96; Osgood and Tucker, 1967: 35–120; Howard, 1976: 94–135). The growing strengths of state structures thus shaped the pattern of global wars, which are also more capable than less extensive interstate wars of accounting for the discontinuous expansion of governmental power (Rasler and Thompson, 1985).

State structures stand in an intermediary position between national societies and the global system. That is why it is possible to argue that 'the key to successful structural analysis lies in the focus on state organiza-tions and their relations both to international environments and to domestic classes and economic conditions' (Skocpol, 1979: 291). A further study of state structures calls for a two-way analysis. On the one hand, it should be specified how these structures in different countries affect inter-national political and economic relations.[4] On the other hand, the degree and nature of a nation's integration into the world economy con-ditions the orientation of domestic interest groups and their mutual coalitions. Effective state intervention may in both cases be important to assure domestic economic and political stability, promote external economic expansion and international political influence. In the core nations the effectiveness of state intervention hinges upon the nature of the predominant domestic power coalition (in this regard France and the United Kingdom provide historically different lessons), while at the semi-periphery a centralized state structure is a more common solution (Garst, 1985: 474–7; Zolberg, 1981, 268–70). The prevalence of centralized state structures in the semi-periphery, as opposed to the market orientation of the predominant coalitions at the core, may explain why interstate wars that fall short of global wars may in general be waged more frequently by semi-peripheral powers than by core powers (see Väyrynen, 1983b, and Wallerstein, 1980, on the war involvements of Sweden and Prussia in their semi-peripheral stage of development).

State structures may contribute to the explanation of the relationship between economics and politics in the state system. Without a consideration of state structures it is difficult to establish whether the stability of the world-system in the nineteenth century was due to the economic hegemony of the United Kingdom or to the balance of power in Europe. Gilpin (1981: 134–8) argues that relative stability was due to British economic predominance and to the increasing impact of economic factors in general. Rosecrance (1986: 99–101), on the other hand, denies that any British hegemony existed and observes that stability was assured rather by the division of responsibilities between major powers. These responsibilities included British economic leadership, on the one hand, and the maintenance of the balance of power by the continental European powers on the other. Stability broke down, however, when the UK could no longer maintain its economic advantage. This can, no doubt, be explained by the stagnation of technological innovation or by a lack of entrepreneurial spirit in the UK, but the impact of her economic decline on the world-system was mediated by state structures.

In nineteenth-century Britain state structures were weak and the economic power bloc, integrating provincial industrialists and London merchants, steered foreign economic policies. The secondary role of the British state made it possible to differentiate economics from politics at the international level. This point is well brought out, long before any world-system analysis, by E. H. Carr (1945: 16–17): 'it was because economic authority was silently wielded by a single centralized autocracy [the City of London] that political authority could safely be parcelled out in national units, large and small, increasingly subject to democratic control'. The 'formal divorce between political and economic power' and ensuing 'pseudo-international world economic order' allowed other states to retain their independence. This formal divorce entered into force by the end of the nineteenth century when British naval supremacy waned. It became evident that sea power and land power were interdependent and that a decline in the former had to be complemented by the strengthening of the 'continental commitment' if the future control of Europe was not to be conceded to the rising land power, i.e. Germany (Kennedy, 1984). German predominance would have threatened the multipolar balance of power on the continent and hence the independence of smaller states.

Such a development, associated with the reinforcement of state structures in Germany, would have reunited politics and economics on the continent. To some extent, this actually happened, a result being the First World War of 1914–19.

The decline of naval hegemony and economic predominance sparked off domestic British disputes between 'navalists' and 'continentalists'. The 'navalists' looked at the Empire and were content with a weak state, while the 'continentalists' saw the need for a stronger state and the reindustrialization of the British economy. Upper-class values and the strong influence of traditional elites account for the victory of the imperial and naval option and for the failure to reindustrialize through a new type of state intervention (see Garst, 1985: 479–81, 487–8). This example illustrates the point that state structures are not merely functions of the state's position in the world-system, but possess a degree of autonomy in modifying the global relationship between economics and politics.

It can be surmised that a similar debate between 'continentalists' and 'navalists' may be boiling up in the United States whose hegemonic economic position appears to be in decline. So far the internationalist orientation has prevailed. Instead of curtailing political and military commitments abroad, as suggested by the incipient group of 'continentalists', recent US administrations, in particular the Reagan administration, have tried to expand resources to meet these commitments. Judging from history the process of hegemonic decline seems to have some inexorable features: with the partial exception of the United Kingdom, no predominant power has been able successfully to extend its period of domination to any noticeable extent. If this is to be the case of the United States as well, it can be predicted that current criticism of political and military overextension will become more vocal. The growth of such criticism, advocating reduced commitments to military allies and resort to protectionism in international trade is already manifest in the United States, but has so far been successfully thwarted by the political leadership.

Conclusion

In the study of global power dynamics and their impact on warfare only scant attention has been paid to the opportunities to avoid wars. This is in part due to the focus on historically rare global wars which diverts attention from everyday wars and collective violence, obviously easier to prevent and manage than global confrontations. The study of global wars has, as a result, been selective and deterministic in the sense that the macro-dynamics of the world-system, be they materialist or political, are seen as leading almost inexorably to major military confrontations. They are comprehended in terms of their theory-specific origins and consequences rather than of their 'autonomous' characteristics (see e.g. Modelski and Morgan, 1985: 398–403).

The stress on structural dynamics and on power as force and control unite all the approaches discussed above. In order to function these theories need hegemonic powers and that is why they are even created by definitional exercises in which the criteria of judgement may be dubious (cf. the debate of Portugal's hegemony and, to a lesser extent, British hegemony in the nineteenth century). The functional nature of the hegemonic explanation of major wars may also lead to empirically unjustified decisions in defining such wars (cf. Modelski and Morgan, 1985: 398). More generally, the focus on predominant powers and major wars only means that large chunks of international dynamics are neglected; parsimony in explanation may be purchased at the expense of the validity of conclusions. Neither international co-operation nor violence can be reduced to the relations between core powers. Equally, the construction of any theory of international relations would be impossible without their inclusion.

It must be realized, as Keohane (1984) among others has done, that co-operative relations between nations can emerge without hegemonies and that their existence does not ensure international peace and security. It has also to be realized that deterrence, even if based on nuclear weapons, cannot be sufficient to prevent future global wars. Deterrence can hardly provide stability in a dynamic economic and technological environment; it is an interim solution in a longer historical perspective. In order to avoid the annihilation inherent in modern war and to permit peaceful transitions of power between states, more flexible and viable alternatives to nuclear deterrence must be developed (see Modelski and Morgan, 1985: 403–14).

To keep on the right track, research on peace and war requires a complex and dialectical view of the world. The definition of power as control, its concentration in core nations and their mutual rivalries are perhaps benchmarks of international relations. They are constantly challenged, though, both by international and national forces of opposition leading to interactive political dynamics. Such dynamics may reflect international power struggles, but beneath them lie confrontations between old and new social orders, forces and ideologies which, as Arno Mayer (1981) has shown, may result in a 'great war'. The complexity of international relations is ultimately crystallized in the unity of two opposing conceptions of power – power as control and power as competence – as well as of social agents using these two forms of power.

Notes

1. Such ideas on the division of labour between state units run counter to the first ordering principle of anarchic international relations, namely functional undifferentiation, suggested by Kenneth N. Waltz. His second principle pertains to the distribution of capabilities and is operationalized, in the first place, by the polarity of the system (Waltz, 1979: 93–101 and *passim*). This aproach seems to deviate from various structural theories in that it aims at a very parsimonious model of explanation comprising only two basic criteria, while other theories tend to be more complex. Waltz's theory can be criticized because of its insensitivity to change; historically, as the change in the functional

differentiation is very rare, the distribution of capabilities remains the only mechanism of transition from one international system to another. Even such transitions from one mode of polarity to another are infrequent; the theory constructed by Waltz is hence essentially static over long periods (see Rapkin, 1983: 250–1). In a similar vein it has been pointed out that Waltz's theory fails to account for the shift from the medieval to the modern international system, and does not, after all, contain any theory of change (Ruggie, 1983: 273–9).

2. There seems to be a tendency to this direction in the world-system tradition as global wars have been defined as military engagements between rival coalitions in which at least one core power participates, instead of defining them as extensive wars between hegemonies and challengers only (see Chase-Dunn and Sokolovsky, 1983: 364–5).

3. A sign of parochialism is some approaches to international relations research even in the United States is that Chase-Dunn and Sokolovsky (1983) do not even list Gilpin (1981) in their references despite many similarities in their conclusions.

4. An interesting path for further research may be offered, for example, by the theory of regulation of domestic economies. Regulation may be based either on competitive or monopolistic practices. This approach starts from the national components instead of the systemic structure and hence provides an opportunity to account for international processes by domestic economic policies and structures (see Aglietta, 1982). Another useful perspective to the analysis of national factors in international development may be provided by the systems of property rights (see e.g. Ruggie, 1983).

References

Aglietta, Michel (1982) 'Capitalism in the Eighties', *New Left Review* 136: 5–54.

Alker, Hayward (1981) 'Dialectical Foundations of Global Disparities', *International Studies Quarterly* 25(1): 69–98.

Arendt, Hannah (1969) *On Violence*. New York: Harcourt Brace Jovanovich.

Ashley, Richard K. (1983) 'Three Modes of Economism', *International Studies Quarterly* 27(4): 463–96.

Beaud, Michel (1981) *Histoire du capitalisme 1500–1980*. Paris: Editions du Seuil.

Beenstock, Michael (1983) *The World Economy in Transition*. London: George Allen and Unwin.

Bergesen, Albert (1985) 'Cycles of War in the Reproduction of the World Economy', in Paul M. Johnson and William R. Thompson (eds) *Rhythms in Politics and Economics*, pp. 313–31. New York: Praeger.

Carr, Edward Hallett (1945) *Nationalism and After*. London: Macmillan.

Carroll, Berenice A. (1972) 'Peace Research: the Cult of Power', *Journal of Conflict Resolution* 16(4): 585–616.

Chase-Dunn, Christopher (1981) 'Interstate System and Capitalist World Economy. One Logic or Two?', *International Studies Quarterly* 25(1): 19–42.

Chase-Dunn, Christopher and Sokolovsky, Joan (1983) 'Interstate Systems, World-Empires and the Capitalist World Economy: a Response to Thompson', *International Studies Quarterly* 27(3): 357–67.

Doran, Charles F. (1983) 'Power Cycle Theory and the Contemporary State', in William R. Thompson (ed.) *Contending Approaches to World System Analysis*, pp. 165–82. Beverly Hills: Sage Publications.

Doran, Charles F. and Parsons, Wes (1980) 'War and the Cycle of Relative Power', *American Political Science Review* 74(4): 947–65.

Garst, Daniel (1985) 'Wallerstein and His Critics', *Theory and Society* 14(4): 469–95.

Gilpin, Robert (1981) *War and Change in World Politics*. Cambridge: Cambridge University Press.

Goldstein, Joshua (1985) 'War and the Kontratieff Upswing', *International Studies Quarterly* 29(4): 411–44.

Hinsley, F. H. (1973) *Nationalism and the International System*. London: Hodder and Stoughton.

Howard, Michael (1976) *War in European History*. Oxford: Oxford University Press.

Jervis, Robert (1985) 'From Balance to Concert. A Study of International Security Cooperation', *World Politics* 38(1): 58–79.

Kennedy, Paul (1984) 'Mahan versus Mackinder: Two Interpretations of British Sea Power', in Paul Kennedy, *Strategy and Diplomacy 1870–1945. Eight Essays*. London: Fontana.

Keohane, Robert O. (1984) *After Hegemony. Cooperation and Discord in the World Political Economy*. Princeton: Princeton University Press.

Kleinknecht, Alfred (1981) 'Lange Wellen oder Wechsellagen? Einige method enkritische Bemerkungen zur Diskussion', in Dietmar Petzina and Ger van Roon (eds) *Konjunktur, Krise, Gesellschaft*, pp. 107–12. Stuttgart: Klett-Cotta.

Levy, Jack S. (1985) 'Theories of General War', *World Politics* 37(3): 344–74.

Maddison, Angus (1982) *Phases of Capitalist Development*. Oxford: Oxford University Press.

Mayer, Arno (1981) *The Persistence of the Old Regime. Europe to the Great War*. New York: Pantheon Books.

Modelski, George (1978) 'The Long Cycle of Global Politics and the Nation State', *Comparative Studies in Society and History* 20(2): 214–35.

Modelski, George (1983) 'Long Cycles of World Leadership', in William R. Thompson (ed.) *Contending Approaches to World System Analysis*, pp. 115–39. Beverly Hills: Sage Publications.

Modelski, George and Morgan, Patrick M. (1985) 'Understanding Global War', *Journal of Conflict Resolution* 29(3): 391–417.

Organski, A. F. K. (1964) *World Politics*. New York: Alfred A. Knopf.

Organski, A. F. K. and Kugler, Jacek (1980) *The War Ledger*. Chicago: Chicago University Press.

Osgood, Robert E. and Tucker, Robert W. (1967) *Force, Order, and Justice*. Baltimore: The Johns Hopkins Press.

Rapkin, David P. (1983) 'The Inadequacy of Single Logic: Integrating Political and Material Approaches to the World System', in William R. Thompson (ed.) *Contending Approaches to World System Analysis*, pp. 241–68. Beverly Hills: Sage Publications.

Rasler, Karen A. and Thompson, William R. (1985) 'War Making and State Making: Governmental Expenditures, Tax Revenues, and Global Wars', *American Political Science Review* 79(2): 491–507.

Rosecrance, Richard (1986) *The Rise of the Trading State. Commerce and Conquest in the Modern World*. New York: Basic Books.

Ruggie, John Gerard (1983) 'Continuity and Transformation in the World Polity. Towards a Neorealist Synthesis', *World Politics* 25(2): 261–85.

Screpanti, Ernesto (1984) 'Long Economic Cycles and Recurring Proletarian Insurgencies', *Review* 7(2): 509–48.

Senghaas, Dieter (1982) *Von Europa lernen. Entwicklungsgeschichtliche Betrachtungen*. Frankfurt am Main: Suhrkamp. (English translation: *The European Experience*. Leamington Spa; Berg Publishers, 1985.)

Senghaas, Dieter (1983) 'The Cycles of War and Peace', *Bulletin of Peace Proposals* 14(2): 119–24.

Skocpol, Theda (1979) *States and Social Revolutions. A Comparative Analysis of France, Russia and China*. Cambridge: Cambridge University Press.

Thompson, William R. (1983a) 'Uneven Economic Growth, Systemic Challenges, and Global Wars', *International Studies Quarterly* 27(3): 341–55.

Thompson, William R. (1983b) 'Cycles, Capabilities and War: an Ecumenical View', in William R. Thompson (ed.) *Contending Approaches to World System Analysis*, pp. 141–64. Beverly Hills: Sage Publications.

Thompson, William R. and Zuk, G. (1982) 'War, Inflation, and Kontratieff's Long Waves', *Journal of Conflict Resolution* 26(4): 621–44.

Tilly, Charles (1985) 'War Making and State Making as Organized Crime', in Peter B. Evans, Dietrich Rueschemeyer and Theda Skocpol (eds) *Bringing the State Back In*, pp. 169–91. Cambridge: Cambridge University Press.

Tylecote, Andrew B. (1982) 'German Ascent and British Decline 1870–1980: The Role of Upper-Class Structures and Values', in Edward Friedman (ed.) *Ascent and Decline in the World-System*, pp. 41–67. Beverly Hills: Sage Publications.

van Duijn, J. J. (1983) *The Long Wave in Economic Life*. London: George Allen and Unwin.

Väyrynen, Raimo (1983a) 'Economic Cycles, Power Transitions, Political Management and War between Major Powers', *International Studies Quarterly* 27(4): 389–418.

Väyrynen, Raimo (1983b) 'Semiperipheral Countries in the Global Economic and Military Order', in Helena Tuomi and Raimo Väyrynen (eds) *Militarization and Arms Production*, pp. 163–92. London: Croom Helm.

Wallerstein, Immanuel (1974) *The Modern World System I*. New York: Academic Press.

Wallerstein, Immanuel (1980) *The Modern World System II*. New York: Academic Press.

Wallerstein, Immanuel (1984) *The Politics of the World-Economy*. Cambridge: Cambridge University Press.

Waltz, Kenneth N. (1979) *Theory of International Politics*. Reading, MA: Addison-Wesley.

Zolberg, Aristide R. (1981) 'Origins of the Modern World System: A Missing Link', *World Politics* 23(2): 253–81.

Zolberg, Aristide R. (1983) '"World" and "System": a Misalliance', in William R. Thompson (ed.) *Contending Approaches to World System Analysis*, pp. 269–90. Beverly Hills: Sage Publications.

7

The Inadmissibility of War in the Nuclear Age

A Theoretical and Historical Analysis

A. Chubaryan and B. Marushkin

Wars provoke both keen interest and sharply negative reactions among people. It could not be otherwise, for the history of mankind abounds in wars, many of which have remained in collective memory as the gravest calamities.

To be sure, we must not forget just wars and wars of liberation, that is, those waged against tyrannies, despotism and oppression, in the name of social progress and national liberation and to protect the sovereignty and independence of countries and peoples. However, history provides a great many examples of predatory and aggressive wars provoked by the mercenary interests of classes, parties and groups, which brought disaster and suffering to many millions of people in every continent.

We know of many cases when wars were responsible for the decline and decay of entire states and civilizations. War and culture are antithetical, being opposite phenomena in the history of humanity. Continuity and communication are the vital conditions for the development of culture, while wars are detrimental to them and threaten the existence of human culture.

The gradual quantitative and qualitative evolution of weapons and armaments has made wars increasingly destructive. And today, in the nuclear age, war has become not just immoral but absolutely inadmissible in the most literal and practical meaning of the word.

The uninterrupted progress of instruments of destruction is today the essence of the arms race and it has acquired a new quality, absolute in its meaning. In the nuclear age, war ceases to be another way to conduct politics as the new weapons have turned it into a means of total destruction, representing a fatal divide for humanity. For the first time the entire world population is faced with the unprecedented threat of being annihilated in no time whatsoever.

The dominant imperative of our era is the inadmissibility of a nuclear war through the elimination of conflicts conducive to it, disarmament and preventing the arms race from spreading into the cosmos. The only reasonable alternative to a nuclear Armageddon is to learn the art and science of living together on one planet, respecting mutual interests and security. The question is how to achieve this objective.

Conceptions of humanism

To respond to Hamlet's question – 'To be or not to be?' – with which we are confronted today, we may turn to historical experience and to the huge humanistic potential accumulated by civilization, so that – to paraphrase the great Russian poet, Alexander Pushkin – one may 'put algebra to the test of harmony'. Evidently, notions of the inadmissibility of wars did not spring into existence like Athena from the head of Zeus, that is, without any connection to the past or present. The best minds over the centuries reflected upon a world without wars and with 'eternal peace'. It was Dante, for instance, in his *Monarchia* who wrote of the need for peace to accomplish the human cause and destiny and that peace is the most vital condition for prosperity.[1]

Humanist reasoning was not confined to wishes cut off from reality, for one can easily detect in it a consistent ethical and political programme for the attainment of the postulated ideal. Desiderius Erasmus of Rotterdam, Sir Thomas More, John Colet and other famous figures of the Renaissance put forward concepts of permanent and inviolable peace which neglected wars as crimes against human nature. These conceptions also incorporated ideas about education in the spirit of loving peace and appeals to take steps to achieve this. Peace was understood as a necessary condition and guarantee of the prosperity of every country and of civilization as a whole. Of great interest in this context are various projects to ensure eternal peace and even to set up international bodies for this purpose which were suggested by Ch. Saint-Pierre and Jean Jacques Rousseau in France, Immanuel Kant in Germany, Alexander Pushkin and V. F. Malinovsky in Russia and other thinkers of the eighteenth and nineteenth centuries.

In the twentieth century the accumulated humanistic potential has become particularly precious in view of the quantitative and qualitative evolution of the arms race. The nuclear explosions over Hiroshima and Nagasaki visually demonstrated a possibly fatal turn in world history. In 1946 Albert Einstein succinctly formulated the problem by noting that 'the unleashed power of the atom has changed everything except our thinking, and we are thus moving towards an unprecedented catastrophe'.[2] Nuclear weapons having transformed the human habitat, the task now is to align thinking with this cardinal fact.

Arguments from historical experience

Social consciousness notoriously lags behind reality and sometimes causes very considerable problems in all epochs. But today the factor of time has become crucial: scientific and technological progress in the military sphere is steadily reducing the available time and options for political decisions concerning matters of war and peace. The reorientation of consciousness and the decisive political steps needed cannot be long postponed.

The Vice-President of the USSR Academy of Sciences, E. P. Velikhov, writes in the *Newsletter* of the Academy that the use of a nuclear weapon cannot be considered as one kind of step in a critical situation.[3] It would be a crossing of the Rubicon and trigger off a chain of irreversible events. The use of nuclear weapons endangers the vital interests of the opposite side and will, most likely, provoke a retaliatory blow calculated to achieve maximum destruction of the enemy. Nuclear war is not a joint enterprise; it is not a game with rules and restrictions known in advance but, owing to the nature of nuclear weapons and the consequences of their application, potentially the greatest catastrophe in the history of mankind.

In the same *Newsletter* a member of the National Academy of Sciences of the USA, D. Hamburg, points in the same context to the conclusions of biological studies on the effects of stress situations on higher nervous activity.[4] He notes, in particular, that acute stress situations entail disturbances in perception and strongly affect the accuracy of analysis of a given situation and its outcomes. There also appears to be a tendency towards a decrease in the flexibility of thinking and the perception of changes in time and space, with notions of 'here' and 'now' moving to the foreground. Under stress there is a growing tendency to shift blame on to the other, i.e. on to the opponent. Historical experience has demonstrated that the normalization of relations in the period of *détente* greatly reduced stress in evaluation and the adoption of appropriate decisions. On the contrary, the aggravation of confrontation causes a sharp increase in feelings of distrust, suspicion and fear which add to the stress-load and consequently intensify confrontation.

In a nuclear environment, traditional concepts of the type *ius ad bellum, Si vis pacem, para bellum* and the like lose their meaning. Many military and political terms have also become outdated. If missiles with nuclear warheads are capable of destroying millions of people in a fraction of a second, are they merely 'weapons'? Is the term 'war' applicable in its old meaning to the exchange of nuclear blows which will inevitably result in the destruction of life on earth? One of the myths of militarist philosophy is that the stockpiling of weapons enhances security. Yet we observe that, while stocks of weapons are constantly growing, security diminishes. It is also clear that confrontation is an abnormal state in international relations when nuclear Apocalypse threatens.

The unceasing perfection of technology for waging wars is a thread of world history. Scales of military operations have increased correspondingly, and in the twentieth century war acquired global scale. War losses in terms of human lives and material and cultural values have become catastrophic. The price of war has risen monstrously. The wars of the nineteenth century took the lives of 5.5 million people, while in the two world wars of the twentieth century over 60 million people were killed and more than 110 million wounded. Such casualties are constantly increasing through the so-called 'local' wars waged in different parts of the world.

While in the past the problem could have been the survival of some particular state, the stake now extends to mankind as a whole. At present there exist over 50,000 units of nuclear weapons, enough to destroy everybody living many times over. The ecological consequences of a nuclear war are inconceivable. Studies by scientists show that the explosion of just a small part of the existing nuclear stockpile can result in a 'nuclear winter'. Soot, ashes and the dust of fires and explosions would screen off the sun and cause a considerable drop in temperature. The ecological crisis to follow would result in the destruction of all life.

In view of the present level of development of the means of destruction and demolition, no military technology is capable of ensuring security. As a matter of fact, the same holds true of many situations in the past. Neither the Great Wall of China nor the Maginot Line – to take but two well-known examples – were able to justify the hopes invested in their construction. No less futile are calculations based on 'super-weapons'. The inventor of the machine-gun, H. Maxim, is known to have believed that it would put the end to wars as 'only a barbarian general would send his men to certain death against the concentrated power of my new gun'.[5] In the opinion of Orville Wright the aeroplane would 'make further wars practically impossible'. The experience of the First and Second World Wars demonstrated the *naïveté* of such hopes. As a result of just one American air raid on Tokyo on 9 May 1945, 80,000 people were killed and a quarter of the city was destroyed, leaving over a million people homeless. The nuclear bombing of Hiroshima and Nagasaki took a toll of over 150,000 lives.

Historical experience further testifies to the illusion of arguments in support of the 'defensive' nature of the 'Star Wars' projects. Conclusions drawn by scientists from many countries show that even the most 'optimistic' calculations of the supporters of the Strategic Defense Initiative do not demonstrate that the efficiency of the 'cosmic shield' would exceed some 80 to 90 percent, yet only 1 percent of the missiles that might reach their targets is equivalent in total power to 5000 Hiroshimas. According to analysis by scientific experts in the USSR and the West, counter-measures to the Strategic Defense Initiative would be cheaper and sufficiently effective to neutralize it It is impossible to hide behind a 'cosmic shield'.

At the same time, the ominous and destabilizing character of the 'Star Wars' project is quite evident as it threatens to undermine strategic parity, and is conducive to a new and open-ended turn in the development of the arms race. The plans give rise to political and military illusions that they offer a way out of the 'nuclear balance' and to win a nuclear war.

The problem of security is, therefore, of a political nature and can be solved above all by political means. To put a stop to the arms race that has become the major potential for a nuclear war, it is necessary to display political will and to initiate disarmament.

An experienced politician and historian, G. Kennan, writes that no goal can be achieved if new weapons and their variants are increasingly produced and stationed over ever more areas. As for strategic comparisons between what and how much is owned by whom and what conclusions should follow, Kennan sees no sense in them, for if the question relates to the huge 'overkill' capacity which can never be used without provoking a universal catastrophe, arguments concerning superiority or inferiority lose all meaning. Even the assertion that intimidation is necessary becomes questionable, for in Kennan's opinion the source of danger is not in the aggressive intentions ascribed to one of the sides but in the arms race itself.[6]

In view of the probable consequences of nuclear war, it can be affirmed that no goal is worth the nuclear risk. A particularly important task in this connection is to establish an atmosphere of trust and the rejection of prejudices, false images and stereotypes. George Washington warned that 'the nation which indulges toward another an habitual hatred. . . is in some degree a slave. . . to its animosity'. Such a country 'disposes more readily to offer insult and injury, to lay hold of slight causes of umbrage, and to be naughty and intractable when accidental or trifling occasions of dispute occur.' Washington was opposed to projecting emotions (i.e. sympathies and antipathies) into the sphere of interstate relations and stressed that they can 'lead it [a nation] astray from its duty and interest'.[7]

Mutual understanding requires communication and interest in each others' history, culture and tradition.

Image studies

In recent years, 'image' studies have become popular. They involve research into how countries and peoples are perceived in the eyes of others. Ethnographers study ethnic and national stereotypes, their stability, mobility and change, while specialists in international relations study images and stereotypes pertaining to foreign relations. History provides numerous examples of the formation of stable, good neighbourly images and perceptions, but there are also many examples of animosity in the attitudes of countries to others which have been a cause or consequence of wars and conflicts.

The process of image formation and stereotyping is not as a rule predetermined or spontaneous: its development is determined by various factors, including the policy pursued by different classes, parties and groups. Often chauvinistic and racist prejudices were instilled and inculcated from 'above'; equally, countries and peoples were set against others.

It is particularly necessary and important today not to repeat such errors and delusions, for even now there are many instances of the cultivation and propagation of feelings of animosity and distrust among peoples, and of the inculcation of ideas about an alleged 'principal enemy and opponent', an 'evil empire' and the like. An important role in these processes is played by the mass media. The press, radio and television of certain countries contribute to the diffusion of such attitudes, myths and opinions. Kindling hatred has a destructive effect on international relations and serves to spread distrustful attitudes among states which impedes the conduct of negotiations on different and particularly on debatable or conflictual issues. But the main point is that it poisons the general political and psychological climate.

In recent years specialists from different countries have been analysing the essence and meaning of an 'international political climate'. In the early 1970s this climate was favourable, providing support for détente by conveying the idea of co-operation and the need for joint efforts by different political forces in the cause of peace and disarmament. The positive influence of such a climate was particularly noticeable and made itself felt by comparison with the many years of the Cold War which had created its own rhetoric and style, its own stereotypes and myths.

But even in those positive years, certain circles were not pleased with the climate of détente, trust, mutual understanding and co-operation. In the second half of the 1970s these forces staged a wide offensive against the policy of détente and its results. At the turn of the 1980s considerable changes occurred in the sentiments of people in the West. Once again, as in the regrettable Cold War years, ideas of distrust and enmity and the theories of 'evil' and the 'main enemy' were revived. As frequently in the past such ideas were accompanied by the general aggravation of the international situation and a new round of the arms race.

Historical experience shows that there is an organic connection between the aggravation of situations and the arms race, on the one hand, and the worsening of the international climate on the other. If, therefore, we speak of the need for a turn for the better, and about the preservation of peace and international security, we should pay particular attention to changes in the political and psychological climate and in public sentiments. The consciousness of millions of people should be imbued with an understanding of the ruin and inadmissibility of nuclear war and of its fatal consequences for mankind.

It is equally important to take measures to cultivate in the public mind a spirit of good neighbourly relations and trust and to overcome prejudices and animosity. It should be understood clearly that peace, security and disarmament are an imperative of our time and that the renunciation of interference in internal affairs as well as equality and recognition of the right of peoples to determine their own future is indispensable, offering the prospect of improving the international situation and the affirmation of the principles of peaceful coexistence in international relations.

The art of living together

Not so long ago remoteness from a site of military operations was sufficient to provide a certain guarantee of security. In the twentieth century the importance of the 'distance factor' is being rapidly eroded: wars that began in Europe grew into world-wide ones. Today the border between national and general security has shrunk to the minimum. Where, when and in what circumstances will a 'Sarajevo' of the nuclear age take place that may detonate the entire huge stock of 'nuclear powder'? Such thoughts about the unthinkable have a real basis. We shall either survive together or perish together. No security can be achieved to the detriment of the other side. The art and science of living in peace is, above all, to care not only for the security of one's own but for the other side, too, so that it feels itself no less secure. In our age of universal interdependence, world indivisibility is an axiom. In the famous report of the Independent Commission on the issues of disarmament and security or (the so-called Palme Commission), it is stated that security cannot be ensured unilaterally:

> From the point of view of economy, politics and culture and, most impor-
> tantly, from the military point of view we live in a world of growing
> interdependence. The security of one state cannot be safeguarded at the
> expense of security of the others. . . . We are faced with a threat to everybody
> and must therefore strengthen our security by the efforts of everybody.[8]

For nations to be able to live together on one planet they need mutual understanding and trust. It is clear that the basic problem is not the ideological differences of systems. In the past as in the present, those with different systems have been able to co-operate successfully. Over millennia interactions and communication between communities were not always smooth, but they have taught people – and it could hardly be otherwise, for the last lesson was too costly – to accommodate their interests with those of their neighbours and to refrain from making the contradictions appear too dramatic. Ideological and political differences, some of them most serious, do naturally exist, but there is also a great fund of political experience that helps to define a common language.

A realistic concept of security must proceed from the fact that there are several dozen states with their own vital interests. Hence, it is necessary to renounce global claims, to take account of the legitimate rights of other peoples and, above all, their right to choose the way of life they like without external interference. Contemporary political thinking should be based not on intimidation but on the new realities that have emerged.

In the solution of the problem of international security, the experience of history is instructive. It includes both studies in the history of negotia-tions on disarmament and an analysis of different past projects and systems of security.

At the turning-points of history various international political systems were generated and designed. For instance, after the defeat of Napoleon the so-called Vienna Congress system was created, and a variation of the European system was set up in the form of the Versailles settlement imposed by the Western powers after the First World War.

These variants of 'security' had a number of common traits. Basic to them were the principle of inequality between peoples and the desire of some countries to gain superiority at the expense of others. The Vienna Congress system aimed to organize suppression of revolutionary liberation movements. The later projects of the West envisaged isolation of the Soviet Union and ignored the principles of equality and peaceful co-existence with the socialist state. 'Security' conferences were accompanied by the accelerating arms race which was reducing to zero any guarantees of national and international security.

The Soviet conception of international security is built upon the principle of equality and equal security, and rejects any seeking of gain, advantage or superiority over others. In putting forward a comprehensive programme of normalizing the international situation, the Soviet Union proceeds from the necessities of the modern era and from the under-standing that the world has reached a critical borderline. The Soviet proposals at the same time comprehend the experience and lessons of history.

Historical experience, both positive and negative, is important. An analysis of the failure to set up a system of security in the 1930s teaches us not to repeat the errors and delusions of those years. A negative experience is important as a historical lesson, as a warning. Under modern circumstances, when miscalculation is not admissible, restraint and discretion in the international behaviour of all states are particularly significant. A diplomacy of blackmailing and threats to bring pressure to bear on sovereign countries has become an inadmissible anachronism. At the same time history has a considerable store of positive experience accumulated during the early 1970s when Europe laid the foundations of a new international political system that found its most distinctive expression in the Helsinki Conference on Security and Cooperation in Europe.

Historical experience offers us numerous examples of interconnected-ness and interdependence between the countries and peoples of the world. In step with the development of human society this interdependence becomes increasingly intimate. The turbulent twentieth century, with its progress in science and technology as in communication and transport, has brought different countries and continents closer together and caused considerably greater economic interrelatedness. Lenin noticed that world economic ties made capitalist countries accept broad economic relations with the socialist state.

Current realities have greatly enhanced economic interdependence. Despite differences in social systems and in defiance of those in certain circles who mean to undermine economic ties and trade with the USSR, the objective trend towards maintaining and deepening co-operation with the Soviet Union is making headway and determines to a considerable measure the direction of events in Europe and elsewhere. Such inter-relatedness involves not only the economic sphere and trade but much wider aspects, too. The dilemma 'to survive or perish', with which we are confronted today, unites people living on different continents, and raises to a qualitatively novel level responsibility for the fate and future of mankind.

There are now two approaches to war and peace and two different modes of thinking. The supporters of the use of force are still proposing to make use of the arms race to pressure the opponent, while the adherents of the other approach believe in human intellect and wisdom and come out in favour of common responsibility for the fortunes of the planet.

In the statement of 15 January 1986, the General Secretary of the Central Committee of the Communist Party of the Soviet Union Mikhail Gorbachev put forth proposals to eliminate nuclear, chemical and other mass-destruction weapons before the end of the century. On 25th February 1986, the 27th Congress of the Communist Party of the Soviet Union proposed to find ways for closer and productive cooperations with governments, parties and mass organizations and movements in order to build an all-embracing system of international security. The world, oversaturated with arms, was offered a real prospect of delivering itself of the deadly burden, uprooting militarism from the thinking and actions of countries, and renouncing the 'enemy image' in their relations.

The joint Soviet-American statement in Geneva in November 1985 is a manifestation of the realistic approach, noting that 'no nuclear war must be unleashed, for there can be no winners in it' and that the two sides 'will not strive to gain military superiority'. This statement can and must become the basis for the prevention of the arms race in space and for its curtailment on earth in order to eliminate international tension. The Soviet-American summit in Reykjavik, to which the Soviet Union came with a package of proposals, illustrated that agreement on the abolition of nuclear weapons is already practicable today.

Moral-ethical and legal prohibitions of wars and the application of force in international relations have become extremely important. It is necessary to elaborate a moral and legal code of behaviour in the foreign policies of the nuclear age which would prevent a nuclear war, renounce propaganda for it, enshrine the obligation not to use nuclear weapons first, allow no proliferation and provide for the reduction of nuclear armaments up to their complete liquidation.

A very important problem seems to be that of education in the spirit of mutual understanding and co-operation, in accord with the decisions of the Conference on Security and Cooperation in Europe, of irreconcilable opposition to wars, and the understanding that force and wars are immoral and inadmissible as methods of solving international conflicts. We may note that the defence of peace has been made a constitutional norm in the USSR. According to Article 69 of the Soviet Constitution 'the international duty of a citizen of the USSR is to assist the development of friendship and co-operation with the peoples of other countries, and the maintenance and strengthening of universal peace'. Article 28 of the Constitution prohibits war propaganda in the USSR.

Public opinion is called upon to play a great role in the awareness of the inadmissibility of wars. From the historical point of view the second half of the twentieth century witnesses a permanently growing influence of world public opinion on the solution of the problems of war and peace. This process is characterized by sharp rises and certain falls, but on the whole there is a general tendency towards strengthening the anti-war movement and sentiments. The reasons are, firstly, a general upsurge in the social activity of the masses and of different social strata which affects various activities and the questions of war and peace, above all. Secondly, beginning in the late 1940s, the experience, lessons and memory of the Second World War produced a great and lasting impact on public opinion. A lasting lesson drawn from that war is that people must fight against it before it breaks out. The practical experience of the Second World War, multiplied by the experience of numerous other conflicts, has sharpened the sensitivity of the world's public to the problems of war and peace and to the linkage between national and international security, thus stimulating more acute public consciousness. Thirdly, the development of nuclear weaponry has qualitatively changed the character of war which threatens mankind with complete destruction. Numerous anti-nuclear movements and sentiments in favour of a reasonable agreement between the East and the West sprang from this realization. In the post-war era and chiefly over the past ten to fifteen years, there was a sharp increase in awareness by the world public at large of its responsibility for the fortunes of the world. This has served as a strong moral and psychological impulse for drawing broad social forces into the anti-war movement. Today this movement has become a permanent factor of the international scene and exercises a real influence on international relations.

The growing importance of the anti-war movement as a component of politics is connected not only with its quantitative but with its qualitative characteristics, that is, with the rise in educational levels and the amount of information available to participants, with increased activity in the perception and reactions to emerging international problems as well as with the elaboration of a firm stand and the taking of appropriate actions. Public opinion has moved along with the evolution of society. During the post-war period many countries have experienced the steady democratization of public opinion and have lost their elitist character. An erosion of 'the silent majority' has occurred. Today's 'new wave' of anti-war sentiments embraces a greater proportion of the electorate in Western countries.

Apart from higher educational levels, public opinion in many countries has acquired wider access to the views of specialists in nuclear physics, biology, medicine, ecology and military specialists who explain the destructive potential of modern nuclear weapons and the terrible consequences of a nuclear war for mankind and its environment.

History is rich in experiences of good-neighbourliness and unification among people. It is important today to take this experience into account and to use it, to develop the traditions of joint efforts in the name of peace and social progress, and to train the population of all countries in the spirit of peace and mutual understanding.

Mikhail Gorbachev, General Secretary of the Central Committee of the Communist Party of the Soviet Union, has said that 'the modern world has become much too small and fragile for wars and a policy of strength. It cannot be saved and preserved if the way of thinking and actions built up over the centuries on the acceptability and permissibility of wars and armed conflicts are not shed once and for all, resolutely and irrevocably'.

The twentieth century has brought mankind two world wars. But this century is nearing its close with the stronger struggle of millions of people for a world without wars and weapons.

Notes

1. Dante Alighieri, *Monarchia*, I, IV, 1–4.
2. Albert Einstein, *Beyond War. A New Way of Thinking* (Palo Alto, 1984), p. 1.
3. E. P. Velikov, *Newsletter of the USSR Academy of Sciences* (1983, no. 9), pp. 24–5.
4. Hamburg, ibid., p. 90.
5. Einstein, op. cit., p. 10.
6. Cited from P. Koch, *Wahnsinn Rüstung* (Hamburg, 1981), p. 13.
7. Cited from Ch. Mathias, 'Habitual Hatred', *Foreign Affairs* (Summer 1983), pp. 1029–30.
8. *Security for All. Disarmament Programme*. A Report of the Independent Commission on Disarmament and Security Issues, chaired by Olof Palme (Moscow, 1982), p. 40 (in Russian).

8

War, Interdependence and Functionalism

Ernst B. Haas

I

In the sixteenth and seventeenth centuries the European countries were
at war 65 percent of the time; in our century the frequency of European
warfare has declined to 18 percent.[1] We like to think that the improvement is related to the growth of international ties of all kinds: trade,
investment, migration, tourism and our common dependence on the same
science and technology as expressed in global publications and co-
operative research. We also like to think that the phenomenal growth
of all types of international organizations, especially of those with non-
political mandate, is causally linked to the decline in warfare.

The purpose of this essay is to show that no such causal connection
can be demonstrated. Freer trade and intellectual cosmopolitanism seem
to have little to do with international violence and international security.
Moreover, I intend to show that even to assert a simple causal connection
between international interdependence and international violence is to
skate on theoretical ice which is too slippery for comfort.

Violence or security?
The issue to be explored is slippery because we tend to talk as if the
avoidance of international violence and the assurance of security were
the same thing. They are not. The recourse to violence by one state
against another, or one social group against its rivals, presupposes the
existence of a specific animus, a motive, a need. When we seek the causes
of war in the demands and fears of a group of leaders we assume that
they are motivated by what Richardson called a 'grievance'. This grievance may flow from the domestic political setting or from some good
withheld by the leaders of another country. It may result from the fear
that unless violence be initiated now, postponing the war may mean that
one's arch-enemy will be stronger at some future time. The desire to go
to war may also result from cognitive failings of the leaders, or flaws
in their country's decision-making system. The potential enemy's messages
may be misunderstood or his policies may be misinterpreted, thus
resulting in war even in the absence of a specific animus. In all these
instances the cause of war is located in the political routines of the
countries involved, in their mutual perceptions, in the history of past
grievances.[2]

An equally prominent approach to the causes of war sees the culprit in the very nature of international relations, to which countries are expected to respond in identical ways irrespective of their domestic peculiarities. Violence is not the problem; the lack of international security is. Violence is merely the means for rationally coping with insecurity; grievances are incidental. The lack of security is the result of the existence of 'anarchy' among states. Since there is no superordinate source of authority to assure security, each must seek to help itself survive as best it can. The world is an interdependent system of autonomous units, each fearing for its own continued safety. The fact that these units are also interdependent with respect to their economic welfare and intellectual sustenance is less important than the systematically institutionalized insecurity in which they must live. War, therefore, is best seen as a means whereby states seek to *reduce* their insecurity. The function of war, in this view, is to assure the survival of one's state. War is the means for maximizing one's expected utility in an anarchic world. A perceived challenge to the balance of international power is likely to be met with a resort to war by the challenged; but the challenger may also see his position in the balance as an occasion for unleashing violence.[3]

Both views are credible. Both can be used effectively to describe and explain international events. What matters for our purposes is that each implies a different theoretical argument about the connection between war and interdependence because each interprets the problem of war in its own unique way. Before proceeding with our case these arguments have to be summarized.

Interdependence limits war
I first examine the argument that relates to the grievances and needs of leaders. Since the argument is familiar I summarize it in the form of a few propositions. (1) Increased trade and cross-national investment, especially free trade and capital flows, result in a more highly articulated international division of labour; any disruption in that division of labour causes the belligerents to incur heavy losses of welfare; fearing such losses, countries are less willing to go to war. (2) Increasing popular demands for services on the part of the government limit the amount available for armaments and war; any disruption of welfare services is resented and will cause domestic strife leaders prefer to avoid. (3) Societies committed to welfare-enhancement spin off interest groups dedicated to safeguarding their entitlements; when the nature of the international division of labour creates mutual dependencies among several welfare states, the groups concerned will organize transnationally and thereby outflank their home governments. (4) The more such groups expect of transnational arrangements, the less they expect from their home governments. (5) The more cosmopolitan the knowledge (on which the deepened international division of labour depends) becomes, the less the beneficiaries of that knowledge are willing to disrupt things by war. In short, increasing international ties

in trade, finance, science, technology and interpersonal contact make war irrational for more and more people. Conversely, grievances that in the past have led to war become less relevant, and compelling fears that promoted the use of violence in the past gradually diminish.[4]

Defenders of the systemic explanation of war can also find reason to associate interdependence with the reduction of anarchy. International security will improve to the extent that states, in their mutual relations, no longer need to fear the Hobbesian state of nature. Economic interdependence would presumably have such an effect. Transnational corporations, for example, become a force for peace because their future solvency depends on uninterrupted international flows of goods, services and capital, quite independently of the security fears of the governments on whose territories these activities take place. To the extent that the states concerned are economically integrated as a result of these trends, fears of enmity and war decline – anarchy recedes. Similarly, long-lived alliances brought into being initially by the condition of anarchy have the effect of reducing anarchy among the allies, though not in relation to the opposing alliance. In short, anarchy becomes a special rather than a general condition.

Interdependence does not limit war
Even if we believe that increasing interdependence side-steps past grievances and fears, the devil could argue that interdependence is too patchy and temporary to permit our insisting on a causal link. The experience of the European Community is not everybody's experience. Substitutes can be found for goods and services that make up the division of labour of the moment. Strategic raw materials can be stockpiled. Lenders of capital are less easily changed, but the borrowers have recently shown that even in the realm of finance the dependencies are mutual, and hence the constraint of creditor power on war may be in doubt. Moreover, the intensity of the ties among the West and East European states, respectively, is not matched elsewhere in the world. So why insist, asks the devil, that a demonstrably more extensive division of labour also implies the disappearance of past fears and grievances? In this perspective, no special causal relationship should be presumed to exist between interdependence and violence.

What about war as a protection against insecurity? Here the argument the devil offers is much the same. If anarchy within NATO is less visible than before 1949, the same cannot be said of relations between NATO and the Warsaw Pact, India and Pakistan, Israel and Syria, South Africa and the rest of the African continent. Far from inferring a lesson from a deepened division of labour, the systemic analyst points to neo-mercantilist practices, strategic embargoes, unrelenting arms races, and successful national efforts to tame multinational corporations by insisting that anarchy is alive and well. The recourse to war remains a protection against insecurity despite the growth in international interdependence.

I intend to show that in the current international environment, some kinds of violence – but by no means all – are indeed reduced by the increase in international interdependence. This has occurred in a few parts of the globe only. I also intend to show that other kinds of interdependence can be shown to have altered the perceived security needs of some countries in relation with some others – not all countries everywhere – and that therefore the extreme case for anarchy is flawed. That accomplished, the fact remains that the devil's arguments, for now, remain the better ones. The enormous growth of international organizations of all kinds, political and functional, universal and regional, public and private, cannot change this conclusion. First, however, it has to be demonstrated that interdependence has increased and that international armed conflict has not declined. Then we can worry about the finer points implied by this mismatch.

II

There is no need to demonstrate once again that world trade has grown to enormous levels, that ever larger percentages of almost every country's gross national product depend on foreign trade (even in the case of the United States and the Soviet Union), and that these levels remain high despite the current global recession. Nor is there need to cite statistics on the ever-growing flood of travel, tourism and telecommunication links, including prominently the establishment of many international computer networks and data banks. The current debt crisis illustrates all too clearly the interdependence of world monetary systems and financial markets. All of this is quite unprecedented even though not all parts of the globe are affected equally. The notion of 'the global village' is rapidly becoming a reality with impact on the daily lives and habits of the citizens of most countries. Growing interdependence is a fact. That, however, does not prove that the fact is related to violence and security.

Significance of interdependence
Advocates of the position that interdependence ought to constrain violence and enhance security also argue that the institutionalization of international politics in public international organizations further limits recourse to war and may even contain civil wars. They suggest that habits of jointly defining and solving common problems will grow as a result of repeated encounters in such organizations. Eventually, the network of ties institutionalized in these encounters may take the place of the sovereign state as the dispenser of valued services. Functional co-operation, triggered by interdependence originally, will become self-sustaining. The rate at which such organizations have multiplied seems to support the argument. In 1865 six public international organizations existed, with a mean number of 9.0 states per organization; by 1965 the

number was 122, with a mean of 22.7 states per organization. The mean number of organizations per state was 1.4 in 1865; but it had risen to 36.4 by 1965, even though the number of states had tripled by then.[5] The growth of private organizations has been even more spectacular, though much of it has been in Western Europe.

Argument based on these statistical trends confuses cause and effect. Organizations develop because states experience a need for the services organizations are expected to provide. Organizations are a result of interdependence. If they develop the kinds of autonomous programmes advocated by functionalists they may take the place of their member governments. But none has. States use the organizations to supplement and strengthen national programmes and policies without deferring to international authority consistently or predictably. The rise of international organizations is evidence of increasing interdependence, but not of increased security. Any future relationship between interdependence and the decline of violence must be based on more than the argument of functionalism.

Why does interdependence grow? Theories about grievances and of anarchy provide answers. For the systemic analyst, the condition that matters is 'strategic interdependence'. States are in a relationship of mutual strategic interdependence when each can move safely only if it understands the motives and appreciates the capabilities of its antagonist, knowing that the antagonist is equally constrained. This leads to rational calculation that constrains each major state to act with extreme caution in dealing with its antagonists because, for example, of the danger of nuclear escalation. Strategic interdependence, when rationally appreciated by the parties, also leads to norms of reciprocity, which in turn can defuse grievances and allay fears of the war of all against all. Strategic interdependence is the condition that permits the conclusion of arms-control agreements, allows the superpowers to use the United Nations to seek peaceful solutions to conflicts among third parties, and to seek détente from time to time. It is a matter of empirical time and circumstance, of course, whether strategic interdependence is really experienced as generally as the theory proclaims.

Theorists who look to domestic society and politics for the sources of international strife find the causes of interdependence in the shifting demands and expectations of ordinary people, as influenced by changing scientific knowledge. The functionalist is correct in locating the impetus for international co-operation in changing demands for economic benefits that are influenced by technological change. He is equally correct in identifying co-operation in public health, transportation, telecommunications and environmental protection as resulting from initial demands at the national level for improved personal welfare, again triggered by science and technology in many cases. Collaboration enters the picture only when it is realized that the solutions to problems cannot be realized through national action alone, but require parallel measures by other states. Only then does interdependence entail collaboration.

This explanation can be applied to other forms of international collaboration. Institutionalized military co-operation is the result of the recognition that modern weapons cost a great deal and that joint weapons-procurement policies are a means for the maintenance of desired welfare levels. Giving foreign aid, though it originated in a desire to influence the future economic and political orientation of the receivers, now has an independent constituency (at least in some countries) that sees it as a means to globalize minimal welfare standards. Humanitarian relief has its origins in the guilty conscience of the rich countries, some of whose citizens seem eager to atone for and correct global inequality. Many things have happened in the industrialized countries since 1865 that now make people identify their welfare with global welfare.

Interdependence as shared meanings

Interdependence is with us, whether seen as strategic interaction and constraint, as global transactions, as expanding values concerned with welfare, or as institutionalized co-operation in organizations. But is the impact of interdependence sufficient to reduce violence and enhance security? Before tackling this issue I want to offer a master indicator of interdependence which I call 'the growth of shared meanings', and then provide some illustrations of its impact. A shared meaning is a consensus among the relevant national elites that a 'problem' exists, that this problem can be defined and circumscribed in terms of agreed criteria, and that 'solutions' requiring international collaboration can be devised which meet the technical criteria while also expressing the shared political values of the participants. Shared meanings combine a convergence of values on *what* is desirable, values that remain rooted in the domestic political experience of the participants, with a convergence of modes of analysis on *how* the values can be realized. Shared meanings are an indicator of how the consequences of interdependence are actually perceived by decision-makers.

My illustrations of how widely meanings may be shared come from the experience of four major conferences held under UN auspices: Conference on Science and Technology for Development (UNCSTD, 1979), conferences of the UN Environment Program (UNEP 1972 and 1982), the deep-sea mining aspects of the Law of the Sea Conference (UNCLOS III, 1972–82), and the World Conference on Agrarian Reform and Rural Development (1979). In each case, the question is: did political objectives and scientific knowledge about problems and solutions converge to result in the elaboration of shared meanings expressed in collaborative programmes?[6]

A major common theme underlies all four. Each conference questions the consensus that had inspired almost all international collaboration on economic welfare prior to the 1970s. The earlier consensus accepted the desirability of a complex international division of labour and the dominance of free trade and free investment abroad. It envisaged increases in human welfare as resulting from these practices, from the trickling-down of economic benefits to the mass of the urban and rural population. Scientific and technological knowledge were crucial in this process. Knowledge was expected to be diffused automatically and therefore require no special intervention by states and international organizations. Efficiency was the organizing concept uniting the processes considered relevant to development. The economic experience of the Western countries inspired it.

Efficiency was challenged in each of the conferences. Equality, national and international, was the most important rival to efficiency, as represented by the ideology of dependency reduction and the programme of the New International Economic Order (NIEO). Other rivals included various efforts to organize international collaboration under the concept of improving the global quality of life. They relied heavily on the ideologies of substituting labour-intensive indigenous technology for imported Western modes of production and on meeting the basic human needs of the poorest in the poor countries, such as food, medical care, shelter and education. At a minimum, the conferences show the move away from the efficiency criterion as the dominant concept and towards a more complex way of understanding human and national welfare.

What were the results of these encounters? UNCSTD does not demonstrate a progressive sharing of meanings. It is true that the OECD countries deferred to the developing countries in abandoning their earlier defence of efficiency criteria for diffusing technology. Dependency-reduction arguments officially won in that the conference endorsed the principle that science and technology had to be treated as an aspect of systematic economic planning to reduce inequality. However, this achievement was not matched by any action programmes really capable of implementing this rhetorically shared meaning. No agreement on the proper way to transfer science and technology was reached.

The case of the two UNEP conferences illustrates a deterioration of shared meanings over a decade. Despite widely divergent initial positions at the 1972 Stockholm conference about the dangers and causes of environmental degradation, the participants achieved very important agreements in the 'environment-and-development' formula, which defined environmental protection in terms acceptable to the industrialized as well as the developing countries. It did so by stressing that such issues as soil erosion, desertification and human settlements are 'environmental' issues just as much as air and water purity. UNEP's action programme was designed to meet all of these objectives, and consequently the developing countries accepted the global environmental monitoring programme which became UNEP's first priority and had been the OECD countries' major objective all along. Ten years later, at Nairobi, everybody expressed disappointment. The intervening recession had dampened the enthusiasm of the OECD countries for growth-restraining policies and dried up funds for development-related environmental policies.

Like UNEP, UNCLOS III began with what appeared to be a new shared meaning regarding the uses of the oceans: the concept of the oceans as the common heritage of mankind. While the later negotiations soon relegated this idea to the background, it survived in the part of the agreement relating to the mining of the seabed outside the 200-mile economic zone. The rules drawn up fully reflect the desire for equity; they also seek to integrate deep-ocean mining, the associated technologies, and the pricing of the minerals to overall economic development planning. The agreement is going into force despite the fact that, for the moment, several of the major countries possessing deep-sea mining technologies refuse to participate.

Nevertheless, the meaning being shared remains very superficial. Access to mining technology, private against public enterprises, expected rents from ocean-mining as opposed to profits from mining the same land-based minerals, national control over siting as opposed to supranational authority – all these issues are mentioned in the agreement without really being integrated and co-ordinated under a consensual master concept. Equality and development of the poor are emphasized without being given an unambiguous dominance. The fact remains, however, that compared with earlier conferences and agreements on the law of the sea, UNCLOS III represents a major illustration of the process of building a consensus that links diverse political objectives with an economic analysis that takes resource use out of the realm of pure profit-seeking.

The conference on agrarian reform and rural development did not result in a new action programme or a new set of legal rules. The conference discussed the best way to end rural poverty by means of national and international programmes. It pitted four distinct schools of thought against each other, each inspired by a different set of values and notions of causation; yet they arrived at an agreed master formula. The contestants were: (1) defenders of private commercial agriculture who identified rural welfare with the better functioning of markets and the activities of multinational firms; (2) advocates of sweeping land reform who equated rural welfare with the social and political enablement of peasants to determine their own lives; (3) spokesmen for overall economic development who saw rural reform largely in terms of its contribution to the industrialization of the Third World under NIEO auspices; (4) advocates of 'integrated rural development' who favoured some land reform but mostly spoke in terms of appropriate technology and basic-human-needs projects. Their formula contained enough of what everybody wanted (except spokesmen for multinational agribusiness) to furnish the basis for the consensus which emerged.

International programmes in the field of public health and the allocation of radio wavelengths and orbits in outer space tell stories similar to the positive experiences recounted; but activities with respect to nuclear proliferation, arms control, the restriction of nuclear testing, and peacekeeping in interstate conflict do not. Clearly, shared meanings do not come about easily or automatically. They do not predict a banishing of violence unless we can demonstrate that a shared meaning in the field of rural welfare or economic equality also presages a decline in other grievances or banishes the fear of the insecure.

III

It is clear that compared with a hundred, or even fifty years ago, cosmopolitan forces have brought about a certain convergence of thought in most parts of the world. These, in turn, have resulted in the growth of shared meanings among countries and their elites in such diverse areas as population control, famine relief, concessional international lending and the duty of the rich to help in the economic advancement of the poor. It is time we matched this evidence with the world's experience in warfare.

Violence and war are increasing

The incidence of war is summarized, for roughly the last century, in Tables 1 and 2. The world has got more violent as interdependence has

TABLE 1
International violence, 1875–1984

	Number of wars	Number of major wars[a]	Major civil wars/colonial revolts	Percentage of countries at war[c]
1875–85	9	1	5	34
1886–95	3	0	3	10
1896–1905	4	1	3	14
1906–15[b]	6	2	3	46
1916–25	2	0	7	11
1926–35	3	0	3	10
1936–45[b]	4	2	1	42
1946–55	11	2	9	29
1956–65	20	3	30	25
1966–75	14	5	19	21
1976–84	26	5	19	25

[a] More than two belligerents and casualties in excess of 10,000; two belligerents and casualties in excess of 100,000.
[b] Only active fighting participants in the First and Second World Wars are counted.
[c] States at war during decade/states in existence during decade. Each state was counted only once even if it participated in more than one war.

Wars are credited to the year in which they began: they are not recounted if they continued in the subsequent decade.

Source: for disputes before 1945, Francis A. Beer, *Peace Against War* (San Francisco, Ca: W. H. Freeman, 1981), p. 281; for disputes since 1945 I have used my own data bank.

TABLE 2
Seats of war, 1875–1984
(percentage of wars during each decade)

	Europe	Western hemisphere	Middle East North Africa	South Asia	East/South-East Asia	Africa	*n*
1875–85	33	22	0	11	22	11	9
1886–95	0	0	0	0	33	66	3
1896–05	25	25	0	0	25	25	4
1906–15[a]	50	17	33	0	0	0	6
1916–25	50	0	50	0	0	0	2
1926–35	0	33	0	0	33	33	3
1936–45[b]	40	0	0	0	60	0	5
1946–55	0	18	18	36	27	0	11
1956–65	5	5	35	15	35	5	20
1966–75	7	7	43	14	0	28	14
1976–84	0	15	35	4	15	21	26

[a] The First World War was credited to Europe.
[b] The Second World War was counted twice, once credited to Europe and once to East Asia.
   Wars are credited to the year in which they began; they are not recounted if they continued in the subsequent decade.
Source: same as Table 1.

increased. Moreover, the relatively low incidence of interstate war before 1946 hides the fact that the casualties incurred in the wars that took place after 1904 were several magnitudes higher than was true previously. On the other hand, since 1945 the world has not witnessed violence of the same magnitude even though the number of major wars has gone up. We should also note that the number of civil and colonial revolts has sharply increased since the Second World War. Moreover, there is some evidence that the increase in interstate and civil wars is causally related because of the tendency towards intervention by outside states in conflicts that originate as civil wars.[7] Finally, it bears noting that since 1945 approximately one-quarter of all states have been at war at least once during each decade.

   Europe has dropped out as a major war zone since the Second World War, while the Western hemisphere remains as relatively peaceful as it has been for most of modern history. In both instances there is an impressive correlation between the decline of warfare and the growth of economic interdependence, as reflected in statistics on foreign trade, as well as in the growth of every type of interstate and intergroup contact through the medium of the increasing number of regional organizations.[8]

   One indicator of future seats of war is provided by the regions most prominent in importing armaments from the United States, the Soviet Union, Britain, France, West Germany and Brazil. The Middle East increased its purchases from US $500 million in 1966 to US $6.2 billion in 1973, declining to US $4.2 billion in 1976, and picking up again after the outbreak of the Gulf War. European imports levelled off at about US $4 billion in 1973. East and South-East Asia declined after the termination of the Vietnam War from US $4.4 billion to US $1 billion in 1976. While South Asia and Latin America remain more or less stable at annual imports of US $500 million, Africa's imports increased from US $200 million in 1966 to US $2 billion in 1976.[9] We must remind ourselves that, while these figures refer to conventional arms only, the weapons in question include some highly accurate and very destructive systems.

Another indicator is the percentage of GNP spent on armaments of all kinds. The situation stands revealed in Table 3. Since their low point

TABLE 3
Defence expenditures as a percentage of GNP/GDP

Country/region	1952	1960	1970	1980	Most recent year
United States	13.6	8.9	7.8	5.6	6.9 (1984)
Soviet Union	13.4	6.4	6.2	8.8[a,b]	8.7 (1982)[a,b]
Israel	4.4	6.6	24.4	20.3[a,b]	16.9 (1983)[a,b]
India	1.7[a]	1.9[a]	3.0	3.1	3.3 (1982)
Pakistan	4.0[a]	2.8	3.7[a]	5.3	6.5 (1983)
South Africa	1.5	0.8	2.1	3.9[a]	3.6[a](1983)
Western Europe	6.8	4.0	3.5	3.4	3.6 (1983)
Latin America	2.0	1.8	1.7	1.5	2.9[c] (1983)
Middle East/North Africa (except Israel)	n.a.	4.1	8.6[d]	8.7[d]	14.1[d](1983)
Africa South of Sahara[f] (except South Africa)	n.a.	0.7	1.9[e]	3.2[d]	2.7[d](1983)

[a] Estimate.

[b] The estimate derived from International Institute of Strategic Studies (IISS), *The Military Balance, 1973-74* and *1985-1986* (London) is substantially higher. Note, however, that Stockholm International Peace Research Institute (SIPRI) and IISS do not use identical methods for arriving at their figures.

[c] Brazil omitted.

[d] Source used is IISS, op. cit., pp. 74-5 (1973) and pp. 17-20, 112, 170-3 (1985). IISS offered a fuller sample of countries for these years.

[e] Nigeria omitted.

[f] Countries included in various years differ; no complete data for all countries is available for each year.

Sources: unless otherwise indicated, these figures were calculated from data contained in SIPRI, *World Armaments and Disarmaments: SIPRI Yearbook 1974*, pp. 205-29, and *World Armaments and Disarmaments: SIPRI Yearbook 1985* (Stockholm), pp. 270-86.

in the late 1970s, American and Soviet arms expenditures have risen modestly. Arms racing in the Middle East has been extreme for fifteen years. Western European expenditures have been stable for the same period. Africa's have risen steadily but remain relatively low, while Latin American outlays have declined steadily until the most recent period. In absolute figures, of course, everybody's expenditures have risen; it is the poor countries of the world, however, for whom the increase is most worrisome.

Does increasing violence mean decreasing security?
The growth in armaments and the increase in the number of wars and civil disturbances are not final evidence that there is less international security – more anarchy – than in earlier times. Has the art of conflict management, whether it employs international organizations or not, kept pace with the level of violence? If so, then the growth in interdependence and organizational ties can still be linked to conflict reduction in a positive way. The evidence, however, tells us that this is not so. While the number of disputes referred to the United Nations and all regional security organizations has kept pace with the number of wars and civil wars that broke out, the success of these organizations in stopping, abating, isolating or settling the disputes has worsened. The UN's success rate declined steadily from a high of 40 percent in 1955–60 to a low of 8 percent in 1980–4. The combined score for five regional organizations declined from a high point of 30 percent in 1970–5 to a low of 16 percent in 1980–4, with major ups and downs before 1970 as well. As for disputes in which attempts at settlement were made outside multilateral organizations, no trend towards improvement could be discerned. In addition, the frequency and effectiveness of peacekeeping operations mounted by multilateral organizations has also declined.[10] The increase in violence seems to match a decrease in international security. Yet since there is no other means of assuring national security, states increasingly resort to violence as a means of protecting themselves while also resorting to war to find satisfaction for their grievances. Our two causal theories seem to tell the same story.

But this is not true everywhere and in all circumstances. There is *less* security now than before 1945 for small states engaging in low-level conflict with their neighbours. The rest of the world tolerates such conflict, without undue worry over escalation or local damage. This is true in the Third World, but not in the First and Second. There, because of the logic of armed deterrence, there is considerably *more* security than before 1945. Moreover, the decline in security for weak African and Asian states exposed to intervention from their neighbours, because it does not endanger the rest of the world, has no marked malign impact on the stability of the international system as a whole.

There is *less* security than earlier with respect to the relations among states with nuclear arsenals. Horizontal and vertical nuclear proliferation poses new dangers to security in the future, unless we make the dangerous assumption that the prudent rules of self-restraint practised by the United States and the Soviet Union will be adopted by all and prevail forever. The escalation of the technological arms race between the superpowers poses the same danger. The failure of post-1945 efforts at disarmament and arms control lessens everybody's security.

But there is *more* security than earlier with respect to serious disputes among middle and smaller states. When there is a danger of escalation in such conflicts, third-party intercession is practised with consistency and considerable success, though not often to the point of removing the grievance from the international agenda altogether.

Something has been learned. Learning has not taken the form of the deliberate design of more effective practices. Governments have stumbled onto the lessons without changing their basic values, and without practising technical rationality. They have stumbled into the mutual recognition of serious constraints on their freedom of action to make war under circumstances which, in the past, did lead to hostilities.

How can we explain the change? I shall argue that an understanding of nationalism enables us to overcome the differences between the two explanations of international strife. Different conceptions of national identity offer clues as to how a nation sees itself with reference to other nations; these conceptions enable us to see how leaders arrive at the preoccupation with a 'grievance' against other nations. The analysis of nationalism also makes us understand why one nation's security often appears as another's insecurity and why both of them therefore find themselves in the situation we call the 'security dilemma'. I now reinterpret international anarchy as an expression of national self-perceptions and conceptions of 'the other'. Today, for instance, the OECD countries no longer experience a security dilemma in relations among each other because they all profess liberal nationalism, though this was not the case until about 1950.

Types of nationalism

Since the advent of mass politics, nationalist doctrines can be divided into two great families: revolutionary and syncretist. The growth of nationalism is directly linked to the processes we sum up under the label of modernization: those who wish to modernize also wish to change drastically the societies in which they live; the modernizers are unhappy with the traditional state of affairs. They develop revolutionary ideologies to explain the changes they want to make and to define the future they wish to introduce. Citizens in other countries are influenced by these modernizers, whether the influence comes in the form of imperialism and colonization or through education, travel and example, and take position with respect to these proposed changes. If they wish to undo their own traditional societies they simply embrace the revolutionary ideologies of the foreigners; but if they wish to rescue something of their own traditions or change more gradually, those affected by foreign revolutionary ideologies respond by creating syncretist doctrines, mixtures of the old and the new.[11]

There are two kinds of revolutionary nationalism, liberal and integral, each subdividable into two variants. The three syncretist nationalisms, synthetic, traditional and restorative, differ from each other in how they respond to the foreign models. Synthetic syncretists are willing to borrow some of the foreign values as well as the institutions and techniques of the revolutionaries. Traditional syncretists reject the foreign values, but are willing to experiment with foreign institutions and welcome the foreigner's techniques. Restorative syncretists reject both values and institutions, but are willing to retain the foreigners' techniques, such as modern armies and factories.

I now pinpoint how the willingness to go to war varies with nationalist commitments. Liberal nationalist states, though committed to a notion of international harmony, also remain committed to a certain amount of evangelism and are willing to use force in pursuit of their Utopia; they felt entitled to become colonizers in the nineteenth century and protectors of democracy today. Marxist integralists do not expect international harmony while the world continues to contain capitalist societies and they expect to use force in the pursuit of their millennium and their security needs. Fascist integralists accept the need for war as a permanent condition; they consider it necessary to demonstrate their evolutionary prowess. All syncretists are concerned with survival in the face of the challenges of modernity, but they differ in their acceptance of war and their perception of insecurity. Synthetics are the most secure, the least fearful, and they entertain the possibility of international harmony. Traditionalists are far more ambivalent and therefore more defensive in attitude and policy in order to ward off the undesired aspects of modern life. Restorers, finally, tend to entertain millenarian ideas of going back to a past golden age and therefore are almost as bellicose towards the outside world as are fascists. Those nationalists who are most distrustful of the outside world are also the ones who are most likely to find a grievance justifying war, and their feelings of insecurity are bound to be strong.

Nationalism and international society
Our world contains all types of nationalists; they agree on only one – albeit a very important – item: they all want the advantages of science and technology as instruments to assure general welfare, good health, higher living standards and national defence, though the syncretists do not necessarily also want the institutional and normative commitments that tend to accompany the acceptance of science and technology as major social forces. To the extent that this commitment really shapes policy, and provided that the perceived need for national defence does not dominate all the other objectives, shared meanings for the conduct of foreign affairs can be developed.

Such meanings developed in relations among the democratic and industrialized countries. Their enmeshment in the ties triggered by technological interdependence goes hand in hand with their common acceptance of liberalism as the definer of social relations. They no longer have grievances against each other serious enough to trigger the fears that lead to arms races. Liberalism, having abandoned messianic imperialism since the Second World War, no longer includes the kind of nationalist commitment that predisposes countries to war. Marxist nationalism, equally committed to the welfare state and dependent on science and technology, is willing to entertain notions of functional co-operation with Western states. Some Marxist leaders see no possibility for a good national defence without global security. At the same time, the Marxist commitment to evangelism in the Third World remains as powerful as does the American zeal. Functional ties among Western countries, among Soviet bloc countries, and between the two blocs have *not* reduced the incidence of war; but functionalism and the reduction of violence are *both* expressions of mass welfare-oriented societies. It is too soon to speak of 'convergence' among the two blocs; it is not too soon to note the moderation in bellicose behaviour, if not in rhetoric.

That leaves us with the Third World areas in which war and violence are now prominent. It is here, of course, that the varieties of syncretist nationalism are mostly to be found, though this was not true before the Second World War. These countries experience the ties of common needs and shared meanings quite intermittently because of their rejection of all but the most instrumental aspects of modernism and cosmopolitanism. Moreover, their dependence on foreign techniques and practices rather than foreign values does not seriously influence their relations with each other since these ties are experienced mostly with reference to the First and Second Worlds. When they make war against each other, Third World countries do not sacrifice their access to foreign investment funds made available by the UN system, nor the services of the World Health Organisation (WHO), the Food and Agriculture Organisation (FAO) and the International Telecommunications Union (ITU), though their ability to make full use of these services and of private foreign funds is clearly reduced by being warlike. Most Third World states have not yet opted with finality for a single type of nationalism. In their domestic political struggles adherents of various nationalist beliefs compete and often fight with each other. I suspect that until they settle down and opt for *either* revolutionary nationalist doctrine, there is little reason to expect Third World countries to act more peacefully than they do now. Hence their increasing enmeshment in functionalist ties remains irrelevant with respect to war and peace, unless that enmeshment links them to each other (as in the Association of South East Asian States (ASEAN)) rather than to the outside world. Cosmopolitan notions of technical problem-solving cannot be expected to moderate the feelings of insecurity until Third World societies have been transformed to a much greater extent by the material and ideological forces that changed the First and Second Worlds. Only then can the types of interdependence which now characterize relations among OECD countries be expected to trigger responses that value economic co-ordination and collaboration in defence over the assertion of national uniqueness. Until that happens grievances and perceptions of insecurity will continue to feed upon each other in the Third World.

The late Hedley Bull saw this clearly.[12] Despite war and violence, there is such a thing as an 'international society' that is recognized and considered essential by the national societies of which it is composed. International society, like any society, is dedicated to the maintenance of some degree of order, which Bull defined as the preservation of such values as security of life, stability of expectations and the security of property. The fact that there are even minimal common rules of conduct is evidence of the recognition by all kinds of nationalists that such an order exists. A common sovereignty is not necessary for the elaboration and implementation of such minimal rules. How can this state of affairs be reconciled with the condition of international anarchy? Bull points out that anarchy is relative: it exists for some purposes but not for others, in some parts of the world more than in other parts. Moreover, since most leaders are committed to some aspects of international order, not every point of contention is equally serious for all at all times. A society is a collectivity that recognizes common interests and values while granting the simultaneous existence of divergent interests and values. The notion of a society cannot accommodate the assumption, however, that the divergent interests always dominate the shared ones.

If we accept this formulation, it should come as no surprise at all that we can see simultaneous, yet contradictory, trends. Interdependence increases, and with it the demands for new rules and a more highly articulated order. The growth in interdependence is expressed, partly, in the increase in international organizations, programmes, staff and rules. However, we must remember that this increase occurs only in those spheres of contact in which egoistic leaders perceive a need: when interdependence seems to dictate an institutional adaptation in the form of new international rules and programmes, the institutional steps will be agreed to; if there is no such perceived need, they will not and anarchy will continue to prevail. The increase in some kinds of interdependence need not entail a general reduction in insecurity or a passing into history of all past grievances. Armed with Bull's analysis, we have no reason to expect that increases in any kind of interdependence mean a reduction in violence.

How can international society become more orderly?

We have explained how two contradictory trends can prevail at the same time. Must they always coexist? Can more powerful rules and more common interests never come about at the global level? Do states never learn from experience and arrive at cumulatively shared meanings until all nationalisms have run their historical course? New definitions of problems can lead to new routines for solving the problems. These things have happened in the economic sphere, in public health, in telecommunications, in the work of the specialized agencies, of the UN Conference on Trade and Development (UNCTAD) and the UN Industrial Development Organisation (UNIDO). They have not yet happened in the realm of conflict management. There constraints on nationalism are recognized but the redefinition of the problem has not yet occurred.

What, then, has been learned? There has been little internalization of discrete lessons from past experience. All the 'errors' of judgement in decision-making to which cognitive psychology calls attention continue to be made. There is no organized institutional memory. Each generation of national and international decision-makers seems to be condemned to relearn the same old lessons. If learning means the collective mastering of a task by profiting from prior trial-and-error or stimulus-response experiences, world politics seems to be the habitat of dunces.

But suppose we think about learning in a different way, following the literature on collective action.[13] Actors, being out to win, are preoccupied with the short run only. Their attitude towards institutions is opportunistic. They cannot be assumed to welcome the help of third parties, show good will, be eager to settle. From the viewpoint of defining and implementing a permanent collective good – international peace – their behaviour is irrational, though from the perspective of safeguarding a private good – national security – it is not. Yet a sequence of episodes involving conflict and its abatement through the UN can also be expected to make actors aware of the fact that they are subject to constraints other than their relative weakness *vis-à-vis* their opponents. Such constraints include the need to justify themselves when attacked in a UN forum, to be threatened with boycotts or ostracism, to be made the subject of peace-keeping against their will. The constraints also include the recognition that persistence in unilateral behaviour can result in eventual isolation and even defeat.

In short, states devoid of altruism can be reasonably expected to become aware of their enmeshment in a situation of strategic inter-dependence, of mutual awareness that their moves depend on how they perceive the perceptions of the antagonist, whose array of options depends on the same double calculation. The policy implication of this constraint is the maxim 'don't push too hard' when conditions are uncertain and there is potential later danger. Paradoxically, this system of interaction imposes rationality on otherwise irrational states. The obverse is also true: if strategic interdependence is weak, so are the constraints on the realization of private goods. In such a case no learning will take place. The real world of conflict management seems to represent both patterns. Compared with conflict before 1945, systemic learning has taken place because things could have been much worse. The fact that learning is not cumulative, not equally internalized by all states, and subject to reversals, should remind us of the fragility of this process, until every state has experimented with its own national problem-solving routines as expressed in its nationalism, and has found them wanting.

Notes

1. Quincy Wright, *A Study of War*, 2 vols (Chicago: University of Chicago Press, 1965), pp. 235, 638. The statistical literature on the incidence of war is summarized by Francis A. Beer, *Peace Against War* (San Francisco: W. H. Freeman, 1981), ch. 2.

2. For recent works exploring this explanation of war see, for instance: Richard Ned Lebow, *Between Peace and War* (Baltimore: Johns Hopkins University Press, 1981); Michael Brecher, *Decisions in Crisis* (Berkeley: University of California Press, 1980); Robert Jervis, *Perception and Misperception in International Politics* (Princeton: Princeton University Press, 1976).

3. The tightest case for this explanation is Kenneth N. Waltz, *Theory of International Politics* (Reading, MA: Addison-Wesley, 1979); see also Bruce Bueno de Mesquita, *The War Trap* (New Haven: Yale University Press, 1981); Glenn H. Snyder and Paul Diesing, *Conflict Among Nations* (Princeton: Princeton University Press, 1977).

4. The best-known proponent of this argument is David Mitrany, *A Working Peace System* (Chicago: Quadrangle Books, 1966). In 1971 he insisted that his functionalist approach applies to war and security as well as to welfare issues. See 'The Functional Approach in Historical Perspective', *International Affairs* (July 1971), p. 539. For a much-qualified version of the functionalist argument see Ernst B. Haas, *Beyond the Nation-State* (Stanford: Stanford University Press, 1964). The psychological dimension of this argument is explored in Louis Kriesberg (ed.), *Social Processes in International Relations* (New York: John Wiley, 1968), and Herbert C. Kelman (ed.), *International Behaviour* (New York: Holt, Rinehart and Winston, 1965).

5. Beer, op. cit., p. 99.

6. The material that follows is more fully discussed in Ernst B. Haas, 'What Is Progress in the Study of International Organization?', *Kokusai Seiji* (May 1984), pp. 11–46 (in Japanese). Also see David M. Leive, *International Regulatory Regimes*, 2 vols (Lexington: Lexington Books, 1976).

7. For evidence on this point see Beer, op. cit., pp. 59ff.

8. For evidence see Ernst B. Haas, *The Obsolescence of Regional Integration Theory* (Berkeley: Institute of International Studies, 1975), Appendix.

9. Helga Haftendorn, 'Die Proliferation Konventioneller Rüstungen – Motive, Folgen, Kontrollmöglichkeiten', in Erhard Forndran and Paul J. Friedrich (eds), *Rüstungskontrolle und Sicherheit in Europa* (Bonn: Europa Union, 1979), p. 83. Purchases are expressed in constant 1975 US dollars.

10. Some of the evidence for this analysis is contained in Ernst B. Haas, *Why We Still Need the United Nations* (Berkeley: Institute of International Studies, 1986).

11. The material that follows is more fully discussed in Ernst B. Haas, 'What Is Nationalism and Why Should We Study It?', *International Organization* (Spring 1986). My discussion, in turn, draws heavily on Karl W. Deutsch, *Nationalism and Social Communication* (New York: John Wiley, 1953) and Ernest Gellner, *Nations and Nationalism* (Ithaca, NY: Cornell University Press, 1983).

12. Hedley Bull, *The Anarchical Society: A Study of Order in World Politics* (New York: Columbia University Press, 1977). For a related argument see Evan Luard, *Types of International Society* (New York: Free Press, 1976).

13. I am especially indebted, among a great many recent works, to Robert Axelrod, *The Evolution of Cooperation* (New York: Basic Books, 1984) and to Russell Hardin, *Collective Action* (Baltimore: Johns Hopkins University Press, 1982). Kenneth E. Boulding's *Ecodynamics* (Beverly Hills: Sage Publications, 1978) remains an inspiration to all who speculate along these lines.

9

Peace Through Emerging International Law

Jost Delbrück

The international debate on how to maintain or establish international peace and security in the post-Second World War period has increasingly focused on the military aspect of the problem. While early post-war planning for international peace concentrated on the role of international organizations such as the United Nations, traditional concepts like a military balance-of-power system between the antagonists of the emerging Cold War became dominant again. In recent decades the stability of the international system based on nuclear deterrence, on the one hand, and the demand for (at least) nuclear disarmament on the other, have been the dominant subjects of governmental and non-governmental debates on the future of international peace and security. At times the outside observer could get the impression that the key to peace lay with the accuracy of the statistics about missiles and other weapons. Recently, however, demands have been voiced that international efforts towards a lasting peace ought to be repoliticized, that is, the problem of maintaining peace is foremost a political one and ought to be treated accordingly. Interestingly enough, though, neither in the early post-war period, nor today has much thought been given to the fact that international peace is also a matter of law or – more precisely stated – that peace properly so-called is a state of law. This is not to say that international peace is primarily or even solely a matter of law. But it is to say that it is necessary to recall the legal dimension of peace and to reconsider the important role which law plays in securing and maintaining peace within social groups whether on the national or on the international level.

In this chapter I will attempt to show where and how the present international system and international law interrelate, what the nature and characteristics of international law are, and where its normative function positively comes to bear on the peaceful conduct of international relations. In the course of such an ambitious undertaking two obvious dangers have to be avoided. On the one hand, one must not add to the bulk of euphoric literature which blinds itself to the shortcomings of an international order which – probably for good reasons – lacks a central enforcement authority and, therefore, more than any other social order, depends on procedures for consensus-building as a basis for the implementation of binding norms of law. On the other hand, in avoiding any idealistic overestimation of present international law with regard to its peacekeeping capacity, one must not intentionally or unintentionally join ranks with those who come close to denying any legal force of international law and view it – rather cynically at times – as a convenient instrument of power politics. In pursuing this ambitious aim, therefore, I will study the way in which international law contributes to the development and maintenance of international peace and security. In analysing this issue, the argument will be developed in three stages. First, a short analysis will be undertaken of the structure of the international system as well as of the role of conflict and the modes of conflict resolution within this system. Second, the foundations and the role of international law, and particularly the relevance of its normative function, will be discussed. And third, attention will be drawn to the present-day body of international law relevant to conflict resolution.

The structure of the international system, the role of conflict and modes of conflict resolution

As the international system is never of a static nature but rather is in a constant process of slow or rapid change, it may be best to start an analysis of the structure of the international system from a historical perspective.

The emergence of the international system before the First World War

The configuration of political actors which we usually refer to as the 'international system' came into being as the result of the disintegration of the medieval feudal order. The central authority of the Emperor of the Holy Roman Empire and that of the Pope gradually vanished, and independent territorial entities with a centralized power structure and clearly defined jurisdictions over their people emerged. The modern state was born. Its characteristics until today have been external and international sovereignty – meaning political independence – territorial integrity and ideally the ability to effectively pursue those political and economic interests which are relevant to furthering the two former aims (independence and territorial integrity). The international or state system thus was constituted by entities freely co-operating or conflicting, as was deemed necessary by the states themselves in pursuance of their national interests. In view of this, the international system in the seventeenth and eighteenth centuries has often been described as anarchic. Yet, as will be shown later, even this system could not dispense with some basic rules of conduct so that, partly at least the characterization of the international system of the time as anarchic is not fully adequate. This characterization is also inadequate in that it overlooks the fact that the international system in the seventeenth and eighteenth centuries, soon after its emergence,[1] tended to develop certain dominant power structures represented by the major powers of the time which ensured at least some degree of stability for the system. The balance-of-power concept, first mentioned in the treaty of Utrecht (1713), adequately describes the stabilizing structural elements which could help to secure peace – at least temporarily – and contribute to the resolution of conflicts. Another such structural element was the delimitation of spheres of interest in areas of colonial expansion and activity. These traits of the international system – which, incidentally, was restricted to the European states – became more pronounced during the nineteenth century. After the failure of French hegemony – an attempt to restructure the international system by the dominance of one nation-state[2] – the multipolar system was re-established. The Vienna Congress again introduced a relatively stable power structure (the Holy Alliance, later developed into the Concert of Europe) which could serve as the socio-political underpinning of the international system. What had been vaguely developed in the eighteenth century, that is, the balance-of-power concept, now became a clearly designed concept of international order which even carried some traits of institutionalization. Inis Claude (1964) expressly points to the Concert of Europe as the forerunner of the institutionalized efforts for securing peace and security in the twentieth century – the League of Nations and the United Nations. The nineteenth-century international system under the guidance of the Concert of Europe provided for a homogeneous political (and legal) order which could effectively cope with conflicts whenever and wherever they arose.

And yet the nineteenth-century international system was unable to overcome the political, social and cultural crisis that marked the turn of the century. The reasons for this crisis and the inability of the system to cope with it were manifold. There were internal factors such as social unrest, increasing demands of peoples or ethnic groups – hitherto integrated in the territorial jurisdiction of great powers – for national self-determination which threatened the internal stability of the very states ensuring the stability of the international system. Also there were external factors such as a sharpening economic rivalry among the major industrial powers, and the increased military capability of the big powers which allowed for more effective political power-projection. With the outbreak of the First World War the international system was precipitated into the abyss of the first global and total war which at the same time signalled the end of the Eurocentric phase of the international system. The process of its universalization was initiated, as the United States and later the Soviet Union became new centres of power and ever more non-European states entered the political scene.

Restructuring the international system: the emergence of International organizations as political actors after the First World War
After the First World War the international system underwent fundamental changes which did not come about abruptly because of the war but which – rooted in developments in the nineteenth century – came fully to bear on the international system only after the breakdown of the Eurocentric system existing until the First World War. First, the universalization of

the system – as already mentioned – became an irreversible fact. Already in the nineteenth century the admission of the Ottoman Empire into the club of the great powers represented a major step forward in opening up the hitherto closed European state system. The independence of the Latin American republics and their participation in international diplomacy was another decisive factor in the process of the broadening of the international system. The Japanese victory over the Russian fleet in the 1905 war was another ominous sign on the wall that the Eurocentric international system was to give way to another power structure. However, at the turn of the century, the system was still dominated by the European great powers. This definitely changed after the First World War when the decline of the Central European powers and the weakening of the Western European powers left a power vacuum which was gradually filled in by the United States and – by the middle of the twentieth century – the Soviet Union. Second, the international system expanded in terms of the communicative functions fulfilled by it. Increased international commerce, rapid development of the means of world-wide traffic (air, land and sea) as well as radio communication, brought about ever more international exchange and co-operation. Third, as a consequence of increased international exchange and communication, the number of actors in the international system not only increased in quantitative but also in qualitative terms. The most important change in this respect was the emergence of new corporate actors: the international organizations. Already at the end of the nineteenth century, national governments felt the need to create institutionalized forms of international co-operation.[3] International organizations were founded in great numbers as entities separate from individual states with organs to act internationally on the basis of their own decision-making procedures. They offered co-ordinating and co-operative services which supplemented the national governments in their efforts to perform their functions in the fields of economic, social, technical and cultural development. After the First World War when the failure of the Eurocentric international system to maintain peace and security became apparent and when it became clear that the individual nation-state was less and less capable of providing for its national security, the international community recognized its collective responsibility for the maintenance of peace and security. The concept of co-ordinating and collectively undertaking the manifold tasks of economic, social and technical development through international organizations was therefore extended to that of maintaining peace and security. The idea of a League of Nations was aired (Schücking, 1909) and then realized within a few years of the end of the First World War, its major function being to provide the means for the peaceful settlement of disputes and thereby to reduce the need for conflict resolution by military means. While the League's Covenant did not completely outlaw war as a means of conflict resolution, the prohibition of war and the use of force or threat of the use of force was further developed by the Kellogg Pact (Treaty of Paris, 1928) and after the Second World War by the United Nations Charter.

Yet until today the attempt to establish an institutionalized central authority charged with the responsibility of maintaining peace and security universally has proved to be relatively ineffective. Thus the international community – especially after the Second World War – has established another kind of organization which serves as a regional centre of power and authority to guarantee peace and security for the states of the respective regions which, in view of the rapid development of military technology, have become more or less incapable of providing for their own defence. These regional institutions – NATO, the Warsaw Pact, the Organization of American States (OAS), etc. – have become the major and most important structural elements infusing relative stability into the international system and also ensuring peace and a fairly high degree of rational, non-military conflict resolution. On the other hand, one must not forget that these new regional organizations have produced another kind of problem with regard to their member states. At least in the cases of the superpower-dominated alliances, e.g. NATO and the Warsaw Pact, member states have to pay for their gains in national security with a considerable loss in their national freedom of action, which is particularly felt by some of the member states of the Warsaw Pact.[4]

Modes of conflict resolution and the role of law
The international system as it was described in the foregoing paragraphs – though characterized by a variety of actors – is still dominated by the state as its principal actor. As it is a major characteristic of the modern state that it is based on the concepts of delimitation in terms of other states and of self-assertion – i.e. the pursuance of its self-interest – conflicts among the constituent members of the international system are an inevitable phenomenon. Such conflict is understood as the struggle between entities for values, rights to status, power and resources (Coser, 1956). The classical, pre-First World War international system did not offer any centralized, authoritative mechanisms of conflict resolution. The system in this respect reflected the structure of the international community of states which was characterized by its independent, sovereign constituent parts. As traditional modes of conflict resolution, therefore, bilateral or multilateral diplomacy and the use of force can be identified. The latter was of utmost importance. War was considered to be a legitimate instrument for resolving conflicts, that is, a solution could be achieved by a victory over the holder of antagonistic interests by pursuing a right against an opponent denying that right and by sanctioning breaches of the law. The international system in this respect may be compared with the late feudal system in medieval times, when the pursuit of rights by the use of force – by feud – was the order of the day because a functioning central authority to adjudicate rights and sanction their implementation was lacking.

Under the impact of the first total wars – the wars fought for the national unification of Italy and the American Civil War – there was a growing realization that war as an instrument of pursuing national interests might have become dysfunctional. At the turn of the century increasing efforts can be observed to provide for institutionalized mechanisms of conflict resolution. In 1907 the Hague Peace Conference established the Permanent Court of Arbitration; the same year saw the establishment of the first Interamerican Court which functioned until 1918. It represented an imaginative, progressive instrument of interstate conflict resolution, but it also had jurisdiction over disputes between states and individuals.

The League of Nations Covenant represented the first major effort to institutionalize and to centralize international conflict resolution. Along with the establishment of the League, the Permanent Court of International Justice was formed, further underlining the League's concept that traditional conflict resolution by war or other forcible means was to be substituted by judicial procedures or other means based on rules of law. This brings us to the problem of the role of law with regard to conflict resolution.

As I have mentioned already, even the classical international system of the seventeenth and eighteenth centuries could not fully dispense with certain basic rules of conduct, i.e. rules of international law, however strongly the sovereign will of the states was emphasized and however emphatically some writers on international law and legal philosophers – both in the eighteenth and nineteenth centuries – contended that sovereign states were not bound by any rules of law or were bound by such rules only as long as they saw fit (international law as the external national law of states – 'außeres Staatsrecht' – as Hegel called it). Looking back upon the development of international law from rather crude basic principles into intricate rules of diplomacy or warfare, we can observe a growing concern among the international community for the development of rules of law regulating their mutual relations in peace and conflict. Especially in the nineteenth century which saw the sovereign state at its peak, the development and codification by treaty of international rules of law, constituting the legal framework of the international system, is of a striking intensity. The Act of the Vienna Congress, the Peace Treaty of 1856 ending the Crimean War, the Acts of the Berlin Congresses (1875 and 1888) and the Act of the Brussels Congress (1890) are important steps in setting up a legal basis for the conduct of international relations, providing also for criteria according to which disputes could be settled.

Having thus described the importance which international law increasingly took on over the centuries on the one hand – a process which is still underway today – we cannot overlook, on the other hand, the fact that, given the structure of the international system, the authority of the law is often disputed and rated low in many quarters, especially when compared with the effectiveness of national laws within the domestic sphere of states. Therefore we have to turn to the analysis of the nature of international law, its foundations and the relevance of its normative function in order to better understand its contributions to and its short-comings in international conflict resolution.

The international system as a legal order

Much of the critical or sceptical perception of the relevance of international law – existing or emerging – for the maintenance of international peace is due to a misconception of the nature and foundations of international law. Quite often the functioning or malfunctioning of international law is measured against the background of the functioning of law on the national or state level where an extensive enforcement machinery is provided and, as a rule, breaches of the law may be effectively sanctioned. Indeed, viewed from such a perspective, international law shows major deficiencies. The view, however, that international law is just an inferior type of law misses the point. In order to explain this in more detail, the nature of international law in general and of particular norms of international law have to be discussed, together with the essential problem of wherefrom international law derives its binding force and validity.

The nature of international law

In the course of the empirical description of the international system, rules of international law were referred to several times as part of the reality of that system. Empirical description, however, cannot produce any sufficient perception of the rule of law in its normative sense. Thus, the empirical description must be accompanied and completed by some insight into the meaning of legally binding norms. If we take a closer look at the notion of 'system', which has become the leading notion of sociological analysis, we realize that the notion is itself a normative one. In its very existence a system is dependent on the provision and observance of certain rules of conduct. Members of a system defend themselves by fulfilling specific functions accorded to them by rules and norms and, furthermore, by relying on a corresponding and reciprocal conduct of the other members participating in the system. A system in this sense presents itself as a configuration of regulated interaction and inter-relations. These regulations, in turn, may be social norms of conduct or they may take on the character of legal norms which may be interpreted as rules of particular importance imbued with a special degree of normativity. Therefore, the international system can be understood as a legal order, the rules of which provide normativity for the necessary degree of stability within the system, and at the same time provide mechanisms or procedures by which the system is enabled to adapt itself to changing circumstances without being violently disrupted. International law is a network of normative rules governing interactions and interrelations in the international system which is considered by the constituent parts of the system as necessary for the maintenance of the system as a safeguard for their own existence. This does not mean that international law provides for rigid norms and principles of conduct. Rather we may understand these rules as allowing for the pursuit of state interests within a relatively wide margin of interpretation which, however, is not unlimited. Even a broadly conceived rule of law has its normative limits which, if transgressed, indicate the boundary between legal and illegal conduct. International rules of law serve as channels through which interests may be articulated – couched in legal terms – and conflicting claims may be lodged with the international community. Only those interests or claims and counter-claims can be legitimately (and legally) postulated which may be brought within the bounds of a rule of law. This introduces a certain degree of stability and reliability into the mutual relations of states and other international actors. On the other hand, if the existing rules of international law evidently do not provide for the possibility of arguing newly arising interests or claims, the accepted process of creating new norms – i.e. the rules of customary or treaty law – allows for the changes necessary. This process can best be observed in the case of the development of a new rule of customary law. A state or a group of states develop a certain practice which gradually becomes supported by *opinio iuris*, that is, the community of states accepts the new practice of the states concerned as a matter of law and thereby opens up new channels of interest articulation and finally of possible conflict resolution. From a different perspective, international law may be defined as being of a primarily advocatory nature.

Having sketched out in rough terms the particular character of international law, it is now necessary to turn to the even more basic problem of the foundation of the normativity of international law and the validity of its norms as distinguished from their formal being in force.

The foundation and validity of the norms of
international law in a pluralistic society of nations
This chapter cannot, of course, deal extensively with the full range of theories about the foundations of international law and its validity as the accepted rules of conduct. These range from theories of individual and common consent as the basis of the normativity of international law to sociological theories of various kinds which try to explain the binding force of international law also on those states which either did not participate in the law-making process or did not consent to a particular rule of international law. International law, however, as the normative, binding legal framework for all states and other actors of the international system, is functional only if its normativity is not made dependent on the consent of a particular state or actor at a particular time. Therefore, only the so-called sociological theories are of interest at this point. The gist of sociological theories may be summarized very pointedly in this way: 'Law is binding because it is necessary' (Dahm, 1958). It is from this premise or axiomatic basis that these theories derive the binding force of international law. At first sight, this theory seems to derive the 'ought' from the 'is' – a methodological step which in modern times has been emphatically rejected

among others by Hans Kelsen because the realms of the 'ought' and the 'is' are categorically different. The binding force of a rule of law may not be derived from an empirical fact, but only from a related value judgement. Yet a closer look reveals that sociological theory goes beyond merely deriving the normativity of law from empirical facts. The axiomatic rule 'law is binding because it is necessary' is itself a value judgement, in that it presupposes a certain notion of what is necessary, that is, the international system – or rather its maintenance and stability – is seen to be of advantage and mutual benefit to its various constituent parts and therefore requires norms binding upon them. These rules must conform in substance to some minimum standards of justice and fairness, for however one may define such values, they are necessary for the maintenance of a social group.

Now while it is conceivable that even a heterogeneous international society such as we have today will universally accept the notion that in the international system certain binding rules of conduct are necessary, the actual problem posed by the pluralism of ideologies and cultural backgrounds arises when it comes to finding consensus as to the substantive elements of these rules of conduct. As the international system lacks an international legislative power and an authority to establish the law in concrete cases (like the courts do in national law), it will always be a major deficiency of international law and its contribution to conflict resolution that in concrete cases of controversy this heterogeneity of values and moral judgements will come to bear. This is clearly borne out by the fact that the present-day body of international law shows various rifts along ideological and socio-political lines. For instance, the group of socialist countries, led by the Soviet Union, maintain the existence of three separate sets of rules of international law, that is, those pertaining to the socialist states only, and those forming the international law of coexistence which is applicable to all states notwithstanding their ideological and political differences. Lastly, there are the old rules of international law which were developed among the capitalist states and which may, or may not, still be applicable to the states adhering to the capitalist system. In addition, a further distinction may be made with regard to the developing countries who tend to adapt international law to their specific needs by introducing concepts of law into the international legal order which were foreign to traditional international jurisprudence and – if accepted as binding upon all states – would transform traditional international law. Outstanding examples of these new concepts are the notions of the 'common heritage of mankind' and of the 'right to development' which have already found their way into various international treaties and other international instruments such as the declarations of UN bodies. In view of these fundamental differences of opinion among states or groups of states about what the international legal order should look like, one may rate the actual and potential peacekeeping capacity of international law fairly low. However, in actual international practice the differences mentioned above are of less importance than one may assume. The fact that states from the various ideological and political quarters of the world are all members of the United Nations, and of most of its specialized agencies, and thereby have subscribed to the law of the United Nations Charter, has contributed to considerable pragmatism in the process of developing international law in accordance with their interests. It has become accepted that the basic dilemma of the international system as a legal order – that is, the existence of a wide heterogeneity of value judgements, on the one hand, and the lack of an obligatory process to establish the law in concrete cases on the other – cannot be overcome normatively by any one group of states or by any other power structure imposing their value-oriented interpretation of a particular norm in a concrete situation. Attempts at this approach were made by the Western countries under the leadership of the United States in the early years of the United Nations, and they are made again by the present vast majority of Third World states in the UN General Assembly and elsewhere. But experience has shown that very little is achieved by this approach in the long run. What is needed, instead, is an obligatory process of international communication or dialogue by which the meaning of the usually broad rules of international law may be established in a concrete case, with the long-range expectancy that this interpretation will guide the future conduct of states in similar socio-political contexts. This means, in other words, that a rule of international law is not only recognized as being formally in force, but that it takes on an agreed meaning and substance or validity in the sense referred to above, and may thereby contribute to the peaceful resolution of conflicts.

Having considered the nature and foundation of international law and its actual or potential peacekeeping capacity, the focus of the chapter must now be turned to the core of present-day international law relevant to conflict resolution and to the failures and achievements of this body of law.

The substance of present-day international law: its failures and achievements in securing international peace and security

The foregoing theoretical considerations have shown that the use of international law to secure and maintain peace is of a twofold nature: the law provides rules regulating interstate conduct in a substantive, material way, and it also contains rules of a procedural nature obliging states to enter into a peaceful settlement of disputes or – viewed from a different perspective – offering states the technical means to seek a peaceful settlement of a given conflict by bringing to bear the communicative function of international law as described above.

The substantive norms of international conduct may be divided into two major categories: on the one hand, there are prohibitive rules obliging states not to engage in activities that are likely to disturb international peace and security, e.g. the prohibition of the use of force. On the other hand, there is a body of law providing positively for those activities of the international community that are conducive to establishing a peaceful order based on social justice and the observance of human rights. In developing the latter, international law has changed from a rather formal set of 'rules of the game' to a value-oriented or value-setting order aimed at overcoming those conflict formations which endanger international peace and security today.

The various categories of the international law of conflict resolution will now be discussed in turn, starting with the prohibitive norms for the maintenance of peace and security.

The prohibition of the use of force and
related norms of international law
Traditional international law until the end of the First World War was characterized by the *liberum ius ad bellum*, the sovereign right of states to go to war. Waging war was not only a legal but also a legitimate means of pursuing national interests. In view of the devastating effects of modern warfare, the international community has progressively turned away from the notion of a *liberum ius ad bellum*. From the League's Covenant, to the Kellogg Pact to the United Nations Charter, international law step by step has outlawed first war as a means of national policy and then any use or threat of the use of force (Article 2 (4), UN Charter), the only exception being the use of force in self-defence (Article 51, UN Charter). As a complementary set of international law norms, treaty provisions in the field of disarmament and arms control, as well as the rules of warfare prohibiting the use of certain weapons, have to be mentioned as being intended to support the primary aim of the international legal order, that is, securing the absence of the use of military force as a means of conflict resolution. Other related prohibitive norms for the maintenance of international peace and security are the principle of territorial integrity and the political independence of states. States are obliged to refrain from any action likely to impair the territorial integrity and political independence of other states. Last but not least, the principle of non-intervention, by which states are prohibited from interfering with the internal affairs of other states, is of relevance here. While all of these norms seem to have a clear meaning and to be an adequate answer by the international community to the problem of securing peace by legal means, it has to be recognized that the prohibition of the use of force and the principle of non-intervention involve many interpretative problems. Thus, there is general agreement that Article 2 (4) of the UN Charter prohibits any use of military force; it is, however, still a matter of dispute whether it also covers other means of power projection, e.g. economic boycotts or similar measures. Even if such a broad construction of Article 2 (4) was accepted, there would still be disagreement about which modes of economic or other methods of power-projection constituted an illegal use of force.

It seems clear that not all instances of economic imbalance, which derives from differences in the economic strength of states and results in an objectively or subjectively felt application of pressure, can be considered as an illegal use of force. Another problem related to Article 2 (4) of the UN Charter is the difficulty of distinguishing the illegal use of military force from the legal use of force in self-defence, since it is often hard to determine whether or not an act of aggression has been committed. The United Nations have tried to solve this problem by working out a definition of aggression (General Assembly Resolution 3314/XXIX), but this has many loopholes which leave ample room for different interpretations and controversy. Therefore, it is necessary not only to provide procedural rules which enable states to solve such interpretative problems, but also to develop substantive rules of international law aimed at overcoming the causes of international friction.

The principles of international law applied to social welfare and the protection of human rights

Within and outside the UN the international community has set out to develop fundamental principles of law which are to provide equal access to political participation and to redress existing inequities. Attempts have been made to control the use of and access to natural resources by safeguarding national sovereignty over such resources, by protecting access to those resources not yet subject to national jurisdiction and by ensuring that the use of such resources is regulated in a way that serves the international community at large. Among these attempts, the concept of 'the common heritage of mankind' (CHOM) figures prominently. The precise meaning of this principle is still a matter of controversy, and so is the question of whether it has already become an established principle of general international law. There are, however, several references to the principle in modern treaty laws which are in force and which indicate the overall direction in which the law is developing (e.g. Space Law, the Law of the Sea, the Antarctic Treaty, the Code of Conduct for Transfer of Technology;[5] a further area where CHOM is of increasing importance is that of the Convention on the World Cultural and National Heritage). CHOM is intended to prevent the extension of national jurisdiction over new or old spaces hitherto not subject to sovereign rights; it aims to secure the use of the resources of those spaces in a way beneficial to all humankind and to provide for solidarity among all states with respect to the fruits of technological developments, with the ultimate aim of attaining a more just international economic, social and cultural order. A principle of solidarity is appearing in various treaty clauses which ask for the progressive fulfilment of the obligations contained in these clauses through the joint efforts of all parties to the treaties, rich or poor, big or small (see International Labour Organization (ILO) practice).

The few references made here to basic principles of international law – relevant to conflict resolution – underline the fact that the international community is setting out to develop a legal order which is designed to cope with the gravest sources of conflict in the present-day international system.

The same tendency is evident with respect to a particular aspect of international relations that has given rise to many serious disagreements – gross violations of human rights. One may safely state that in this field a most impressive and, technically speaking, most developed body of international law has been created over the last three decades. Besides the UN Covenant on Civil and Political Rights as well as the Covenant on Economic, Social and Cultural Rights, a number of universal and regional conventions on human rights have been adopted and have come into force: the Convention on the Elimination of All Forms of Racial Discrimination (CERD), the European Convention on Human Rights (ECHR), the American Convention on Human Rights (ACHR) and, only recently, the African Charter on Human Rights, the so-called Banjul Charter. Furthermore, some of the UN specialized organizations such as the ILO and Unesco have also worked out important human rights instruments. As the international community has increasingly recognized that gross violations of human rights have given rise to international conflicts, the implementation of these international human rights instruments by appropriate international machinery has become an important part of international conflict resolution. It is worth noting that within this area the most sophisticated means of non-violent conflict resolution have been developed like, for instance, the reporting system of the ILO and the judicial processes provided by the regional human rights instruments in Western Europe and in the Americas.

One has to acknowledge, however, major deficiencies in this field. Despite widespread formal acceptance of the human rights instruments, there is a considerable lack of consensus as to the meaning of these human rights norms in particular socio-political contexts. The ideological and cultural rifts of the world fully come to bear on the validity of these norms. This is especially true with regard to the East–West ideological conflict. But there are also major discrepancies between the Old World's and the Third World's perception of some basic human rights which Western democracies are used to refer to as individual rights and freedoms. Yet one may safely state that the existing procedural mechanisms in the human rights field have served adequately to gradually build more consensus, at least with regard to basic rights such as the right to life and to freedom from torture.

The development of international law as described in this section may be adequately summarized by stating that the international community is setting out to establish a new set of frameworks for the conduct of states, examples of which have become known as the new international economic order or the new information order. Each of these orders is highly controversial in many details, but the trend towards such a reconstruction of the international legal order is clearly established.

Principles and procedural aspects of non-violent
conflict resolution in international law
The need to provide procedural means to establish the concrete meaning
of norms of international law as the binding rules for conflict resolution
(dispute settlement) has been increasingly recognized in the international
community, especially after war as an accepted means of pursuing
national interests was illegalized. Yet it must be admitted that a major
problem has not been solved satisfactorily so far, that is, the establishment
of a binding principle in general international law obliging states to engage
in the peaceful settlement of disputes. Chapter 6 of the UN Charter
(Article 33) imposes such an obligation on the member states, but the
actual acceptance of this obligation by the international community is
low, especially with regard to the many potential conflicts lingering on
without the protagonists engaging in any attempt to bring about a non-
violent solution before the conflict escalates.

Despite this rather negative state of affairs, it should not be overlooked that procedures and mechanisms for the non-violent solution of
international conflicts are well developed and at times are being used
successfully. It is no wonder that in the era of international organization
the emphasis is on institutionalized mechanisms of dispute settlement,
although extra-institutional means – such as bilateral or multilateral
negotiations – are still of high importance. Mediation, arbitration and
judicial settlement of disputes are usually named as the best known means
of dispute settlement based on the rules of international law (Judicial
Settlement of International Disputes, 1974). However, the range of means
for conflict resolution provided by international law has become much
wider. International organizations have opened a large number of forums
where international conflicts may be dealt with. These conflicts are not
only those that figure most prominently in the daily headlines, but also
those that arise in the economic, social and cultural fields.

Among those forums we find the UN General Assembly, the plenary
organs of the other organizations of the UN family and the regional
organizations and various sub-organs of these organizations. In the bigger
forums the emphasis is on political considerations, although more often
than not this is couched in legal terms. In the smaller forums – such
as committees of experts in the human rights field – legal considerations
prevail. It is in those committees that the most fruitful work with regard
to the development of more consensus on the norms of international law
in important fields is accomplished.

Besides solving conflicts according to existing rules of law, a major task
for the international community is to create new norms of international
law dealing with vital conflicts of interest, for example, the distribution
of resources not yet subject to the national or sovereign rights of individual
states, or the provision of access to technological know-how, to name
but a few of the long list of disputed fields in present-day international
life. Quasi-legislative conferences with new forms of consensus-building

are an accepted means of accomplishing this norm-creating task, the Law of the Sea Conference being one of the most prominent examples in recent years. The new treaty law – or customary law – originating from these conferences, which is more precisely phrased than older norms, may be considered as an especially valuable contribution of international law to conflict resolution, mainly because these new rules are usually accompanied by elaborate procedural means of dispute settlement.

Concluding remarks

In summing up we may observe that there are a considerable number of rules of international law coping not only with the foremost problem of present-day international relations, that is, restricting or even eliminating the use of force, but also aiming at establishing a more just and peaceful order. These value-setting norms, together with the procedural rules described above, form the essence of the notion of peaceful change which is the most prominent aim of international law, present or emerging. A last caveat may be allowed, however. Since the focus of this chapter has been on the contribution of international *law* to the maintenance of international peace and security, it was appropriate that international law figured prominently in the considerations. However, we must not forget that conflicts and conflict resolution are intrinsically of a political nature (Grewe, 1985). So the message of this chapter is that conflicts are law-related and conflict resolution is not only a political but also a legal problem. Whether or not the law can be applied effectively to maintaining and securing international peace is to a large extent dependent upon the readiness of the international community to recognize the political *and* the legal nature of an international peace order.

Notes

1. The year 1648 (Westphalian Peace Treaty) is usually referred to as the formal recognition of the modern sovereign state and thereby as the birthday of the modern international system. For many reasons the developments described here may be dated back to much earlier phenomena, e.g. the city state system of northern Italy or the attempts by Spain to establish a Spanish hegemony. For a comprehensive history of the early periods; see Grewe (1984).

2. This is a recurrent feature of the development of the European state system up to the Second World War; see Grewe (1984).

3. The formation of the Universal Postal Union in 1874 and of the International Telegraph Union (now International Telecommunications Union) in 1865 are outstanding examples in point.

4. The so-called Brezhnev Doctrine on the one hand, and United States interventions in the OAS region, on the other hand, are examples in point

5. See Wolfrum (1983) for further references.

References

Aron, Raymond (1962) *Paix et guerre entre les nations*, 3rd ed. Paris: Calmann-Lévy.
Bowett, Derek W. (1963) *The Law of International Institutions*. London: Stevens.

Brownlie, Ian (1963) *International Law and the Use of Force by States*. Oxford: Clarendon Press.

Clark, Grenville and Sohn, Lewis B. (1958) *World Peace through World Law*. Cambridge: Harvard University Press.

Claude, Inis L. (1964) *Swords into Plowshares. The Problems and Progress of International Organization*, 3rd edn. New York: Random House.

Coser, Lewis A. (1956) *The Functions of Social Conflict*. New York: Free Press.

Dahm, Georg (1958) *Völkerrecht*, Vol. I. Stuttgart: W. Kohlhammer.

Delbrück, Jost (ed.) (1984) *Friedensdokumente aus fünf Jahrhunderten. Abrüstung-Kriegsverhütung-Rüstungskontrolle*, 2 vols. Kehl, Strasbourg, Arlington: N. P. Engel.

Deutsch, Karl W. and Hoffman, Stanley (eds) (1968) *The Relevance of International Law: Essays in Honor of Leo Gross*. Cambridge: Schenkman.

Dupey, René Jean (ed.) (1981) *The New International Economic Order. Commercial, Technological and Cultural Aspects* (Hague Academy of International Law, Workshop 1980). The Hague, Boston, London: M. Nijhoff.

Falk, Richard A. (1970) *The Status of Law in International Society*. Princeton: Princeton University Press.

Falk, Richard A. and Black, Cyril E. (eds) (1969) *The Future of the International Legal Order*, 4 vols. Princeton: Princeton University Press.

Falk, Richard A. and Mendlovitz, Saul H. (1966) *The Strategy of World Order*, Vol. II: *International Law*. New York: World Law Fund.

Friedmann, Wolfgang G. (1964) *The Changing Structure of International Law*. London: Stevens.

Grewe, Wilhelm G. (1984) *Epochen der Völkerrechtsgeschichte*. Baden-Baden: Nomos.

Grewe, Wilhelm G. (1985) *Friede durch Recht?* Berlin, New York: Walter de Gruyter.

Judicial Settlement of International Disputes. An International Symposium (1974). Berlin: Springer.

Kelsen, Hans (1928) *Das Problem der Souveränität und die Theorie des Völkerrechts*, 2nd edn. Tübingen: Mohr.

Knorr, Klaus and Verba, Sidney (eds) (1961) *The International System – Theoretical Essays*. Princeton: Princeton University Press.

MacDonald, Ronald St John (ed.) (1978) *The International Law and Policy of Human Welfare*. Alphen aan den Rijn: Sijthoff & Noordhoff.

MacDonald, Ronald St John (ed.) (1983) *The Structure and Process of International Law*. The Hague, Boston, Lancaster: M. Nijhoff.

McDougal, Myres S. and Feliciano, Florentino P. (1961) *Law and Minimum World Public Order. The Legal Regulation of International Coercion*. New Haven: Yale University Press.

Mosler, Hermann (1980) *The International Society as a Legal Community*, rev. edn. Alphen aan den Rijn: Sijthoff & Noordhoff.

Northedge, F. S. and Donelan, M. D. (1971–2) *International Disputes*, Vol. I: *The Political Aspects*; Vol. II: *The Legal Aspects*. London: Europa Publications for the David Davis Memorial Institute of International Studies.

Raman, K. Venkata (ed.) (1977) *Dispute Settlement through the United Nations*. Dobbs Ferry, NY: Oceana Publications.

Reuter, Paul and Combacau, Jean (1980) *Institutions et relations internationales*. Paris: Presses Universitaires de France.

Schermers, Henry G. (1980) *International Institutional Law*, 2 vols., 2nd edn. Alphen aan den Rijn: Sijthoff & Noordhoff.

Schücking, Walther (1909) *Die Organisation der Welt*. Leipzig: Kröner.

Sohn, Louis B. and Buergenthal, Thomas (1973) *International Protection of Human Rights*. New York: Bobbs-Merrill.

Waldock, Humphrey (1962) 'General Course on Public International Law', *Recueil des Cours 1962* II: 1ff. The Hague: M. Nijhoff.

Wolfrum, Rüdiger (1983) 'The Principle of Common Heritage of Mankind', *Zeitschrift für ausländischer öffentliches Recht und Völkerrecht* 43: 319ff.
Wright, Quincy (1961) *The Role of International Law in the Elimination of War*. Manchester: Manchester University Press.

10

Lessons from 'Disarmament' Negotiations

Yoshikazu Sakamoto

The four decades since 1946 have been characterized by two apparently contradictory developments. On the one hand, there have been almost continuous talks, whether at the bilateral or multilateral level, on arms control and disarmament, including 'the regulation of armaments' in UN parlance. On the other hand, there has been almost complete failure to halt and to reverse the arms race and to achieve the goals not only of disarmament but also of arms control (except on peripheral issues).

A glance at this lack of achievement precludes an optimistic outlook that still further negotiations would bring about disarmament. A more plausible response would be an interpretation in reverse – a cynical view that the negotiations have played no more than a cosmetic role in concealing by propaganda the reality of uninterrupted arms build-ups. Apart from the possibility that the talks have been merely for cosmetic purposes, the continuation of the negotiations for four decades is inconceivable unless the parties concerned have found a degree of common interest in so engaging themselves. What is this common interest? It seems to be at least twofold.

Firstly, the states involved seem to have preferred arms races coupled with arms control and disarmament talks to untrammelled unilateral arms build-ups. In the nuclear age, when the survival of each state is in common danger, states share a common interest in maintaining a sufficient level of communication to prevent the arms race from getting out of control to the detriment of everybody's interest. Just as the superpowers did not leave the United Nations even at the height of the Cold War (or hot wars such as the Korean War, for that matter), they did not totally discontinue arms control and disarmament talks. Since their interests were in sharp conflict, negotiations were 'war' by other means; but it is important that 'war' took the form of negotiations.

Secondly, the states engaged in negotiations were not always interested in the negotiations as such, but used them for the purpose of propaganda. Spanier and Nogee, in their early analysis of the 'politics of disarmament', interpreted the disarmament negotiations in terms of 'gamesmanship' and even 'psychological warfare'. In their view, while 'compromise is inherent in any diplomatic negotiations...there can be no compromise with a totalitarian state' (Spanier and Nogee, 1962: 34). One can readily point out that this mode of thinking is in itself a component of the Cold War, turning negotiations into propaganda. Accordingly, a number of proposals were put forward not for serious give-and-take negotiation but for propaganda with hypocritical implications, occasionally with the result that the initiator of a proposal was embarrassed by its unexpected acceptance by the opponent (Frye, 1961: 30). But this should not lead merely to a cynical view of disarmament negotiations since, in the words of Reinhold Niebuhr, hypocrisy 'is the tribute which morality pays to immorality' (Niebuhr, 1949: 95). Propaganda is a contest over legitimation; and the recognition of the use of propaganda is an admission of the value of and the need for legitimation. And to the extent that the success or failure of legitimation depends on the reactions of the people, the holders of the power of propaganda are constrained by the popular will.[1]

Thus, there are two major constraints on the arms race – one is the physical imperative to avoid annihilation, the other is the political need to acquire legitimacy. The former calls for communication, and the latter legitimation. It must be noted that what is generally considered or labelled as negotiation is frequently not, nor is it intended to be, a process for diplomatic compromise, but aims to be communication and legitimation. In fact this is a reflection of the reality that these two constraints are embedded in the structure of the contemporary world, the former constituting the technological constraint, the latter the political. Both are of vital importance.

This absence of substantive negotiation in 'disarmament negotiations' leads to the question of whether negotiations are relevant to arms control and disarmament and, if so, in what sense. This query makes a sharp contrast with the view, widely shared by the general public, that tends to equate disarmament with disarmament through negotiations. In this view, disarmament, unless it is imposed by victor states on the vanquished, such as the demilitarization of Germany and Japan at the end of the Second World War, should be disarmament by consent; and consent means agreement through negotiations. Thus, the most realistic and rational approach to disarmament is to seek an agreement through negotiations. But our experience over the last four decades reveals either that something different from negotiation has frequently been undertaken under the name of 'negotiations' or that, if serious efforts were made to negotiate, they did not bear the intended results. We must, therefore, examine why arms control and disarmament through negotiations have been futile so far, and what lessons should be drawn from the failure.

Dilemmas of 'disarmament' negotiations

The view which tends to equate disarmament with disarmament through negotiated agreements is generally based, explicitly or implicitly, on the following two premises. Firstly, it is based on the assumption that armaments and military force are negotiable since they are measurable and comparable. Secondly, it presupposes that at least one party to the negotiations (and it is generally taken for granted that 'one party' is 'we', not 'they') actually takes a non-offensive, non-expansionist stand genuinely seeking disarmament (implying that the 'sincerity' and the intention of the other party is ambiguous), and that 'our' bona fide non-agressive intention is communicable to 'them' through disarmament talks.

The first premise is best illustrated by the idea of 'balance' which has been widely accepted as the basic criterion for post-Second World War disarmament negotiations. It is argued that 'balance' is essential for disarmament by negotiated agreements because, if an agreement were to tip the existing 'balance of power' in favour of one party, the other party would not give consent to it. Thus, during the early period of post-war disarmament talks 'balanced and phased disarmament' was used as the key symbol, representing the guideline for the regulation and reduction of armaments. 'Balanced' refers to synchronic equilibrium, 'phased' to diachronic. A more recent, familiar term which refers to arms reduction is 'balance at a lower level of armaments'.[2] The cardinal concept 'balance' presupposes the measurability and comparability of military power.

In reality, even military power, which at first glance can be quantified without difficulty, is not easily measured for comparison. During the first decade of post-war negotiations, the USSR demanded the abolition of, or a ban on, nuclear weapons first, while the US called for the reduction of the Soviet conventional forces first. How many soldiers with what kind of conventional arms are equivalent to a single atomic bomb? Given the fact that the USSR, unlike the US, has a long border with hostile or unfriendly countries, how many Soviet divisions with conventional weapons can be balanced with how many US divisions? Besides the difficulty of comparing existing military capabilities, uncertainty involved in calculating and forecasting the military implications of future developments in science and technology enters the picture. The manufacturing of missiles with multiple warheads outdated arms-control proposals limiting the number of missiles alone. The delay in talks on strategic arms caused by the Strategic Defense Initiative (SDI) programme, which is characterized by technological uncertainties, is also a case in point. How should these uncertain or unknown factors be taken into consideration when 'balance' is discussed?

Given these ambiguities with regard to the present and the future, a search for 'balance' will of necessity mean securing a margin of safety and thus attaining solid superiority precisely for the purpose of holding a 'balance'. This drive for superiority can be unscrupulously justified by a state which is convinced, in good faith or in false consciousness, that it is genuinely oriented to peace and disarmament and is wholeheartedly ready not only to sign a disarmament treaty but also to abide by its provisions. This state is so deeply convinced of its own sincerity that it looks at the other party as the only source of uncertainty and possible defection. If the danger of cheating and defection by the other party cannot be ruled out, justice dictates that the security of the bona fide state be protected by entitling it to possess a military force which should be sufficiently superior to that of the potential defector to make it impossible for the defector to gain any advantage through the violation of the agreement. Accordingly, the more confident a state is that its heart is pure and white, the more strategic superiority it thinks it deserves. This moralistic superiority complex, frequently revealed in the US posture *vis-à-vis* the Soviet Union, starting from Bernard Baruch's insistence on the need for 'condign punishment' (Herken, 1980: 172-3) through Ronald Reagan's notion of the 'evil empire', has contributed to equating 'balance' with US superiority, making it difficult for the other party to come to terms with the United States, on the grounds that the US proposal is not compatible with 'balance'.

This search for strategic superiority on both security and moralistic grounds forecloses the chances of reaching a disarmament agreement, because it not only contradicts the notion of 'balance' and even that of justice held by the other party; is also contradicts 'our' own second premise on which 'our' rationale for disarmament through negotiations is founded – that is, it is obvious that 'our' intention is genuinely oriented towards peace and disarmament, and that this intention can be communicated to the other party through disarmament talks. The actual results, however, are the reverse. The belief in 'our' sincere intention will reinforce 'our' rationale for pursuing strategic superiority, which will be perceived by the other party as a serious threat to its security and an audacious defiance of its equal sovereignty. Moralistic affirmation of 'our' sincerity will be taken merely as a malicious disguise of aggressive ill-will, for good reasons. Thus, the other party, which may have been originally committed to peace and disarmament, will find itself forced to pursue strategic superiority over its adversary in order to maintain the 'balance', to protect its security and to let justice be done. Hence the well-known action-reaction dynamics.

It is clear that the classic policy of a 'balance of power' gave rise to a positive feedback or a vicious cycle of increased tension, arms races and ultimately an occasional outbreak of war. Since the outbreak of an all-out war will undoubtedly be self-defeating to all parties in the nuclear age, 'balance of power' has been pursued under the guise of the arms race coupled with arms control and disarmament negotiations. If the actual function of the classic arms race was to attain assured strategic superiority over the adversary by increasing one's armaments, arms control and disarmament negotiations have been used to attain assured superiority over the adversary by regulating or reducing one's armaments less than the adversary is expected to do. Whether one will increase or decrease armaments is, in this sense, a secondary question. The crux of the matter is how to attain or retain superiority relative to the adversary, whether at a higher level of armaments or a lower level. Thus, arms control and disarmament negotiations have largely been the arms race by other means. The crucial question, therefore, is how to make disarmament talks, not a mere reflection of the dilemma or arms races, but a solution to it.

Evidently a disarmament agreement is not feasible as long as the distrust and the concomitant 'worst case' analysis of one party justifies and reinforces the distrust and the concomitant 'worst case' approach of the other. To break and reverse this vicious circle of the arms race and futile disarmament negotiations, two behavioural conditions have to be met as systematically put forward in Charles E. Osgood's idea of 'GRIT', that is, graduated and reciprocated initiatives in tension reduction (Osgood, 1962: ch. 5; United Nations, 1985). Although his GRIT is intended to apply to international tension reduction in general, it is applicable more specifically to disarmament.[3]

The first behavioural condition is for one party to take a 'graduated unilateral initiative'. It is imperative to take a unilateral disarmament step within the bounds of maintaining one's own fundamental security, even in the absence of a watertight disarmament agreement of reciprocal consent. Uncertainty remains as to whether the other party will correspondingly disarm. Yet the rationale for doing this is that, under such conditions of uncertainty, it will serve to overcome the dilemma of arms races if one unilaterally acts by taking a chance on the possibility that the other party will correspondingly disarm. This increases the chances of the other party's arms reduction by removing those obstacles to the other's disarmament which can be attributed to one's own behaviour of demanding the other to unilaterally yield (i.e. 'Show your credibility first by deeds, not by words'). This unilateral invitation to corresponding disarmament may be coupled with the promise of a further unilateral disarmament step that will follow the other party's positive response. The second behavioural requisite is for the other party to reciprocate the unilateral initiative. Obviously, unless one of the parties takes a unilateral initiative, nothing will begin to facilitate disarmament. But, unless the initiative is reciprocated, nothing will be achieved in terms of disarmament. Reciprocation is essential for generating a negative feedback or a cycle of tension reduction, laying the groundwork for productive negotiations.[4]

One of the well-known examples of a unilateral initiative is the declaration President Kennedy made on 10 June 1963, in which he said that 'the United States does not propose to conduct nuclear tests in the atmosphere as long as other states do not do so. We will not be the first to resume' (Kennedy, 1964: 463–4). This unilateral initiative proved successful because 'Russia reciprocated by not testing in the atmosphere, so that . . . both sides refrained from such testing under an understanding achieved without negotiations but rather through unilateral-reciprocal moves' (Etzioni, 1967).[5] The result was the Partial Test Ban Treaty signed on 5 August 1963. As underground nuclear tests have continued, many people have expressed cynical views on the value of this treaty

(Myrdal, 1976: 94–5). Although these reservations are quite valid, we should also ask why even this modest achievement has not been attainable despite protracted negotiations, and why the treaty came into being at that particular moment. Another example of a unilateral initiative is that taken by General-Secretary Gorbachev who stated on 29 July 1985 that, starting from the fortieth anniversary of Hiroshima (6 August), the USSR would stop all nuclear tests until the beginning of 1986, and would be ready to extend this period if the United States would do likewise. The United States did not reciprocate and conducted a test. Gorbachev then extended the period twice until the end of 1986. There was no sign of US reciprocation, and Gorbachev began to indicate irritation, giving a warning that the USSR could not unilaterally halt the tests indefinitely while the US was conducting them and that the unilateral moratorium would come to an end if the US continued the tests after 1 January 1987. This development underscored the crucial importance of reciprocation.

The question arises then as to why a unilateral initiative was taken at one time by one party despite a certain risk involved but not at another time, and why it was reciprocated at one time and not at another. A quick answer would be that it depends on which option was considered subservient to the 'national interest' of the party involved. We should, then, ask who defined what interest as the 'national interest' of the respective parties.

Structural obstacles to disarmament
Granted that reduction of arms will serve the interest of the people of each state, and that reciprocation of the unilateral initiatives taken by one's adversary will not impair one's security and interest, the unilateral initiative is an effort to identify and materialize the common interests of the parties concerned. In the terminology of game theory, it is an option for getting out of the 'Prisoner's Dilemma' in search of both parties' common interest (Rapoport, 1964: 48ff.). One may, therefore, well suspect that refusal to opt for a unilateral initiative or its reciprocation is the output of those social forces whose interests are incompatible with those not only of the decision-makers of the adversary state who have taken the initiative but also of the people of that state and, more importantly, the people of their own state. Further examinations should be made regarding this point by treating the industrialized military powers, particularly the superpowers, and the developing countries, first separately and later jointly.

State power complex
The disrupting impact of the domestic forces on disarmament negotiations took a dramatic form in 1955–7. In the course of protracted talks at the Sub-Committee of the UN Disarmament Commission, the Soviet Union presented a detailed plan which accepted the basic position of the West, including the installation of control posts in the territories of all states

concerned. This was on 10 May 1955, 'The Moment of Hope', in Philip Noel-Baker's words (1958: 12ff.). Despite the immediate favourable response of the British and French delegates, the United States made a volte-face with the result that the original Western proposals were finally withdrawn by the Western powers themselves. According to Alva Myrdal, Eisenhower and his emissary Harold Stassen met with strong opposition 'in the Congress, the Pentagon, the State Department and the United States Atomic Energy Commission' (Myrdal, 1976: 83).

It may also be noted that, in the autumn of 1957, the secret Gaither Committee report to President Eisenhower warned of the alleged 'missile gap' and regarded 'an attack by Russian' intercontinental ballistic missiles (ICBMs) as 'a late 1959 threat'. The Committee recommended drastic acceleration of US missile programmes (Gold, 1981: 25). Although Eisenhower did not fully implement the recommendations, he was led to warn, in his farewell address three years later, against the 'unwarranted influence, whether sought or unsought, by the military-industrial complex' and the 'potential for the disastrous rise of misplaced power' (Eisenhower, 1961: 1938). A series of dubious 'missile gap' debates served to accelerate the formation of those forces with entrenched vested interests in arms build-ups and arms races.

Following the first 'missile gap' hysteria in the late 1950s, a second controversy about the 'antiballistic missile (ABM) gap' flared up towards the middle of the 1960s, rationalizing the decision to manufacture missiles with multiple warheads (MIRVs) and a third 'missile gap' alarm was staged in 1969 in support of the development of the Sentinel/Safeguard ABM system to counteract the Soviet SS9 missiles which allegedly had first-strike capabilities against the US ICBMs (York, 1970: 125ff., 173ff.). Even the intermediary nuclear force (INF) debate in the 1980s was somewhat phony in the sense that, while the SS20s do not reach the United States, the Pershing II and cruise missiles are strategic weapons for the USSR. The dramatization of these 'gaps' contributed to forestalling serious disarmament negotiations. Thus the SALT I and II agreements, which were concluded during this period, could be no more than 'a mutually agreed continuation of the arms race, regulated and institutionalized' (Myrdal, 1976: 106). Now there is the issue of SDI. What is new about the SDI debate is that the proponents no longer cite gaps as its original rationale. American superiority is taken for granted, making the SDI non-negotiable.

These developments clearly point to the domestic structural roots of the forces with vested interests in the arms race. They may be the military, the military-industrial complex, the military-industrial-bureaucratic complex, the military R and D establishment, and so forth (Adams, 1981: 105ff.). It is well known that not only the bureaucratic complex but also bureaucratic politics and rivalry have an important affect on these developments. Which agents come into the picture, and how, varies according to the specific circumstances. But they share one feature in common; they are the beneficiaries of the arms race and arms build-up even when the rest of the people would benefit from disarmament. This does not mean that these forces are of necessity a *bête noire* acting out of selfish material incentives. They may seek power, social status, access to scientific facilities, national glory, ideological propagation or even 'world peace', but their intention is beside the point. What is crucial is that they are structurally located in the present political and economic system in such a way that they will profit from the arms race and arms build-ups. Although it is not easy to substantiate, similar forces seem to exist *mutatis mutandis* under the Soviet socialist regime, defending bureaucratic vested interests (Khrushchev, 1974: Epilogue; Holloway, 1983: 159, 171–2).[6]

To the extent that these forces profit from the arms race at the expense of the rest of the populace, the role they play is incompatible not only with disarmament externally but also with democratic governance at home. In fact, the nuclear weapons system erodes the foundation of democracy in two respects. Firstly, it is a grotesque paradox that the citizens in a democracy, through the classic channel of democratic participation, elect a person to whom the power to exterminate the people themselves is entrusted. Obviously, this 'secular absolutism' (Falk, 1982: 262–5) is nothing but a horrible mockery of popular sovereignty. Secondly, the nuclear powers in the industrialized North have gained such a high degree of productivity and efficiency that they can simultaneously develop an enormous power of destruction and an enormous power to sustain affluence. Before 1945, an attempt to acquire military capabilities to destroy the world many times over would have cost a state fiscal bankruptcy, economic breakdown and the large-scale impoverishment and starvation of its people. Today these two kinds of power, destructive and productive, stand side by side without apparent conflict (though recently the limits and incompatibilities have become increasingly more visible). Thus, the people can afford to be apathetic about the problems involved in arms build-ups, weakening the power of popular, democratic control. It is in these two respects that democracy has been undermined by nuclearism. The lack of popular awareness of the erosion of democracy is the most alarming sign of the erosion of democracy. It is evident that activation of democratic processes and popular movements, which do not have to be focused on disarmament issues alone, is precisely a *sine qua non* for the elimination of the domestic structural obstacle to disarmament in the North.

Hegemonic dominance

The hierarchical structure that can be observed within the superpowers, which consists of asymmetric and often vertical relationships between the advantaged and the disadvantaged, is projected externally onto their relations with smaller nations. Among these smaller nations, those on which a superpower has special bearings are (1) its allies and (2) Third World nations. The arms build-ups which have hampered disarmament agreements between the superpowers are not always (or not only) targeted at each other, but are directed to these two categories of smaller states so that the superpowers can maintain their hegemonic dominance.

In fact when the Second World War came to an end, the principle of hegemonic dominance was not abolished; on the contrary, it was sanctified in the status of the permanent members of the UN Security Council.[7] The big five were presumably endowed with might and right. It may well be that the arrangement stemmed from the lesson of the failure of the League of Nations where right without might prevailed. But power-political considerations are bound to be affected by the change in power relations. Apart from changing East–West relations, the altering power constellations within each of the two blocs were dramatically illustrated by the two explosive incidents that took place in the autumn of 1956. The Suez Crisis revealed that the two major allies of the United States were slipping out of the control of the dominant power of the Western alliance; and the Hungarian incident showed a similar challenge to the hegemonic power in the Easten bloc. Apparently one of the major reasons for the lack of progress in disarmament talks in the mid-1950s, despite the advent of the first détente in the post-war period – that is, the 'thaw' which followed Stalin's death, the truce in Korea and Indochina, the termination of the occupation of Austria, and so forth – was the reluctance of the superpowers to reduce their armaments at the time their respective hegemonic positions were challenged by the allies. No doubt the first détente weakened the dominant control of the superpowers, facilitating the evolution of 'polycentrism' within the East and the West. But this did not contribute to the disarmament of the superpowers.

The second détente during the late 1960s and the early 1970s also witnessed the erosion of the respective alliances. In the West, the EEC and Japan began to acquire competitiveness, challenging the economic hegemony of the United States. In the East, the Soviet hegemony was abortively questioned by Czechoslovakia and Poland, but successfully challenged by Mao's nuclearized China. The joint response of the super-powers was the establishment of the Non-Proliferation Treaty regime in 1968, which obviously is not a disarmament arrangement but a device which serves to consolidate their nuclear hegemony. Another important development was the increasing neglect of multilateral disarmament negotiations in favour of bilateral talks. Thus, disarmament negotiations tended to be equated with the SALT process from 1969 through 1979. Insofar as these talks were intended, at least in part, to stabilize the hegemonic position of the superpowers, there is small wonder that they could not be more than an 'institutionalized arms race'. It is clear that the SDI, which amounts to a new round of spiralling arms races, aims to maintain the military and technological hegemony of the United States *vis-à-vis* the Western allies as well as the USSR. At a time when the United States is exposed to the non-military economic and technological competitiveness of Japan and the EEC, one of the few areas where the United States still enjoys an unrivalled 'comparative advantage' is military R and D.

Not much need be said about the hegemonic dominance of the superpowers *vis-à-vis* Third World countries in terms of modern armaments and military technology. As compared with the period up to the 1970s when most of the arms transferred or given by the superpowers to Third World nations were obsolete, the period which followed was characterized by the export of modern, sophisticated weapons. Thus, the import of arms by Third World countries rose from US$2.9 billion in 1970 to US$9.6 billion in 1979 in constant dollars (SIPRI, 1985: 370–1). The purpose of arms sales is to exert influence over the recipient countries through the local elites, to retain bases for military, intelligence and communication operations, and to gain economic profits and secure supplies of resources (Pierre, 1982: 14–38). In short, arms sales serve a twofold purpose – to gain or retain hegemonic dominance *vis-à-vis* Third World countries and to gain or retain a sphere of influence *vis-à-vis* the other superpower. As compared with US policy (and to a lesser extent, Soviet policy) towards its allies in the North, its policy towards Third World nations gives much higher priority to the second purpose than to the first. This is because the political and economic conditions in the Third World seem so volatile that, in the eyes of the superpowers, a decline of influence over a Third World country would lead not only to a greater degree of independence from one of the superpowers but also to a higher degree of dependence on the other superpower. Thus, the means used by the superpowers are not confined to military assistance and arms sales; there are a number of instances of military intervention – the Bay of Pigs, Vietnam, the Dominican Republic, Grenada, Nicaragua, Angola, Afghanistan – where indigenous conflicts were transformed into East–West conflicts.

To the extent that the sale and use of modern weapons are considered an indispensable means of the hegemonic rivalry, disarmament is hampered. Whereas the Geneva Convention of 1925 was produced to regulate, if not reduce, the arms trade,[8] no arrangements have been agreed upon in the post-war period. One of the major reasons for this failure is the opposition of recipient Third World countries to the perpetuation of the North–South gap in military technology.[9] But since what they are against is not disarmament as such but the inequality and inequity that will be maintained under the guise of arms sales regulations, the Northern arms exporting states are to be equally or mostly blamed for the failure to reduce the arms transfer to the South. For various reasons, the volume of arms transfers to the Third World is decreasing for the period 1980–4 (SIPRI, 1986: 323ff.). If this trend continues, it will give rise to two alternatives for the exporting countries: they may either find arms sales less profitable and lose the incentive for arms build-ups in this respect, or, by utilizing their 'comparative advantage', develop more sophisticated and more competitive weapons for export to the Third World. Unless action is taken to halt it, the second alternative is likely to prevail.

What action should be taken? What is essential for both the allies in the

North and nations in the South is to reduce as much as possible their military dependence on the superpowers in order to undermine the political importance of the latter's military hegemony. This does not necessarily mean a formal or immediate termination of the alliance. It can first take the form of adopting the policy of nuclear non-alignment, as has been done in various ways by some NATO countries and New Zealand. This would encourage similar moves on the Eastern side, again in various forms. The same approach can be applied to another flash-point – the Korean peninsula. Secondly, in the process of *de facto* de-alignment, each country should reduce and reorganize its conventional forces so that they will serve only non-provocative, defensive purposes. Thirdly, it is important that this process of *de facto* de-alignment should be implemented on the basis of defensive and collective military self-reliance at the regional level and between regions. Collective action and mutual co-ordination will strengthen the bargaining position of smaller nations *vis-à-vis* the superpowers; it will also minimize the possibility of intraregional conflict and the danger of intervention by the superpowers. For instance, China has decided to reduce its armed forces by 1 million and has stopped increasing its military expenditure. Japan has so far kept its military expenditure around 1 percent of GNP. If these two countries jointly act to facilitate tension reduction and arms reduction on the Korean peninsula and to develop a regional network of nuclear non-alignment in co-operation with the South Pacific nuclear-free-zone countries, both politically and economically, each country can become more independent of the superpowers and be in a position to bring pressures to bear on them to promote disarmament in East Asia and the Pacific. Similar action can be taken in other regions as well in accordance with their specificities. More fundamentally, these measures will call for re-examination of the concept of the state-system. Although this point cannot be elaborated here, it is based on the recognition that we live in a world where the nation-state can survive and develop only if it modifies and eventually transforms the nation-state system. The initiative for building a new co-operative international order should come from smaller nations which badly need it, rather than the superpowers which have vested interests in the obsolescent present world order. But a demand for strong statehood and strong military power is prevalent in the Third World, constituting another obstacle to disarmament. We shall now turn to this point.

Militarized development
As is well known, of the approximately 140 wars to have occurred during the period from 1945 to the early 1980s, almost all took place in the Third World. Over 75 percent of the wars are what Istvan Kende categorizes as 'internal anti-regime wars' and around 20 percent 'internal tribal . . . wars'; nearly 70 percent of all wars are accompanied by 'foreign participation' (Kende, 1980: 269ff.). These figures indicate that the role played by Third World nations in obstructing disarmament has not taken the form of their being the subject or arms build-ups but rather they have been the object

of foreign intervention, including colonial wars. It is also evident that these wars are closely intertwined with the internal instability of Third World societies which in turn are affected by the process of unequitable development.

As the contradictions inherent in the development process have intensified the instability of political regimes, the privileged elites have resorted to repressive measures to keep law and order in the name of 'national security'. Hence, according to Ruth Sivard, 56 of 114 'developing' countries have come to be placed under military control (Sivard 1983: 11). Unlike in the big military powers in the North, the problem is caused more by the militarization of political regimes and the increasing peacelessness of society as a whole than by the quantity or quality of weapons. The fundamental question concerns the political and economic structure rather than the military hardware – namely, disarmament in the sense of demilitarization rather than arms reduction. But as long as unequitable development continues, resulting internal conflict will provide room for external intervention by big military powers which will hinder their own disarmament. In this sense, one may say that the structure of militarized development in the Third World countries has an important bearing on the arms race of the superpowers. Nevertheless, disarmament negotiations between the superpowers have failed to deal properly with the arms race, armed conflict and military tension that are rooted in the militarization – particularly the militarized development – of the Third World. On the contrary, disarmament talks have often been deliberatedly separated from 'regional conflicts' on the grounds that the linkage between the two categories of issues would make an accord on disarmament all the more difficult.[10]

It is true that the linkage would hinder disarmament talks if it is used to obstruct disarmament that could be agreed upon otherwise. But the linkage would promote disarmament if a settlement of regional conflict went hand in hand with arms reduction and vice versa. In other words, there are two modes of linkage – one negative and mutually defeating, the other positive and mutually reinforcing. What has been missing in disarmament negotiations is a quest for a positive linkage; and, evidently, the lack of this linkage is one of the reasons for the futility of post-war disarmament talks. The task of the non-militarized, equitable development of Third World societies should be undertaken by both the North and the South, and should include a transnational network consisting of non-governmental forces in both regions. But the primary agents for demilitarization will be the people in the Third World.

From the perspective of the people in the Third World, violence exercised by the repressive regimes in their locality has much more direct bearing on the survival and human rights of the marginalized masses than the sophisticated missile systems in the North do. Whereas in the North, arms and the military are primarily for external use, the military and the means of violence in the South are, in most cases, directed against the masses at home. In this sense, unlike in the North, military power and its inhuman implications are far more tangible to the people. There is no room for them to be indifferent to state violence and addicted to affluence. It is against this background that the symbol of 'democracy' or 'democratization' has increasingly gained a massive mobilizing power comparable to that of the symbol of 'independence' or 'decolonization' in the past. The power to demilitarize Third World societies should be, and actually is being, generated by the people of the Third World who are engaged in a variety of grass-roots social movements in search of alternative equitable development and non-militarized democratic governance.

It may also be noted in this connection that militarized development has international sources within the Third World as well as domestic ones. One pitfall the popular movement for nation-building must avoid is the danger of becoming a captive of the state system, falling victim to militarization at the moment state power is seized – the self-same state power by which it establishes a state of its own. We have seen a number of liberation movements, national and social, which transformed themselves into a system of state violence, giving rise to internal oppression and external aggression.

The popular liberation movements have legitimate reasons for striving to build a 'strong state' (Wallerstein, 1979: 274) in order to achieve autonomous development by resisting and eliminating the penetration of hegemonic powers. But the agents of this social change should be on guard against the danger of the militarization that many of their predecessors failed to overcome at the post-independence or post-revolutionary stage. Further, autonomous development in and by one country is a goal hardly attainable for Third World nations without generating tremendous stress and strain, internally and internationally. Hence the urgent need for a radical re-examination of the state system and an innovative reconceptualization of international order in search of co-operative self-reliance. It is through this process that Third World nations can promote disarmament and non-militarized development in the South. This in turn will contribute to empowering them with the means to challenge the hegemonic dominance of Northern powers, not through the military build-ups in the South but, on the contrary, through demilitarizing North–South relations. For militarization in the South is both an effect and a cause of unequitable development in the South, the hegemonic dominance of the North over the South and the rivalry between the superpowers.

Concluding summary

The following lessons can be drawn from the observations made above. Firstly, it is clear that the dynamics of the arms race and disarmament are, in the final analysis, embedded in the structure of world order. This does not mean, however, that behavioural options such as unilateral initiatives and their reciprocations cannot serve as an independent variable. The actions taken by Kennedy and Khrushchev demonstrate that a certain range of unilateral and reciprocal options are at the disposal of decision-makers despite the fundamental structural constraints which largely remain intact. In this sense, disarmament is 'a matter of will'. At the same time, the requisites for disarmament that can be fulfilled by voluntary behavioural changes on the level of decision-makers alone are quite limited unless coupled with public pressures for structural transformation.

Secondly, the pressures for structural change are, by nature, unlikely to come from the advantaged. The privileged position of the military-industrial-bureaucratic complex and the military R and D establishment will not be altered by the beneficiaries of the structural vested interests in arms build-ups. The initiative for undermining hegemonic dominance will not be taken by the superpowers. The privileged elites in developing countries will not spontaneously give up the fruits of inequitable development. The agents of change must be identified among those nations and people who are disadvantaged and deprived under the system of asymmetric, vertical relationships, both domestic and international. It is noteworthy that at the two UN Special Sessions on Disarmament in 1978 and 1982, even the governments recognized the importance of the mobilization of 'public opinion'.[11] Responsible leadership on the level of decision-makers and the popular movements for structural change will reinforce each other in their joint efforts to bring about disarmament and demilitarization.

Thirdly, the structural transformation for attaining equitable development and democratic governance on the domestic and international levels is an absolutely necessary, if not sufficient, condition for disarmament. An equitable international order consisting of the nations of equitable social order will definitely facilitate disarmament and co-operation among the nations concerned. The emergence of a 'security community' in Western Europe is a case in point. Today few people would anticipate an arms race and war between, for instance, France and West Germany, even in the absence of the perceived common threat of the USSR.

Finally, although it is true that the structural change necessary for world disarmament is an enormous task and cannot be brought about overnight, we should not lose sight of the dialectic processes that are under way in today's world. Modern history is characterized by 'development', which is based on a rapidly increasing mobility of commodities, capital, persons and information. This process has given rise to a fundamental contradiction – unequal economic and technological development, on the one hand, and the growing demand for equal rights on the other. These two are contradictory, but stem from a common dynamic. The keen military competition between the superpowers, with the United States having an edge over the Soviet Union, and the accumulation of the unprecedented power of annihilation in the hands of the two hegemonic giants are a manifestation of unequal economic and technological development. At the same time, the demand for equal rights has manifested itself in the contemporary world on an unprecedented scale in the form of the movements for peace, national liberation, social change, women's liberation, racial equality, ethnic identity, and so forth – in short, popular movements for democratization of society on a global scale. It is in the context of this dialectical transformation that disarmament dynamics find their place. It is as part of this transformative process, in which the survival and dignity of human beings are at stake, that disarmament negotiations can assume a positive role of historic significance.

Notes

1. The term 'disarmament' negotiations as used here includes 'arms control and disarmament' negotiations. 'Disarmament' is preferred not only for the sake of brevity, but also because of the general awareness that arms control should not be an end in itself but a step towards disarmament. It is interesting to note that, under the Reagan administration, a rhetorical shift for legitimation was adopted from the Strategic Arms Limitation Talks (SALT) to the Strategic Arms Reduction Talks (START).

2. The widespread acceptance of the notion of 'balanced' disarmament is illustrated by the following passage: 'The adoption of disarmament measures should take place in such an equitable and balanced manner as to ensure the right of each State to security.... At each stage the objective should be undiminished security at the possible lowest level of armaments and military forces' (United Nations, 1978: paragraph 29).

3. Herbert York (1970: 230) pointed out the significance of unilateral actions in a reverse way by saying, 'Our unilateral decisions have set the rate and scale for most of the individual steps in the strategic-arms race. In many cases we started developments before they did...'.

4. The unilateral initiative Egyptian President Sadat took by speaking before the Knesset in 1977 did not lead to an overall settlement of the Middle East conflict, largely because the initiative was not appropriately reciprocated by Israel, particularly in terms of the Palestinian issue.

5. While Etzioni seems to hold the view that unilateral initiatives were taken solely by Kennedy, it can be argued that Khrushchev had also taken a unilateral initiative prior to Kennedy's speech in June 1963. The Russian decision to remove missiles from Cuba was an initiative taken without prior official commitment of the other side in two respects. First, it was not a decision made in response to unambiguous American commitment that the missiles in Turkey would be removed. Secondly, it was a decision even without unambiguous prior commitment of the US that the US would not invade Cuba. Obviously, the process was so complex that one cannot regard Khrushchev's decision as surrender.

6. Holloway cautiously inclines towards emphasizing that the military and defence of the USSR have been placed under the control of the Communist Party leadership. At the same time, he recognizes the pre-eminent role played by them at the expense of other legitimate needs of Soviet society such as economic reform and development. The emphasis on the role of the military-industrial complex in the US context is not necessarily based on the idea that the complex prevails over, for instance, the President of the United States. The crux of the matter is the disproportionate, and often hidden, influence exerted by the complex over the decision-making process.

7. Put conversely by Luard (1982: 86), 'the universal veto available within the League, which had weakened its effectiveness in a number of crisis...was now replaced by a far more limited veto power, restricted to the permanent members alone, which even in their case allowed them to prevent only positive action, not discussion, by the Council.'

8. 'See the Convention of June 17, 1925, for the Supervision of the International Trade in Arms, Munitions and Implements of War, which, although it has been ratified by a considerable number of States, including Great Britain, France, and the United States, has not entered into force owing to the nature of the conditions and reservations attached to the acts of ratification. In this Convention the parties undertook, subject to some exceptions, not to export or permit the export of arms and munitions as specified in the Convention except to the Governments of States or governmental authorities in pursuance of properly signed and executed orders.' L. Oppenheim, *International Law*, Vol. II, 7th edn. (London: Longman, 1952, p. 123, note 2).

9. It was as late as 1978 that the UN for the first time made a recommendation on this question as follows: 'Consultation should be carried out among major arms supplier and recipient countries on the limitation of all types of international transfer of conventional weapons,...taking into account the need of all States to protect their security as well as the inalienable right to self-determination and independence of peoples under colonial or foreign domination and the obligations of States to respect that right...' (United Nations, 1978: paragraph 85).

10. The Independent Commission on Disarmament and Security Issues (ICDSI) (the Palme Commission) took the position that 'the task of diplomacy is to limit, split, and subdivide conflicts, not to generalize and aggregate them.... The Commission consider the notion of political linkage an unsound principle which should be abandoned' (ICDSI, 1982: 140). But it is noteworthy that the Commission's report contains a somewhat inconsistent but sound remark as follows: 'At the same time it must be recognized that significant movement towards disarmament will proceed only with difficulty in the absence of broader political accommodation. The two interact and must move together' (ibid.: 10).

11. 'In order to mobilize world public opinion on behalf of disarmament, the specific measures set forth below, designed to increase the dissemination of information about the armaments race and the efforts to halt and reverse it, should be adopted' (United Nations, 1978: paragraph 99).

References

Adams, Gordon (1981) *The Iron Triangle*. New York: Council on Economic Priorities.

Eisenhower, Dwight D. (1961) *Public Papers of the Presidents of the United States, Dwight D. Eisenhower*. Washington, DC: GPO.

Etzioni, Amitai (1967) 'The Kennedy Experiment', *The Western Political Quarterly* 20(2): part I. Reprinted in *Peace Research Review* 8(1): 53–89.

Falk, Richard A. (1982) 'Political Anatomy of Nuclearism', Robert Jay Lifton and Richard Falk *Indefensible Weapons*, pp. 128–265. New York: Simon and Schuster.

Frye, William R. (1961) 'The Quest for Disarmament since World War II', in Louis Henkin (ed.) *Arms Control*, pp. 18–48. Englewood Cliffs: Prentice-Hall.

Gold, David, Paine, Christopher and Shields, Gail (1981) *Misguided Expenditure*. New York: Council on Economic Priorities.

Herken, Gregg (1980) *The Winning Weapon*. New York: Alfred Knopf.

Holloway, David (1983) *The Soviet Union and the Arms Race*. New Haven: Yale University Press.

Independent Commission on Disarmament and Security Issues (ICDSI) (1982) *Common Security*. New York: Simon and Schuster.

Kende, Istvan (1980) 'Local Wars 1945–76', in Asbjørn Eide and Marek Thee (eds) *Problems of Contemporary Militarism*, pp. 261–285. London: Croom Helm.

Kennedy, John F. (1964) *Public Papers of the Presidents of the United States, John F. Kennedy*. Washington, DC: GPO.

Khrushchev, Nikita S. (1974) *Khrushchev Remembers*. (Tr. and ed. by Strobe Talbott.) Boston: Little, Brown.

Luard, Evan (1982) *A History of the United Nations*, Vol 1. London: Macmillan.

Myrdal, Alva (1976) *The Game of Disarmament*. New York: Pantheon Books.

Niebuhr, Reinhold (1949) *Moral Man and Immoral Society*. New York: Scribner's.

Noel-Baker, Philip (1958) *The Arms Race*. London: John Calder.

Osgood, Charles E. (1962) *An Alternative to War or Surrender*. Urbana: University of Illinois Press.

Pierre, Andrew J. (1982) *The Global Politics of Arms Sales*. Princeton: Princeton University Press.

Rapoport, Anatol (1964) *Strategy and Conscience*. New York: Harper.

Sivard, Ruth Leger (1983) *World Military and Social Expenditures*. Washington, DC: World Priorities.

Spanier, John W. and Nogee, Joseph L. (1962) *The Politics of Disarmament*. New York: Praeger.

Stockholm International Peace Research Institute (SIPRI) (1986) *World Armaments and Disarmament*.

United Nations (1978) *Final Document of the General Assembly Session on Disarmament*. New York: UN.

United Nations (1985) *Unilateral Nuclear Disarmament Measures*. Department for Disarmament Affairs, Report of the Secretary-General, New York.

York, Herbert F. (1970) *Race to Oblivion*. New York: Simon and Schuster.

Wallerstein, Immanuel (1979) *The Capitalist World-Economy*. Cambridge: Cambridge University Press.

PART IV

Military, Political and Economic Dynamics

11

Conflict Escalation and Conflict Dynamics

Anatol Rapoport

Escalation as a consequence of the 'logic' of power struggle
Carl von Clausewitz in his magnum opus, *On War*, distinguished between war as it would be if its 'essence' were allowed to manifest itself and war as it actually occurs. The 'essence' of war is stated by Clausewitz in the opening statements of his treatise: 'War is an act of violence intended to compel our opponent to fulfil our will' (Clausewitz, 1968).

In our age, characterized by greater intellectual weight of empirical science compared with that of speculative philosophy, such definitions, expressed as pronouncements concerning 'essences', are taken less seriously than they once were. Traditionally, however, philosophers did just that: they purported to answer questions in the form 'What is *X*?' suggested by the tacit assumption that something that has been *named* exists for that very reason. The business of the philosopher was supposed to be that of discovering the 'true nature' of *X*.

Clausewitz, regarded by many as the foremost philosopher of war, wrote in that mode. War, to his way of thinking, was something given, and it was his job, as one who thought long and seriously about war, to discover what it 'really' was.

Definitions in the form of pronouncements about essences have consequences. Clausewitz drew them. If in its 'essence' war is an act of violence aimed at compelling our opponent to do our will, then the same aim must govern the behaviour of our opponent. Further, since success of one of the combatants is incompatible with the success of the other, each will exert his utmost effort in attempting to overcome the other, because only if one of the combatants is rendered completely helpless, can the other impose his will on him. It follows, according to Clausewitz, that 'moderation in war is an absurdity'. If the forces of the opponents are balanced but do not yet represent their utmost capabilities, it will seem to each that by increasing his effort just a little, he can achieve total victory. But by the symmetry of the argument, his opponent will come to the same conclusion. It follows that escalation in war is inevitable and will proceed until one or the other of the combatants will have mobilized his entire effort. Then any remaining discrepancy in the power applied will result in a total victory of the advantaged side.

Such is the 'logic' of war, according to Clausewitz. He was, however, not seduced by 'logic', as many philosophers are, into losing touch with the realities. He recognized that actual war fell far short of the ideal war, and he attributed this discrepancy to factors analogous to friction in mechanics. Just as the laws of classical mechanics, valid in a frictionless world, seem to be violated in the real world, so actual war, Clausewitz thought, fails to come up to the expectations based on the knowledge of the 'essence' of war. The effort mobilized often falls short of the effort of which a state is capable. Human foibles provide grounds for missing opportunities of achieving a total victory. Although the 'true aim' of war is the annihilation of the opponent's armed forces (in order to make him helpless), many generals conduct wars with the view of achieving limited goals or minimizing risks. All these departures from total war Clausewitz believed to be violations of the 'logic' inherent in the 'essence' of war.

Today we usually distinguish between descriptive and normative modes of discourse. A descriptive theory purports to give an account of some aspect of reality in terms general enough to reflect some theoretical concepts, but still in a way that is corroborated by observations. A normative theory depicts events not as they are but as they ought to be or else how they would be under idealized conditions. That Clausewitz's discussion of total war belongs to normative theory is clear by his own admission. What is not clear is whether he was talking about war as it *would* be if it were not for the disturbing influences, or about war as it *should* be, that is, as something to strive for.

Clausewitz's essentially metaphysical mode of thinking about war is antiquated. However, his suggestion that escalation is built into the dynamics of war reflects a profound insight. Today we would derive the same conclusion in a different way. We would say that the system representing the dynamics of a struggle for power between two states is inherently unstable and that escalation is a consequence of a 'positive feedback' engendered by the instability of the system.

A mathematical model of an arms race

The first mathematically rigorous model of an arms race governed by the positive-feedback principle is attributed to Lewis F. Richardson, a British meteorologist, who devoted much attention to the escalation of arms races. He constructed mathematical models purporting to represent idealized 'psychologies' of rival states (Richardson, 1960).

The building blocks of such models, now called Richardsonian, are quantities representing the armament levels of states participating in an arms race and the rates of change of these quantities. Actually, it is possible to interpret these quantities in various ways, for example, as 'indices of hostility' of the states towards each other or the destructive potentials of their arsenals, of their defence budgets. The content of these variables is not important. The essential feature is the mathematical form of the model, which links the variables characterizing the respective states with each other. It is this linkage that depicts the arms race as a system.

To fix ideas, we will refer to the variables of the Richardsonian model as armament budgets.

In the simplest version of this model, the rate of change of the armament budget of each state depends on the weighted difference between one's own and the other's armament budgets. This difference is the mathematical representation of the perceived 'gap', the standard justification of increasing armament budgets. The two terms in the difference represent respectively the 'threat' of the other's military potential, weighted by the relative importance ascribed to it, and the 'security' of one's own potential, similarly weighted.

In addition, the rates of change depend on a pair of constants, depicting the 'residual' hostilities. These represent, perhaps, grievances that the states have against each other, which may persist even if both were to disarm.

All these assumptions are embodied in a pair of *differential equations*:

$$dx/dt = ay - mx + g \tag{1}$$

$$dy/dt = bx - ny + h \tag{2}$$

The left side of each equation represents the rate of change of the armament budget, x or y, of the respective states. The right side represents the weighted difference between the other's budget and one's own and also the constant residual hostility (g or h). The positive constants a, b, m, and n represent the weights assigned to the threat of the other's potential and to the security provided by one's own potential.

One further remark will complete our description of the Richardsonian model. As has been said, the variables x and y can be interpreted as indices of hostility. As such, they could be positive or negative. If negative, they could represent indices of 'friendliness'. The same applies to the constants g and h. If 'hostility' manifests itself in levels of armaments, 'friendliness' could manifest itself in levels of trade. At any rate, in order to test the model, the variables x and y would have to represent observable quantities. These could be taken as levels of armaments or levels of trade or the differences of these in some appropriate common units, e.g. money. In this way, extending the meanings of x, y, g, and h to include negative values, Richardson was able to formulate his conjecture (to be presently discussed) concerning the arms race between European powers preceding the First World War.

The other conclusion of a more general nature is about the *stability* of the system represented by the model. A system of this sort is said to be *stable* if there is a state of the system, represented by a pair of values of the variables x and y, to which the system will be driven by its dynamics and in which it will persist once it gets there. This state will then be called a *stable equilibrium* of the system.

Clearly, if a system is to persist in an equilibrium state, then the rates of change of the variables associated with that state must be zero. Accordingly, given the values of the constants a, b, m, n, g, and h, we can find the values of x and y that would represent an equilibrium by setting the left sides of equations (1) and (2) equal to zero and solving the resulting algebraic equations for x and y.

The equilibrium will be stable if any disturbance that takes the system away from that state will generate forces that will bring the system back to it. Conversely, the equilibrium will be unstable if any disturbance will generate forces that will magnify the effect of the disturbance and thus drive the system away from the equilibrium.

It turns out that the stability of the system represented by equations (1) and (2) does not depend on the values of g and h, but does depend on a relationship between the values of a, b, m, and n. Specifically, the system will be stable if $mn>ab$ and unstable if $mn<ab$. It is easy to see intuitively why this is so. The constants a and b represent the importance assigned to the 'threat' posed by the other's military potential, while m and n represent the importance assigned to the 'security' provided by one's own potential. The system is unstable if the product of the weights representing the importance of the perceived threat levels is greater than the product of the weights representing the importance assigned to the perceived security levels.

The first test of Richardson's arms race model was made with reference to the arms race in the years preceding the First World War, that is, the race between the Russo-French alliance and the Austro-German. The values of the constants were estimated by taking readings of the combined armament budgets for two of the four years examined. The armament budgets of the other two years turned out to be very nearly equal to those predicted by the model (Richardson, 1960).

Actually, this confirmation is not very impressive. Many more such confirmations would have to be observed to justify taking this exceedingly simple model seriously as an accurate representation of a phenomenon as complex as an arms race. Of greater interest is the conclusion that Richardson drew about the stability of the system. Using the values of a, b, m, and n to fit the theoretical time-course of the arms race to observations, he calculated the difference $mn - ab$ and found it to be negative, which, in accordance with the criterion mentioned above, revealed that the system was *inherently* unstable. In other words, a conclusion suggested by the model was that the arms race preceding the First World War *could not* be stabilized (without changing the conceptions that the adversaries had about each other).

There are two alternatives to the persistence of a Richardsonian system in an equilibrium state. The values of x and y may tend either towards positive or towards negative infinity. Which way they will tend depends on the values they started from or else, if the system started from an (unstable) equilibrium, the direction depends on the direction of the initial disturbance.

In view of what the variables x and y represent, the movement towards ever larger positive values can be interpreted as a runaway arms race, which we can expect to erupt in war. Conversely, if x and y keep decreasing, eventually becoming negative, this could be interpreted as disarmament followed by increasing co-operation, for instance, an increasing volume of trade between the erstwhile rivals. In the international arena, escalation of hostility is, of course, the more common or, at any rate, the more conspicuous phenomenon. But cases of 'escalation' of co-operation are also known. For example, following the establishment of the American republic, Britain and the US were for several decades potential enemies. They fought one war and came to the brink of another over some boundary dispute in the American north-west. During the American Civil War, Britain was on the verge of intervening on the side of the Confederacy. (Ironically, Russia dispatched a small naval task-force as a gesture of support for the Union side.) Since the last decade of the nineteenth century, however, relations between the two empires steadily improved until they culminated in a firm alliance.

A psychological implication of Richardson's model

The Richardson model points to another important principle, which he himself did not enunciate but which fits well into the formal structure of the model. Recall that we interpreted the parameters a, b, m, and n as weights assigned to *perceptions*, specifically to the relative importance assigned by the states (regarded as actors) to the threat posed by the other's armaments and to the security provided by one's own military potential. These subjective factors can also interact in a Richardsonian manner. In particular, positive-feedback interaction leads to what psychologists call the 'self-fulfilling assumption'.

As a simple example, consider two individuals, A and B, initially strangers, who come together in some social interaction. If A for some reason assumes that B is hostile towards him, his assumption may be reflected in his own hostile manner towards B. If B replies in kind, A's original assumption will have been corroborated. Conversely, if A's initial assumption is that B is friendly, this assumption can also be reflected in A's manner, evoking a similar response from B. Then this assumption, too, can be corroborated. This system behaves like a Richardsonian unstable system.

The principle of the self-fulfilling assumption applies not only to the assumptions that an actor may make about the attitudes of another but also to the assumptions that he may make about the *assumptions* that the other makes about his own attitudes. This 'higher order' of self fulfilling assumption is an especially dangerous feature of the present 'balance of terror' which has resulted from the build up of the nuclear arsenals of the superpowers and from the perfection of delivery systems. The rationale offered in support of this situation is that it constitutes 'deterrence'. Since each side is now in a position to completely destroy the other, in the sense of decimating its population, wrecking its production capacity and disrupting its social organization – in short inflicting 'unacceptable damage' – it follows logically that neither side can rationally undertake any action that would provoke this sort of chastisement. In particular, each side is supposedly deterred from launching a nuclear attack, so long as this attack is insufficient to completely annihilate the other's retaliatory capacity. However, the argument loses its force if the retaliatory capacity *can* be destroyed by a sufficiently sudden and sufficiently devastating 'first strike'.

It stands to reason that if the leaders of the superpowers think that sooner or later the present confrontation will erupt in war, they will turn their attention to the possibility of achieving such a 'first strike capability', either by their own side or by the adversary.

In the context of 'pure' military values, a knock-out blow of the sort envisaged would be the best possible outcome of the present confrontation, for it would be tantamount to a 'total victory', as victory is defined in military terms. Whatever else may be entailed in an event of this sort is of no concern to the military. To the extent that the present international situation is conceived predominantly in military terms, the military mode of thought becomes dominant in the thinking of political leaders. Thus, the achievement of a first strike capability appears as an attractive goal.

At this point, the escalation driven by the higher order of self-fulfilling assumptions sets in. Even if the leaders of a superpower do not seriously contemplate the notion of launching an unprovoked first strike, they may be driven to contemplate it if they think that the leaders of the adversary superpower entertain such a notion. For assuming that a completely devastating first strike is a possibility, the only 'defence' against it is a pre-emptive strike. And, of course, to be effective, the pre-emptive strike must be completely devastating. Thus, the pressure to develop such a capability becomes well-nigh irresistible.

And this is not all. Suppose superpower A neither contemplates a first strike nor supposes that superpower B contemplates one. However, A may have reason to believe that B thinks that A is contemplating a first strike. Then, according to the logic inherent in 'first strike thinking', A must conclude that B contemplates developing a first strike capability 'in self-defence'. But a first strike 'in self-defence' is in no way distinguishable from an offensive first strike. Then A, who originally neither contemplated such a course nor assumed that B contemplated it 'on his own', is driven to assume that B nevertheless is contemplating it ('in self-defence'). Thus, A is likewise driven to contemplate it.

The important implications of the Richardsonian model of escalation are conceptual rather than predictive. The successful fit of the model to the arms race preceding the First World War may well have been fortuitous. Subsequent attempts to fit Richardsonian models to arms race data (e.g. Lambelet, 1971; Wagner et al., 1974) met with mixed success. On the other hand, the principal concepts of the approach – e.g. system stability, the relative importance of mutual stimulation and self-inhibition

– suggested further explorations of qualitative rather than quantitative aspects of escalation. For example, O'Neill (1970) examined the pattern of instability among nations in the light of Richardson's model. Wagner et al. (1975) made the interesting discovery that *self-stimulation* rather than mutual stimulation appears to have been a prime mover in the Arab–Israeli arms race of 1950–70. This result points to the important role of the so-called 'technological imperative' to be discussed below. The fundamental instability of the arms race concomitant to the Cold War deserves special attention.

Nuclear doctrines as generators of instability
At one time it was thought in some defence circles in the United States that the so-called 'mutually assured destruction' capability (MAD) would provide security through deterrence. The MAD stance was based only on a 'second strike capability', that is, a destructive potential sufficient to deter the adversary from attacking (provided he did not possess a first strike capability). This posture was once advocated by the 'moderates' on the Dove–Hawk spectrum of American military policy. MAD appeared moderate because it required only a 'minimum' retaliatory capacity, namely, just sufficient to inflict 'unacceptable damage'. Thus, it seemed to hold out a promise of stabilizing the balance of terror.

From another point of view, however, the MAD posture appeared horrendously immoral. Consider the nature of a retaliatory second strike in response to an all-out attack. Assuming that in order to ensure as nearly a knock-out blow as possible, the adversary will fire all his intercontinental ballistic missiles, there is no point in retaliating against the now empty missile sites. To achieve credible deterrence, the retaliating strike must be directed against the population centres of the adversary. This amounts to holding civilian populations hostage.

The advocates of the so-called 'counter-force' strategy have argued that the charge of intended genocide cannot be made against this strategy, inasmuch as it is not primarily the population centres that are threatened by it but the military installations of the adversary. That is to say, the counter-force strategy would be in accord with the 'rules of civilized warfare', which prohibit slaughter of civilians. On the other hand, there is no disguising the fact that a counter-force strategy, intending to deal a knock-out blow, must be a first strike strategy, i.e. an unprovoked attack. Whether this strategy is or is not more in accord with rules of civilized warfare or with humanitarian concerns is left for the reader to decide.

The idea of preserving a minimal capacity for mutually assured destruction may now be regarded as virtually dead. Both superpowers are now in possession of arsenals that confer a thirty to forty fold overkill capacity on both. That is to say, each superpower is in a position to completely annihilate the population of the other thirty or forty times over. Apparently, it takes willingness on both sides to limit their arsenals in order to stabilize the mortal threat. Why this willingness is difficult, if at all possible, to achieve can be seen by once again examining the concrete meaning of 'stability'.

As has been said, a system is stable if it can remain close to a state of equilibrium. This will be the case if any disturbance that moves the system away from the equilibrium generates forces that drive it in the opposite direction. That the balance of terror envisaged by the advocates of the mutually-assured-destruction stance cannot reflect a stable system can be easily seen by imagining what happens when the balance is disturbed. Given the determination of each side to achieve at least parity (preferably superiority) in military potential, the inequality resulting from a minute disturbance of a balance (assuming that a balance can be achieved) cannot possibly be cancelled by the momentarily stronger side voluntarily reducing its potential. At any rate, this has never been observed to happen. What does happen is that the side that perceives itself to be the weaker tries to catch up. But catching up means that the rate of change of military potential becomes positive, which is immediately interpreted by the other side as an attempt to achieve superiority, which under no circumstances can be permitted. The Richardsonian escalation sets in. Given the present parameters of the system linking the two superpowers, a stabilization of the arms race seems impossible.

As a matter of fact, what is meant by 'stabilization' in some discussions of arms control is not keeping the *levels* of the destructive potential constant but rather keeping the *rates of change* of this potential constant and, naturally, positive. The idea is probably taken over from the context of inflation. Inflation is sometimes said to be 'stabilized' when its rate no longer increases, say remains at 5 percent. This does not, of course, mean that *prices* have been stabilized. A constant inflation rate means that the prices increase exponentially. In the case of prices, the effects may not be noticeable if all the related indices (e.g. wages) increase at the same rate. In the case of armaments, however, an exponential increase is something quite different. The fact that the armament levels *have* been increasing exponentially during several considerable stretches of time since the beginning of the present arms race suggests that escalation is built into the present superpower confrontation. It is unlikely to be brought under control by means short of a complete reorientation in the thinking of political leaders or short of their being replaced by others who think in different categories.

So far, we have examined escalation as the behaviour of an unstable system. Instability is usually a consequence of loss of control. Then the tendency of some variables associated with the state of the system to increase at an accelerated rate away from the equilibrium state is usually associated with a catastrophe leading to the disintegration of the system. Such is the case with living systems, for example. These systems possess control mechanisms which hold certain physiological indices (e.g. temperature, concentration of substances in the blood) within tolerated limits. Typically, the viability of such a system is assured only if those variables stay within those limits. If the limits are exceeded, the system becomes unstable, the indices can no longer be brought within the tolerated ranges, and the organism dies.

The notion that the 'international system' may also be subjected to destabilizing fluctuations (whereby its demise is represented by a general war) appears disturbing to those who regard war, particularly one fought with weapons of total destruction, as a disaster. There is, however, a profession with practitioners in every country who do not see war necessarily as an unmitigated disaster. In our age, it is not altogether respectable (as it once was) to speak of war as a legitimate instrument of foreign policy. Consequently, the profession whose business it is to prepare for and conduct wars projects an image of an institution whose business it is to prevent war. All ministries of war have been converted to ministries of defence. All wars, meticulously planned for, are called defensive wars. The motto adopted by the United States Air Force is 'Peace is our profession'.

The extent to which this representation of military establishments is credible is a question beyond the scope of this chapter. We will, however, note one circumstance that is directly relevant to this discussion, namely, that escalation has been included as a deliberate manoeuvre in the repertoire of strategies developed by at least the American defence community.

The strategic dimension
As we shift from system analysis to strategic analysis, we introduce the concept of the 'rational actor', one who presumably responds to the environment by deliberately choosing among available courses of action, taking into account their consequences as well as the circumstance that the consequences depend not on his choices alone but also to some extent on the current state of the world and (most important) on choices of actions taken by other actors as rational as he. In particular, 'the other' may be an adversary, whose preferences for the outcomes are diametrically opposed to his. Analysis of situations of this sort is taken up in the theory of games.

Restricting for the moment our attention to situations of this kind involving just two participants (players), we note an important distinction between *antagonistic* games and so-called *mixed-motive* games. In the former, the interests of the players are diametrically opposed. The better an outcome is for one, the worse it must be for the other. In mixed-motive games, there are always outcomes that *both* players prefer to other outcomes. So with respect to these, the interests of the players coincide. However, among these outcomes, preferred by both players, some favour one, some the other. With respect to these, the interests of the players are opposed.

Mixed-motive games provide a natural setting for bargaining. Note that bargaining serves no purpose in an antagonistic game, since there is no way for *both* players to profit from an agreement. The principal events in bargaining are threats and promises. Threats indicate an action disadvantageous to the other that an actor will undertake if the co-player fails to behave as he is told. Promises are indications of·actions advantageous to the other, which will be undertaken if the other behaves as he is told.

The appearance of weapons of total destruction has turned the attention of strategists to the new opportunities provided by bargaining in international relations. Understandably, the threat of extinction shed doubt on Clausewitz's classical definition of war as 'the continuation of politics by other means'. The definition may have been enlightening in the days when the objectives of politics were to win the usual prizes of power struggle: acquisition of territory, assurance or demise of dynastic continuity, etc. The value of such prizes compared with the costs incurred in a war fought with weapons of total destruction dwindled. To be sure, the loss of meaningfulness of conventional war aims did not render 'military science' obsolete, since a mode of thinking, once rooted in a profession, acquires a dynamics independent of any applications external to its own development. We see ample evidence of this 'law' in the history of academic disciplines and in the arts (all of which were once nurtured by mundane utilitarian concerns). Military science, as a discipline, has undergone the same autonomous development. Practitioners of this modern military science call themselves 'strategists' (cf. Gray, 1982).

The necessity of justifying social support of military establishments in an age when there can be no meaningful defence against total destruction turned the attention of strategists to uses of military power aside from its destructive potential. Indeed, the most persistent and persuasive rationale for piling up arsenals, which, if activated, can only destroy civilization, is 'deterrence'. Weapons are declared by each side to be essential as means of preventing their use.

Now deterrence can be effective only if the deterring power is able to effectively communicate its intentions to the power deterred. Furthermore, once the 'game' depicting the 'interests' of the powers confronting each other is recognized as a mixed-motive game, i.e. one in which the interests are only partially opposed (and partially coincident), communication in bargaining acquires an added significance.

Consider a highly simplified model of a 'crisis', that is, a confrontation between two hostile powers, each intent on having its own way and each in a position to destroy the other. Assume that each must choose between 'giving in' and 'standing firm'. If both give in, a compromise results which each side can interpret as a moderate gain or, perhaps, a moderate loss. If one side stands firm and the other gives in, then the former emerges 'victorious', while the latter is 'defeated' or 'humiliated'. If both sides stand firm, war breaks out in which each side loses much more heavily than if it had given in.

In these circumstances, communication can be used in two ways. Each side can point out to the other that avoiding war is in their common interest and that therefore a compromise is the prudent outcome. Or else communication can be used to try to convince the other side that one is absolutely committed to standing firm, so that the other has no choice but to give in, if it wants to avoid disaster. In other words, communication can be used either with the view of establishing co-operation to defuse the crisis or with the view of intimidating the adversary and so ensure victory.

It is this latter power-play aspect of communication that has received most attention from the strategists. The opportunities for conflict resolution offered by the insight into the nature of mixed-motive conflicts evidently appeared less attractive to the professional strategist than the opportunity to carry on the power struggle (business as usual) 'by other means', i.e. to realize Clausewitz's maxim in reverse. Strategic bargaining held out the promise of achieving victories without incinerating the world.

That this opportunity has been grasped can be seen in Thomas Schelling's discussion of international strategy. After pointing out that in the context of a mixed-motive conflict, 'winning' need not necessarily have a strictly competitive meaning, that the result of mutual accommoda-tion can also be sometimes regarded as a gain, Schelling goes on to discuss what he believes might be the most important contribution of the theory of mixed-motive games to the rational conduct of strategic conflict. Whereas military science has been traditionally concerned with the rational application of force, in strategic bargaining the focus of interest is on the rational application of the *threat* to use force. In particular, a theory of deterrence, as Schelling conceives it, is a theory 'of the skilful *non-use* of military capacity to pursue a nation's objective' (Schelling, 1960: 6).

In assessing the contributions of strategic bargaining to the theory of deterrence, Schelling writes:

> We have learned that a threat has to be credible to be efficacious, and that the credibility may depend on the costs and risks associated with the fulfil-ment for the party making the threat. We have developed the idea of making a threat credible by getting ourselves committed to its fulfilment, through the stretching of a trip wire across the enemy's path of advance, or by making fulfilment of matter of national honour and prestige. . . . We have considered the possibility that a retaliatory threat may be more credible if the means of carrying it out and the responsibility for retaliation are placed into the hands of those whose resolution is strongest. (Schelling, 1960: 6)

It would seem that strategic thought has acquired a new dimension. 'Victory' has come to mean successful intimidation of the enemy. In this battle of wills or of 'resolve', as brinkmanship is sometimes called, escala-tion is effected by raising the stakes so as to make the opponent lose his nerve.

Herman Kahn, in his book *On Escalation Metaphors and Scenarios* (1965), spells out the reasons why a nation might deliberately seek to escalate a crisis. For example, '. . . threaten the other side with all-out war, to provoke it, to demonstrate committal to recklessness . . . to prepare for likely escalation on the other side . . .'.

Escalation suggests a calibration of conflict intensity, and this is just what *On Escalation* is about. The book is built around an 'escalation ladder' consisting of forty-four 'rungs'. The lowest represent 'subcrisis maneuvers' (political, economic, and diplomatic gestures). Then come 'traditional' crises (show of force, significant mobilization); 'intense crises' comprising large conventional war; 'barely' nuclear war; 'bizarre' crises (e.g. declaration of limited nuclear war), etc. When we consider that nuclear strikes occur already on rung fifteen and that there are still twenty-nine rungs to go until the climax is reached in the form of a 'spasm' (all-out) nuclear war, we can see how complex the game of escalation can be and how much expertise is required to play it well.

It seems that *On Escalation* was meant to make two points: first, that the popular conception of nuclear war as 'the end of everything' is an oversimplification, an overreaction, engendering crippling fear, blocking coolheaded analysis, which in Kahn's estimation, is indispensable for dealing with the 'problem' posed by nuclear weapons; second that escalation (and incidentally de-escalation) ought to be regarded as an option in dealing with the adversary. Apparently Kahn intended to convey the impression that the situation could be 'controlled' and that it was the business of the strategist to learn how to control it to advantage, for example, by sliding up and down the escalation ladder as the situation requires. In the light of sophisticated strategic analysis, the nuclear age could be presented as a fountainhead of opportunities instead of a paralysing threat.

Kahn did a great deal of lecturing on matters of nuclear strategy, his audiences consisting, as he writes, of 'college students, businessmen, members of the League of Women Voters, etc.'. To illustrate the point about exercising control, Kahn would ask them what they thought would (or should) happen if a single hydrogen bomb were dropped on New York. In the early stages of this informal education programme, the answer would usually be that the President should order a crushing retaliatory blow on the Soviet Union. A few years later, however, Kahn notes with satisfaction, the audiences became more sophisticated. A lively discussion would ensue. Searching questions would be asked. Some one would suggest that the President get the Soviet leader on the hot line and ask him why there was only one bomb. Where were the others? Kahn would stimulate further discussion by explaining that the one bomb on New York was indeed a deliberate act of the Soviet Union and that the Soviets could destroy the US completely by an all-out attack. Then, Kahn writes,

> almost all would agree that there should be retaliation but that it should be limited. Most suggest that Moscow should be destroyed, but many object to this on the grounds that this city is much more important to the Soviet Union than New York is to the United States. These usually suggest that the destruction of some smaller city, such as Leningrad or Kiev, would be an appropriate counterescalation.

Kahn concludes that

> In the past five years almost every one in the U.S. who has any interest in these problems or is even modestly well informed has, as a result of both serious and fictionalized discussions, learned that there are possibilities for control in such bizarre situations. (Kahn, 1965: 185–6)

In the light of historical evidence, it is highly unlikely that once escalation has passed a certain point, any meaningful control can be exercised. In the last days of July 1914, frantic efforts were made by both sides of the impending war to reverse the escalation triggered by mobilization orders. The efforts were futile, because *both* the efficiency of the German war machine *and* the unwieldiness of the Russian war machine made it impossible (for different reasons) to stop the plunge into war. Four years of futile carnage followed, and the stage was set for a bigger bloodletting twenty years later.

In those days, it took several days for the fuse to set off the explosion. With long- and medium-range missiles posed to trigger a nuclear holocaust, decisions must be made within minutes. In fact, the crucial decisions must inevitably be delegated to automata, to 'whom' the fact of humanity is of no consequence.

An aborted attempt to de-escalate the arms race

A somewhat ironic example of 'loss of control' was the aborted attempt to reverse the arms race in 1963. The idea was suggested by the so-called graduated and reciprocated initiatives in tension reduction (GRIT) programme proposed by Professor Charles E. Osgood. The expectation was that small *unilateral* (i.e. non-negotiated) initiatives in the direction opposite to escalation would stimulate reciprocal initiatives by the adversary. Thus, the frustrating negotiation process, invariably blocked by rigid postures prescribed in advance and by chronic distrust making rejection of all proposals of the adversary a foregone conclusion could be bypassed (Osgood, 1962).

An attempt to initiate a GRIT-type de-escalation was actually made by the US in 1963. The first (unilateral) step was in the form of a moratorium on testing nuclear weapons in the atmosphere. The Soviets reciprocated by announcing cessation of production of a new bomber. The process continued.

> For each... move that was made, the Soviets reciprocated.... Further, they shifted to multilateral simultaneous arrangements once the appropriate mood was generated...
>
> A danger that seems not to have been anticipated by the United States Government did materialize: the Russians responded not just by reciprocating American initiatives but by offering some initiatives of their own... Washington was put on the spot: it had to reciprocate if it were not to weaken the new spirit, but it could lose control of the experiment. (Etzioni, 1967)

Apparently, 'to lose control' was an unbearable prospect for the military mind. At any rate, the process was aborted and soon afterwards Kennedy was assassinated and Khrushchev removed from office.

The compulsion to be in control at all times, that is, to keep the initiative, to dominate the course of events including negotiations, diverted whatever efforts may have been made to reverse the nuclear arms race into the old channels, that is, to desultory manoeuvring and bickering. The process of 'normal' disarmament negotiations was vividly described by Alva Myrdal (1976), then Sweden's Minister of Disarmament. The picture that emerges from this charade suggests that the superpowers *institutionalized* the arms race. A major factor in this process was the so-called technological imperative.

The technological imperative

The significance of Richardsonian models of arms races has been greatly diminished in the nuclear age, because qualitative factors have now over-shadowed the quantitative ones. For example, armament budgets no longer represent the destructive potential of states, because nuclear weapons are actually cheaper than conventional ones when the amount of destruction per unit of money spent is taken into account. ('More bang for a buck; more rubble for a ruble.') Even the destructive power no longer suffices as an index of military potential, as it is conceived by strategists. Technological break-throughs now occur in several directions, for instance, in the accuracy of missiles sent to hit targets several thousands of kilometres away, in the development of 'invisible' offensive weapons, i.e. undetectable by radar or similar techniques. The neutron bomb, laser beams, completely new horrendous chemical and biological weapons have rendered all the usual indices of military capability meaningless.

The technological imperative can be seen as a massive compulsion to engage the full potential of scientific knowledge in the service of the war machine. The compulsion is inherent in the self-propelling dynamics of burgeoning technological progress. The ever-increasing complexity of weapons systems necessitates a further increase in the complexity of supporting systems, which, in turn, creates opportunities for making weapons systems even more sophisticated. For example, intercontinental ballistic missiles were made possible by the development of guidance systems, which, in turn, depended on the development of computer technology. But the development of computer technology has had its own break-throughs, which made possible further advances in automatic control of weapons systems of ever greater sophistication. The development of offensive weapons stimulates the development of defensive systems on both sides, because one can safely assume that whatever new ideas for offensive weapons have occurred to one side will have also occurred (or will inevitably occur) to the other. The escalating interaction between the technological imperative, strategic theory, and policy has been repeatedly emphasized by strategists (cf. Gray, 1982).

In the 'qualitative' arms race between the United States and the Soviet Union, the former appears to have been the initiator in most of the innovations (see Table). However, it is also possible to explain the process in terms of its built-in self-stimulation: each advance suggests the next. Each successive step must be taken, because the very ethos of technical progress demands it: whatever is possible must be realized, just as mountains must be climbed 'because they are there'. The lag of Soviet military technology is naturally explained by a lag in most other branches of Soviet technology. The fact that the Soviets have led in two instances (the orbiting satellite and the anti-ballistic missile) shows that their following the US lead is only apparent. The prime mover of the arms race is its own inner dynamics.

When we consider that by analogy with similar processes in other fields of endeavour, the burgeoning complexity of weapons systems is conceived as 'progress', we realize how strong are the pressures for escalation. Prospects of progress inspire energetic and creative people, and the virtually unlimited budgets of the defence establishments of the superpowers are for many an irresistible attraction. An equally attractive prospect is that of exercising control over awesome power. Technological progress creates the illusion of attaining such control – perhaps the most dangerous delusion of our age.

TABLE
The qualitative arms race:
chronological development of weapons systems
by the United States and the Soviet Union

Date of innovation by US	Weapons system	Date of innovation by USSR
1945	Atomic bomb ⟶	1949
1948	Intercontinental bomber ⟶	1955
1954	Deliverable hydrogen bomb ⟶	1955
1958	⟵ Orbiting satellite (Intercontinental ballistic missile)	1957
1960	Submarine-based ballistic missile ⟶	1968
1970	⟵ Anti-ballistic missile	1968
1972	Multiple independently targeted re-entry vehicle ⟶	1975
1982	Long-range cruise missiles ⟶	198?

Note: the direction of arrows is from initiator to follower.
Source: Craig and Jungerman, 1986.

References

Craig, P. P. and Jungerman, J. A. (1986) *Nuclear Arms Race*. New York: McGraw-Hill.

Etzioni, Amitai (1967) 'The Kennedy Experiment', *The Western Political Quarterly* 20: 361–80.

Gray, Colin S. (1982) *Strategic Studies and Public Policy*. Lexington: University Press of Kentucky.

Kahn, Herman (1965) *On Escalation Metaphors and Scenarios*. New York: Frederick A. Praeger.

Lambelet, J. C. (1971) 'A Dynamic Model of the Arms Race in the Middle East, 1953–1965', *General Systems* 16: 145–67.

Myrdal, Alva (1976) *The Game of Disarmament*. New York: Pantheon Books.

O'Neill, B. (1970) 'The Pattern of Instability among Nations: A Test of Richardson's Theory', *General Systems* 15: 175–81.

Osgood, Charles E. (1962) *An Alternative to War or Surrender*. Urbana: University of Illinois Press.

Richardson, Lewis F. (1960) *Arms and Insecurity*. Chicago: Quadrangle Books.

Schelling, Thomas C. (1960) *The Strategy of Conflict*. Cambridge: Harvard University Press.

Von Clausewitz, Carl (1968) *On War*. Harmondsworth: Penguin Books.

Wagner, D. L., Perkins, R. T. and Taagepera, R. (1974) 'Fitting the Soviet–U.S. Arms Race Data to the Complete Solution of Richardson's Equations', paper presented at the Western Regional Peace Science Meeting, San Diega, California, 22 February.

Wagner, D. L., Perkins, R. I. and Taagepera, R. (1975) 'Complete Solutions to Richardson's Arms Race Equations', *Journal of Peace Science* 1: 159–72.

12

Peace, Violence and War

From the Viewpoint of Cybernetics and Computer Modelling

Karl W. Deutsch

Cybernetics is part of the general theory of systems (Miller, 1977). Within that theory, it deals with structures and processes of communication and control, which are the basis of steering and self-steering (Wiener, 1961). These in turn are at the core of the conflict behaviour of individuals, groups, organizations, nation-states or larger alliances of nation-states, and of the escalation of such conflicts, up to the extreme intensities of violence and war, or of their de-escalation away from such extremes.

Some terms of systems theory and cybernetics
The basic concepts of systems theory and cybernetics are well stated in the relevant literature (Wiener, 1967; Deutsch, 1963; Steinbrunner, 1974; Galnoor, 1982). Here only a few basic notions can be recapitulated briefly. Readers familiar with them may go to the next section of this chapter.

A 'system' is a set of elements or components linked by three properties:

1. 'Interdependence', such that a change or manipulation in element i will be followed by a predictable change in element j; the structures and processes through which this interdependence is transmitted may be called 'couplings' and may be strong or weak, symmetrical or asymmetrical, in their effects.

2. Markedly higher frequency and effectiveness of 'interactions' within the system.

3. 'Boundaries' or boundary zones, across which such interactions drop markedly in frequency and strength, or where some important side-effects change.

The elements in such a system may be physical structures, units of information, organisms or human beings and their smaller organizations. Each component may be, and usually is, a 'subsystem' with components of its own.

Two systems in conflict may be considered as the components of a larger system, sometimes called 'suprasystem'. Marx and Engels wrote in their *Communist Manifesto* of 1847 that class struggles tended to end with the victory of one class or the other, 'or with the common doom of both contending classes'. The French poet Henri Barbusse wrote in 1918 that two armies fighting each other were one large army committing suicide. Such awareness of a common membership in a larger system may sometimes save people from the murderous provincialism of their smaller one.

Dynamic systems are characterized by an inner disequilibrium or 'drive'. This moves them towards a change of state, away from their current one, relative to their external environment or to the internal arrangement of their components, so that its inner disequilibrium is less. This tendency towards a change of state may lead to aimless fluctuations unless the system has some capacity to be steered or to steer itself to a 'goal'-state where its inner disequilibrium is reduced. In simple physical or chemical systems, such drives and goals may be physical or chemical. In social systems, they may be sociological, economic, psychological or political, or some combination of all these.

The most important components of all systems of steering are 'feedback' circuits and processes. Through these information about the results of a previous action of the system is fed back into the decisions about what the system will do next. If this feedback enhances the current behaviour, it is 'amplifying feedback'; if it reduces or reverses that behaviour, it is called 'negative feedback'. Amplifying feedback occurs in the early stages of conflicts, arms races and wars (Richardson, 1960; Rapoport, 1974). If it continues at constant or increasing increments, amplifying feedback will eventually lead to the breakdown of the system or the exhaustion of its resources, or to some other limiting condition. If amplifying feedback occurs at steadily decreasing rates of increment, it is likely to come to a virtual halt when the increments become negligibly small. This could be one way in which conflict escalations and arms races could be halted before crossing some threshold to breakdown or destruction.

Negative feedback constitutes the essence of goal-seeking. A 'goal' is an internal or external state of the system such that its internal disequilibrium is at a relative minimum, as compared with neighbouring states, in the sense of Herbert Simon's notion of 'satisficing' rather than in the sense of some absolute optimum (Simon, 1969). In this process, information about the distance of the system from its goal-state is fed back to the system. If the system's current behaviour is reducing this distance, it is continued, but if it increases that distance, it is reversed. This produces a sequence of corrections which may lead the system towards its goal. It does not always do so, however. The goal may change its position, as does a rabbit chased by a dog or an aircraft tracked by an anti-aircraft battery, or the system itself may do so, as in the case of a slalom skier.

The changes required of the steering arrangement of the goal-seeking system in such cases per unit of time are called the 'load' upon it. The delay with which it responds constitutes its 'lag' and the size of the corrective action taken is its 'gain'. If the lag is too large, the system may fail to catch up with its goal. If the gain is too large, it may overcorrect its action or overshoot its mark, ending up dithering or 'hunting'. Such oversteering may occur in machines, organisms and societies.

Both lag and excessive gain or overcorrection may be avoided by an appropriate choice of 'lead', as in the case of a duck hunter who aims not at the point where the duck is when the hunter squeezes the trigger but at the point where the duck is likely to be at the time when the pellets of shot reach its flight-path. This practice of 'leading' a moving target also has applications to anti-aircraft fire and anti-missile defence, and it has parallels in politics and economics.

Autonomy and sovereignty

The behaviour of a system may be thought of as consisting of three categories of components. The first comprises the inner dynamics of the system, that is, those parts of its behaviour that are due to the processes among the subsystems within it, largely regardless of what happens in its environment. The second category refers to the proper dynamics of its environment or suprasystem, largely independent of what happens within this smaller system. The third category consists of those parts of the behaviour of the system and of the environment that are the results of the interaction of those first two categories. The inner dynamics of the system are then the result of the interaction among the components or lower-level subsystems within it. We are then in effect using a very simple three-level model, with our first and second categories corresponding to its second and third levels, respectively.

The degree of autonomy of the system then consists in the degree of freedom left for the interaction between the components in the system and between the system and its environment. A system has no autonomy if it moves entirely with its environment like a piece of driftwood; nor has it autonomy, if it remains wholly a slave of its past, like a high velocity bullet with such momentum that at least in the early stages of its flight the influences of gravity and air resistence remain relatively small.

Seen from this point of view, a system is at the first level of autonomy if its behaviour cannot be predicted even from a complete knowledge of its environment. It is at a second, higher level of autonomy, if its behaviour cannot be predicted from a perfect knowledge of its own past and of its environment. It is at a third, highest level of autonomy if its inner structure includes one or several 'random input sources', so that no complete prediction of its behaviour is ever possible.

Here the mathematical model of a 'random-walk process' becomes relevant. According to the classic image, a drunk is standing in a field, sober enough not to fall down but drunk enough to make his next step in any direction fortuitous. A group of mathematicians at the edge of the field is making bets as to when and where the drunk is most likely to leave it. Rational bets of this kind can be made with the help of random-walk models. Significant variables are the man's distance from the edges of the field, his length of stride, and the slope of the field, making his downhill strides somewhat longer. In this way, random-walk models can unite regularity and chance, deterministic processes and random ones. Different kinds of system output are then generated by the proportions in which they are being influenced by these two factors, determinism or very highly skewed probability, on the one hand, and randomness or relatively flat distributions on the other (Bharucha-Reid, 1960; Feller, 1957; Marma and Deutsch, 1973).

The inner dynamics of an autonomous system may go more in one of these directions or more in the other. But the same principle also applies to the suprasystem: the autonomous dynamics of the environment also may resemble random-walk processes, and so do the processes of cross-level interaction.

Subsystems: classes, strata, groups, regions, sectors, media and memories

Most often in today's world, only nation-states are capable of waging major war in the sense of organized warfare claiming more than 1000 battle deaths. Sometimes, however, subsystems of nation-states can wage civil wars of similar size and duration, claiming similar numbers of victims (Singer and Small, 1974; Small and Singer, 1982). In the course of history, some such civil wars have been mainly between social classes or strata, or between ethnic, religious or regional groups or among occupational sectors. Most often, however, such major civil wars involved coalitions of diverse elements of such groups, with most members of such a group on one side of the conflict, but with a minority of the same general group fighting on the other. In this way, a majority of French peasants in 1793 supported the French Republic but a minority, mostly in the regions of Brittany and La Vendée, remained on the side of the monarchy. A major role in these alignments is often played by experiences and memories of different subgroups and by the mass media of communication, from the traditional networks of religious preaching to the modern means of printing and electronic communication.

Most often interactions among subsystems do not lead to civil wars but to non-violent contests for influence on the behaviour of the nation-state as a whole towards other nation-states – contests that then lead to international warfare. Competitive armaments and the escalation of conflicts to the level of military or naval confrontations and from there to open warfare – as occurred in roughly one-tenth of such confrontations during the twentieth century (Siegmann, 1986; Yamamoto and Bremer, 1980) – initiated by an entire nation acting like a single monolith. Most often they are first promoted by individuals and small groups, and then backed by larger groups whose perceived interests appear to be served by the more militant policies proposed.

These 'interests', in turn, are 'subjective' expectations of larger rewards or smaller deprivations, contingent upon particular events or conditions, and like all such expectations, they are highly fallible. Moreover, some of these rewards to be sought, or deprivations to be reduced or averted, need not consist of tangible goods and services, but may be symbolic and psychological in nature, in accordance with the perceptions and preferences learned in the past and stored in the memories of individuals, the culture patterns of a community and the facilities of a state for information storage and recall – all of which are again subject to error.

In so far as it is possible to ascertain the objective probability of such positive or negative rewards, one may also speak of 'objective interests', but such judgements, too, by observers or historians are fallible.

More complex processes: memory, filtering, consciousness, will and learning

More elaborate cybernetic systems include facilities for the storage of information and for its recall, not only in the associations in which it was originally received, but also for its 'dissociation' into separate items, their 'recombination' into new patterns not previously encountered in experience, and their application to new ways of behaviour.

Complex cybernetic systems also are able to 'filter' the information coming into the system through its receptors, as well as the orders going out to its effectors and the information going into its memory or being recalled from it.

Each of these subsystems and processes can malfunction, and so can any connection between them. This possibility makes it useful to monitor their functioning, specifically and in their ensemble. Such monitoring requires the feeding back of highly abbreviated secondary information about the state of the parts of the system and about the primary messages moving through its channels, so as to bring together these summary secondary messages at some central facility for simultaneous inspection and decision. This is the process we may call 'consciousness'. The situation room in the White House of the United States is such a facility, intended to present at all times to the President and his advisers the current location and movements of all US armed forces and of all challenges currently posed to them. Analogous facilities exist on a smaller and less comprehensive scale on warships and in some government agencies and major private corporations.

It would be desirable for such facilities for awareness also to monitor the filtering facilities and processes in the system, so as to let the decision-makers know what kinds of information are not reaching them, but in practice this is often omitted in favour of avoiding or reducing delay, congestion, uncertainty and information overload at the level of the decision-makers. Even so, such omissions are dangerous, and even more so is omission of adequate monitoring of receptors and effectors. In such cases, governments may not know to what extent they are being misinformed and their intention misdirected. In the case of effectors being left unmonitored, perhaps for the sake of 'deniability', rulers then actually may not know what they and their governments are doing. Clandestine operations, carried on by some governments in East and West, leave these governments subject to built-in risks of this nature.

Filtering facilities and processes have another major function in complex cybernetic systems. Such systems may have to pursue some goal by means of a sequence of actions. Before these have been carried out, they form a 'program' of actions, stored in memory and to be fed to the decision-centre and the effectors for its implementation. That part of such a program of action of the system, to which the system is already committed but which has not yet been carried out, may be thought of as the equivalent of the 'intention' of the system (Miller and Chomsky, 1963). In this sense, it resembles the program tape that is already in a running computer but whose instructions have not yet been completely carried out.

In many human organizations, and perhaps in some automatic systems, such a preformulated plan may still be modified by additional information received from the outside or recalled from memory. Therefore 'will' can be defined as a state of the filtering system such that no additional information is permitted to change the course of the system once the appropriate decision has been taken. Since that decision was taken, of course, in the light of information received earlier, will is the process of subordinating post-decision messages to pre-decision ones. A system with vast effector-power may not need to learn in many situations. But a system with extreme will power will not learn and cannot learn. Adolf Hitler's orders in April 1945 to the remnants of his troops to continue fighting in the middle of Germany carried the theme of the Nazi party congress of 1936, 'The Triumph of the Will', to its macabre conclusion. In many situations, political will plays a major role in the initiation and continuation of warfare.

Where will does not reach such extremes, processes of learning are possible. 'Learning' is a stable modification of behaviour as a result of gains in information. 'Learning capacity' therefore is twofold. It is the capacity to accept information and the capacity to change behaviour (Deutsch, 1975). In both aspects it is proportional to the amount of recommittable resources in the system. These resources need not to be idle but they must be available for new combinations of communication intake and memory contents. With the help of these facilities, a learning system may develop new responses to repetitions of old stimuli. If these new responses in their turn become stable, then the system has learned something.

From the cybernetics of channels to the cybernetics of memory

What has been said so far about cybernetic models has emphasized channels of communication and their capacities much more than it has the 'content' of the messages passing through them, and their meaning to their recipients. The 'meaning' of any message depends on the amounts and kinds of information stored at the receiving system and triggered off into recall by the arrival of that message. The same message, therefore, may have different meanings for different recipients, depending on the state of the memory of each of them. Differently put, meaning is context; and context most often is mainly supplied from memory and only to a lesser extent from association with other currently arriving information. The word 'red' in a message may mean a colour, a political tendency, an intense stage of heat or of anger, or a military plan, depending on the context stored and now recalled as relevant to it by the receiver.

As first steps towards an analysis from this point of view, fifteen questions might be asked about every incoming message (Deutsch, 1981). For convenience, these questions may be divided into three groups, according to their main area of reference for the receivers: cognitive, emotional and pragmatic. The first five of these are mainly cognitive:

1. In what code is the message formulated; in what language, secret encoding, or picture transmission? Or is it a trace of some natural event, such as a flight of birds that once was interpreted by the North American Radar Defense System as an attack by Soviet bombers, until the error was discovered?

2. What is the source of the message? Is it something that the ambassador of one's own nation reports as having seen with his own eyes, or is hearsay offered by some notorious rumour peddler?

3. To whom is the message addressed or directed? Who are its intended recipients?

4. What is the context of the message? What is it about? It is a joke, a serious item of military intelligence, a love letter or a business proposal? What are the intentions of its sender and/or transmitter? Or could it be disinformation, spread by some international actor as part of some programme of deceit?

5. What is the actual text of the message, together with its decoding, if appropriate? What does it say?

The next six questions deal with emotions, as seen from the point of view of the receiver:

6. Is the message pleasant or unpleasant? This comes close to using Freud's Id or 'pleasure principle'.

7. Is the message true or untrue? This uses what Freud called his 'reality principle'.

8. Is the purport of the message moral or immoral? This asks about what Freud called the particular 'Superego', that every culture teaches its children.

9. What difference, if any, would the acceptance of the message make to the self-respect of the receiver and to his enjoyment of the respect of the community that is relevant to him or her? This relates to Freud's notion of 'Ego-strength'.

10. Is the message fact-oriented or emotion-oriented or is it a combination of the two?

11. Does the message appeal mainly to the inner-directedness or the outer-directedness of the receiver?

The last four questions are pragmatic:

12. What difference would the acceptance of this message make to the previously accepted plans and intentions of the receiver?
13. If the message is accepted, what, if anything, is to be done about it?
14. What is the expected cost in resources, time and opportunities?
15. How soon?

To every one of these questions there is at least one answer that would cause the message to be rejected and thus stop it from influencing thereafter the decision-making of the receiver in the sense of the burden of its text.

War-promoting and war-retarding feedback processes: external and internal

There exists today no adequate comprehensive theory of the origins of modern wars. Efforts in the tradition of Thomas Hobbes to blame wars of the innate aggressiveness of human nature fail to account for the absence of war among Scandinavian nations since 1815, and claims that abolishing the diversity of sovereign states in favour of a single government fail to account for the frequency and extent of civil wars, which since 1815 have been about as numerous as international wars, and have claimed about as many victims (Small and Singer, 1982).

Marxist theories that see the main cause of present-day wars in the existence of bourgeois and capitalist classes find it difficult to account for the warfare in the 1980s between China and Vietnam and between Vietnam and the Pol Pot regime in Cambodia, and for the high levels of military preparations at the border between the Soviet Union and China, since each of these countries is ruled by some form of communist regime, so that bourgeois class-rule cannot be held responsible for military conflicts and tensions among them. At the same time, some capitalist countries, such as Sweden and Switzerland, have not been at war for more than 170 years. At most the Marxist theory would have to be re-examined in terms of relative frequency or probability in order to test to what extent it would then be compatible with the facts.

Neither the classic pacifist theory, that high levels of armaments cause wars, nor the opposite classic view that a strong national defence prevents wars, according to the ancient Roman slogan 'If you want peace, prepare for war', are compatible with the record. Sweden and Switzerland have high levels of armaments and did not go to war, but other highly armed countries did. Denmark after 1928 was disarmed and became a victim of aggression in 1940, but many other countries with low or zero levels of armament did not.

More modern theories are based upon interaction processes and feedback models. External interaction processes between rival states are stressed in the two-party arms race models by L. F. Richardson and Kenneth Boulding. These models use pairs of differential equations which include some domestic terms such as 'grievance' on the war-promoting side, and 'cost' or 'fatigue' on the war-retarding one. In addition, Boulding's model includes the external condition of distance as a war-retarding factor. None of these early models said much about the inner structure of the contending countries (Boulding, 1968; Richardson, 1960; Rapoport, 1974).

A more sophisticated model by the Soviet scholar F. X. Gause, reported widely by Anatol Rapoport, included in its equations terms for 'self-inhibition' and 'other-inhibition' in the performance of each party (Rapoport, 1974). All these models, according to Rapoport, described wholly automatic 'fight processes', with no choice of goals or tactics on either side.

In another type of conflict, which Rapoport identifies as 'games', the parties have some choice of tactics but their goal – to win – remains unchanging. Only in a third type of conflict, called by Rapoport 'debates', can the parties learn enough from each other to create the possibility of a change of goals on one side or the other, or on both (Rapoport, 1974).

Only the last of these three conflict types, the debates, admit possible changes in the goal-setting and goal-seeking inner structures of the participating systems. Even there, however, Rapoport says little or nothing about the details of such inner structures and the changes that would have to be brought about in them.

In the 1970s, two sketchy attempts were made to show some of the major internal structural elements and feedback processes that in their interplay might decide the willingness of the government of a nation-state to go to war, or to enter situations of high risk of escalation to warfare, and the readiness of the elites and masses of the country's population to accept such a course of policy.

Dieter Senghaas and I made the first attempt (Deutsch and Senghaas, 1973). We identified six major subsystems which in their interplay might lead to the acceptance of a national strategy and foreign policy:

1. human nature and personality, as developed within the prevailing general culture; i.e. model personality and the distribution of personality types in different social strata and levels of influence;
2. the main large social groups and interest groups in the country;
3. the main elites, leading these interest groups but sometimes with distinctive backgrounds and interests of their own;
4. the mass media of communications;
5. the national political system and political culture; and
6. the civil and military government and bureaucracy, their institutional organizations and behaviour.

These elements are linked to each other by asymmetric two-way feedback processes, as shown in Figure 1.

FIGURE 1
Ten stages in the production of war (feedbacks shown)

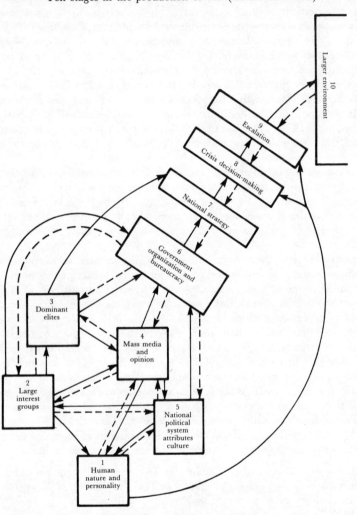

Source: Deutsch and Senghaas, 1973: 29.

The interplay of these domestic elements, together with salient experiences in foreign affairs, will led to the formulation and acceptance of a 'national strategic doctrine'. That doctrine itself will be stored in the memories of the civil and military organizations of the government, and in the minds of many of its officials and legislators. It will be disseminated and reiterated by the mass media, accepted by many members of the elites and eventually by larger social groups. In extreme cases such a doctrine may even come to modify the general culture of the population and influence the personalities and character structure of many of its members. The changes in Japanese political culture between 1895 and 1945, in German culture from about 1900 to 1945, in South African culture from 1938 to the present are examples of the complexities of this process. Some less extreme doctrines may remain largely limited to the realm of foreign policy, such as the British doctrine of the 'balance of power', or the Monroe and 'Open Door' Doctrines in the United States. Even long-established and pervasive doctrines may be modified or abandoned under the cumulative impact of experience, as were colonialism and racism in Western Europe and the United States in the decades after 1945.

When one national strategy has been abandoned, usually another takes its place. When in the nuclear age all doctrines of military victory over a superpower become implausible, doctrines of deterrence and 'mutually assured destruction' may take their place, supplemented by notions of 'competitive coexistence', where each side expects, more or less confidently, the economic and social decline or collapse of the other.

Once a nation has accepted a strategic doctrine, that doctrine will influence the behaviour of its government and bureaucracy, its armed forces, its mass media and large parts of its public opinion. This may become crucial when the government finds itself in a crisis in foreign affairs. 'Crisis decision-making' is decision-making under extreme pressure, with reference to fewer and simpler patterns of information from the present or recalled from the past (Deutsch, 1973). Consequently, crisis decisions are likely to be cognitively impoverished, and appeals to the 'nation will' may only make this situation worse.

If the crisis is international, at least one other nation-state must be involved, and its decisions are not likely to be much better. The results may easily be the amplifying feedback process of 'vertical escalation', with each state increasing the intensity of its conflict behaviour. The tendency to do so is increased by the search of each state for 'escalation dominance', that is, for a more intense level of conflict at which it hopes to gain some significant advantage over its rival. But there may be also 'horizontal escalation', with additional states entering the conflict on one side or the other (Kahn, 1965).

Continuing the escalation process, with the actors of each side serving as input for the decisions of the other, may lead to war and/or to the intervention of other powers, or to a halt, followed often by steps towards 'de-escalation' and détente. These latter processes are how wars between equally strong rivals may end, or how they may be prevented from erupting. Cases of successful détente include the Fashoda crisis between Britain and France in 1898, and the tension between the United States and the Soviet Union in the early 1970s.

This schematic representation, of course, is extremely primitive. Little or nothing is said about the inner structure of these large elements within each country, their intake of demands and experiences, their memories and goals. I presented an only slightly less primitive scheme in 1978 (see Figure 2). The limits of graphic representation, however, make it unlikely that this method will be capable of describing the complexity of the cybernetic processes determining peace or war. In the first scheme, the main elements were treated as 'black boxes' with identified input and output channels but with no inner structure of their own. In the second scheme, published in 1978, the boxes labelled 'government', 'elites', 'media', etc., had not only inputs and outputs, but also memories and decision-making areas. The elements, furthermore, were arranged in a cascade pattern, and connected by a complex web of backward and forward

FIGURE 2

Communications flow in a five-level system and its environment

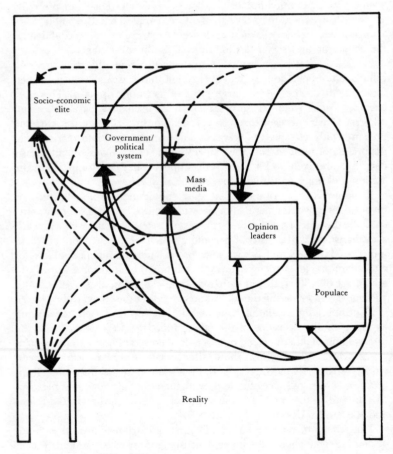

Source: Deutsch (1978: 129).

feedback channels (see Figure 2). This entire scheme, however, was still mainly channel-oriented, showing few or no traces of the content-oriented approach that became part of my interests from 1979 onwards (Deutsch, 1981).

From feedback diagrams to computer simulation

Common to all approaches discussed so far is the severely limited number of elements, channels, circuits and other data that can help us to imagine visually. According to George A. Miller, the number of units we can easily survey at one and the same time in many cases has been found to be 7 ± 2 (Miller, 1956). According to Herbert Simon we tend to perceive much larger numbers of items as hierarchies of subcategories or subsystems, each composed of an intelligible number of subassemblies, which in turn may be composed in a similarly hierarchic manner (Simon, 1965). Even this way of thinking, however, falls short of accounting for the manifold dynamic processes that in their interplay produce the behaviour of complex systems.

A way to surmount many of these difficulties has come through the mathematical method of simulation and the large capacity of modern computers. Large computer-based world models were developed by Jay W. Forrester and Dennis and Donella Meadows, then by Ivan Mesarovic and Eduard Pestel, and also by Carlos Mallmann, Hugo Scolnik and their associates in the Bariloche group of Latin American scientists (Meadows, 1975; Herrera et al., 1976; Kappel, et al., 1983; Mesarovic and Pestel, 1976). The first of these models focused on world population, food, energy, raw materials and the pollution of the environment for several decades ahead. The Bariloche model, intended to represent a view point from the Third World of developing countries, concentrated on the satisfaction of basic needs, mainly by the year 2000, and did not include data about pollution. None of these models dealt explicitly with politics and questions of peace and war.

Other world models followed. Surveys in 1985 counted between twenty and twenty-seven major world models (Meadows, 1985; Siegmann, 1986), but only one of them was explicitly political, the GLOBUS world model of the Berlin Science Centre for Social Research (Deutsch, 1979a; Bremer, 1984, 1985; Deutsch and Bremer, 1985). The GLOBUS model is based on simulation. (Bremer, 1976; Guetzkow and Valadez, 1981; Deutsch et al., 1977). (Its name, proposed by Stuart A. Bremer, is an acronym for 'generating long-range options by using simulation'.) This approach starts from the known input and output data of a process of which the inner structure and subprocesses are not completely known, and it then attempts to construct a model of these inner workings that will produce input-output relationships similar to the observed ones. This method treats a real-world process as an opaque 'black box' of which only the inputs and outputs are known, and it attempts to construct a transparent 'white box' whose inner arrangements are specified and can be inspected.

Simulation is subject to at least three major difficulties. First, the model to be constructed may turn out to be very complex and laborious. Second, the range of real-world input–output data may be limited, and any extrapolation from the model to situations beyond this range – such as to some possible future – may be hazardous. Third, no complex simulation model is likely to be unique. Some slightly or strongly modified versions of the 'same' model might fit the totality of known input–output data to the same approximate degree, and even a very different alternative model might do so.

Despite these difficulties, computer simulation has been applied successfully to a wide variety of problems. If it has proved possible to simulate the behaviour of a river throughout the climatic changes of the seasons and the years – as has been done in the case of the Chalk River in Canada – why should it not be possible to simulate the behaviour of a system of states?

This is just what GLOBUS is about to do. It is the first model to treat the world as a set of nation-states, each with its own national political and economic system, instead of treating the world as an undifferentiated whole or as a small set of regions that have no governments and make no decisions. Of the 160-odd states of the world, GLOBUS includes a selection of 25 nations that account for 75 percent of world population, 80 percent of world income and 85 percent of world armaments. These states also represent a range of different qualities. Among them are Western and non-Western nations, market-oriented and centrally planned economies, large countries and small ones, highly industrialized nations and those on the way towards industrial development. The remaining 135 or so small nations are lumped together into an artificial 'country' called 'Rest of the World'. It seems plausible that any policy that works among these 25 key nations might work in the world as a whole, and that what would not work among those 25 would not be practical world-wide, but future research will have to test this.

The twenty-five key nations and the Rest of the World are held together by two process models: (1) 'trader' (for short TRDR), representing the exchange of goods and services, and (2) 'swapper' (SWPR), showing the exchange of friendly and hostile acts between pairs of countries. Each year these data add up to the total exports and imports of each country, and to the total of acts of foreign co-operation and hostility experienced by it, and they add up also to similar totals for the world as a whole insofar as GLOBUS represents it, that is, without the trade and the co-operation and hostility exchanged within the small countries in the Rest of the World.

Each of the twenty-five key nations has an inner structure, consisting of six sectors. Five of these sectors within each nation are connected by feedback processes. The sixth, population, feeds into each of the other five but is not fed by them – it is supplied externally. For reasons of space, time, resources and lack of a generally accepted theory, GLOBUS does not attempt to simulate population dynamics. Instead, and after consultation with some leading demographers, the population projections of the United Nations Statistical Office – 'high', 'medium' and 'low' – are used as alternative inputs for each country, from which estimates of their impact on each of the other five sectors is computed.

These five interacting sectors are:

1. the national economy,
2. the national political system,
3. the foreign economic relations sector,
4. the sector of foreign policy and foreign affairs, and
5. the governmental budgetary process.

The second, fourth and fifth of these sectors deal directly with political matters. Each sector, in turn, includes about 15 ± 10 variables which in their interplay produce the output of that sector and its feedback relationships with the other sectors within the national model of that country. In this way, the GLOBUS model includes about 15,000 variables, connected by an even larger number of equations.

Thanks to the two world-wide submodels – world trade and international politics in terms of co-operation and hostility – different national models can be plugged into GLOBUS within the limits of the information storing, processing and programming capacities available. Thus different versions, more or less elaborate, of a national model for the same nation can be used, mainly depending on the availability of data. Elaborate national models for some countries can be used side by side with simpler models for others, or an entire country might be dropped out and another one plugged in, so long as the representative character of the entire world model is preserved.

The basis of GLOBUS is empirical, consisting mainly of actual data for 1960–78. From these data, coefficients of the relationship of changes in one variable to changes in another were computed by means of equations of estimation, if sufficient information was available for doing so. By such methods, thousands of such coefficients – similar to what economists call 'elasticities' – were computed for couplings in either direction between pairs of variables. Where this could not be done, coefficients were estimated more freely with the help of such social science literature as was found to be relevant. In this way, GLOBUS is more broadly empirically based than any other world model now in existence.

The actual changes over time in the world of GLOBUS and in the interdependencies among its parts are then the basis for projecting developments into the future. This does not mean merely a simple projecting ahead of every variable. Since variables change at different rates, the proportions among them also change. Majorities may become minorities, small variables may later become large and even preponderant, and the model must represent also such qualitative changes.

Most data from the past are available on an annual basis; only some are available by quarters or by months. Changes over shorter periods of time must be computed therefore by interpolation, so as to permit the use of faster interaction and feedback processes. GLOBUS computes its interactions ten times per year, or for about every thirty-six days, but ordinarily only annual figures are printed out.

In its time series, GLOBUS deals essentially with trends. It does not try to match specific figures for any single year between 1960 and 1978, nor does it aim to do so in its projections for the future. In terms of such trends, however, GLOBUS has projected the state of the world to 2010, and it may be extended to 2025.

A first use of GLOBUS consists in computing a 'standard run' or better, a 'continuity run'. This run is based on the assumption that there will be no major discontinuous changes in the world larger than those that occurred between 1960 and 1972, such as the Vietnam War of 1965–75, the October war between Egypt and Israel in 1973, and the Oil Crisis of the same year. Only the cumulative effects of relatively gradual changes until 2010 are being highlighted by this run, including the possibility, of course, that even these effects may lead the world to the threshold of some catastrophe.

A next step is then introduced by the use of 'scenarios'. Here a major change of natural conditions or of the political policy of one or several major nations, as specified in a 'scenario card', is incorporated into the model, so that its expected effects on the further course of events can be studied. The effects of two major changes arriving simultaneously or closely together in time could also be studied in this manner, but so far this has not been done.

GLOBUS includes no explicit representation of wars or civil wars. These are treated as relative discontinuities, and they appear only indirectly in the model through their antecedents – the fast or slow gradual development of conditions leading to their outbreak – and they appear again through their consequences in the changes in the stream of events that follow and are included in the model. A research effort to identify certain pre-conflict indicator levels, such as acts of hostility, tension or conflict escalation, and the actual outbreak of war or civil war is currently under way. It might then be possible to see when and how often dangerous threshold levels in these indicators will be reached in the continuity run or in some of the scenario runs of the model between now and 2010.

So far GLOBUS represents the latest application of the approaches of cybernetics, systems theory and computer modelling to political science. At different levels of its system and subsystem, it incorporates a large number of theories and research results from the various social sciences. In this sense it is fundamentally interdisciplinary in its present form.

A micro-GLOBUS model designed to run on IBM XT and AT personal computers is under development and should become available in 1987. This version sacrifices very little of the detail of the main-frame model, but requires much longer running times. Tracing the development of world politics within the limits of micro-GLOBUS from 1970 to 2010 is expected to take up to 6 hours on the IBM XT computer and still 2 to 3 hours on the more powerful IBM AT machine. In part, these longer running times might be offset by using the IBM AT, or an equivalent machine, as a 'dedicated computer', that is, one available at any time for running the model without any of the problems of waiting or congestion.

In its concept and methods, GLOBUS has come a long way from the pioneering peace research of L. F. Richardson, Quincy Wright and J. David Singer, from the general systems theory of Ludwig von Bertalanffy and from the cybernetics of Norbert Wiener, and from the earlier attempts to apply cybernetic thinking to politics by John Steinbrunner, Izhak Galnoor and myself. Even so, it is only a beginning. As space navigation has begun to turn astronomy into an experimental science, so computer modelling will make, in time, much of political and social theorizing experimental, through computer experiments in which no human being need be killed.

So much for description and perspective. But what about results? What has GLOBUS taught us so far about politics and policy, about dealing with the problems of large-scale violence and war and peace?

Some provisional research results

The results from GLOBUS, as available in the spring of 1986, are provisional and tentative, since the model is still being tested and adjusted. Subject to this caution, here are some of them.

The world is more resilient than the early models of the Club of Rome supposed. Processes which, considered by themselves, might lead to catastrophe, usually tend in time to meet with countervailing processes that greatly reduce their impact. Using average values, GLOBUS shows no tendency towards world-wide catastrophe by 2010 nor, apparently, by 2025.

According to the best estimates available, Malthus was wrong: world population will not grow indefinitely to the point of catastrophe. Its growth is expected to come to a halt by 2080, or at some time between then and 2140. The next 100 years, however, will be dangerous.

The world will be mainly in danger of what might be called 'gambler's ruin', not from the averages but from the variations in its development. Gamblers in a casino are ruined most often not by the house odds but by the fluctuations of the game, which may come to exceed their reserves. In politics, the inequalities and tensions may be enhanced by such fluctuations from country to country, from income group to income group, and from time to time. These risks are underrepresented in the present version of GLOBUS but must be borne in mind.

GLOBUS has projected three possible scenarios for the course of conventional world armaments, initiated in each case by a policy decision of the NATO countries and followed by responses of the other countries, similar to those observed between 1960 and 1978.

First, the freezing of conventional arms expenditures. This would leave more resources for investments and welfare policies and reduce somewhat the frequency of perceived threats and hostile acts, but it would shift the relationship of conventional forces in favour of the Eastern and Southern groups of countries.

Second, an increase of NATO arms expenditures by 6 percent annually in real terms (allowing for inflation), in accordance with the policies urged by President Reagan. Together with the expected responses of other countries, this would produce by 2010 a world in which the United States would be spending 18 percent of its gross national product on conventional armament, and the Soviet Union would similarly spend 17 percent of its GNP. Neither of these superpowers would collapse, but there would be few or no resources left for investments, innovations or improved welfare policies. A great deal of stagnation would become pre-programmed for both countries. At the same time, levels of hostility and perceptions of threat would increase. Altogether, the world might be expected to become more unpleasant and more insecure, but the West would gain in the balance of conventional forces.

Third, by contrast, a more moderate increase in the conventional arma-ment of NATO countries of only 3 percent each year in real terms. This might leave the East–West relationship of conventional forces substantially unchanged, as well as the present levels of hostility and threat perception, and it would not lead to a major change in the burden of defence spending as a proportion of GNP on either side. It was surprising to us to note that this more moderate and less unsafe policy is in fact what many NATO members, including the Federal Republic of Germany, have adopted.

Another GLOBUS scenario deals with protectionism. A strong growth in this practice was assumed to amount to an average increase in the OECD countries of the present excess of domestic prices of services and agricultural and manufacturing products over world prices by another 40 percent; a more *moderate* increase was assumed to amount to only 20 percent more. Both increases would by 2010 hurt the United States hardly at all in terms of trade flows and GNP, and they would hurt the Federal Republic of Germany only slightly, but some other NATO countries would suffer more. Losses would be inflicted by increased Western protectionism on the East bloc to a moderate extent, and much more drastically on the Third World. If most of these developing countries, being market-oriented, are counted as parts of what has sometimes been called the free world, then a rise in Western protectionism would bring an increase in economic conflict within that entire market-oriented sector of the world. These results hold for both the 40 percent and the 20 percent increase of protectionism, but are less severe in the latter case.

GLOBUS projects a general increase in the militarization of the world to 2010, with increases in military participation and manpower, mainly in the Third World countries, and similar trends in the proliferation of conventional – and presumably of nuclear – weapons. This will reduce the military power differential in favour of the West, which was at its peak about 1900, but has been declining since about 1950. By 2010, much of this power differential is likely to have disappeared (Sonntag, 1981; Eberwein and Reuss, 1982; Eberwein, 1981).

The upshot of these provisional analyses, as well as of parallel studies carried out at the Berlin Science Center, suggests a thesis of untenability. Between now and 2050 it seems unlikely that it will be possible to maintain the present, highly unequal patterns of the distribution of income, health, power and prestige among the peoples of the world.

Major changes in the present world system seem inescapable. Whether they will occur through mounting crisis, frustration and large-scale violence or through timely non-violent reforms is a question that cannot be pursued fully within the limits of this study. However, a few of the policy implications suggested by the cybernetic and modelling perspective can be listed briefly here.

Some implications for policy

It must be repeated that the present results of GLOBUS are provisional and so are the policy implications developed from them and from other research data. But we are living in a world that is in danger, a world in which we must seek a balance between waiting for more research results and applying whatever knowledge we have here and now. The present model is based on the processing and analysis of a great deal of social science information. It would be hazardous to accept it blindly, but perhaps no less hazardous to ignore it.

The list is obviously incomplete. Readers may disregard items they consider impractical, but they may – and indeed should – add other items which they consider promising.

The implications that follow are based on the proposition that violence is a primitive and dangerous form of damage control and an attempted escape from intolerable frustration (Dollard, et al., 1980). A frustrated laboratory rat may bite the bars of its cage; a fox with its leg caught in a steel trap may bite it off in order to escape. The larger the number of frustrated people, the more intense their frustration and their perceived opportunity to act on it, the greater the violence, whether it is spontaneous or organized by governments and states.

Our world is in danger of becoming an engine for the production of mass support for large-scale violence and war. This may happen because of the vast poverty and inequality in the world, and because of the demonstration effects of technology and wealth – the effects of the mass media. There is also a mounting sense of the needs, the deprivation, the potential power and frustration which is produced by social mobilization among millions of people for whom traditional doctrines of passivity and resignation are losing their meaning.

Together with the system of competitive armaments and states, these developments are producing an engine for the generation of large-scale violence and war, both within nation-states and among them. During the last 170 years, this system has produced about every eighteen months somewhere in the world an international war with at least 1000 battle dead, with an estimated total of about 30 million battle dead plus another 30 million civilian victims. It has also produced on average every eighteen months a civil war causing about the same number of combat dead, totalling another 30 million victims (Small and Singer, 1982; Singer and Small, 1974). With new victims being added every year, the grand total since 1816 is moving towards 100 million victims of large-scale violence. And all these figures would be dwarfed in any future all-out war among major powers disposing of nuclear weapons and other means of mass destruction.

To weaken and eventually dismantle the present war-producing system, attacks will be needed on many of its parts and links. An incomplete list of suggestions, influenced by a cybernetic viewpoint but not exclusively so, looks as follows.

Primarily tangible measures
Reduce the appalling poverty of three-quarters of mankind, and of the poorest strata even in the world's richer countries (Taylor and Jodice, 1983; Sivard, 1985; Brown, 1985; Barney, 1984). This would require more production, and hence more savings and more productive investments, a reduction in the extreme world-wide inequalities of distribution, and more capital for science, technology, innovation and new initiatives. Most of the world's people are already rising from the extreme levels of poverty that are associated with resignation and passivity, and they are rising now towards the secondary levels of poverty and social mobilization, where frustration breeds a propensity to violence. They must be helped to reach those levels of minimal equality, economic security and welfare, at which the propensity to violence declines.

Reduce defence spending to a world-wide average of 1 or 2 percent, or to about half its present level, since arms expenditures and the freezing of manpower and equipment in large armed forces compete directly with the purposes I have just listed.

Reduce drastically all publicity for deterrence, and increase publicity for reassurance that no first strikes or similar attacks are being prepared, facilitated or intended. Deterrence also has a recoil effect. The more credible a threat of nuclear war is made to seem to some foreign political adversary, the more it may also frighten large parts of one's own population into passivity, resignation or active opposition. In particular, it may demotivate a significant part of the youth of one's own country, who may despair of any viable future for themselves.

Ensure verifiable reductions of arms spending by international agreement between two or more powers on alternative positive expenditure programmes, or else on tax reductions. Such verifiable alternative spending might be on improvements to a country's infrastructure of roads and transport facilities, or on national programmes of health or education, or on the production of more consumer goods, which might be popular in the Soviet Union. Consumers and taxpayers might serve as additional forces of inspection.

Reduce the manpower of professional armed personnel and shorten the terms of service of conscripts. This will not only reduce threat perceptions of other nations but will also weaken domestic pressures towards hawkish policies implying higher risks of war. Surveys have shown that in the United States, such hawkish sentiments are strongest among professional military officers and businessmen (Russett and Hanson, 1975; Russett, 1970).

Stop all testing of nuclear weapons and of vehicles for their delivery; proceed similarly in regard to all weapons of mass destruction.

Shift from end-use defence goods, such as guns, shells and warheads, to intermediate goods and facilities, such as computers, civil aviation, span rockets for research, etc., which could be shifted to defence uses in a crisis.

Shift from the forward deployment of troops, rockets and military airfields, pointing at a single adversary, to more generally usable locations nearer to home from where different alternative deployments would be possible in case of need. In this way, Britain and the United States after 1819 shifted the deployment of their forces away from the Canadian–United States frontier.

Primarily intangible measures relating mainly to information
Organize spectacular non-war enterprises which in the imagination of people may function as a 'moral equivalent of war'. Space navigation since the 1960s may have had this effect. Such enterprises should be soundly planned, economically and ecologically, and they should be carefully conducted, to avoid disastrous disappointments like the *Challenger* catastrophe of 1986, and they should be demonstrably useful in their own right. A counter-example is the long-standing Soviet project to reverse the course of some major rivers in Siberia, which was abandoned in 1986.

Separate strictly all governmental organizations for intelligence acquisition from those engaged in clandestine activities, such as agitation, subversion, sabotage, supporting uprisings and civil wars, etc., in the territories of other countries. Intelligence acquisition is a vital need of all major governments, if they are not to act blindly. Clandestine activities are in their essence marginal (Hoopes, 1973; George, 1971). They are effective at most in small countries or among politically passive and apathetic populations or as political theatre to please this or that sector of home opinion. But so long as such activities are being carried out by the same agency that has to inform its government objectively about what is actually going on abroad, its fulfilment of that vital task is being distorted by the need to justify those clandestine activities, both past and present.

Mass media can whip up pro-war sentiments and brand all dissenters as traitors to the nation. William Randolph Hearst claimed credit for having brought about the war between the United States and Spain in 1898. An incident, a vessel, a small piece of territory can be magnified into a vital test of national honour and resolve, instead of leaving the matter to be quietly adjusted by diplomacy, or simply left in its present state in favour of other national interests less likely to lead to war. But how could international agreements help in such matters? While preserving the substantial freedom of their press and similar media, nations could agree to give them the freedom to whisper but not to shout. Complaints about other nations could then be voiced, but not in banner headlines, or on the front page or in the lead news bulletins on the radio or television. Limits might have to be agreed on to prevent inflammatory repetition of conflict issues in the media. In this way, people could be kept informed freely, but not inflamed to the point of no return (Deutsch, 1957).

Use the transition towards the historic stage of the information society as an opportunity to reduce mass impulses towards war. Learn to mitigate the effects of information overload and cognitive dissonance, which are a part of that transition and which could give rise to feelings of fear and rage and to the short-circuit response of fundamentalism. Work to prevent the coincidence of material deprivations on a mass scale, such as hunger or unemployment, with such cognitive and emotional pathologies, and use the growing resources of the emerging information age on the side of peace (Otto and Sonntag, 1985; Deutsch, 1986).

Use and support for this purpose the emerging non-agressive culture among parts of the young generation and in the growing social and political influence of women. According to French opinion researcher Jean Stoetzel, survey data from the early 1980s show that as many as 40 percent of respondents in France, Germany and Italy declared themselves unwilling to fight for their country (Stoetzel, 1985).

Possible interaction effects
Several of these policies, if applied simultaneously, might turn out to have synergic effects, that is, joint effects larger than those indicated by their mere addition.

It is likely that the current and coming conflicts and issues for decision will not let themselves be ordered neatly into a single main issue, eventually drawing upon itself most of the attention and resources of society, national or international. Rather we already see, and must expect in the future, a plurality of major issues that may require strategies for simultaneous responses, similar to some of the problems of linear programming.

All this will require increased resources for knowledge, awareness, thinking and decision-making. For these tasks, the developing fields of cybernetics, systems theory and computer modelling, which today are still in their beginnings, will not provide automatic answers, but they will be major aids for human cognition, decision and commitment.

References

Barney, Gerald O. (ed.) (1984) *Global Two Thousand Report to the President of the U.S.* – *Entering the 21st Century*, 3 vols. Elmsford, NY: Pergamon.

Bharucha-Reid, A. T. (1960) *Elements of the Theory of Markov Processes and Their Applications.* New York: McGraw-Hill.

Boulding, Kenneth (1968) *Conflict and Defense: a General Theory.* New York: Harper and Row,

Bremer, Stuart A. (1976) *Simulated Worlds.* Princeton: Princeton University Press.

Bremer, Stuart A. (1984) 'Modelling the Political Globe', *Intermedia* 12(4/5): 46–9.

Bremer, Stuart A. (1985) *The Globus-Model: History, Structure, and Illustrative Results.* IIVG-dp 85–104.

Brown, Lester R. (1985) *The State of the World: A Worldwatch Institute Report on Progress Toward a Sustainable Society.* New York: Norton.

Deutsch, Karl W. (1957) 'Mass Communication and the Loss of Freedom in National Decision-Making', *Journal of Conflict Resolution* 1(2): 200–11.

Deutsch, Karl W. (1963) *The Nerves of Government.* New York: Free Press.

Deutsch, Karl W. (1973) 'Zum Verständnis von Krisen und politischen Revolutionen: Bemerkungen aus kybernetischer Sicht', in Martin Jänicke (ed.) *Herrschaft und Krise: Beitrage zur politikwissenschaftlichen Krisenforschung*, pp. 90–100. Opladen: Westdeutscher Verlag.

Deutsch, Karl W. (1975) 'On the Learning Capacity of Large Political Systems', in Manfred Kochen (ed.) *Information for Action: From Knowledge to Wisdom*, pp. 61–83. New York: Academic Press.

Deutsch, Karl W. (1978) *The Analysis of International Relations*, 2nd edn. Englewood Cliffs: Prentice-Hall.

Deutsch, Karl W. (1979a) 'On World Models and Political Science', *Government and Opposition* 14(1): 1–17.

Deutsch, Karl W. (1979b) 'Uber Weltmodellarbeiten im Internationalen Institut für Vergleichende Gesellschaftsforschung', in *Jahrbuch der Berliner Wissenschaftlichen Gesellschaft*, pp. 123–30. Berlin-West: Duncker & Humblot.

Deutsch, Karl W. (1981) 'Von der Industriegesellschaft zur Informationsgesellschaft', *InMEDIASres*-Prize Address, pp. 98–109. Offenburg: Burda-Verlag.

Deutsch, Karl W. (1986) 'Einige Grundprobleme der Demokratie in der Informations-gesellschaft', in Max Kaase (ed.) *Politische Wissenschaft und Politische Ordnung.* Opladen: Westdeutscher Verlag.

Deutsch, Karl W. and Bremer Stuart A. (1985) 'Berliner Wissenschaftler stellen ein neues Weltmodell vor: GLOBUS', *Bild der Wissenschaft* 7: 100–6.

Deutsch, Karl W. and Senghaas, Dieter (1973) 'The Steps to War', in Patrick McGowan (ed.) *Sage International Yearbook of Foreign Policy Studies*, Vol. 1, pp. 275–329. Beverly Hills, London: Sage Publications.

Deutsch, Karl W., et al. (1977) *Problems of World Modeling: Political and Social Implications.* Cambridge: Ballinger.

Dollard, John, et al. (1980) *Frustration and Aggression*, Reprint of 1939 edn. Westport, CT: Greenwood.

Eberwein, W.-D. (1981) *Kriegsgefahr? Eine Prognose bis zum Jahr 2000.* Berlin: WZB. IIVG-dp 81–112.

Eberwein, W.-D. and Reuss, Folker (1982) *Doomed to Violence. Power, Mobility, and Serious Disputes, 1900–2000.* Berlin: WZB. IIVG-dp 82–115.

Feller, W. (1957) *An Introduction to Probability Theory and Its Applications*. New York: Wiley.

Galnoor, Itzhak (1982) *Steering the Polity: Communication and Politics in Israel*. Beverly Hills, London: Sage Publications.

George, A. L. (1971) *The Limits of Coercive Diplomacy*. Boston: Little, Brown.

Guetzkow, Harold and Valadez, Joseph (eds) (1981) *Simulated International Processes: Theories and Research in Global Modeling*. Beverly Hills, London: Sage Publications.

Herrera, A. O., et al. (1976) *Catastrophe or New Society? A Latin American World Model*. Ottawa: International Development Research Centre.

Hoopes, Townsend (1973) *The Limits of Intervention: An Inside Account of How the Johnson Policy of Escalation was Reversed in Vietnam*, rev. edn. New York: Longman.

Kahn, Herman (1965) *On Escalation*. New York: Praeger.

Kappel, Rolf, et al. (1983) *Technologieentwicklung und Grundbedürfnisse. Eine empirische Studie über Mexiko*. Saarbrücken, Fort Lauderdale, FL: Verlag Breitenbach.

Marma, Victor J. and Deutsch Karl W. (1973) 'Survival in Unfair Conflict: Odds, Resources, and Random Walk Models', *Behavioural Science* 18(5): 313–34.

Meadows, Donella H. (1985) 'Charting the Way the World Works', *Technology Review*, February/March.

Meadows, Donella, et al. (1974) *The Limits to Growth: A Report for the Club of Rome's Project on the Predicament of Mankind*, 2nd edn. New York: Universe Books.

Mesarovic, M. and Pestel, E. (1976) *Mankind at the Turning Point*. New York: New American Library.

Miller, George A. (1956) 'The Magical Number Seven, Plus or Minus Two: Some Limits on Our Capacity for Processing Information', *Psychological Review* 63: 92–5.

Miller George A. and Chomsky, Noam (1963) 'Finitary Models of Language Users', in D. Luce (ed.) *Handbook of Mathematical Psychology*, Vol. 1. New York: Wiley.

Miller, James G. (1977) *Living Systems*. New York: McGraw.

Otto, Peter and Sonntag, Philipp (1985) *Wege in die Informationsgesellschaft. Steuerungsprobleme in Wirtschaft und Politik*. Stuttgart: Deutscher Taschenbuch-Verlag.

Rapoport, Anatol (1974) *Fights, Games and Debates*. Ann Arbor: University of Michigan Press.

Richardson, Lewis F. (1960) *Arms and Insecurity: A Mathematical Study of the Causes and Origins of War* (ed. by Nicolas Rashevsky and Ernesto Trucco). Pittsburgh: Boxwood Press; Chicago: Quadrangle Books.

Russett, Bruce M. (1970) *What Price Vigilance?* New Haven: Yale University Press.

Russett, Bruce M., and Hanson, Elizabeth C. (1975) *Interest and Ideology: The Foreign Policy Beliefs of American Businessmen*. San Francisco: Freeman.

Siegmann, Heinrich (1986) *Recent Developments in World Modeling*. Wissenschaftszentrum Berlin and Unesco.

Simon, Herbert (1965) 'The Architecture of Complexity', in *General Systems Yearbook*, Vol. 10, pp. 63–76.

Simon, Herbert (1969) 'Some Problems of Strategy in Theory Construction in the Social Sciences', in Paul Lazarsfeld (ed.) *Mathematical Thinking in the Social Sciences*, reprint of 1954 edn. New York: Russell.

Singer, J. David and Small, Melvin (1974) *The Wages of War: 1816 to 1965*. Ann Arbor, MI: Inter-University Consortium for Political and Social Research.

Sivard, Ruth L. (1985) *World Military and Social Expenditures*. Washington, DC: World Priorities.

Small, Melvin and Singer J. David (1982) *Resort to Arms: International and Civil Wars, 1816–1980*. Beverly Hills, London: Sage Publications.

Sonntag, Philipp (1981) *Ein Planet verteidigt sich – Politometrische Untersuchung der globalen Aufrüstung*. Berlin: Wissenschaftszentrum, IIVG-dp 81–115.

Steinbrunner, John D. (1974) *The Cybernetic Theory of Decision: New Dimensions of Political Analysis*. Princeton: Princeton University Press.

Stoetzel, Jean (1985) 'The Willingness to Fight for the Country: A Comparison of Nine Western Countries', typescript.

Taylor, Charles L. and Jodice, David A. (1983) *World Handbook of Political and Social Indicators*, 3rd edn. New Haven: Yale University Press.

Von Bertalanffy, Ludwig (1969) *General System Theory: Essays on Its Foundation and Development*, rev. edn. New York: Braziller.

Wiener, Norbert (1961) *Cybernetics: Or Control and Communication in the Animal and the Machine*, 2nd edn. Cambridge: MIT Press.

Wiener, Norbert (1967) *The Human Use of Human Beings: Cybernetics and Society*. New York: Avon.

Yamamoto, Yoshinobu and Bremer, Stuart A. (1980) 'Wider Wars and Restless Nights: Major Power Intervention in Ongoing War', in J. David Singer (ed.) *The Correlates of War II, Testing Some Realpolitik Models*, pp. 199–229. New York: Free Press.

13

Roots of War:
The Master Variables

Nazli Choucri and
Robert C. North

Introduction

'Where are the causes of war to be found?', by now a classic query in
the study of international relations, resorted to three levels of explanation:
'man, the state, or the international system'. While theories abound to
explain war at each of these levels, the evidence remains confusing,
confounded largely by the particular theoretic paradigm or explanation
chosen (Waltz, 1959).

Those arguing for man as the real root of war have confronted the
complexities of distinguishing between 'good' and 'bad' men; querying
whether specific features of human nature makes men particularly prone
to war. Those arguing for the state, as the correct level of analysis, have
yet to resolve whether 'good' states make more war than 'bad' states,
distinguishing between democratic and authoritarian politics for those
purposes (Chen, 1984; Russett, in press). Those arguing for explanations
at the international level face the type-of-system predicament: whether
bipolar, multipolar, or other types of systems are more or less conducive
to war (Rosecrance, 1969).

Interestingly, however, seldom has the choice of level of analysis alone
provided a satisfactory explanation for violence or war. More often than
not, the underlying paradigm guiding the enquiry serves as the lens for
explaining the nature of the evidence – to determine whether organized
violence is caused by man, the state or the international system.

Theoretical developments in the study of international relations have
been numerous, often reflected in terms of competing theories of relations
among nations. Such developments have been particularly reactive to
events in the international arena which make it even more difficult to
identify empirically the appropriate explanatory level.

By the mid-decade of the 1980s, the dominant paradigms – beyond
specific explanations of particular events or processes – could be
characterized roughly as follows: a realist-state centric view of the world;
a Marxist perspective, broadly defined; a periphery paradigm, including
dependence and related perspectives; and idealist-communitarian orientations, covering earlier functionalism, integration views and collaboration

perspectives. Each differs in its views of motivation, processes and outcomes, and in their reliance on the nature and type of socio-economic and political factors that lead to war. These contending perspectives are both paradigms of state behaviour in international politics, as well as statements of political economy, making it difficult to distinguish between theories of international relations and paradigms of political economy. The real world does not respect distinctions between politics and economics, nor does it conform to acknowledged disciplinary differentiations. Each of these paradigms takes cognizance of the interconnections between the two domains of activity, to a greater or lesser degree, as the case may be.

The purpose of this chapter is to delineate socio-economic and political causes of violence. We present the variables, processes, sequences and connections that relate man and the state in order to locate, where appropriate, the underlying causal factors that lead to international conflict in a way that transcends contending perspectives of international relations and of political economy. Our purpose is to delineate generic relationships across levels of analysis and highlight some particular characteristic features, such as specific state profiles, to provide some linkages between man, the state and the international system that enhance propensities for conflict and violence.

The 'master variables'

Our point of departure centres around the most basic elements defining states, namely 'master variables', whose linkages characterize the basic features of statehood in any particular case and at any point in time. Three master variables and interconnections generate the profiles of states. These are *population, resources* and *technology* – in the generic sense of their aggregate representations as well as in the specific sense of their distinctive manifestations.

The population variable, as an example, has specific manifestations such as size, rate of change, composition, distribution, mobility and so forth. Resources, defined broadly as a natural source of wealth or revenue, are conventionally distinguished in terms of minerals, fuels, arable land and so forth. Resources can also be viewed in terms of inputs into productive processes, or inputs for generating bases of human survival. Complexities abound, however, when considering definitions and dimensions of technology. The conventional distinction between products and processes, useful for some purposes, may obscure the fact that technology refers to knowledge and skills that are mechanical as well as organizational. Skill levels are often difficult to measure, yet they often determine what can in fact be done given the resources and the population at hand. Technology, in the generic sense, provides the means of conversion of inputs into outputs; the level of technology thus referring to the efficiency of conversion.

These elementary observations are designed to highlight the reality that each state, or society, at each point in time, is characterized by a particular set of master variables that define the empirical parameters of polity, on the one hand, and provide the basis for the policy agenda, on the other. For example, a state like Japan, 'born' with few raw materials, has throughout modern experience acquired access to raw materials from the external environment. This pattern shaped state policy irrespective of the political regime or government in power. While Japan may be an extreme case in this regard, there are others whose reliance on external resources also defines their objectives in the most elementary sense. Each master variable cannot be viewed in isolation from the other two. It is their interconnections – each with reference to the others – that define state characteristics. The same numerical value for population size may be considered a problem in one context, but hardly an issue in another.

The recognition of master variables leads to three distinct lines of enquiry: what is the relationship of master variables within a state to external international behaviour? How do master variables generate differences in patterns of international behaviours? What processes, deriving from the above, may be linked with 'antagonizing behaviour' spiralling to violent conflict? By way of illustration, we then turn to ways in which master variables generate differences in national profiles. These three lines of enquiry, and the illustrations, constitute the agenda of this essay.

The master variables, the state and international behaviour

The master variables provide the basis for delineating linkages from the individual to the state. The initial proposition is that the roots of war are to be found in population growth which, when combined with other master variables may affect dispositions towards conflict, as well as the intent and ability to wage war successfully. The starting point is the individual (the 'discrete statistic').

Every individual (each 'statistic') has basic needs and requirements, and a set of demands. For example, to ensure minimal survival, food, water, air and living space are required. As a population grows, the demand for these basic resources increases. This expansion of demand is a claim on the environment and the social context. Whatever the minimal amount of basic resources needed by a single person, multiples thereof will generate corresponding demand. The functional form of the process of growth – of people and demand – is basically an empirical question. The point here is that demand invariably entails uses of resources.

To obtain and use resources effectively, people rely upon technology, the application of knowledge and skills; technology facilitates acquisition of new resources and development of new uses for known resources. Interactive effects are embedded in the fact that the development, maintenance and use of technology also require resources. On the one hand, technological growth serves to 'relax' productive constraints; on the other, it may also create new constraints.

Generally the more industrialized the technology, the greater the magnitude and the wider the range of resources required. Technological developments almost invariably have social outcomes; furthermore, organizations and institutions of the society are likely to become more complex. To speak of technology without recognition of intense interdependence and reciprocities with its social context is very misleading, yet often resorted to for simplification.

For all societies, at all levels of development, security, cohesion and access to resources are a necessity for sustaining basic needs and demands. Sustained access is a prerequisite for meeting demand generated on all levels of the social order, as well as for the maintenance of social capabilities and institutions, and even the state itself.

Threats of being cut off are often the most credible and powerful in creating national antagonisms and feelings of insecurity – irrespective of the empirical basis for these perceptions. Such threats (and perceptions thereof) serve to link the social system and its demands to the external environment, and assist in defining obstacles to meeting demands. The nature of the linkage (and the underlying perceptions) will shape the disposition to subsequent action and the nature of that activity.

To meet particular demand, people develop specific capabilities and particular institutionalized arrangements in two generic ways: by developing and applying technical knowledge and skills, and/or by co-operating with others, organizing and even bargaining. Bargaining is generally a useful means of articulating 'interest' and exercising leverage.

The important point here is that *demand* as well as the availability of *capabilities* to generate activity (or behaviour) is such that if *either* demand or capability is zero no activity can take place. However, it is possible that the strength of one may compensate for the weakness of the other. (For example, religious or ideological fervour can be used as a compensatory mechanism, much as economists specify substitution effects. Witness, therefore, the Gulf War of the mid-1980s, where one state, Iran, uses its population and their demands as the core element of its strategy to compensate for limitations of other capabilities, such as weapons, infrastructural facilities and so forth.) Actual behaviour is the outcome of the interaction of demand on the one hand and capability on the other.

But these relationships are neither simple nor linear: population growth can contribute to demand and to the expansion of capability; depending upon resources and technology, it can also constrain capability. In other words, population can be an asset or a liability, depending on its position in the context of the master variables in question.

The driving fact, however, is that a growing population, especially when combined with advancing technology and industrialization, cannot be sustained in a resource base or a limited environment. Expansion beyond the environment (or extension of the boundaries of the environment) itself is almost always necessitated to reduce attendant constraints. It is this extension and expansion of behaviour outside an initial environment or established boundaries that defines the socio-economic roots of violence.

The political system – and policies – serve largely to interpret this extension (as 'good', 'bad', 'necessary', or whatever) and to aggregate and articulate social demands. The behaviour of a state will be shaped by its institutions and capabilities, and patterns of international activity delineated accordingly (Choucri and North, 1975).

As domestic resources are depleted (or resources of a particular sector), costs tend to rise. This is a generic relationship, irrespective of the particular resource in question. Rising costs generate strains of their own. When the gap widens between the demand for resources and the resources locally available, the external environment becomes salient in the national policy space.

Lateral pressure and international behaviour

With rising demands and expanding capabilities, states reach out – directly and indirectly – for resources beyond home borders and demand some degree of security for the maintenance of access routes. The protection of a wide range of associated activities and interests becomes a salient feature of outward orientation. The process of outward expansion is termed 'lateral pressure'.

In principle, lateral pressure due to domestic constraints can be 'solved' in several generic ways: (1) control of territories beyond national boundaries (various forms of colonialism); (2) permanent out-migration – some members move into a new resource environment (e.g. the English colonists in the thirteen colonies, Europeans to the United States generations later, European settlers in South Africa); (3) temporary out-migration (e.g. Turks, Portuguese, Spaniards and Algerians to Western Europe, Arabs and Asians to oil-rich countries of the Middle East); (4) forced expulsion of population (displacement and refugees in a variety of conflict situations); (5) external exchange of goods and services (international investments, foreign direct investments, transnational economic services, in private and/or public modes); (6) expansion of national boundaries outward (such as the US historically, or Tsarist Russia, or Israel following wars with Arab states); or (7) combinations of the above (adapted from North, 1986).

Historically, lateral pressure has often taken the form of territorial aggrandizement; however, the attempt to relax or reduce domestic constraints imposed by territorial boundaries or limitations of space generally entails outward expansion which can be manifested in many other forms as well. Again, interactive effects of the master variables are at work. For example, technological advances may contribute to domestic resource expansion and availability, but they also create new demands and new claims on resources.

The actual patterns of expansion (or the specific modes of lateral pressure undertaken) are conditioned by geopolitical location, the levels of population and technology, and the resources available for external activity. For example, the phenomenon of corporate investment abroad is illustrative of a contemporary mode of lateral pressure (Gilpin, 1975), and some have suggested that this form competes with national sovereignty (Vernon, 1971), while others have stressed its transnational characteristics (Keohane and Nye, 1977).

The point here is that lateral pressure has been expressed variously, in both peaceful and violent activities – as exploration and peaceful settlement, as conquest, often as trade and financial influence. Whatever the mode, the consequences may be expected to depend upon the capabilities of the expansionist country relative to the capabilities of its neighbours. In general, states with high capability, those we refer to as 'major powers', tend to influence, dominate, possibly exploit and on occasion conquer societies of significantly lower capabilities. At times, trade as a mode of lateral pressure is used as an instrument of power and control (Hirschman, 1969; Sideri, 1970). There are also instances of limitations of lateral pressure imposed by others and reversals in power relations can occur (as we have seen in the US war in Vietnam).

In each historical situation, the expansion of a society's activities and interests into far-off places has been an indicator of its domestic capabilities and power (and some would say political 'will'). Similarly, each substantial contraction or withdrawal has tended to mark the diminution – relative if not absolute – of the society's capability on critical dimensions.

When the master variables themselves harbour sources of social conflict, more complex forms of violence can emerge. For example, ethnic differences in the population structure of Lebanon culminating in civil war created a conflict system whose dynamics are so robust as to entail wide-ranging regional implications.

National interest, intersections and antagonizing processes

State behaviour, however, is not only the outcome solely of a demand for resources, markets, services or other economic considerations. Other objectives are pursued. The reality is that motivations are mixed: some groups support a policy with one goal in mind, others support the same policy as a means of achieving other objectives. As long as capabilities exist to translate motives into behaviour, actual motivation may not be important.

In general the external activities of a society tend to derive from demands and activities that are generated internally and that cannot be met or successfully carried out without some reference to the external environment. International competition and conflict are thus closely linked to the domestic growth of countries, with the result that domestic and foreign activities are effectively interconnected. What may be construed as foreign policy for one audience may be interpreted as domestic politics for another. Issues and issue-areas can become blurred. The important aspect of national interests is less their existence (or their specific content) than the emergent feeling that they must be defended. States do not 'stand still' relative to one another, some are growing while others are declining. Under such circumstances a rapidly growing society may threaten the established international order.

When two countries extend their respective interests outward, there is a strong probability that such interests will be in opposition, and the activities of these nations may collide. Competition among the colonial powers in Asia and Africa prior to the First World War is the classic case. The US presence in Vietnam and its justification as part of a containment doctrine is an 'intersection' of the military presences of two (or three) major powers, and the violence in the conflict makes it a collision *par excellence*. In this context one can also interpret the Soviet presence in Cuba as an intersection with the US in a part of the world that is considered as an American sphere of interest.

National leaders, making assumptions and claims for the sovereignty of their respective states, tend readily to perceive other states as rivals. Not all collisions are inevitably violent; however, when collisions do occur, they are likely to become violent. 'Apparent cause and underlying cause do not necessarily agree' (Aron, 1967: 87).

As an intersection intensifies, there are many possible outcomes. Collisions of activities and interests can lead to the withdrawal of one (or both) of the parties, an agreement between them or continuing conflict (Choucri and North, 1975: 9). Opportunities for identifying strategies of potential co-operation may occur if the costs of conflict are perceived to be high. Any one of these options is shaped by their respective demands, capabilities and interests.

When two societies are mutual rivals and a military gap between them is perceived as wide or widening, efforts to catch up may be undertaken, and feelings of threat ensue (Ashley, 1980; Choucri and North, 1975). A threatening move by one party in an interactive situation often evokes a comparable response from the other party, whether or not the purpose of the first was to threaten or inflict an injury. This escalation generates a conflict spiral. The arms race is a special type of escalation wherein an increase in one state's military capabilities is viewed by the leadership of a rival state as a threat to its security (Richardson, 1960). Interactions 'interlock' and yield action–reaction processes. Perceptions of threat and suspicions then abound.

The empirical evidence to date suggests that arms race phenomena are generally fuelled by two sets of underlying processes: those involving competitive international action–reaction processes; and those generated by domestic factors, such as technology, budgetary, bureaucratic or interest-group pressures. Clearly, domestic factors and action–reaction dynamics, rather than being contradictory may well be mutually reinforcing (Choucri and North, 1975, 1987). In sum, then, international crises generally exhibit escalatory or action–reaction processes. Some crises escalate into war, others de-escalate; in all cases, however, lateral pressure lies at their origins. In turn lateral pressure is rooted in the disposition of the master variables.

Interactions among master variables
It must be stressed that population growth, advancement in technology, rising demands, increases in military capabilities, and expansion of national activities and interests are seldom the immediate or proximate explanations of war. They generate demands, constrain capabilities, arm the antagonists and contribute to the stances of the opponents, but seldom are they the direct cause of violence. The more proximate explanations are likely to include confrontations or provocations, alliances, counter-alliances and an arms race. Thus, from the perspective of states interacting in an international context, conflict and war are rarely, if ever, directly explained by the master variables alone. (Exceptions are considered below.)

Master variables provide the parameters for the players; they are often contributory to, not determinant of, conflict. It is the intersection in spheres of influence, action–reaction processes and their perceptual and psychological underpinnings that are among the more immediate causes of violence. However, all these processes originate with numbers in the population profile of a state – the discrete statistics, the individual human beings. Over the longer range differences in population levels and rates of change of technology and access to basic resources may literally generate demands, capabilities, leverages and behavioural outcomes as states relate to each other. The master variables thus provide the socio-economic roots of the processes leading to war.

Considering the master variables in their aggregate manifestation may obscure their particular manifestations. For example, ethnicity is a demographic characteristic that may have explicit implications for conflict and violence. Elsewhere we examined the role of ethnicity as a determinant of violent conflict between states and found that a large number of interstate conflicts show ethnic differences within and between the combatants to be a significant feature of the conflict (Choucri, 1974, 1984).

The example noted earlier is akin to a textbook case: the Lebanese Civil War in 1976 and the subsequent invasion by Israel were the outcome of changes in differential rates of growth among ethnic groups, dislocating the earlier communitarian basis of the polity and calling into question the viability of the social contract. The obvious superiority of Israeli technology and military power was irrelevant to the conflict or to its outcome at each point in time.

Considerable evidence regarding another facet of population, namely the age distribution, suggests that age contributes to domestic conflict, and the notion of 'population-at-risk' refers to those populations (groups or societies) whose characteristics are more conducive to overt conflict (Kelly and Galle, 1984). Further, to some extent, and in certain contexts, crowding is found to be a conflict-producing phenomenon (Proshansky, 1984).

Of the many population variables, that which is least explored is the mobility of populations across national boundaries and the way in which relations among nations might be affected. International relations theory and analysis harbours serious gaps with regard to migration across national boundaries. Considerations of the rules of entry and rules of exit appear to provide an empirical link between the fact of such mobility and the efforts of states to regulate or formalize the mobility (Weiner, 1985). It is more important, however, to explore the process by which states regulate cross-border mobility. Why a particular state sets in place particular rules of entry and exit remains to be determined (Choucri, 1987).

The resource variable, so central to survival, is by the same token subject to specific manifestations yielding 'constraint' or 'availability' as the case may be. For oil-rich states, the demand for a critical raw material combined with their access to technology (to convert oil in the ground to actual production) was historically the outcome of corporate management and control (Tanzer, 1969). The increase in their own knowledge and skills, and expanded technical capacities enabled them to exert pressure and assume control over national resources (Choucri, 1976). The resultant interdependence in the world oil market eventually led to market changes allowing producers to influence prices. Consumers responded, individually and collectively – at all levels of social organization – shaping new behaviours and resulting in new 'demand' schedules (see Choucri, 1981, for the analytical and simulation structures).

The deteriorating oil prices throughout the early 1980s are the apparent outcome of dramatic change in individual behaviour (consumers and governments) over the decade of 1970s. In this set of events, actions and counter-actions, the master variables were a central part of the story. Population played a role by influencing consumption and demand, but technology set in place new patterns of resource utilization and threatened to separate the pattern of GNP growth and traditional patterns of energy utilization.

Technology is the master variable most difficult to untangle from its context. None the less, it provides the critical differentials in capabilities, the leading edge in international transactions. Whether in trade, military activities, investment strategies, or whatever, those with a 'technological edge' have a relative advantage. (The Lebanon–Israel conflict is an important exception, confounding expectations.)

Master variables, state profiles and international behaviour

The actual behaviour of any state is shaped by the underlying profile created by the master variables. The following examples illustrate how the interaction of population characteristics, resource endowments and levels of technology lead to different types of international behaviour, and how some of these may be more conducive to conflict than others. These comparisons are presented in terms of 'state profiles' to illustrate broadly the linkages between internal characteristics and external activities.

Profile A: high population, high technology, high resources
Today the United States and, to a lesser extent, the Soviet Union are illustrative. This profile allows, perhaps even necessitates, outward-oriented activities. Expansion of state behaviour outside territorial boundaries occurs in a wide variety of ways – trade, military activity, diplomatic interactions, investments, violent confrontations and so forth. The types of external behaviour are very broad. A Soviet Union with the level of technology of China would be less threatening to the US today. Although there are differences between the US and the USSR along the master variables, and differences in levels and type of international behaviour, they represent a profile fundamentally different from other generic types.

Profile B: high population, low technology, low resources
This state profile is commonly associated with the large former colonies of Asia and Africa, and provides little opportunity for international behaviour. India in the 1950s is a case in point, as is China at the same point in time. Thirty years later the profile of India shifted notably when their technology advanced dramatically and resource constraints were reduced. Today, we could not characterize India's profile in the same manner as in the 1950s. This change entails an expansion of the domestic resource base ('development' to be sure, as well as application of 'technology'), but unlike the Japanese case where domestic resource constraints are severe, the Indian profile had significant resource potential which was realized over the past three decades.

Profile C: low population, low technology, high resources
This state profile is one of resource abundance, as illustrated by the oil-exporting countries of the Gulf in the Middle East. The real constraints are low population size and low levels of technology: population and technology must both be imported. The fact that states rely on imports for two of the master variables raises substantially the degree of dependence on the external environment.

Profile D: low population, high technology, low resources
Israel and Singapore illustrate this type of state profile. The distinctive feature is high technological advances relative to size and to domestic resources. The foreign policy thrust is to use national capabilities to

obtain access to resources, which then enable the expansion of activities outside territorial boundaries. Some of these activities may lead to conflict Consider, for example, the implications of an Israel with low technology; its external behaviour and military stance would be quite different from the one of today. So, too, a Singapore with the level of technology of a Gabon would not be a credible producer or exporter of high-tech materials.

Profile E: low population, low technology, low resources
Many of the smaller developing countries are of this type. Survival is a primary objective. The agenda is stark. The bounds of permissible behaviour domestically and internationally are constrained relative to the other state profiles considered here. Examples include Chad and Niger.

Profile F: high population, high technology, low resources
Japan represents this profile, where 'carrying capacity' concepts illustrate the constraints, and where the demand for resources persists as a salient element that cannot be alleviated simply by economic development. The greater the Japanese industrialization over the past century, the more pronounced became the domestic resource constraints and, by extension, the initial necessity of access to external resources. States like Japan, born with few raw materials, regard unimpeded access to resources as a prime objective irrespective of the political regime or government in power.

Profile G: low population, high technology, high resources
Canada, Sweden and Norway today illustrate this profile. Their distinctive feature is relatively low population levels in conjunction with high levels on the other variables. A major thrust of external activity is trade and diplomacy. (Historically, of course, Sweden was not always a 'peaceful' state.)

These illustrations can be thought of as 'comparative statics', one-point-in-time snapshots. They indicate only some broad implications of a state's population-resource-technology profile for its international activity. State profiles, however, are not static, but highly dynamic, and there is a change over time of profile and of consequences. Comparative statics – profiles of states – provide only an initial view of the relative positioning of the master variables setting the broad parameters of international behaviour. The processes of lateral pressure and the political framework mediate between the stark profile and the external behaviour, whether tending towards conflict or towards co-operation.

Conclusion
Returning to the questions asked at the onset of this chapter, the concluding propositions, are these: the roots of war are found in man making

claims on an environment within the structures of states. Demands are generated and capabilities are marshalled to assist in meeting these demands. To the extent that behaviour extends beyond national boundaries, the interactions of states then shape the nature of subsequent outcomes. We reiterate that master variables are seldom the immediate or proximate causes of war. Even when the conflict has an obviously demographic base, the influence of population does not occur overnight.

In this process, man recedes in importance, being no longer a proximate cause of subsequent events or processes. But there are exceptions. In cases of ethnic divisions or cross-national migration, population variables may constitute the immediate determinants of conflict. The mode of lateral pressure and the constraints on such pressure imposed by other states or by the international environment will define the emergent policy agenda and the articulation of national interests.

The master variables, the comparative statics of state profiles, and the process of lateral pressure are generic in the sense that no society is immune, and no political regime or ideology can eradicate their impacts. They transcend the nature of a particular political system, or the ideology or belief system prevailing among the leadership or the population. Nor are these processes hostage to the requirements of a particular paradigm in international relations or of political economy.

When defending national interests becomes salient, the costs of defence are not always assessed appropriately. History has shown many examples of miscalculations of costs. How far states are willing to go to defend their perceived interests and when they decide to opt out of strategic interactions has sometimes been referred to as 'the search for peace systems'. This search generally follows a transformation in the disposition of the master variables.

Master variables seldom change rapidly. They generally evolve over a long period of time. The reality, however, is that their interaction literally defines the bounds of permissible behaviour, and determines what a state can or cannot do at any point in time. This interaction is the fundamental constraint on statehood, relaxed only to the extent that the critical variables themselves are modified. Relaxing the constraints can occur within national boundaries, or through expansion of behaviour outward (lateral pressure) or both. Propensities towards conflict and violence are determined by the mode of lateral pressure and its international consequences.

References

Aron, Raymond (1967) *Peace and War*. New York: Doubleday.

Ashley, Richard K. (1980) *The Political Economy of War and Peace*. New York: Nichols.

Chen, Steve (1984) 'Mirror, Mirror, on the Wall...: Are the Free Countries More Pacific?', *Journal of Conflict Resolution* 28: 617–48.

Choucri, Nazli (1974) *Population Dynamics and International Violence*. Lexington: D. C. Heath.

Choucri, Nazli (1976) *International Energy Interdependence*. Lexington: D. C. Heath.

Choucri, Nazli (1981) *International Energy Futures: Petroleum Prices, Power, Payments.* Cambridge: MIT Press.

Choucri, Nazli (ed.) (1984) *Multidisciplinary Perspectives on Population and Conflict.* Syracuse, NY: Syracuse University Press.

Choucri, Nazli (1987) 'International Relations and International Migration: Delineating the Connections', unpublished MS, Massachusetts Institute of Technology.

Choucri, Nazli and North, Robert C. (1972a) 'Dynamics of International Conflict: Some Policy Implications of Population, Resources, Technology', in Raymond Tanter and Richard H. Ullman (eds) *Theory and Policy in International Relations.* Princeton: Princeton University Press.

Choucri, Nazli, with the collaboration of Robert C. North (1972b) 'In Search of Peace Systems: Scandinavia and the Netherlands', in Bruce M. Russett (ed.), *Peace, War, and Numbers*, pp. 239–75. Beverly Hills, London: Sage Publications.

Choucri, Nazli and North, Robert C. (1975) *Nations in Conflict: National Growth and International Conflict.* San Francisco: W. H. Freeman.

Choucri, Nazli and North, Robert C. (1987) 'Lateral Pressure and International Conflict: Japan Before World War II and After', MS.

Gilpin, Robert (1975) *U.S. Power and the Multinational Corporation.* New York: Basic Books.

Hirschman, Albert O. (1969) *National Power and the Structure of Foreign Trade.* Berkeley: University of California Press.

Hobson, J.A. (1938) *Imperialism: A Study*, rev. edn. London: George Allen and Unwin.

Kelly, William R. and Galle, Omer R. (1984) 'Sociological Perspectives and Evidence on the Links Between Population and Conflict', in Nazli Choucri (ed.) *Multidisciplinary Perspectives on Population and Conflict*, pp. 91–122. Syracuse, NY: Syracuse University Press.

Keohane, Robert O. and Nye, Joseph S. (1977) *Power and Interdependence.* Boston: Little, Brown.

Lenin, V. I. (1968) *Imperialism: The Highest Stage of Capitalism*, new edn. New York: International Publishers.

North, Robert C. (1986) 'War, Peace, and Survival', unpublished MS.

Proshansky, Harold M. (1984) 'Population Change and Human Conflict', in Nazli Choucri (ed.) *Multidisciplinary Perspectives on Population and Conflict*, pp. 59–90. Syracuse, NY: Syracuse University Press.

Richardson, Lewis F. (1960) *Arms and Insecurity.* Pittsburgh: Boxwood Press.

Rosecrance, Richard N. (1969) 'Bipolarity, Multipolarity, and the Future', in James N. Rosenau (ed.) *International Politics and Foreign Policy*, pp. 325–35. New York: Free Press.

Russett, Bruce (in press) 'Economic Change as a Cause of International Conflict', in Frank Blackaby and Christian Schmidt (eds) *Peace, Defence, and Economic Analysis.* London: Macmillan.

Sideri, S. (1970) *Trade and Power.* Rotterdam: Rotterdam University Press.

Tanzer, M. (1969) *The Political Economy of International Oil and the Underdeveloped Countries.* Boston: Beacon Press.

Vernon, Raymond (1971) *Sovereignty at Bay: the Multinational Spread of U.S. Enterprises.* New York: Basic Books.

Waltz, Kenneth (1959) *Man, the State, and War.* New York: Columbia University Press.

Weiner, Myron (1983) 'International Migration and Development: Indians in the Persian Gulf', *Population and Development Review* 8(1): 1–36.

Weiner, Myron (1985) 'On International Migration and International Relations', *Population and Development Review* 11(3): 441–55.

14

An Economic Contribution to the Analysis of War and Peace

Christian Schmidt

Introduction: from economic analysis of military expenditures to the economic modelling of war and peace

The interest economists have taken in war and peace is not at all new. Without referring back to the mercantilist debates, the history of economic thought is dotted with specific contributions on such topics.

A glance at the classic school of political economy is suggestive enough. Adam Smith not only developed a synthetic analysis of the economic specifics of military expenditures among other public expenditures in Book V of *The Wealth of Nations*, but also discussed extensively the economic impact of technological armament improvement and argued in favour of a standing army rather than a militia (see Smith 1976: 698 ff.). Classic economists presented the main features of war, pre-war and peace economies. Certain suggestive analyses have been conducted on the process of accumulation of an economic surplus during pre-war periods and the risk that it might lead to war. Such acceleration towards warfare is well explained (Hume, 1752). Furthermore, the negative economic consequences of amassing a surplus in peacetime, by withdrawing capital from productive use has been clearly demonstrated, along with the final weakening of national economies (MacCulloch, 1863). Military expenditures were then mainly viewed from an exclusively financial point of view, as a key problem, alternatives being proposed such as borrowing or taxation, with their specific effects on economic growth (J. S. Mill, 1967).

The change of international scale during the First World War induced fresh reflections among economists concerning the nature of the relationships between war and the economy. The first picture of the burden war represented for economic activity was delineated in a book published in 1914 under the title of *Economy of War*, which anticipated events to come (Hirst, 1914). Some of the major contradictions between a war system and economic activities were argued with the support of many statistical figures and data. It anticipated an active debate between economists mainly in the United Kingdom about political economy and preparations for war and peace which opened up between the two world wars.[1] But the best-known contribution came from J. M. Keynes, when the author of *The General Theory of Employment, Interest and Money* tried to interpret the economic problems arising from war and post-war situations in terms of the relevant aggregates he had analysed. In a number of publications, received in different ways (Keynes 1939–40), he analysed the 'inflation gap' as generated by wage bills increasing on the one hand, and the reduction of aggregate consumption on the other, since the distribution of income for military purposes does not have a sufficient counterpart. Some of Keynes's suggestions concerning the macro-economic effects of the defence system were reformulated subsequently by several American economists (Galbraith, 1964, 1969; Melman, 1971, 1975).

If we approach the economic contributions on war and peace from a more analytical point of view, two principal pieces of work emerge, which could respectively be called 'defence economics' and 'war-and-peace economic modelling'. The general concern of the first one is to study how, and to what extent, an economic system is affected (or can be affected) by a wartime or a peacetime environment, including pre-war, post-war and mixed situations, such as cold war. The core is obviously military expenditures as an economic aggregate. The first step therefore is to set up a theoretically well-founded and econometrically relevant matrix for such concepts as defence expenditures, the military burden or security cost (Smith 1977, 1980). Starting with national accounts, economists have tried to enter empirical estimates of these concepts into econometric models at a world level (Leontief and Duchin, 1983) as well as of national or comparative ones (Smith, 1980; Fontanel, 1982). The purpose is to show the relationships between military expenditures and the main aggregates, such as GNP consumption, investment, prices, imports and exports. This material is used firstly to locate the economic parameters of defence activities (Pilandon, 1982; Maizels and Nissanke, 1984), and secondly to assess their impact on economic growth and fluctuations (Schmidt, 1986). Defence economics is now part of positive economics and has discovered several relations at a macro-level in the absence of any particular assumptions covering individual behaviour.

The second group of studies is, on the contrary, characterized by the applications of micro-economic tools to war-and-peace situations, through individual decision-making processes. The suggestive analogy on these grounds between an economic calculus and a military and diplomatic one goes back to Edgeworth at the end of the nineteenth century (Edgeworth, 1967).

The foundations of such research programmes lie in several crucial assumptions: (1) war-and-peace decision-makers are *rational*, adopting the minimum requirements of economic logic, that is, they strive to attain an expected value (maximum or minimum) along a scale of preferences. (2) The content of decisions in strategic and diplomatic matters is to choose an allocation of resources consistent with criteria in accordance with (1). On the basis of (1) and (2), some of the key concepts in micro-economic theory, as well as utility and cost functions, equilibrium solutions and optimum situations can easily be extended to international conflict, defence, war and negotiation.

The application of this economic approach to war and related phenomena was significantly advanced by the mathematical framework of game theory in its close links to economic modelling (Morgenstern, 1948; Shubik, 1959). Indeed, pioneering work along these lines using both game matrices and economic reasoning began in the United States during the early 1960s (Schelling, 1960; Boulding, 1962). Since then economists have built many theoretical models in order to reflect the international arms situation (Brito, 1972; Brito and Intriligator, 1987), the logical transition from arms races to the outbreak of war (Lambelet, 1975; Intriligator and Brito, 1976; Brito and Intriligator, 1987) and even war dynamics (Intriligator, 1967; Shubik, 1983). The outset of the nuclear age certainly opened broad scope for such theoretical economic models. Nuclear strategic doctrines are indeed basically conceptualized on grounds of relatively few options. Their main variables can easily be translated, at least at first glance, into economic terms (missile utilities, damage estimations) and strategic calculations into economic computing (maximization of expected utility, cost-benefit analysis).

The meaning of the information provided from this second source is highly questionable. Generally, despite the empirical content of the variables and parameters, such modelling is rarely testable. It must be viewed as tentative simulations of the logical implications of the phenomena addressed. Their content is therefore generally normative. Some sceptics might even argue its purely metaphorical meaning. But even if decision-makers only roughly adhere to this way of thinking about wars, these economic models can also, at least indirectly, convey a positive meaning.[2]

Are these two groups of studies closely linked to provide consistent results, or on the contrary, are they completely disconnected? The question is clearly related to the general problem of micro/macro-economic relationships. This framework can be used, for instance, for arms dynamics, because a purely decisional dynamic armaments model, derived from a differential game (Simaan and Cruz, 1975) can, in principle, be tested against relevant samples of macro-economic data.

But certain additional difficulties must be solved in that case. Despite the formal apparatus, criteria and preferences attaching to decision-makers are defined in different spheres, referring to economic strategic or military considerations. Variations in military expenditures have two different meanings, an economic one, accounted in economic units, and also a military meaning interpreted in military units (e.g. technical efficiencies or potential casualties). Not only must the second measure be constructed, but the transformation of the economic variables and parameters into military ones (and the reverse) is by no means a trivial problem (Schmidt, 1986).

The micro-economic and macro-economic dimensions are not identical.

Peace and war are not intrinsically macro-economic categories, but security and defence can be investigated as public goods (for more details see p. 221) like education or health in a welfare perspective. Yet war-and-peace situations can be deduced at a very abstract level from micro-economic concepts. But no bridge has been constructed, like aggregation procedures in welfare economics, to link up these two approaches.

We thus propose to examine each of these two contributions separately before offering a few more synthetic remarks in conclusion.

Defence viewed as a dynamic subsystem within national economies and the world economy

There is, as yet, no good accounting system to compute data about military expenditures, arms production and arms transfers. Such a lack has weakened the meaning and reach of empirical investigations. The political barriers to the construction of a clear statistical framework is unanimously underlined by specialists, but is also the consequence of conceptual deficiencies.

Let us consider, for example, aggregate military expenditures which serve as the starting point for the majority of empirical studies. First of all, national defence budgets are not correct estimations. Some defence activities often fall under other administrative categories (such as home affairs, foreign affairs, research and industry). Furthermore, where a national arms industry exists, the public budget does not cover its complete range. On the contrary, one can find some inputs in defence budgets not directly linked to military output. The construction of a relevant aggregate involves two preliminary operations, namely, the choice of a meaningful criterion to support the definition, and a correct identification of components consistent with economic categories.

The traditional purpose of military expenditures is to protect people and the national territory from external threats. But it can be also used, especially when a state is not well established, to protect it against internal threats (revolution, armed uprisings, etc.). Such an extension can be observed in many developing countries, and more particularly in some Latin American ones. More generally, major trends of conflicts during the last twenty-five years reveal a predominance of the '*intra-state*' type over the traditional '*interstate*' type, often with an additional complex international dimension (as in the case of terrorism).[3] This observed evolution tends to upset the distinctions between military forces for international uses and other forces for home purposes and requires the best possible statistical translation. Certain researchers, working in developing countries, have consequently proposed to follow Boulding's suggestions and to utilize a broader categorization, often called 'security-related expenditures' rather than the traditional military expenditure heading (Ball, 1984).

From an economic point of view, such aggregates combine hetero-geneous components. Payment of different salaries (conscript and/or professional soldiers), arms procurement from abroad (imports), weapon construction (including logistic material and equipment), operations and maintenance, research and development do not all have the same macro-economic impacts. The weighting of each of these components varies greatly from one country to another, not only as between industrial and developing countries but also between similar economies. A comparison between Brazil and India, two major arms producers among the developing group, is very suggestive. Until 1980, despite big military programmes, the share of arms production in Brazil never exceeded 2.3 percent of the total aggregate GNP; meanwhile in India it has some-times gone beyond 20 percent (Daeger, 1986: 43). Therefore, the close relationship between security expenditures and other macro-economic aggregates (Fontanel, 1982) can be imputed, at least in part, to differences in their structural components. It is even arguable that the economic meaning of this aggregate stays obscure so long as it is not disaggregated into well-defined economic categories. Unfortunately, among the 150 countries of the world, hardly 25 can provide disaggregated figures, which do not exist even for a military power as important as the Soviet Union.

The two limitations just discussed in the context of military expen-ditures also apply more or less to the arms industry and arms transfers. The improvement of our knowledge is perhaps not mainly a purely statistical data problem, but rather requires us to delineate the features of the defence system more precisely. As already mentioned, this system emerges from three principal sources: a domestic, public source (military expenditures), designated P1, and related to the national decision-making process; an industrial one (the arms industry), designated P2 and related to industrial policies and major technological choices; and an interna-tional one (arm's trade), designated P3, and connected both to the strategic facet of world politics and to international economic constraints. Each source is correctly identified as a specific and unique mixture of military and economic variables. Even for the first, a degree of inter-national involvement exists, because in many developing countries, part of the economic burden is borne by financial assistance, through military aid, the final consequences of which for public finance are often difficult to estimate correctly. The system itself is multi-levelled and its dynamics can be considered from various angles (national, regional or even world economies).

Before analysing their relationships, it is useful to examine briefly the principal characteristics of P1, P2 and P3.

P1: military activity as public expenditure

According to Samuelson's classic polar-case approach (Samuelson, 1958), national security as well as space are pure public entities entering *irreducibly* into the utility function of every fellow citizen in a given country. It is more questionable to consider peace as a good in the strict economic meaning related to the difficult definition of its price, but for defence the picture seems to be the reverse – defence can be regarded as an economic commodity without any difficulty. Meanwhile its pure public denomination has to take two more peculiarities into account: (a) the pattern of the relationship between defence input (expenditures) and defence output (security) is hardly shaped into a single value function (production function); (b) the international environment requires us to consider the opportunity of alliances and the burden of sharing of defence costs among nations. These two complications are of a very different kind. It is noticeable that Samuelson's criterion does not imply that every fellow citizen must be affected by defence in exactly the same way. The existence of positive utilities for only a few members of the national community and negative for others does not rule out the pure public good classification. Therefore, such a denomination cannot be limited to the deterrence case, as the ground of a general principle to relate defence to security. The second point is more cumbersome. The alliances problem opens a hole in the non-excludibility principle traditionally attached to a pure public good (Sandler, 1977). But such consideration modifies the topic and moves from a micro-level to a macro-level. The subjects are now the nations themselves analysed as individual units upsetting the aggregate process. Therefore the phenomena of alliances do not affect the pure public good characteristic of defence as long as the restricted point of view of the fellow citizens or individual consumers is assumed to be the only relevant one for the purpose.

As a production activity, whatever its legal organization, defence is public-oriented perhaps more radically than any other social goods. While, for example, private education and health services exist, war preparations and defence systems (except for a militia) seem difficult to manage as a market goal, at least in its human component.

All these very peculiar properties which characterize the economics of defence activity explain why and to what extent military expenditures, whatever their scale, affect all variables and all the functions of national economies: they are thus best apprehended at a macro-economic level.

Furthermore, security and its defence-expenditure translation are generally perceived by governments as a top collective priority in the more or less informal hierarchy of their public responsibilities. Now it can be demonstrated that, except under very particular conditions, this top priority is not theoretically consistent with a maximally obtainable rate of national income growth.

Aligning these characteristics provides a tentative explanation of trends in military expenditures in different environments. Despite expectations sometimes supported by biased computations (Pryor, 1968), no real trade-off takes place between military and social expenditures, such as education and health. (Applying a substitution logic between these categories of public expenditure as an approximation of opportunity cost in order to estimate the military burden for a nation must be considered wrong (Russet, 1969, 1970).) It seems, on the contrary, that in the case of many industrial countries, such as the United States, a complementary relation often exists between fluctuations in military expenditures and education and health budgets, if the sample extends over a sufficiently long period (Russet, 1982). A negative correlation between military and social aggregates does not seem to contradict a positive one between their respective budget totals. The peculiarities of military expenditures relative to other social ones is consistent with the fact that the evolution of military budgets is more closely linked to economic growth and its fluctuations and to governmental expenditures as a whole than to any particular social budget. In other words, the decision to fix the amount of military expenditures partially escapes the budget-bargaining process. But this does not mean that military expenditures have no consequences for other social activities through macro-economic linkages and often only after relatively long delays (lag time). This impact is clearer, but most often different for obvious reasons, in developing countries (Daeger, 1986).

P2: weapons as industrial products
The classic economic laws do not operate in the arms production sector. Weapons, indeed, are not common commodities. Fortunately only a small proportion of produced armaments are actually used in the battlefield, storage being their main fate except in times of war. Under these conditions, their obsolescence cannot match ordinary commodity life. Broadly speaking, military material becomes obsolete quicker than civil equipment, and its technological turnover is not determined by market conditions, but by strategic considerations deduced from assessments of the adversary's material, that is to say, by a mixture of technological and military perspectives. The economic consequence is, first, a very peculiar R and D spin-off, and second, high unit costs. Calculations in industrial countries show that the average unit cost of military material is from 3 to 8 percent higher than for civil material using the same technology (Gansler, 1980). The sophistication of weapon systems and their deterrent function, as for nuclear weapons, tend to exaggerate this trend.

Another peculiar characteristic of arms production is its monopsonistic structure. Indeed, at least for domestic needs, demand is exerted by only one buyer, the national government, which conveys the demands of the military staffs (even if competition can be observed between different staffs according to the public choice schema). Consequently, most frequently, industrial and commercial risks are reduced for firms, which are, on the other hand, also more or less controlled by governmental authorities. One of the main results of this situation is a strong incentive to export. Except for the two superpowers, domestic outlets are generally limited, mainly by budget constraints, hence export and more recently international co-productions becomes economic necessities in order to reduce unit costs by lengthening the production run. This is why profits are mainly in foreign markets. But foreign demand tends to diverge more and more from domestic production, which introduces further complexity.

Finally, there is a strong linkage between civil and military industrial activities, thanks to the organization of the industrial arms sector. Everywhere arms production is highly concentrated in relatively few large groups which are articulated to a wide and complex network of sub-contracting firms, often relatively small. Most of the main groups expand both for military and civil production, in order to seize the opportunities of substitution effects (e.g. aircraft production, helicopters, etc.). It is often difficult to establish the precise connections between civil and military sectors within industrial groups (Boston Consulting Group, 1979; Dussauge, 1986), but the best way to scrutinize the final industrial impact of arms production is to analyse organization and management around the military programmes (Dussauge, 1986). If 'militarization' has any meaning, it must be viewed in that perspective.

P3: arms transfer as international trade
To refer to arms transfers as a market is nothing more than a metaphor. If something like supply and demand exist, there is no clearing mechanism which would tend to standardize weapon prices for each category. The same material can be bought at very different prices according to the importing country and to other specific conditions (credit, offset arrange-ments, etc.). Moreover, there is no transparency concerning prices and financial conditions. Each military contract is the result of a unique negotiation process, though directly or indirectly related to other contracts. This does not mean, however, that arms transfer is not a business since, on the contrary, the share of arms gifts from the US and the Soviet Union has declined drastically over the past fifteen years. Recent studies have shown, for instance, that a key role of Soviet arms exports is to earn hard currency (Despree, 1985).

It is difficult to evaluate the share of major weapons, the transfer of which are controlled by governments (large public contracts), and that of minor weapon transactions, which are really uncontrollable. In any case, the registered contracts have two interesting economic characteristics: firstly, their time horizon is medium-run and sometimes even long-run, with consequences for credit and banking, and secondly they often induce trade flows in lateral sectors, for instance, public works which can be considered as by-products of the bargaining processes. Another illustration is provided by the links between oil and arms con-tracts which represent a specific offset case. The final economic impact of the arms trade is thus often largely indirect and diffuse.

Another distinction must be introduced between 'political market spaces' which are closed and dominated by political relations between buyers and sellers (alliances, assistance agreements, etc.) and 'economic market spaces' which are more open and where a sort of competition operates. In extreme cases of the first type, arms transfers are no more than the by-product of military alliances. The borderline is not firmly fixed and fluctuates with the international climate and regional trends.

The détente period in East–West relations, during the 1970s, brought a tendency to enlarge economic open spaces for political reasons. Furthermore, a developing country rarely turns immediately from one major seller to a rival: more often it passes through an intermediate stage corresponding to open space (Neuman and Harkavy, 1979). Further, there is a strong tendency for non-arms-producing countries to diversify their sources, which also tends to reduce closed areas in the world arms trade.

P1, P2 and P3 are interrelated in various ways. As the economic defence subsystem described here is an open one, each of their linkages are also related to the socio-political environment. The relations between P1, P2 and P3 are hence subject to adjustment processes with these environmental variables. The main features of these complex relationships can now be sketched.

Military expenditures and arms production relationships
Military industrial programmes are principally supported by defence budgets, and have medium-run consequences on public finance. The major macro-economic problem is the imputation of arms programmes to overall budgetary deficits. The Reagan administration's defence plan provided a good illustration of the difficulty of making a correct evaluation. First, the presidential target was to increase the share of the Department of Defense (DOD) in the US federal budget from 24 percent (1981) to 29 percent (1985). At the same time, the real increase of the different appropriations between 1981 and 1984, corresponding to the nominal increase from the previous year minus deflator, were estimated respectively at 59.6 percent for arms procurement, 44.2 percent for research, development, testing and evaluation versus only 9.8 percent for military personnel and 4.9 percent for retired military pay. But these data do not suffice for a correct quantitative estimation of the weapon programme's weight in the federal budget deficit, mainly because of the 1981 tax cut and the extension of federal borrowing from the private sector over the same period. The better way to ask the question is rather to start from a given general economic context characterized by a structural deficit, where a large part of arms procurement and military research and development is not paid for by taxes, which leads to a broader question concerning the macro-economic impact of the affordability of the industrial defence programmes.

In developing countries with arms industries, a specific mechanism tends to transfer the internal debt burden to external debts. This occurred in many countries such as Brazil, Argentina and, even if on a smaller scale, the Republic of Korea (Schmidt, 1984). It must be noted that this indirect effect of military production is more significant for the external debt than the direct impact of arms imports for non-arms-producing countries.

In all situations, the linkage between P1 and P2 is largely determined by bureaucratic interactions which are sensitive to domestic politics. For the United States the decision-making processes, resulting from interactions between Congress, the Pentagon and the arms industry, were first studied over a long period (Peck and Sherer, 1962; Fox, 1974) and partially formalized into models (Rattinger, 1975, 1976; Orstrom, 1978). These researches supported a convincing explanation of arms procurement and R and D variations which have fluctuated, according to the DOD figures, between 29 and 48 percent of total military expenditures over the period 1960–82. More recently other researchers, starting from case studies, also illuminated internal trade-offs between industry and bureaucratic groups in developing countries, especially in Latin America (Grindle, 1984).

From arms production to arms transfers

There are strong export incentives for the arms producer, but contradictions can occur between economic and political points of view. Furthermore, credit terms often complicate the export deal. From a very large variety of situations, two constraints seem to emerge. Exporting is a compelling economic necessity for every arms producer. Such imperatives are specially hard for developing countries and explain the situation even when production is mainly domestically oriented as in India (Wulf, 1983). Exporting as an economic necessity can also have diplomatic implications – Israel is a good example – and generate new international tensions and difficulties. Secondly, in a first phase, often prolonged, military programmes in developing countries increase arms-related imports more quickly than corresponding exports, and consequently enlarge the arms trade deficit, as could be observed in Argentina and even Brazil from 1975 to 1979. This is an additional argument to support the paradoxically negative impact of internal arms production programmes on the external debt of developing countries.

Arms trade and the financial burden

One of the major innovations in arms transfers is the rapid extension of credit terms making the linkage between P1 and P3 a more purely financial one. According to a recent estimation, arms transfer credits have multiplied five times between 1972 and 1982. But the consequences in terms of the financial burden on buyers cannot easily be calculated because of the lack of information on the financing of arms transfers. Case studies, however, reveal that arms contracts are often not only directly or indirectly linked to military aid but also to more general borrowing facilities and trade counterparts. It can thus be advanced as a hypothesis that a portion of credits extended to the supplier for the sale of arms is, in many cases, used to lighten the weight of short-term external debt. Some indirect indices can be related to this. For example, Israel's debt-financing deficit shifted in contrast with the general trend of private versus public financing from 1970 to 1980, the share of public credit (mainly bilateral) increasing from 47 to 70 percent of the total external credits. More recently, a similar trend occurred in Morocco. Such paradoxical short-run effects of arms purchases on public finance do not imply a positive impact, but underline the complexity of the mechanism.

Another phenomenon reduces the burden of arms imports on buyers' budgets: 'offset' arrangements, i.e. conditional compensation practices for military-related exports (Neuman, 1985). They can take the form of counter-trade, technology transfers, overseas investment and also certain types of joint production or licensed production counter-trade. Such practices have for long been a significant feature of Soviet arms supply. The United States has equally resorted to military offset recently. Despite the difficulty of making even a rough approximation of US military agreements, one-third of them are often said to fall into this category. The rising cost of military material combined with the IMF's restrictions on debitors' imports is the main reason for increasing offsets, principally in Third World countries. Their major economic consequences are to reduce the burden on public finance in the short run and to shift constraints on trade and production to the medium and long run. Novel forms of dependency also arise through such arrangements.

Despite appearances, these two trends are not contradictory at all, but converge to complicate the strict accountancy links between arms procurement expenses and arms import flows.

Are the economic dynamics of defence related to international conflicts?
Defence economics as a subsystem is related both to the economy and to strategy. Some researchers have even tried to derive a general framework to model the whole situation (Lambelet and Luterbacher, 1987). The crucial question of the role of this dynamic in international conflicts and tensions can be explored in two complementary directions. The first concerns the direct interactions between P1, P2 and P3, on the one hand, and the outbreak, duration and end of wars on the other. The second is focused on indirect effects, via their economic consequences, at national as well as world levels. For both approaches, the adoption of a single determinant is quite inadequate and a simple causal chain cannot provide a correct framework.

In spite of many limitations, certain major features emerge from studies of those topics. Firstly, for developing countries, or groups of countries in conflict situations (potential or real), the well-known action–reaction dynamics between military expenditures (and arms import flows) seem to be closely related to the outbreak of wars at a regional level, in partial confirmation of Richardson's hypotheses on the arms race.

Recent statistical tests are significant for Israel and the Arab countries, as well as for Iraq and Iran (Majeski and Jones, 1981), but there is no significant correlation for Indian and Pakistani movements between 1950 and 1976. Different international linkages between arms dynamics and regional conflicts are revealed by quantitative studies. For instance the arms race between Israel and Arab countries has taken a symmetrical form, while the interactive process is asymmetrical in the case of Iran and Iraq. Two factors can explain the counter-intuitive situation for India and Pakistan, firstly if China is introduced into the model so that an indirect connection is established and secondly because both are arms producers. The action –reaction schema does not operate as clearly for arms producers as for arms importers. Lastly, the 'perception coefficient' and the 'grievance coefficient', to adopt Richardson's terminology (see Rapoport, Ch. 11 in this volume), are most frequently positively correlated, which is consistent from a rational point of view and probably tends to exacerbate instability.

The economic constraints on these countries seem relatively flexible, or at least not sufficient to arrest arms race dynamics. Arms transfers with their related financial and counter-trade conditions may have significant effects in various ways. But arms production imposes a burden which, over the long run, inhibits national economic capacity. For instance, economic problems in Israel – the decline in private investment, the slow-down of economic growth and rising inflation – followed immediately upon tremendous arms-industry performances. Egypt provides an illustration of overall economic constraints on military efforts over a long period, which surely facilitated the negotiation of the Camp David Agreements in 1978.

Secondly, there is no statistical evidence of an interactive process between US and Soviet military expenditures. Some scholars have advanced technical arguments to explain such an unexpected situation as, for instance, the irrelevance of flow evaluation (military expenses) versus the relevance of stock evaluation (weapon accumulation), raising the difficult problem of arriving at a correct assessment of the stock (Gregory, 1974; Lambelet and Luterbacher, 1979). One may also argue by referring to the difference between economic and strategic evaluation (see below). In any case these negative relations are reinforced by the positive showing of domestic bureaucratic models applied to both countries (Rattinger, 1976; Cusack, 1981). Obviously, the significant variables are not identical for the two superpowers, because of the asymmetry of the regimes. Responding to the electorate's changes in aggregate demand and previous military spending are determining for the US, while competition for leadership tenure, economic performance (related to the planning cycle), and previous military spending in the USSR yield more significant statistical results than interactive international modelling.

Indeed, the US and USSR are the leading arms producers of the world. The strong technological constraints of their more and more sophisticated arsenals consequently restrict freedom for mutual adjustment. On the other hand, investment in military equipment establishes a close link with domestic economic cycles and bureaucratic processes of resource allocation for defence, which are quite different in the two cases (Nincic, 1983; Cusack, 1981; Holloway, 1983). Attempts by these means to regulate economic growth and fluctuations in a neo-Keynesian spirit have been observed for the USA (Schmidt, 1974). More recent studies also shed light on a possible counter-cyclical effect of military expenditure in short-term Soviet economic fluctuations (Nincic, 1983). Even if, as seems to be the case, domestic factors chiefly govern military expenditure in the two countries, impacts on East–West relations cannot be neglected. These do not appear as one-to-one relations between arms programmes, strategic talks and trade negotiations. The matter is much more complicated. In terms of system analysis (see Deutsch, ch. 12 in this volume), one can observe certain sequences where the negative feedback loops dominate with regulating effects (as from 1970 to 1977) and other sequences dominated by positive feedback loops with cumulative impacts (as between 1978 and 1983). In short, arms and trade can be viewed as two simultaneous games, where the United States and the Soviet Union operate by reference to their own constraints and strategic designs. Weapons deployments in that perspective can be seen as signals in ceaseless debate, contributing to the non-war, non-peace state of current affairs.

Finally, the regional dynamics of non-arms-producing developing countries and the domestic dynamics of big industrial arms-producing powers are quite different. Arms transfers are the linkage between them. Arms imports to developing countries have grown faster than world military expenditures over the past fifteen years. According to the United States Arms Control and Disarmament Agency figures, the share of developing countries in world imports has risen from 71.5 to 81.9 percent. Over the same period, the USSR and the US have accounted for 65 to 70 percent of total world exports. These data must be interpreted very cautiously, but suggest the relative magnitude of transfers. Not only do such transfers induce macro-economic consequences, but they also have certain crucial influences on conflict evolution. In the Gulf War from 1981 arms supplying appears as a key variable to interpret action on the battlefield. Through their arm supplies, the Soviet Union, France and, more indirectly, the US try to control the continuing limited war between the two adversaries. But simultaneously, a complementary regional network has been set up, mainly via Libya, Syria and even Israel and the US, to support Iran on one side, Egypt and Saudi Arabia to support Iraq on the other, without taking into account the private flow of small arms and munitions.

In order to escape this dependency, many developing countries, such as Israel, India and the Republic of Korea, have built up national arms industries over the last twenty years. Unfortunately, by a perverse effect, the benefit expected in terms of political autonomy is often more than compensated for in the long run by increased economic dependency, especially through indebtedness.

Economic rationality and decision-making analysis for war and peace

To explain such economic phenomena as exchange and production from a rigorous analysis of individual behaviour is one of the main assumptions behind micro-economic theory. More precisely, one goal of micro-economic theory is to derive economic categories from a limited set of hypotheses about the logic of individual decisions. The same method can also be applied to the formal study of the logic of war. Rapoport, in his introduction to the masterly work of Clausewitz, identifies as the 'rational' prospect of war this underlying philosophy (Von Clausewitz, 1968: 13–15). The question of the extensions of economic definitions of rationality to conflicts and war is thus opened.

One of the first economists to be sensitive to this potential use of economic calculation is Edgeworth who wrote about it as early as 1882: 'Deferring controversy, let us glance at the elements of *economic calculus*; observing that the connotation (and some of the reasoning) extends beyond the usual denotation; to the political struggle for power as well as to the commercial struggle for wealth' (Edgeworth, 1967: 16). Such an extension of the economic calculus seems legitimate to Edgeworth via the principle of self-interested action as the key to economic rationality. In other words, in economics, the outcome of every action is to be assessed exclusively from the point of view of the decision-maker's interest. If economic competition is an example of conflicting interest between individuals or institutions such as firms and groups, the battlefield is another example of fighting resulting from the opposing interests of nations or peoples. If we grant an analytical separation between aggressiveness and violence (individual as well as collective), several features of economic rationality may contribute to a general logical approach to conflicts of interest.

Let us see what alternative principle could be substituted for self-interest to support a rational calculation. Edgeworth himself opposes the utilitarian calculus based on the principle of a 'maximum universal utility'. Utilitarian criteria are not the only way to take into account the interests of opposing parties and literature on welfare economics is rich in alternative formulations to justify collective economic decisions (Sen, 1982). Such principles also operate at a micro-level during negotiations in economic as well as in diplomatic arenas (Raiffa, 1982).

In order to focus on the main differences between these two kinds of social rationality, Edgeworth summarizes them in the following terms: 'The economical calculus investigates the equilibrium of a system of hedonic forces, each tending to maximum individual utility; the Utilitarian Calculus, the equilibrium of a system in which each and all tend to maximum universal utility' (Edgeworth, 1967: 15). As a first approximation, the individualistic assumption in traditional economic calculation might illuminate the logical background of conflicts and wars viewed as national conflicts of interests, while the social criteria of welfare calculations could improve the logical grounds of peace research viewed as the outcome of fair negotiation between competing national interests. But the question of relevance is indeed more complex.

The same situation can often be seen from two points of view, so perspectives are not mutually exclusive. Sometimes the result is the same, but more often it is different. A good illustration is a non-zero-sum game situation with only two decision-makers, for instance, a bilateral monopoly. According to purely individualistic rationality, a non-co-operative Nash game can lead to a logical solution based on the power of threats by one player *visà-vis* the other and the reverse, but according to the alternative assumption of collective rationality, the situation can also be modelled as a 'fair decision' problem. The first solution could be characterized as the result of a conflict-oriented rationality, the second could be seen as the outcome of a rationality of fair sharing. But there is no direct correspondence between these two categories and concepts of war and peace. Finally, in some cases these two kinds of rationality appear contradictory. One example is the well-known 'Prisoner's Dilemma' (see Eskola, ch. 2 in this volume); another is the logical impossibility of deriving a hypothetical aggregation procedure (Arrow, 1983).

A pure, economic-modelling approach to defence
To clarify the opportunities and limits of micro-economic calculation to improve understanding of wars, crises and international conflicts, it is appropriate to examine in greater detail what Schelling has called 'the strategy of inflecting cost' (Schelling, 1967). The first step requires the translation of the main elements of international conflicts of interest into the formal language of economic theory, to provide an explanation based on a subsequent cost analysis. In a recent one, it can be convenient to test this economic apparatus with some defence doctrines in order to formulate methodological suggestions for their evaluation.

Choices, preferences and expectations in the strategic domain. The economic decision-making approach uses three major tools, namely, a logical treatment of individual preferences, a quantitative evaluation of the state of affairs and a probabilistic calculation of risk.

Concerning preferences economists generally assume: (1) that each decision-maker has perfect knowledge of his own preferences; (2) that all individual preferences can be well ordered on a complete map; and (3) that well-ordered preferences defined as the set of every possible state of affairs suffices to choose one consistent path of action among the whole set of possible actions.

In international political matters, warfare (or armistice) decisions involve not a single person but several persons or services, for instance, ministries of defence, ministries of foreign affairs and heads of governments (presidents or prime ministers). All these players do not necessarily have the same preference system, and the preferences of countries often result from a bureaucratic bargaining process which can itself be analysed as 'a game within the game'. An interesting distinction can be introduced between pre-war situations, where a well-ordered preference system often need not be assumed, and a developing war situation, where the military staff dictates its preferences. Another aspect of this preference approach is the distance between the preferences of political authorities and those of the population at large. Many situations where international tensions uncovered and intensified these preference conflicts explain how international and domestic disputes are often closely interlinked. The Falkland/Malvinas War of 1982 pointed to this kind of opposition in Argentina. Finally, knowledge of the other's preference is not necessary for each economic player to enable him to choose consistent action according to point (3) above. But a rational choice on that basis implies the computation of too many strategic cases because of the high complexity of states of affairs. Furthermore numerous strategic doctrines, such as deterrence, necessarily refer to the preference system of others. Such strategic doctrines introduce fresh logical difficulties into the preference approach (i.e. the possibility of an infinite regression), in the determination of both preference systems (Schelling, 1960). But the preference approach also provides a fruitful analytical framework to study misperceptions which play such a crucial role in East–West tensions. The Cuban Missile Crisis of 1963 provides one of the most relevant examples of such perceptions and misperceptions with their consequences.

Is it possible to derive a utility function from these preferences? Weapons destroyed and human casualties seem to provide simple bases for the measurements to be applied in a theoretical economic model of war (Intriligator, 1967, 1976). But one must immediately note the tremendous differences between *ex ante* and *ex post* war-cost evaluations. Hence the assumption that the price of a war corresponds to its utility (or more precisely, its dis-utility) remains highly questionable. Correct economic empirical estimations of such recent international conflicts as the Falklands and the Gulf War are as yet very few. The linkage between acts and their consequences is not as easy to formalize as in the traditional economic domain. On the other hand, for many strategic doctrines, there is no need for a smooth function derived from preference relations, because their logical foundations are quite different and refer to an alternative, discontinuous schema (Schmidt, 1982). That is the case of nuclear deterrence doctrines, the logic of which is based on 'threshold values' corresponding to 'unacceptable casualties' or more precisely, what are supposed to be unacceptable casualties for the potential adversary, as perceived by the deterring side. But a correct formulation of the deterrence schema leads to a difficult problem of cross-expectations (Walliser, 1985). Mutually assured destruction's strategic situation thus provides an intuitive illustration of an infinite regression. Its solution requires mathematically sophisticated treatment in order to escape a logical paradox (definition of the convergence conditions).

Towards an economic evaluation of defence systems

At this stage, economic reasoning leads to a method to conduct a kind of cost-benefit analysis relevant to strategic purposes (Hitch and MacKean, 1960; Enthoven and Smith, 1971). The meaning of 'benefit' must be understood here as an expression of a 'security goal', which concretely corresponds to a no-casualties case. The key difficulty of finding a positive content for this definition is then related to the deterrence dimension of security. If such a problem is at the core of nuclear doctrines, it is really more or less contained in every strategic calculation. But its role becomes crucial with nuclear power owing to the magnitude of potential casualties.

Deterrence, by definition, cannot be directly tested. In other words, weapons never used, such as stockpiles of missiles, can only be assessed by reference to formal deterrence models, which are normative and purely hypothetical.[4] From a logical point of view, however, assuming that a set of a few reasonable conditions exists, a fruitful distinction can be proposed between a 'sure' deterrence strategy, where the damage threatened deters the adversary from attack under all circumstances, and an 'uncertain' one where the damage threatened is not sufficient to deter an attack, if the decision to wage war is based on grounds other than economic ones (grievances, retribution, etc.).

To scrutinize the tentative reaction of a country to the perception of increasing armament by an adversary, Schelling has proposed the distinction between a 'coercion' effect, which tends to start or to resume an international bargaining process, and a 'diversion' effect, which changes domestic resource allocations between military and non-military uses, or between alternative military options (for instance, first and second strikes). Their consequences for security are obviously quite different. Let us consider, for example, the Reagan military programmes and try to anticipate their final impact on US security according to (1) the quality of US deterrence itself and (2) induced reactions from the Soviet Union. The coercion effect here implies a resumption of strategic negotiation processes, while the diversion effect corresponds to change in strategic Soviet military options (defensive and/or offensive missile deployments). Economic calculation can here only provide a logical framework to explore the question, interests being given from outside.

Furthermore, there are two extreme kinds of deterrence. The first is offensive because it is based only on the threat of retaliation. The second is defensive because it is based on protection which rules out the relevance of the targets in a decision to attack. These two types of deterrence are not mutually exclusive and the second being only able to operate in combination with the first (i.e. the second-strike assumption). From Foster Dulles to James Schlesinger and Harold Brown, the nuclear deterrence debate has been mainly focused on the first type, specially during the 1970s, but Reagan's Strategic Defense Initiative (SDI) programme has now reopened scope for the second type. Viewed from an economic angle, the problem of deterrence evaluation becomes extremely difficult because these components of the US deterrence system do not refer to the same economic model and are hence hardly comparable in cost evaluation (the threat of billions of casualties on the one hand and the waste of billions of dollars on the other).

Finally, the efficiency of a defence system in terms of security can be pictured from the starting point of the relationship between defence investment and damage. If such a relationship is sufficiently well established, it becomes possible to compare this efficiency-measurement of defence to its economic cost in terms of monetary units. Economists now have some ideas about the general evolution of costs in the defence sector but, the precise shape of the efficiency curve of defence remains no more than purely conjectural (Olvey et al., 1984). Therefore, pure economic defence modelling can only be improved by information provided by political scientists and resulting from joint research programmes.

Concluding remarks: the meaning of economists' messages

Is war more suited to economic analysis than peace? Looking at the published studies the answer would certainly be yes. Except for some brilliant pamphlets (Galbraith, 1964) and several researches on military-to-civilian conversions (Olivier, 1967; Kaldor, 1980; Gleditsch et al., 1983), economic contributions to peace studies are relatively rare by comparison with contributions to war and international conflicts. This striking asymmetry is all the more surprising because many well-known economists involved in defence economics and conflict studies, such as Boulding and Isard, are also personally more or less active in intellectual peace movements.

To explain this paradoxical situation, one can identify certain common features between economics and conflicts as communication systems (social codes and communication decision-making processes) which do not immediately appear in the peace domain. Another reason can be found in the apparently zero price of peace versus the heavy price of war, which does not mean that peace must simply be taken for a free good. If defence is assumed to be the positive price of security, this argument is ruled out, but such an assumption remains questionable and requires a detailed discussion beyond the scope of this chapter.

Finally, the true topic for economic analysis is neither war nor peace but rather the dynamic of war preparation, which can be understood from an aggressive military point of view as well as from a cautious civilian one, according to non-economic considerations. Therefore the semantic content of economists' messages in these fields should be reinterpreted by the other social science disciplines.

Notes

1. With the participation of Cole, Einzig and Durbin.
2. The use of economic concepts as a background for military strategies can be

observed in the USA during Robert McNamara's period as Secretary of Defense. The influence of C. J. Hitch and T. C. Schelling on American doctrines provides an illustration of such positive consequences of normative economics in those fields. For a critical evaluation, see Brewer and Shubik (1979).

   3. Such a distinction was extensively developed by G. Bouthoul's team at the Institut Français de polémologie.

   4. From a Popperian point of view, the absence of war between nuclear powers does not prove that deterrence calculation is correct, but only shows that its falsity is not demonstrated. More precisely, the deterrence statement can only be indirectly falsified.

References

Arrow, K. J. (1983) *Social Choice and Justice*. Cambridge.

Ball, N. (1984) *The War Security: A Statistical Compendium*. London.

Boston Consulting Group (1979) *The Price of Defense*. New York.

Boulding, K. E. (1962) *Conflict and Defense*. New York.

Brewer, G. D. and Shubik, M. (1979) *The War Game: a Critique of Military Problem Solving*. Cambridge: Harvard University Press.

Brito, D. L. (1972) 'A Dynamic Model of an Armament Race', *International Economic Review* 13.

Brito, D. L. and Intriligator, M. D. (1987) 'Arms Races and the Outbreak of War: Applications of Principal Agent Relationships', in Schmidt and Blackhaby (1987).

Brody, A. (1987) 'Defense Spending as a Priority', in Schmidt and Blackhaby (1987).

Cusack, T. R. (1981) 'Military Spending in the United States, the Soviet Union and the People's Republic of China', *Journal of Conflict Resolution* 25(2).

Daeger, S. (1986) *Military Expenditure in Third World Countries*. London: Routledge and Kegan Paul.

Despree, L. (1985) 'Les ventes d'armes et la coopération militaire entre l'U.R.S.S., les pays socialistes européens et les pays en voie de développement', Paris, mimeo.

Dussauge, P. (1986) *L'industrie Française d'armement*. Paris.

Edgeworth, F. Y. (1967) *Mathematical Psychics*. London. (Originally published 1882.)

Einzig, P. (1934) *The Economics of Armament*. London.

Enthoven, A. and Smith, K. W. (1971) *How Much is Enough? Shaping the Defense Program, 1961–1969*. New York.

Fontanel, J. (1982) *Military Expenditures and Economic Growth*, New York: UN.

Fox, J. R. (1974) *Arming America: How the U.S. Buys Weapons*. Cambridge.

Galbraith, J. K. (1964) *The Report of Iron Mountain*, preface.

Galbraith, J. K. (1969) *How to Control the Military*. New York.

Gansler, J. S. (1980) *The Defense Industry*. Cambridge.

Gleditsch, N. P., Bjerkholt, O. and Cappelen, A. (1983) 'Conversion: Global and National Efforts', *Cooperation and Conflict* 18.

Gregory, P. R. (1974) 'Economic Growth, U.S. Defense Expenditures and the Soviet Defense Budget: A Suggested Model', *Soviet Studies*, 26.

Grindle, M. C. (1984) 'Civil–Military Relations and Budgetary Politics in Latin America', mimeo.

Hirst, F. W. (1914) *The Political Economy of War*. London.

Hitch, C. J. and MacKean, R. N. (1960) *The Economics of Defense in the Nuclear Age*. Santa Monica.

Holloway, D. (1983) *The Soviet Union and the Arms Race*. London.

Hume, D. (1752) *Essays and Treatises on Several Subjects*. Edinburgh.

Intriligator, M. D. (1967) 'Strategy in a Missile War', Los Angeles, UCLA, mimeo.

Intriligator, M. D. (1976) 'Strategic Considerations in the Richardson Model of the Arms Race', *Journal of Political Economy* 83.

Intriligator, M. D. and Brito, D. L. (1976) 'Formal Models of Arms Races', *Journal of Peace Science* 2.

Kaldor, M. (1980) 'Technical Change in the Defense Industry', in *Technical Innovation and British Economic Performance*. London.

Keynes, J. M. (1936) *The General Theory of Employment, Interest and Money*. London.

Keynes, J. M. (1939–40) *How to Pay for the War*. London.

Lambelet, J. C. (1975) 'Do Arms Races Lead to War?', *Journal of Peace Research* 12.

Lambelet, J. C. and Luterbacher, U. (1979) 'Dynamics of Arms Races: Mutual Stimulations vs. Self-Stimulation', *Journal of Peace Science* 4.

Lambelet, J. C. and Luterbacher, U. (1987) 'Conflicts, Arms Races and War: a Synthetical Approach', in Schmidt and Blackhaby (1987).

Leontief, W. and Duchin, N. (1983) *Military Spending: Facts and Figures, Worldwide Implications and Future Outlook*. Oxford.

MacCulloch, J. R. (1863) *Treatise on Taxation*, 3rd edn. London.

Maizels, A. and Nissanke, M. K. (1984) 'The Determinants of the Military in Developing Countries', mimeo.

Majeski, S. J. and Jones, D. L. (1981) 'Arms Race Modeling, Causality and Model Specification', *Journal of Conflict Resolution* 2.

Melman, S. (1971) *The War Economy of the United States: Readings in Military Industry and Economy*. New York.

Melman, S. (1975) *The Permanent War Economy*. New York.

Morgenstern, O. (1948) 'Demand Theory Reconsidered', *Quarterly Journal of Economics*, February.

Mill. J. S. (1967) 'War Expenditure', in *Collected Works*, Vol. IV. Toronto. (Originally published 1824.)

Neuman, S. G. (1985) 'Offsets in the International Arms Market', in *World Military Expenditures and Arms Transfers*. Arms Control and Disarmament Agency.

Neuman, S. G. and Harkavy, R. E. (1979) *Arms Transfers in the Modern World*. New York.

Nincic, N. (1983) 'Fluctuations in Soviet Defense Spending: a Research Note', *Journal of Conflict Resolution*, December.

Olivier, O. R. (1967) 'Employment Effects of Reduced Defense Expenditures', *Monthly Labor Review*, September.

Olvey, L. D., Golden, J. R. and Kelley, R. C. (1984) *The Economics of National Security*. New Jersey.

Ostrom, C. (1978) 'A Reactive Linkage Model of the U.S. Defense Expenditure Policy Making Process', *American Political Science Review* 72.

Peck, M. J. and Sherer, F. M. (1962) *The Weapons Acquisition Process and Economic Analaysis*. Boston.

Pilandon, L. (1982) 'Rapport Dépenses Militaires Développement économique à partir de quelques corrélations économétriques', *Revue d'Economie Politique* 4.

Pryor, F. (1968) *Public Expenditures in Communist and Capitalist Countries*. London.

Raiffa, H. (1982) *The Art and Science of Negotiation*. Cambridge.

Rattinger, T. H. (1975) 'Armaments, Détente and Bureaucracy: the Case of the Arms in Europe', *Journal of Conflict Resolution* 19(1).

Rattinger, T. H. (1976) 'Econometrics and Arms Races: a Critical Review and Some Extensions', *European Journal of Political Research* 9.

Russett, B. (1969) 'Who Pays for Defense?', *American Political Science Review* 2.

Russett, B. (1970) *What Price Vigilance? The Burdens of National Defense*. New Haven.

Russett, B. (1982) 'Defense and National Well Being: Vigilance and Ignorance', *American Political Science Review* 76.

Samuelson, P. A. (1958) *Collected Scientific Papers*, Vol. II. Boston: MIT Press.

Sandler, T. (1977) 'Impurity in Defence: an Application to the Economics of Alliances', *Kyklos* 30(3).

Schelling, T. C. (1960) *The Strategy of Conflict*. Cambridge.

Schelling, T. C. (1967) 'The Strategy of Inflecting Costs', in R. N. MacKean (ed.) *Issues in Defense Economics*. New York.

Schmidt, C. (1974) 'Guerre et Economie', *Etudes Polémologiques* 14, October.

Schmidt, C. (1982) 'Logique de la décision économique, logique de la dissuasion nucléaire', *Revue d'Economie Politique* 3, July/August.

Schmidt, C. (1984) 'Depenses militaires industries d'armement et endettement du Tiers Monde', *Revue Défense Nationale*, December.

Schmidt, C. (ed.) (1986) *Military Expenditures, Economic Growth and Fluctuations*. London.

Schmidt, C. and Blackhaby, F. (eds) (1987) *Peace, Defense and Economic Analysis*. London.

Sen, A. K. (1982) *Choice, Welfare and Measurement*. London.

Shubik, M. (1959) *Strategy and Market Structure*. New York.

Shubik, M. (1983) *Mathematics and Conflict*. Amsterdam.

Simaan, M. and Cruz, J. B. (1975) 'Formulation of Richardson's Model of the Arms Race from a Differential Game Point of View', *Review of Economic Studies* 42.

Smith, A. (1976) *An Inquiry into the Nature and Causes of the Wealth of Nations*, Vols I, II (edited by Cambell and Skinner), London.

Smith, D. and Smith, R. (1980) 'British Military Expenditure in 1980's', in Thompson and Smith (eds) *Protest and Survive*. Harmondsworth: Penguin.

Smith, R. (1977) 'Military Expenditures and Capitalism', *Cambridge Journal of Economics*, September.

Smith, R. (1980) 'Military Expenditures and Investment in O.E.C.D. Countries 1954/1973', *Journal of Comparative Economics*, March.

Tullberg, R. (1986) 'Military Related Debt in Non Oil Developing Countries 1972/1982', in *SIPRI Year Book*. London.

Von Clausewitz, Carl (1968) *On War* (edited and with an introduction by A. Rapoport). Harmondsworth: Penguin.

Walliser, B. (1985) *Anticipations équilibres et rationalité économique*. Paris.

Wulf, H. (1983) 'Developing Countries', in N. Ball and M. Leitenberg, *The Structure of Defense Industry*. London.

PART V

Inequality and Violence:
Regional and Global Perspectives

15

The Geography of Violence and Premature Death: A World-Systems Approach

R. J. Johnston, J. O'Loughlin and P. J. Taylor

As with all other human and societal phenomena, violence is not equally distributed across the earth's surface, whatever criterion one uses to define the norm against which the empirical distribution is to be compared. The goal of the present essay is to provide a tentative explanation for the unequal distribution. This is done by using the world-systems approach developed by Immanuel Wallerstein (see Wallerstein, 1979; Taylor, 1985, 1986) as the framework for analysis. Within it, two types of violence are studied – structural and behavioural. In this way, the causes of violence will be situated in their root causes, which we identify as the structure of the global world-economy, rather than in their proximate origins, which is the goal of many other studies but which we view as the context.

Geography and the capitalist world-economy

The world today comprises a single economic system, the capitalist world-economy, which is global in its coverage and universal in its impact. This has evolved over a period of some 400 years, and has been successively regional, international and global in its scope.

The key feature of the capitalist world-economy is its basis in the circulation of capital. It is driven by the desire to accumulate wealth, which can only be met through the selling of commodities (goods and services) for more than they cost to produce; wealth is accumulated from the difference between the cost of production and the selling price. Initially, in the era sometimes referred to as mercantile capitalism, it was in the sphere of exchange that wealth was chiefly accumulated. This economy soon developed into an agro-industrial production system, in which the goal of accumulation was pursued directly in the sphere of production as well as exchange. Capital – the results of prior rounds of accumulation – was invested in production, through the purchase of both the needed materials and labour; the output was sold to yield a profit, to increase the investors' stock of wealth, thereby providing capital for the next round of investment. Increasingly the investment capital needed involved the development of financial institutions which aggregated individual capital holdings, in that way providing sufficient for further investment. Thus there are two types of capital – financial and industrial – and each is invested in the production of commodities to advance the wealth holdings of those with capital.

A full presentation of the operations of the global capitalist world-economy is beyond the scope of this chapter. (Harvey (1982) provides a detailed treatment, and in a later essay (1985) he identifies ten 'core features'.) For the present purpose, three features of its operation are of particular importance.

1. Global capitalism is predicated upon a class relation. Basically this relation involves two separate groups implicated in the buying and selling of labour. The first group, the buyers, use capital to purchase labour-power in order to produce commodities and to accumulate wealth. The second, the sellers, offer their labour-power to the buyers in order to obtain an income, with which to purchase the means of survival (or reproduction). Many people are now in a strict sense both buyers and sellers, since some of the latter invest part of their 'surplus income', through financial institutions, in the search for wealth. But the great majority of the world's population are sellers only (or are the dependants of sellers). Their relative prosperity is a function of how successful they are in conflict with the buyers over the returns that they receive; in the final analysis, they are at the mercy of the buyers to a greater extent than the buyers are at the mercy of the sellers. Here, we will generally present a simplified view of the class structure of the capitalist world-economy as divided into a dominant class (buyers plus their political agents) and a dominated class (sellers of labour plus their dependants).

2. The process of development is spatially uneven. In most analyses of capitalism, development is equated with increasing levels of production and consumption, which in turn are predicated on increasing levels of wealth; if profits were not forthcoming, commodities would not be produced and made available for production. Profits are only made, and wealth accumulated, through what is termed exploitation of labour: the buyers (the capitalists) obtain their wealth at the expense of the sellers (labour), who receive only a proportion of the wealth that they create. Thus development is uneven, since some (a minority) benefit much more than others (a majority).

Such uneven development, according to Harvey, Massey (1984), Smith (1984), and others, is necessarily spatial: some places benefit more than others because profits expropriated from labour in one place are taken elsewhere to form the basis for consumption and further rounds of investment, which may be placed somewhere else again. This spatial structure produces what several analysts have identified as *a core–periphery pattern of spatial organization*. The focus of that organization, and the locus of power within it, is the core, that is, relatively prosperous areas characterized today by high wages, advanced technology and a diversity of economic activities (Taylor, 1985). Opposed to it is the periphery, where wages are relatively low, technology is more rudimentary and activities are much more specialized. Between the two is the semi-periphery, which has no particular characteristics but combines elements of core and periphery; according to Wallerstein it is the dynamic area of the world-economy, where restructuring is most active during the periods of recession discussed below.

It is common to map this core–periphery structure in terms of the individual states so that, for example, most countries of north-western Europe, plus North America and Japan, are allocated to the core, much of Africa, Asia and Latin America to the periphery, and others – such as several southern European countries and Brazil – to the semi-periphery. But Wallerstein argues strongly against such an over-simplification. The core–periphery model is one of a process built on class relations: as Taylor expresses it,

> areas, regions or states. . . only become core-like because of a predominance of core *processes* operating [there]. . . . Space itself can be neither core nor periphery in nature. Rather there are core and periphery processes which structure space so that at any point in time one or other of the two processes predominate. (Taylor, 1985: 16–17, orginal emphasis)

Thus a country can contain both core areas and periphery areas (as argued by Hechter (1975) in his thesis on internal colonialism), and also a semi-periphery, an area of active restructuring. And individual places, too, can reflect uneven spatial development, as the social geography of many large cities clearly demonstrates (see Coates et al., 1977).

3. *Capitalism is inherently unstable*, because it contains within it the seeds of its own destruction: the processes which are used to increase profits and stimulate accumulation lead eventually to the decline of profits and an end to accumulation, because of problems of overproduction (or under-consumption). This instability leads to crises which are solved by the devalorization of investments and restructuring. Major crises occur approximately every fifty years according to most empirical analyses (these fifty-year cycles are widely known as Kondratieff cycles), and these are the periods of major restructuring. Frequently, though not necessarily, such restructuring involves a spatial restructuring, as the core processes become dominant in a new set of places.

States and the world-economy

The capitalist world-economy involves a single market, organized and controlled from the core which develops (i.e. accumulates wealth) by exploiting the periphery. Occasionally, major crises in the operation of that market in the buying and selling of commodities lead to a substantial restructuring, which can involve the emergence of a new core-zone which had risen to that position through the semi-periphery.

The operation of that world-economy requires the existence of a state, a necessary institution for the regulation of the multiplicity of operations that drive capitalism (Johnston, 1984a). States are not simply dependent on capitalism. They are to some extent autonomous from it, and the source of that autonomy, according to Mann (1984), lies in the fact that the state is necessarily a place, a bounded territorial unit (Johnston, 1986). States, in Harvey's (1985) term, are regional alliances, local coalitions of either capitalists or labour or both which seek to advance their interests against those of other states. Thus those who operate states seek to distort the operations of the global market, and the competition between sellers for shares of that market becomes a competition between states.

States, as already noted, are not to be equated with the core/semi-periphery/periphery structuring of the global world-economy; they can contain elements of all three, and indeed most do, in differing proportions. Thus the conflict between core and periphery, between the dominant and the dominated class, is both interstate and intra-state. In many cases, the latter is enhanced because the class relations of core and periphery are linked to other aspects of the population structure, such as ethnic, linguistic and religious differences. The pattern of states, a system of territorial containers (Giddens, 1985), is almost never spatially coincident with the pattern of nations, a system of groups created around common racial, linguistic, historical or other ties and frequently associated with a territory. (The exception is Iceland.) Exploitation of one nation (or a majority of it) by another is a source of conflict, which may be intra-state if the territory accumulated by a state covers that (or part of that) of two or more nations.

One final aspect of the pattern of states at the present time concerns those usually termed the 'socialist states'. Opinion differs as to whether these should be considered as part of the global capitalist world-economy or separate from it (see Chase-Dunn, 1982). Ideologically, they are separate, for their goal is to replace capitalism by communism, via socialism. Empirically, however, they are increasingly a part of the global capitalist system (see Johnston, 1982), because they have been unable to solve the problems of production, which should form the basis for a successful socialist economy, without imports of capital and commodities and exports of commodities.

Violence and premature death

The usual dictionary definition of violence refers to the use of physical force leading, in a human context, to damage and, possibly, premature death. In its turn, premature death refers to the cessation of life earlier than the individual concerned could anticipate on the basis of existing norms. Thus, if the average life expectancy is 50 years, a person who lives for only 35 dies prematurely; the premature death may be brought about by physical violence or it may have been the result of other forces external to the individual concerned. Those two causes of premature death are presented here as the results of behavioural and structural violence.

(This separation was suggested by Galtung (1969) and developed by Galtung and Høivik (1971).)

Behavioural violence leading to premature death refers to aggressive acts against the person, intended to cause physical injury, if not death. Three types of behavioural violence can be identified:

1. *Personal behavioural violence*, in which the victim is known to the aggressor and the attack is usually the outcome of either a disagreement or a desire to discipline. Death may not be intended, but injury is; the result is termed either murder or man-slaughter.

2. *Property-related behavioural violence*, in which the violence is part of a process of removing something from the victim. In many cases, death is not intended, and is a by-product of violence employed to advance the theft.

3. *Politically-related behavioural violence*, in which the violence is an integral part of a political campaign. It may be directed against particular individuals, as in some terrorist activities; it may affect individuals simply because they happen to be at a certain place at a given time, rather than because of who or what they are; and it may be aimed at a large number of individuals – usually all those in a particular place. The last is clearly a characteristic of acts of interstate aggression and war.

The first two of these types are usually related to the inequalities created by the processes of uneven development, and the frustrations that they engender: many are intra-periphery (or dominated class), especially those of the first type; some involve core–periphery (or dominant–dominated) relations, mainly in the second type. The third type involves large numbers of people, and is almost invariably the product of state action.

Structural violence leading to premature death is not the consequence of direct aggression against the individual but is rather the outcome (necessary according to most analyses) of the processes of uneven development that are inherent to capitalism. (Kohler and Alcock (1976: 343) write that 'whenever persons are harmed, maimed or killed by poverty and unjust social, political and economic institutions, systems, or structures, we speak of structural violence'.) Through those processes, the average life-expectancy of members of the core exceeds that of those in the periphery because of the processes of expropriation. As a result of the conditions (environmental and otherwise) in which they work and live, the level of their wages relative to the costs of necessities such as food, clothing and shelter, and of inequalities in the provision of utilities (such as clean water, heating, removal of sewerage and garbage) and facilities (particularly health care), members of the periphery are exposed to more hazardous conditions and are likely to suffer greater morbidity and earlier mortality than are members of the core, who are relatively much better provided for.

The extent of structural violence reflects the levels of mortality in every place relative to the most favoured, which is the norm. Thus, if the average life-expectancy in the favoured place is 75 years, then where it is only 45 each person is being denied 30 years of life by the operation of an unequal system. Multiplied by the number of individuals involved (i.e. the population of the relatively deprived place), this gives the total amount of structural violence over any period – the number of years of life lost.

These four types of violence leading to premature death – three types of behavioural violence plus structural violence – are all related in their spatial distributions to the geography of the global capitalist world-economy. Elucidating and evaluating those relationships is the function of the next section of this chapter.

The geography of politically-related behavioural violence
States, as argued above, are necessary territorial units within the global market of the capitalist world-economy. One of their basic roles is to promote accumulation of wealth (Taylor and Johnston, 1984), not accumulation in general but accumulation by local capital in particular. For this, the relevant state apparatus (Clark and Dear, 1984) must ensure social cohesion within the state's territory, which involves legitimating the capitalist mode of production. It must also invest in providing the infrastructure within which accumulation strategies can prosper, and in the reproduction of a labour-force fitted to undertake the production and consumption of commodities.

Capitalism, as already stressed, is a global system, so that these strategies, and especially that involving the provision of an infrastructure for accumulation, involve policies relating to areas outside the state's own territory. The state must promote the pursuit of profit wherever it may be sought, through actions that advance the interests of local capital. A wide range of actions is possible. In the past, colonialism and imperialism have been common, whereby the territories of other states have been dominated in order to advance the search for cheap materials and labour and the expansion of markets. (Such states were frequently created, removing earlier state forms, in order to advance such goals.) Today, those strategies are rare and they have been replaced by neocolonialism and neo-imperialism, which seek the same goal but without the imposition of direct rule; the relevant states are subordinated but allowed the empirical appearance of autonomy.

A successful core-area requires a periphery, an underdeveloped aureole to sustain the privileged centre. That periphery may involve areas within a single state, or, more likely, it can involve parts of several or many states. Both involve geopolitical strategies, the expansion of the core's sphere of influence. They require the subjugation of the peripheral population, which could be achieved without any explicit display and/or use of political force, but rarely has been or is. Maintenance of that subjugation is an increasing cost to the core-state, which as a result finds its position in the world-economy increasingly threatened. Other states are promoting the productive, commercial and financial activities of their cores (O'Loughlin, 1986a), and to counter this the state with the extensive periphery must act to protect its interests by investing in restructuring. But its ability to invest in this way is limited by its high level of spending on subjugation; insufficient capital is available to spend on restructuring to counter the new competition. Hence, as Taylor (1985) argues, Kondratieff cycles can be associated with eras of economic hegemony for particular core-states; any one state's hegemony is associated with a pair of Kondratieff cycles (Britain was the hegemonic state in the first two pairs and the USA in the second, with its hegemony now in decline), so that the geography of the world-economy provides a framework for understanding global geopolitics (Parker, 1985). (Note that Modelski (1978) has proposed an alternative model of cycles of hegemonic power, based not on Kondratieff cycles but on long cycles each of about 100 years; each of his 'centuries' has been dominated by a single power, successively Portugal, the Netherlands, Britain, Britain again, and the United States.)

Such geopolitical models set the foreign-relations role of the state in the context of the operations of the global world-economy. The exploitative interstate relationships between core and periphery necessarily require various forms of military action by the state, thus producing a variety of foci of politically-induced behavioural violence. These models involve states challenging for hegemony within the global system. At the present time, that process is extended by the development of a further geopolitical core (a superpower in the usual parlance) based in the USSR, which Taylor situates in the economic semi-periphery. Thus there are two major areas of conflict: the various states in the core compete in the periphery (this is often termed the North–South division); and the two superpowers (the East–West conflict) compete for political hegemony, with each superpower having a bloc of allied states, plus a third (largely, though not exclusively, in the periphery) bloc occupying 'non-aligned' positions. This twin division (North–South and East–West) of the world provides the matrix within which politically-induced behavioural violence occurs.

Most of this violence occurs in situations usually referred to as conditions of *war*. According to Ardrey (1969: 361) war 'has been the most successful of all our cultural traditions' because it fulfils all three of the basic human needs that he identifies – for identity, stimulation, and security. Each is linked to territoriality, the need for spatial expression of self and society. If, as it can be deduced from his writings, plus those of others such as Black (1975), Mann (1984) and Sack (1983), territoriality is necessary to human life, the state (or the rule of law in Black's terms) is similarly necessary, and since the state is necessarily a territorial strategy, then war, as the expression of contests over territory, appears necessary to human societies. In the present context, that necessity is firmly linked to the need for territorial strategies in the creation and maintenance of cores and peripheries in the world-economy. For geopolitics, therefore, war and its associated violence are usually the products of economic competition. (States are autonomous actors within the capitalist framework (Mann, 1984) and they may embark upon wars that have no proximate economic rationale.) Our focus, then, is on the 'where' of this activity, not in the absolute sense of where on the face of the earth but rather in the relational sense of where within the core–periphery spatial structure and the dominant–dominated class system. To this end, we have identified eight types of politically-induced behavioural violence (see Figure 1).

1. Frontier violence involving extending world-systems, when states already in the global capitalist system seek to extend the territory that they control or possess, as in the initial Iberian expansion into America and the extension of the frontiers of the United States into Indian territories. One state is claiming the land that is occupied, though not claimed in the sense of state-sovereignty, by a non-state group. That state may be part of the core, but not necessarily so – as with the eastward extension of the USSR and the extension of Brazilian control into the Amazon basin.

2. Imperialist violence involving the extension of the core's spheres of influence, as in the many processes of colonialism and imperialism that have characterized world history. A core-state comes into conflict with a peripheral nation-state that it wishes to subjugate. Occasionally, two core-states may be in competition, as recently in the Horn of Africa (O'Loughlin, 1986a). At the present time, most of such conflicts are being played out at some distance from the core-states, in parts of Africa, Latin America and South-East Asia, but in the past they have been much more local, as in the British conquest of Ireland; in either case, they provide the context for further violence, as discussed in the following types.

3. Colonial violence involving the maintenance of spheres of influence, when people in peripheral countries seek to overthrow the hegemony of the core. The long issue of the 'Irish question' in British nineteenth- and twentieth-century history vividly illustrates this, as do the 'invited invasions' of Hungary in 1956 and Czechoslovakia in 1968 by the USSR. Basically, these are repressions of anti-colonial rebellions, which are being 'put down' by core-force. They usually involve indigenous activity against external occupation, but can – as in the Falklands/Malvinas War of 1982 – be stimulated by a third party which wishes to oust the occupants from territory that it lays claim to.

4. Neocolonial violence involving the support of 'puppet regimes', whereby the core-countries act to keep friendly governments in power and, where it is perceived necessary, to oust those considered unfriendly. Such action can range from covert destabilization activity (as in the US efforts to overthrow the mildly socialist government of Michael Manley in Jamaica by creating a climate of violence that led to electoral defeat), which may be followed by armed assistance for a coup (as in the overthrow of Salvador Allende in Chile), through overt military aid to insurgents (as

FIGURE 1

Politically-induced behavioural violence in the world economy: a model of eight types

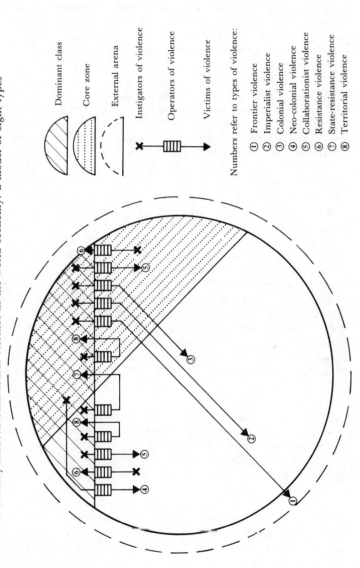

in Nicaragua at present), to direct military incursions (such as the US invasion of Grenada in 1983).

5. *Collaborationist violence involving state repression*, largely involving elimination of national dominated-class institutions (such as trades unions) and collaboration with international dominant-class institutions (e.g. multinational corporations); some recent Latin American dictatorships are classic examples of the purveyors of this type of violence (Harman, 1982).

6. *Resistance violence*, representing class antagonisms within an individual country and usually focused on the government (the core) and its associates. Such violence may involve long-term low levels of guerrilla activity (as with the Tupamaros in Uruguay and similar groups in other Latin American countries), which sometimes erupts into major episodes, as in Uganda, Sri Lanka and, especially, South Africa at the present time. The state may react by using violence, as with the actions of the Argentinian government in the late 1970s.

7. *State-resistance violence involving anti-core activity, often through terrorism*, by which states in the periphery attack those of the core within their own territories; in 1986, such activity was associated by the states of the Western core (focused on the USA) with the governments of Libya and Syria, and led to reprisals against the former.

8. *Territorial violence* usually reflecting dissatisfaction with the outcome of previous conflicts. Many of these disputes are minor, and only rarely are elevated so that violence ensues (as with the Argentina–Chile border disputes); the present Gulf War between Iran and Iraq – focused on the Shatt al 'Arab – is an excellent example of territorial violence. They are especially characteristic of post-colonial situations, as in Africa, where newly-established states are seeking to obtain territory (often on dubious grounds), thereby boosting both their resource base and their charisma. A few are both long-established and frequently characterized by violence, with the conflict between Israel and its neighbours being the most obvious example.

Over the last forty years, most of the violence in the world associated with these eight types has occurred in the periphery of the global world-economy, as the maps produced by Kidron and Smith (1983) indicate; indeed, war seems to be endemic outside the core according to their maps. (Figure 2 shows the number of deaths in a single year.) The vast majority have been limited in both time and extent, producing relatively few casualties (the exceptions have been the wars in Korea, Vietnam and the Gulf), although their number has been so substantial that the total sum of casualties is far from insignificant. The main exception to this has been violence of the eighth type, for nationalist movements involving physical violence are typical of many core-countries, in Europe at least, as well as those of the periphery (Kidron and Smith, 1983). In many cases, such intra-core violence is interpreted as periphery–core at the national scale, but this is not necessarily the case, as the examples of Belgium and Catalonia indicate (Williams, 1980).

Attempts to explain this geography of violence have focused on models of interstate conflict, and therefore exclude both intra-state (types 5 and 6 above) and those involving 'third party' states (types 1–4). Most use geography as a basic predictor variable, producing a one-dimensional view of international relations (see O'Loughlin, 1986b); thus one concludes (according to O'Loughlin, 1984: 212–13) that 'borders are an attribute, borders produce contact, contact generates conflict, conflict leads to international violence'. Such oversimplification is readily discredited – Switzerland has borders with four countries, for example, the same as Israel. All we can argue here is that the core–periphery structure of the global world-economy, divided as it is into a multitude of states and many more nations, provides a context within which violence is not infrequent; how and why that violence comes about reflects individual acts at particular times, set in their spatial and historical contexts as they are interpreted.

The geography of personal and property violence

Violence against the person, either directly or indirectly as part of an assault on property, is generally considered a criminal activity, although in many circumstances crimes involving property are punished more severely (i.e. by larger fines and longer prison sentences) than are crimes against the person. (The exceptions are murder and, increasingly, rape and other sexual assaults.) Most studies show that there is a geography of such crimes but, as a debate showed (Harries, 1975, 1976; Peet, 1975, 1976), much of the research conducted is concerned with the proximate causes of crime rather than its origins. For example, Haynes (1973) has shown that in the United States the larger the city and the greater the population density the greater the crime rate, and Newman (1973), Coleman (1985) and others have related the details of urban design to various aspects of criminal activity. Such studies imply an environmental causation, that particular situations produce crime rather than, as we would argue, provide the context within which it is easier to commit crimes than it is in others.

Most analyses of criminality within a country show that crimes of violence are much more likely to be committed by people in the lower income groups, who have uninteresting jobs, less secure employment, and poorer housing conditions, than those who are more prosperous. They are trapped in a cycle of poverty (Johnston, 1984b), the frustrations of which can lead to crimes of personal violence. They are more likely to be predisposed to crime, hence the correlations with housing and other conditions, which are also part of the cycle of poverty. Since those in that cycle are in dominated rather than dominant classes, and since the processes of distancing and housing-market manipulation produce spatial segregation of such people into particular regions and residential districts of cities (Johnston, 1984b), the geography of crimes of violence usually

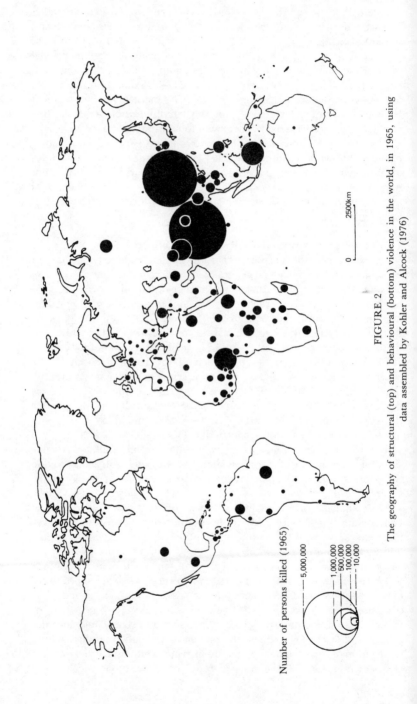

FIGURE 2

The geography of structural (top) and behavioural (bottom) violence in the world, in 1965, using data assembled by Kohler and Alcock (1976)

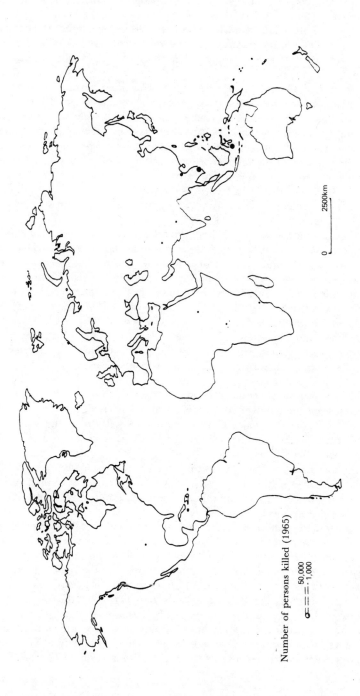

Number of persons killed (1965)

o — 50,000
o = = — 1,000

correlates closely with that of the geography of inequality within countries and cities (Smith, 1979).

Although there is a clear correlation between the geography of the class structure and the geography of these two types of behavioural violence, that correlation does not imply a deterministic link. People are put in a situation where violence may be a consequence, but it is not a necessary consequence. Other factors intervene, such as those relating to environmental opportunities and encouragements (see Baldwin and Bottoms, 1976). Further, there are important cultural variations which are reflected in the geography of crime, since culture is very much a place-bound phenomenon. In some cultures, crimes of violence are common; exposure to them is part of the process of socialization which leads to their continued commission. In other cultures, such crimes are rare and social controls restrict their occurrence. Again, because there is a geography of culture so there tends also to be a geography of criminality (as Harries (1974) suggests).

The class model employed here provides insights to the geography of personal violence, therefore, because those in the dominated class are more likely to commit such crimes and they are spatially separated, at a variety of scales. This does not mean either than no such crimes are committed by residents of dominant classes or that dominated-class areas are necessarily associated with high crime rates. Other social, cultural and environmental factors are involved too, so that the model provides a partial understanding only. Nevertheless, in its broad outlines the geography of violent crimes against the person is a clear consequence of the spatial structuring of the capitalist class system.

The geography of structural violence
Apart from the relatively brief periods of major wars (such as 1914–18 and 1939–45) the major cause of premature death in the world is structural violence, as Figure 2 makes very clear. It comes about because of inequalities in diet, environmental conditions and health care, and results in many millions of deaths annually. Occasionally, as with the major famines of the early 1980s in Africa, it reaches very high levels and becomes a focus of international attention and activity. But these are only peaks on a very high plateau.

Most discussions of structural violence are phrased at the international scale and use countries as the units of analysis, if for no other reason than that data (albeit crude) are readily available. Two indices are frequently used – the life-expectancy of a child at birth and the infant mortality rate. Both show the same pattern: life-expectancy is lowest, and infant mortality highest, in the countries of the periphery, with the converse for those of the core. For life-expectancy, the extreme rates vary by a factor between two and three; for infant mortality, the factor is closer to four.

Two factors are related to this pattern – the availability of food (see Grigg, 1985) and of health care (Smith, 1979; Harrison, 1979). The first reflects population pressure on the environment, but not entirely, since many areas where the majority of the population suffer malnutrition leading to premature death are not necessarily areas of food deficit in what they do or could produce. The problem, as Bradley (1986) makes clear, lies not so much in the environmental base for food production as in its social organization. Increasingly, agriculture in the periphery has been incorporated into the capitalist sytem, which is organized to produce commodities that can be sold at a profit (usually in the core) not to meet local food needs. Cash crops of little nutritional value locally replace subsistence crops – as was the case in Ireland in the early nineteenth century, leading to the widespread famine during the failure of the staple food crop (the potato) at a time of good harvests for the export staple (wheat). Thus structural violence resulting from food shortages is frequently a consequence of the organization of agriculture in the periphery rather than the inability of the land there to support its population (Watts, 1985) – although many of the commercial agricultural practices also lead to environmental deterioration and declining fertility (Blaikie, 1986).

Health care in a capitalist society is a commodity that must be bought, either directly (as in the United States and France) or indirectly – through taxation – in countries with substantial welfare state provision (as in New Zealand). In general, then, the more prosperous the country the greater its ability to afford health care, and the greater the likelihood that people will be trained for it as an occupation that will yield a substantial income. Thus the dominant class is not only better fed, because it can exploit food from the dominated; it is also better cared for, using the benefits of that expropriation to buy care and longevity (or the possibility of). Attempts have been made to remove some of the inequality that results, by the provision of better services, in part out of altruism and in part out of self-interest – a healthier work-force in the periphery is more exploitable and, perhaps, less ready to resist exploitation (because it is being 'given' equality, or so it seems). But these attempts are often counter-productive in that better care, by reducing infant mortality rates, for example, leads to a larger population putting greater demands on the agricultural system for food which it is not organized to provide. As a consequence, at the international scale, the core encourages birth control in the periphery as a way of reducing such demands, a policy that is increasingly mistrusted in the periphery as a manifestation of the core's control.

The geography of uneven development at national and local scales is also related to variations in structural violence. This was clearly demonstrated by Bunge, for example, who mapped infant mortality rates in the various parts of Detroit in 1969 (Bunge and Bordessa, 1975). He showed that in the suburbs the rates were at or below the US rate (21.7 deaths per 1000 births; the lowest was 10.7, equivalent to that of Norway), whereas in the inner city they were typical of countries of the global periphery (Guyana, 43.9; Trinidad, 36.8). In short, he had discovered a 'Third World within the First'. This led him to divide that city into three zones: an inner zone, which he termed the city of death; an intermediate zone, or the city of need; and an outer zone – the city of superfluity (Bunge, 1975). Regarding the first, he describes it as a zone of deterioration: 'its homes, its streets, its schools and its children's teeth fall apart as the money is sucked out' (p. 162). Within Detroit, as in most capitalist cities, the more peripheralized workers live in segregated areas and are subject to structural violence. The same occurs at the regional scale: in the UK, there are substantial variations in standardized death rates, and Northern Ireland has an infant mortality rate 25 percent above that of England and Wales (Compton, 1982). And the dominated-class areas are in many cases the worst supplied with health-care services. Many empirical studies have provided strong evidence of an 'inverse-care law' – the further that people live from a health-care facility the less use they make of it (Smith, 1979), so that the poorer the provision the lower the usage and the greater the deleterious consequences.

Summary

Premature death through violence, whether behavioural or structural, is much more likely to occur in some parts of the world than in others, in some parts of countries than others, and in some parts of cities than others. Figure 2 shows this at the international scale, using the data for 1965 assembled by Kohler and Alcock (1976). The relative insignificance of behavioural violence as a cause of death is clear; the concentration of structural violence in the periphery of the world-economy stands out.

These spatial variations are not simply the result of environmental influences. They are a product of the socio-political structure of the world in the exploitation of that environment. The world today is a single economic system, the global world-economy of capitalism. In it, there are major class differentials, between exploiters and exploited, dominant and dominated. The former are better fed and housed, more protected from crime and, for most of the time, less likely to be involved in warfare. Thus it is among the exploited that the highest levels of violence and premature death are to be found (as Alcock and Kohler (1979) have shown).

This differentiation between exploiters and exploited is expressed spatially in the core–periphery structure of the world-economy. The exploiting class are spatially concentrated at all scales, creating a pattern of uneven development. The geography of structural violence very largely follows that pattern; people in the periphery tend to die younger than those in the core. The geography of physical violence against the individual follows a similar pattern; people in the periphery are more likely to die as a result of crimes against their persons.

The other geography of violence is that of politically-related behavioural violence. In recent decades that, too, has been closely linked to the core–periphery structuring of the international system of states. This is not always the case, because occasionally in the past major wars have been fought between core-states, leading to a large number of deaths there. At present, however, the core is largely free of such violence (because, it is claimed, of the deterrent provided by nuclear weapons), and intra-core conflicts are being enacted within the periphery. Should another intra-core war be fought, the likelihood is that the entire population of the world will be victims of such violence.

What we have shown, therefore, is that an understanding of the geopolitics of violence and premature death requires an appreciation of the geography of the world's economic order. It is not the outcome of that order, for the fashioning and refashioning of the global world-economy is itself a continuous process of spatial structuring. As we organize the world according to capitalist dictates, so we organize the geography of death.

References

Alcock, N. and Kohler, G. (1979) 'Structural Violence at the World Level: Diachronic Findings', *Journal of Peace Research* 16: 255–62.

Ardrey, R. (1969) *The Territorial Imperative*. London: Fontana.

Baldwin, J. and Bottoms, A. E. (1976) *The Urban Criminal*. London: Tavistock.

Black, D. (1975) *The Behavior of Law*. New York: Academic Press.

Blaikie, P. (1986) 'Natural Resource Use in Developing Countries', in R. J. Johnston and P. J. Taylor (eds) *A World in Crisis? Geographical Perspectives*, pp. 107–26. Oxford: Basil Blackwell.

Bradley, P. N. (1986) 'Food Production and Distribution – and Hunger', in R. J. Johnston and P. J. Taylor (eds) *A World in Crisis? Geographical Perspectives*, pp. 89–106. Oxford: Basil Blackwell.

Bunge, W. (1975) 'Detroit Humanly Viewed: the American Urban Present', in R. F. Abler, D. Janelle, A. Philbrick and J. Somner (eds) *Human Geography in a Shrinking World*, pp. 145–82. North Scituate, MA: Duxbury Press.

Bunge, W. and Bordessa, R. (1975) *The Canadian Alternative*. Downsview, Ontario: York University Geographical Monographs.

Chase-Dunn, C. K. (ed.) (1982) *Socialist States in the World System*. Beverly Hills: Sage Publications.

Clark, G. L. and Dear, M. J. (1984) *State Apparatus*. Boston: George Allen and Unwin.

Coates, B. E., Johnston, R. J. and Knox, P. L. (1977) *Geography and Inequality*. Oxford: Oxford University Press.

Coleman, A. (1985) *Utopia on Trial*. London: H. Shipman.

Compton, P. A. (1982) 'The Changing Population', in R. J. Johnston and J. C. Doornkamp (eds) *The Changing Geography of the United Kingdom*, pp. 37–74. London: Methuen.

Galtung, J. (1969) 'Violence, Peace and Peace Research', *Journal of Peace Research* 6: 167–91.

Galtung, J. and Høivik, T. (1971) 'Structural and Direct Violence: a Note on Operationalization', *Journal of Peace Research* 8: 73–6.

Giddens, A. (1985) *The Nation-State and Violence*. Cambridge: Polity Press.

Grigg, D. B. (1985) *The World's Food Problem*. Oxford: Basil Blackwell.

Harman, E. S. (1982) *The Real Terror Network*. Boston: South End Press.

Harries, K. D. (1974) *The Geography of Crime and Justice*. New York: McGraw Hill.

Harries, K. D. (1975) 'Rejoinder to Richard Peet', *The Professional Geographer* 27: 280–2.

Harries, K. D. (1976) 'Observations on Radical Versus Liberal Theories of Crime Causation', *The Professional Geographer* 28: 100–3.

Harrison, P. (1979) *Inside the Third World*. London: Penguin.

Harvey, D. (1982) *The Limits to Capital*. Oxford: Basil Blackwell.

Harvey, D. (1985) 'The Geopolitics of Capitalism', in D. Gregory and J. Urry (eds) *Social Relations and Spatial Structures*, pp. 128–63. London: Macmillan.

Haynes, R. M. (1973) 'Crime Rates and City Size in America', *Area* 5: 162–5.

Hechter, M. (1975) *Internal Colonialism*. London: Routledge and Kegan Paul.

Johnston, R. J. (1982) *Geography and the State*. London: Macmillan.

Johnston, R. J. (1984a) 'Marxist Political Economy, the State and Political Geography', *Progress in Human Geography* 8: 473–92.

Johnston, R. J. (1984b) *City and Society*. London: Hutchinson.

Johnston, R. J. (1986) 'Placing Politics', *Political Geography Quarterly* 5: 563–78.

Kidron, M. and Smith, D. (1983) *The War Atlas*. London: Pan.

Kohler, G. and Alcock, N. (1976) 'An Empirical Table of Structural Violence', *Journal of Peace Research* 13: 343–56.

Mann, M. (1984) 'The Autonomous Power of the State', *European Journal of Sociology* 25: 185–213.

Massey, D. (1984) *Spatial Divisions of Labour*. London: Macmillan.

Modelski, G. (1978) 'The Long Cycle of Global Politics and the Nation-State', *Comparative Studies in Society and History* 20: 214–35.

Newman, O. (1973) *Defensible Space*. New York: Architectural Press.

O'Loughlin, J. (1984) 'Geographic Models of International Conflicts', in P. J. Taylor and J. W. House (eds) *Political Geography: Recent Advances and Future Directions*, pp. 133–48. London: Croom Helm.

O'Loughlin, J. (1986a) 'World-Power Competition and Local Conflicts in the Third World', in R. J. Johnston and P. J. Taylor (eds) *A World in Crisis? Geographical Perspectives*, pp. 231–68. Oxford: Basil Blackwell.

O'Loughlin, J. (1986b) 'Spatial Models of International Conflict: Extending Current Theories of War Behavior', *Annals of the Association of American Geographers* 76: 63–80.

Parker, G. (1985) *A History of Western Geopolitical Thought*. London: Croom Helm.

Peet, R. (1975) 'The Geography of Crime: a Political Critique', *The Professional Geographer* 27: 277–80.

Peet, R. (1976) 'Further Comments on the Geography of Crime', *The Professional Geographer* 28: 96–100.

Sack, R. D. (1983) 'Human Territoriality: a Theory', *Annals of the Association of American Geographers* 73: 55–74.

Smith, D. M. (1979) *Where the Grass is Greener*. London: Penguin.

Smith, N. (1984) *Uneven Development*. Oxford: Basil Blackwell.

Taylor, P. J. (1985) *Political Geography: World-Economy, Nation-State and Locality*. London: Longman.

Taylor, P. J. (1986) 'The World-Systems Project', in R. J. Johnston and P. J. Taylor (eds) *A World in Crisis? Geographical Perspectives*, pp. 269–88. Oxford: Basil Blackwell.

Taylor, P. J. and Johnston, R. J. (1984) 'The Geography of the British State', in J. R. Short and A. Kirby (eds) *The Human Geography of Contemporary Britain*, pp. 23–39. London: Macmillan.

Wallerstein, I. (1979) *The Capitalist World-Economy*. Cambridge: Cambridge University Press.

Watts, M. (1985) *Silent Violence*. Berkeley: University of California Press.

Williams, C. H. (1980) 'Ethnic Separatism in Western Europe', *Tijdschrift voor Economische en Sociale Geographie* 71: 142–58.

Williams, C. H. (1986) 'The Question of National Congruence', in R. J. Johnston and P. J. Taylor (eds) *A World in Crisis? Geographical Perspectives*, pp. 196–230. Oxford: Basil Blackwell.

16

Arms, Technology, Violence and the Global Military Order

Giri Deshingkar

King Xiang of Wei asked Mencius: 'How could we get a world settlement?'
'By unification', Mencius said.
'Who is capable of uniting the world?', the king asked.
'If there were a single ruler', Mencius said, 'who did not delight in slaughter, he could unite the whole world'.
'And who would side with him?', the king asked.
Mencius said, 'Today among those that are shepherds of men there is not in the whole world one who does not delight in slaughter. Should such a one arise, then all people on earth would look towards him with outstretched necks. If he were indeed such a one the people would come to him as water flows downward, in a flood that none could hold back.'

from *The Book of Mencius**

Collective violence in the twentieth century has been of a qualitatively different nature to previous eras in history. It is no longer just limited to acts of killing or physical coercion on the battlefield or elsewhere. Nor is it just a matter of structural violence in the form of slavery or patriarchy within and outside the family, for example. Certainly, the collective violence of our time does express itself in terms of both war and structural violence, witness the estimated sixteen million deaths in Third World conflicts since the Second World War.[1] But it also goes further. Human collectives today practise violence against nature through ecologically damaging technologies, against animals in the form of vivisection in medical research, against traditional cultures in the name of modernization and even against knowledge-systems to establish the 'universal truth' of modern science. The methodology of accelerating and 'smashing' nuclear particles may not, at first glance, appear to be violent in the strict sense of the term, but it symbolizes the quest for conquering nature by dismembering it to examine each one of its constituent parts. All these are discrete acts of collective violence; together they form a violence-system which runs through our intellectual, political, economic, cultural, social and productive pursuits. Seen from this perspective President

---

* Book of Mencius (Meng Tzu), I. 1. VI. The quotation is adapted from a translation by Arthur Waley; see his *Three Ways of Thought in Ancient China* (London: George Allan and Unwin, 1953), pp. 125–6.

Eisenhower's Atoms for Peace programme could not have been more inappropriately dubbed!

This violence-system is at work, continuously and inexorably, even in the now rare absence of overt violence – acts of war or physical repression. Directly or indirectly conventional wars may inflict tens of thousands of casualties. But a nuclear war would exterminate millions. But, even in the absence of such wars, millions of poor people are subjected to a process of slow death, a result of misguided economic policies, maldistribution, anti-people development strategies and outright corruption. And when wars occur they create untold problems for those caught in the crossfire who have to survive long after the cessation of fighting.

In the process of nation- and state-building in the plural societies of the Third World, autonomous ethnic groups and cultures are drawn in. In many cases the upshot of this process is oppression by the state – nationality and citizenship are forced upon those who may not want it. The post-Second World War era is littered with examples: South American Indians, Ibos, Armenians, Australian Aborigines, East Timorese, Kurds and Sikhs. Other, such as the Palestinians and the Asians in East Africa, are denied identity when they do not fit into the national design. Statelessness is a dilemma more awkward than being a refugee.

Modern agricultural processes cause desertification and unprecedented famines which lead to the loss of human and animal life. Even where there is ample food for animals, thousands of animals are sacrificed every year for cosmetic, medical and military research.

Increasing integration into the global market creates a very large number of dependent economies; global economic crises hit hard and create unemployment on a massive scale in both the North and the South. In the West this may mean long-term dependence upon the welfare state, a miserable and fruitless existence. But in the Third World, unemployment is slow starvation for marginal workers and landless labourers.

Above all, a relentless process of cultural destruction is at work. In the North, consumerism, television, the advertising industry and the welfare state have overturned cultural values. The urban nuclear family has destroyed social cohesion and severed the transmission belt of culture which, in human history, always ran between grandparents and grandchildren. In the South, the reigning ideology of modernization treats tradition as an impediment. Such cultural destruction – it is not always simply cultural change which takes place in history – has impoverished human civilization. To its victims, it can be a fate worse than death; the South American Indians said of their Spanish conquerors: 'If, as you say, our Gods are false, we see no point in living.'

The human predicament in this century cannot be understood without a broad definition of collective violence. At the outset it is necessary to understand the system of modern war which has undergone a qualitative transformation in recent decades. Wars are no longer fought only between states by soldiers on the battlefield; we now have 'total war' in which entire societies, their production-systems and cultures must participate. Moreover, such participation does not end with the termination of war. Cold wars continue during what is only legally a time of peace. Such cold wars exist not only between the two military blocs headed by the United States and the Soviet Union but between many other potential adversaries, China and the Soviet Union, India and Pakistan, the two Koreas, Egypt and Libya, for example.

The combination of total war and cold war has transformed every human collectivity into a permanent war-system. Such a system continuously prepares itself for war against one enemy or another. Thus, the distinction between war and peace has broken down. Collective violence, or at least the intent to practise it, has become a permanent fact of life for people everywhere.

That is the state of affairs between states. But in many parts of the world, the state itself is more often than not at war with the society and the cultures it constitutes. This phenomenon is not unknown in Western countries; witness the insurgencies in Northern Ireland and of the Basques in Spain. The adversarial relationship between the state and society is much more widespread than in the countries of the East. But there the state has much more elaborate and comprehensive systems of control over the citizens. In the Third World the state is often at war with the society.

The process of nation- and state-building in the plural societies of the Third World invariably involves a degree of violence, the type of which this analysis is attempting to define. The concept of a nation-state was taken from Europe where it was invoked as a means of marshalling and organizing peoples and the means of production primarily for the purposes of war.[2] When transferred to the Third World, the process of nation-building has involved a more significant demand for political loyalty to the centre over and above loyalties to ethnicity, religion, language and culture. Moreover, at the expense of everything else, there is a single commitment to build a strong state which implies a greater degree of complicity from the margins. Often, this process of nation-building leads to the adoption of development strategies which involve forced capital accumulation, the import of polluting and damaging technologies, the imposition of alien concepts of science which condemn all local knowledge to superstition, and the adoption of a nation-wide 'official' culture. This inevitably involves coercion and, frequently, the use of violence. Sooner or later, state-violence meets with counter-violence by the affected people and in the process the state, society and culture become militarized and coercion becomes the preferred instrument for dealing with external and domestic problems.

In a militarized world, peacekeeping and order are primarily achieved through coercive means. At the lowest level, this means the adoption of Draconian laws and the use of a repressive law-and-order machinery to maintain domestic order. At the highest level, there is the international arms race designed to maintain deterrence between military blocs headed by the United States and the Soviet Union. To supplement the nuclear threat from the blocs there are the independent nuclear deterrents of China and those being established by the 'near-nuclear' powers such as India, Israel, Pakistan and South Africa.

It is, therefore, a global military order which has come into being since the Second World War. At its apex stand the two superpowers with their overwhelming military superiority, both nuclear and conventional. At present, the United States is seeking to exploit its technological capability to break the prevailing parity of mutually assured destruction (MAD) through the Strategic Defense Initiative (SDI), popularly known as 'Star Wars'. If successful, the SDI will create another step in the hierarchy whereby the United States alone occupies the peak, at least until SDI begets its antidote from the Soviet side. Elsewhere, there are military hierarchies within blocs, within regions and, of course, coercive hierarchies within states. But these hierarchies do not dovetail neatly. Nuclear weapons may confer power upon the possessor, but also impotence. 'Subimperial' states can develop in unpredictable directions and upset patrons – witness the effects of the Iranian revolution. States buy arms to maintain security and sovereignty and then promptly surrender their sovereignty to international finance organizations in order to reduce the indebtedness engendered by the arms purchases. Colonial interests linger on in the post-colonial world and create crises when they conflict with subimperial interests and/or intra-state crises – the Falklands/Malvinas War and French activity in Africa are examples. These in turn may conflict with superpower interests. Hence, the global military order often shows signs of disorder. Moreover, the military disorder has been increasing over time and international order has been transformed into anarchy.[3]

The global military order, such as it is, runs parallel to several other global orders – the technological, economic and cultural orders. Those countries on the upper rungs of the military order are likely to be technologically much more developed than those on the lower rungs. And by the generally accepted definition of 'culture' by contemporary Third World elites, those on the lower rungs of the ladder would count as culturally backward. Once again, the correspondence between the hierarchies is not entirely neat. Thus, Japan is highly developed in terms of its economy and technology but not on the corresponding military rung. Similarly, the Soviet Union is much lower down on the (non-military) technological and economic rungs than its military strength would warrant. Until the recent (early 1986) fall in oil prices, the OPEC countries also displayed such a mismatch. Although they sought to climb the military ladder through massive arms imports they stayed well down on the non-military technological rungs. For the self-appointed global policemen, these anomalies represent a form of global disorder which they find difficult to manage; witness the Oil Crisis from which the West suffered for nearly a decade after 1973.

In spite of these elements of disorder, one fact remains constant. It is that people, particularly the overwhelming majority of the people of the Third World, occupy the lowest rung of all the different global hierarchies. Even if the demand for a new international economic order (NIEO) were to be realized, a hope that was optimistic at the outset, their situation would remain fundamentally the same; NIEO would merely strengthen the states, not the societies and cultures. The people would remain just as vulnerable as before to the violence-system. A successful SDI would offer them no security. Nor would any form of arms limitation. More development would simply mean the continued destruction of the natural resources upon which they depend directly. More modernization would destroy their cultures and social cohesion. More science would increase the threat to their knowledge- and meaning-systems. Nothing short of challenging the wider interlinking system of collective violence can offer them, and the life-system of which they are a part, the hope of survival.

There are two possible ways in which humankind may be able to transcend collective violence and war. The first is to seek to change the hearts and minds of those who operate the violence-system. The second is to change their interests.

An example of the former way is what occurred in the case of Emperor Ashoka (*c.* 273–232 BC) of India. Having made many conquests on the battlefield, he suddenly experienced an awakening about the futility of it all. He then embraced Buddhism and became a *chakravarti* emperor (one who behaved according to the wheel of *dharma* which preached *ahimsa* or non-violence). Of the latter way, many examples can be cited from everyday life. In a dispute between factory owners and workers, for example, the workers often resort to industrial action (strike) after rational argument and other means of persuasion have failed. The strike does not bring about a change in the attitude of the management towards the workers, but it does adversely affect their interests (profit margins). Occasionally, it can happen the other way around: the management may declare a 'lockout', thereby adversely affecting the interests of the workers. In either case, the two parties sooner or later get down to the negotiating table. A compromise is struck and the immediate conflict is resolved.

Examples of the first kind are rather rare in history, although less so at the individual level. In our everyday experience we do transcend conflict by forgiving and being forgiven. This can occasionally happen at the group level as well; after group violence or even a war, members of the group often undergo a change of heart and learn to live with each other. However, religious, racial, historical and cultural factors can exert a significant negative influence. Obversely, a change of heart on the part of the wielders of state power is extremely rare. King Hui of Wei, whose son's conversation with the sage Mencius has been cited earlier, was one of the few in Chinese history. Similarly, Emperor Ashoka was among the very few of his kind in India, although Indian mythology speaks of many kings who gave up the luxuries of life and warfare to live an ascetic life. One can, perhaps, find a few more instances of a change of heart on the part of the wielders of state power in the rest of the world – a plethora of retired decision-makers in the West are now reacting against nuclear weapons. But the verdict of history seems clear. Collective violence is rarely transcended through a change of heart.

During this century a series of attempts have been made to persuade decision-makers to bring about disarmament at various levels, ranging from nuclear and conventional arms limitation and control to general and complete disarmament (GCD). Of these attempts, those that have been directed at securing arms control on a modest scale have had some amount of success. Thus, the Washington Treaty of 1921 did bring about a ceiling on the expansion of naval power among its signatories. Over fifty years later, after the horror of the Cuban Missile Crisis, an atmosphere of détente yielded a series of arms control agreements. The Limited Test Ban Treaty of 1963 prohibited nuclear testing in the atmosphere. This was followed by the Outer Space Treaty of 1967 which put the brakes on the militarization of outer space. The Nuclear Non-Proliferation Treaty of 1968 was aimed at preventing the horizontal proliferation of nuclear weapons beyond the existing five nuclear-weapon states: the Soviet Union, the United States, Britain, France and China. Thereafter, the Biological Warfare Convention of 1972 outlawed the development, production and stockpiling of bacteriological weapons. Finally, in the same year, the two superpowers reached an agreement on the quantitative limitation of strategic nuclear weapons and anti-ballistic missile systems (Strategic Arms Limitation Talks (SALT) I Accord of 1972).

This is an impressive record in some respects. But it is difficult to argue that it can be traced to a change of heart on the part of policy-makers. Perhaps by the mid-1960s the leaders of the two military blocs, NATO and the Warsaw Pact, did acquire a more sober understanding about the destructive power of thermonuclear weapons. This was prompted perhaps by a combination of the memory of the destruction of Hiroshima and Nagasaki and the near uncontrollable drift towards nuclear war over the Cuban Missile Crisis. In addition, thermonuclear weapons' tests had revealed their frightening and unlimited destructive potential. There was also the development of intercontinental nuclear missiles which placed the metropolitan territories of the two superpowers, the United States in particular, within the reach of the other.[4] The marriage of high technology and weapons systems had produced a situation unprecedented in human history. A nuclear war threatened to exterminate the entire human race and much more. It may have been this understanding which led the United States and the Soviet Union to put forward a joint statement of agreed principles for disarmament negotiations in 1961. And in 1962 they followed this with the tabling of drafts for a multilateral treaty on GCD.

At the same time the international situation was displaying signs of turmoil and anarchy and, predictably, the superpowers became entangled. The 1950s witnessed the Korean War, the Quemoy Crisis, the beginning of a wider war in Indochina, tension in the Middle East and between China and the Soviet Union and a host of other disputes in the Third World. In the 1960s there were more crises – the Sino-Soviet split, the Cuban Missile Crisis, the Sino-Indian War, the Indo-Pakistan War, escalation in Vietnam and the Six Day War. At times the superpowers respected the problems of the other. At other times they confronted each other face to face and on one occasion, eyeball to eyeball.

But if global turmoil and the threat of anarchy nudged the superpowers towards détente and agreement, it was flawed on two counts. First, it commanded little respect among other military powers. China refused to sign the Limited Test Ban Treaty and, together with India, Pakistan, Israel and France, the Nuclear Non-Proliferation Treaty. In fact, most Third World states defied superpower attempts to impose a global military order to avoid curtailing their own military freedom *vis-à-vis* their regional adversaries. Moreover, they quickly discovered that they could bite the hand that fed with virtual impunity.

Consequently, for these and other reasons military expenditures in Third World countries increased progressively during the 1960s. While the superpowers may have been inclined to reduce inter-bloc tension, their global political rivalry continued. Hence they made no attempt to curb their arms sales and transfers to Third World countries. And by the 1970s the United States could not have done so had it wished, such was the economic dependence upon arms sales after 1971. The flow of ever more sophisticated weapons to the Third World went on rising. It assumed alarming proportions during the 1970s after the rise of the petro-dollar problem. In 1973 military expenditure in the Third World stood at US $44,225 million. By 1978 it had risen to US $72,953 million and by 1982 it had reached US $103,713 million, according to the Stockholm International Peace Research Institute.

The second flaw was that the superpowers could not rise beyond the level of a quantitative and cosmetic arms control. There was a treaty to demilitarize the Antarctic but not the Arctic. SALT I restricted the numbers of missiles but not warheads. The Non-Proliferation Treaty aimed to prevent the horizontal spread of nuclear weapons and vertical proliferation only by implication. The Test Ban Treaty prevented over-ground but not underground nuclear tests. Thus, the relatively sober understanding which American and Soviet leaders had acquired was offset by the rapid development of military technology which began with the launch of Sputnik by the Soviet Union and was perpetuated by interest groups of both sides. Space technology, combined with the miniaturization of nuclear warheads and the astonishing advances in electronics, promised a 'technological fix' encouraged by a 'can implies ought' mentality and produced the hope of breaking the nuclear deadlock, the balance of terror. Although no specific claims were made about winning an all-out thermonuclear war, technological advances seemed to offer several choices short of such a 'spasm'. For example, a highly sophisticated nuclear force would deter the adversary from launching a strategic nuclear attack but the same technology would enable one to win a 'limited' nuclear war. Alternatively, technology could permit a totally disarming first strike against the enemy's strategic nuclear forces. To be sure, much of the thinking of the era was technically and conceptually flawed, but technological change altered the perceptions of the decision-makers of the two superpowers.

Technological advances in weapons systems gradually transformed the notion of 'prevention' into one of 'management'. The superpowers seemed willing to discuss GCD in 1962. But, one decade later, they had given up the thought of reversing the nuclear arms race; they were content to manage it, and institutionalize it. Today, few who wield state power refer to the goal of GCD with any conviction.

China and some of the Third World countries occasionally invoke the goal of GCD, but never for themselves. Recently China has embarked upon a programme of 'Regularizing and modernizing' its armed forces. Third World countries have taken to massive transfers of military technology. In so doing they have pushed the technological fix much further. By importing inappropriate production technologies, organizational methods, information gathering (surveillance) and dissemination systems (propaganda) and management techniques for production and social control, these societies are adopting a completely new violence-system. The visions of Buddha, Mencius and Gandhi have been overshadowed by those of Bacon, Metternich and Kissinger.

Perhaps it was not a change of heart which made the leaders of the two superpowers think in terms of GCD, beginning with arms limitation and control. In retrospect it seems that advances in military technology at the turn of the 1960s had affected the national and global interests of both superpowers equally adversely. It was a technological deadlock. Hence the willingness to arrive at a compromise. But during the subsequent decades, military technology, which itself possessed an independent momentum, developed in such an uneven way that at times it seemed to affect the interests of the enemy far more than one's own. This was the era of the follow-on system which was based on the worst-case analysis. The implications of the Sputnik launch and the greater megatonnage of Soviet thermonuclear weapons tilted the balance in favour of the Soviet Union. But greater sophistication in multiple targeting (MIRV), tertiary guidance for lower circular error probability (CEP), precision-guided munitions and a host of other innovations tipped the balance in favour of the United States in some areas and conferred balance, or stalemate, in others. In time, the Soviet Union was able to catch up and even surpass the United States, but only to be overtaken once again.

But these are not descriptions of reality. They are examples of the blinkered perceptions of national leaders shaped by the development of military technology. In this sense, the issues of war and peace, collective violence and its transcendence have already passed out of the hands of the political decision-makers and into the diffused realm of modern technology which is in itself an integral part of the violence-system. The more diffused and impersonal the system, the less chance of a change of heart.

The process of replacing diplomacy with high technology has reached its acme during the 1980s. Since this situation is likely to continue into the foreseeable future, it is necessary to consider what it portends in some detail. The new technological leap began with Ronald Reagan's visit to Cheyenne Mountain in 1980, just before he was elected to the US Presidency. There he learnt that the launch of Soviet missiles could be detected within minutes. His subsequent question about what could be done after the launch was detected elicited no satisfactory reply.

Three years later, on 23 March 1983, Reagan launched the concept of ballistic missile defence in his now famous 'Star Wars' speech. At the time he did little more than call upon the US scientific community to explore the possibilities for a defence against ballistic missiles. But in so doing he removed the lid from an already boiling pot of vested interests spanning the armed forces, the scientific community and the anti-Soviet ideologues. The Reagan administration then proceeded to back the Strategic Defence Initiative with sufficient research and development funds to explore the workability of the concept in detail.

At the time of writing US $30 billion has already been committed to develop a system based upon a mix of laser, particle beams and projectile weapons. But many scientists and strategists have expressed reservations and opposition to SDI – they believe that a staggeringly complex system based upon unproven technologies will create more problems than it will solve. Some believe that the system will not work because the required level of accuracy and reliability is unattainable. But, even if it works, the greater fear is that, despite the rhetoric, there is an implied drive towards deterrence through a mix of offensive and defensive systems. This is bound to meet with reactive measures from the Soviet Union. The result will be to push the nuclear dilemma, the problems of arms control and deterrence into another dimension all together. The goal of GCD recedes even further.

The Strategic Defence Initiative is intended to exploit US superiority in 'high frontier' technology about which General Daniel Graham had written during the late 1970s.[5] Beyond the desire to 'end-run' the Soviet Union, there was no policy framework. The capability which prompted the vision was vacuous – it was high technology in search of a policy. It is in the nature of modern technological systems that such a policy does not aim to reverse but to escalate the arms race. And if the technological system is autonomous of any particular reigning social system, as has been suggested, the logic of escalation will work in the case of the Soviet Union, China and the Third World as well. The escalating arms races among Third World countries which emphasize modern science and technology for development bear witness to this.

But Third World countries have to pay a relatively much higher price for the acquisition of military technological superiority over their enemies. Many of them have been weighed down with high debt burdens. Also, the OPEC countries have seen massive reductions in their revenues over the last few years. Meanwhile, pressures on the state from the international finance organizations, on the one hand, and the impoverished populations in the Third World, on the other, have been growing steadily. Externally, Third World countries have been forced to make adjustments and economies to accommodate the demands of their creditors. Internally, increased coercion and outright state-violence is beginning to show diminishing returns. In short, the people's demands for 'people's security' are forcing a change of interests on those who hitherto thought primarily in terms of 'national interests' and 'national security'. Consequently, the statistical series on arms sales to and military expenditure in Third World countries has shown a decline over the past five years.[6]

Policy-makers will begin to think of transcending collective violence when their interests change or when their positions are threatened. This can happen in two ways. First, historic and economic forces at work over a protracted period can force such a change. The second way is through politics or concerted action by the people.

The role played by technology in escalating the arms race has already been discussed. But the momentum of technology can also undermine the arms race because of its escalating cost. In the decades since the Second World War two concepts have dominated the development of military technology. The first is the rise of the weapon system in place of the weapon itself; a weapon system combines a weapon, a platform and a system of command, control and communication. The second concept is that of a follow-on system whereby technological improvements in each of these components are planned, researched and developed even before a specific need is identified for a improved replacement system. The combination of these two concepts has created systems of astonishing complexity and sophistication – in order to justify its existence a replacement weapon system must display one or several improved performance characteristics.[7] It would be extremely difficult to find a decision-maker who is not extremely impressed with the technological solutions that modern weapon systems can provide for problems on the battlefield.

But such complex and sophisticated systems have also become increasingly expensive. Those involved with innovation per se are not too concerned with this aspect. It is not their responsibility. But the policy-maker who must find the money for the systems cannot evade the issue, particularly in a democracy. For example, an F15 aircraft today costs more than a hundred times more than the best US combat aircraft did in 1944; and the costs are growing by a factor of four every decade. The cost of a modern battle-tank has increased sevenfold during the same period. The most advanced nuclear-powered aircraft-carrier now costs as much as five times more than their Second World War ancestors (all comparisons in constant prices).[8] Prevailing trends suggest that a point will be reached by the year 2036 when the US Department of Defense will only be able to afford one aircraft. Fortunately, by sharing this air-craft among the military services on alternate days of the week, it will be possible to accrue enough money to replace it roughly every fifteen years thereafter.[9]

Particularly in the near-nuclear countries, it is sometimes argued that the cost of a nuclear weapon has gone down. This is a highly misleading argument. Purely in terms of the weapon itself, the cost of destructive power per equivalent ton of TNT has indeed gone down. But the costs of nuclear weapon systems has increased dramatically. Moreover, the costs of the new technologies of the 'Star Wars' type have not been calculated. The result of such escalating costs is that even the richest country in the world, the United States, can only afford a limited number of copies of the most advanced systems, even though there is great pressure to acquire more.

Another problem with complex and sophisticated conventional weapon systems is their protection. A US $35 million combat aircraft can be destroyed by a missile costing only US $1 million or less. A US $2 million tank can be immobilized or destroyed by a barrage of anti-tank missiles costing only tens of thousands of dollars. Cheap aluminium 'chaff' can confuse extremely expensive radars into making equally expensive mistakes. In the Vietnam War, very sensitive US sensors were rendered totally useless by Vietnamese guerrillas who used the simple device of hanging 'shit-pots' on trees and herding buffaloes in the areas where the sensors were planted. To an extent, just as weapon systems do beget their antidotes, there are usually counter-antidotes. But they can only be procured by increasing the cost of the weapon system.

A third problem with high-technology weapon systems is that they give a false sense of security to policy-makers and may thereby precipitate a war. The policy-makers are always given demonstrations of the efficacy of a weapon system under non-combat conditions. Invariably, the systems perform spectacularly. This gives confidence that in a given situation the use of military force will be a smooth and successful venture. However, one only has to recall the abortive attempt to rescue the American hostages in Iran or the element of luck that accompanied the British task-force during the Falklands/Malvinas conflict to realize how 'cosmetic' performance characteristics may be in the 'fog of war'.

The expense of acquiring and maintaining complex and sophisticated weapon systems is high enough in peacetime. But once conflict breaks out, maintenance and other costs multiply several-fold. If there is no decisive outcome at an early point, policy-makers may not be able to continue the war. Their interests are adversely affected and they contemplate a compromise. With a few exceptions, such as the Gulf War, modern wars among Third World countries tend to last for a very short period or change their form.

The combination of the three systemic problems of cost escalation, the cost-effectiveness of counter-measures and the availability of weapons creating occasions for highly expensive wars has led to a crisis of the conventional war-system – a defence dilemma. In fact, the interests of the policy-makers have changed. Yet such is the grip of the violence-system on the minds of the decision-makers that they are nowhere near abandoning the use of collective violence to preserve their interests. But the interlocking crises have created an opportunity for political intervention by the people.

A similar crisis has affected other aspects of the violence-system. Modern medicine is an excellent example. Here, high technology is utilized to counteract disease in contrast to most traditional medical systems which put a high premium on the body itself being helped to manage a disease. Modern medicine has its own variety of technological 'fixes' – modern hospital complexes, computerized diagnostic aids, broad-spectrum drugs manufactured by highly complex processes and sophisticated surgical techniques. But the cost of health care, where the onus is on cure rather than prevention, has escalated. To this must be added the problem of bacterial and virological resistance; each new broad-spectrum, anti-biotic drug loses its efficacy in a short period because the bacteria develop new strains which are resistant. To overcome new forms of resistance, expensive research, development and manufacture of broader-spectrum drugs is needed. This compounds the cost crisis. The third problem is that of iatrogeny; modern medical practice itself leads to a whole range of illnesses. Drugs, surgery and intensive therapies have side-effects which must be countered by further medication. As a result of these problems the delivery of medical care has suffered. This is why people who must pay for medical care are increasingly exploring alternative systems of medicine. And in countries with welfare states, governments are finding it harder to meet the costs. But the modern medical system has not collapsed – 'war on disease' is still the reigning ideology. However, the cost-resistance-iatrogeny crisis has created opportunities to think about transcending the ruling system of medicine. An optimum mass of people actually taking to alternative medical systems would force medical researchers, practitioners and the policy-makers in health ministries to reverse the present trend.

To a certain extent, patients have already started to desert modern medicine, witness the sustained interest in the West for alternative medicines during a period when the prevailing cultural trend is more 'modern' than it has been for many years. Recently, the British Medical Association, the doctor's trade union, has published a report denying the efficacy of alternative medicine on the grounds that it is scientifically unproven. Whether or not the medicine works appears to be something of a secondary consideration!

What has happened in the case of high-technology armament and medicine has also occurred in other areas. Development has benefited a few and impoverished many more and in the process violence has been unleashed against nature. Integration into the world-market has destroyed the political and cultural autonomy of a large number of groups. All these historical changes have created a whole range of opportunities for political intervention by the people.

It is not just a question of planning and engineering political intervention. That would be a Utopian undertaking; even if it succeeds there could be unintended consequences which could be worse than the status quo ante. Intervention by the people is already taking place in almost all societies at almost all levels. In industrialized Western countries, a series of movements are reacting against the violence-system: peace movements, 'green' movements, groups in support of minority rights, women's rights, animal rights, local autonomy and against nuclear energy. In Third World countries, where such movements are permitted to exist, they are struggling against political oppression, deforestation, displacement due to dams, mines and industries, pollution of watercourses, mechanization of fishing, automation, imposition of the 'official' language, ethnic oppression, commercialization of natural resources, cultural autonomy, decentralization of power and administration, a just return for rural produce and labour, fair distribution of land and water and, ultimately, survival. In socialist countries, the people's reactions are often less visible in the form of movements, but expressions do take shape, albeit in different forms; the Solidarity movement in Poland, ethnic assertion in the Soviet Union, expressions of religious piety, underground literature networks, 'big character' posters, once a favoured form of protest in China but now banned, physical flight from Kampuchea and Vietnam – even consumerism is sometimes an expression of dissent in socialist countries.

At first glance, it may seem that such grass-roots movements are so fragmented and so localized that they have nothing in common. Thus, with the exception of France, Western Europe has a growing movement against nuclear weapons, but in no Third World country, with the minor exception of a few urban centres, is there an anti-nuclear movement. Similarly, movements for cultural autonomy are largely found only in the multi-ethnic societies of the Third World. Little of the feminist movement exists in the Third World countries and the 'greens' in these countries take on a different hue.

But that is only the appearance. On closer scrutiny it seems that the overwhelming majority of such movements are reacting to that specific aspect of the violence-system which is most salient in their concrete situation. The struggle of a tribal group in, for example, India for cultural survival and against deforestation is highly complementary to the struggle of US groups against highly centralizing nuclear power stations and for decentralized renewable power sources. This in turn complements the movement against the Union Carbide insecticide plant at Bhopal which recently suffered a leak of poison gas. The protest against mechanized fishing in Malaysia has its counterpart in the resistance to robotization in Britain. The movement for disarmament is informed by the anti-macho values of the feminist movement whether its members are male or female.

These grass-roots movements are in need of two factors which would enable them to gather an optimum mass whereby they can decisively change the interests of policy-makers. They need a theory or a philosophy which knits together their fragmented concerns into a critique of the modern violence-system, a theory which also offers a liberating and inspiring alternative. Secondly, they need guidelines to action whereby they not only link up within their regions but also across them. It is the synergy of theory and action across states, societies and cultures which will enable them to challenge the violence-system and transcend it.

This is not a plea for a Leninist party-inspired plan for a revolution. No seizure of power is involved. No single event would herald the change of interest of the policy-makers. It would be a gradual process of changing the hearts and minds of individuals and groups, of evolving a liberating alternative to the violence-system and then acting in concert on the basis of the critique as well as the alternative vision. As discussed earlier, the contradictions within the violence-system have provided the people with opportunities for political intervention. Given such opportunities, if only 5 percent of the people have a change of heart, the new inspiring alternative could become unstoppable. When some 20 percent of the people link up in a synergy of theory and action the interests of the policy-makers would be decisively changed.

Admittedly, the grass-roots people's movements everywhere in the world are on the periphery. But, over the long term, generational change is on the side of the movements. While the old generation has imbibed the perspective of the violence-system, the sensibilities of the younger generation are quite different; they constitute the backbone of the people's movements. The question now is how to help the process towards a new vision for transcending collective violence before it is too late.

Since the channels of formal education and communication are almost wholly under the control of the policy-makers, the aspirers of change must utilize all available channels of informal education and people-to-people communication. Fortunately, the communications revolution has made this task much less difficult than hitherto. One of the characteristics of the modern violence-system is that a great deal of the violence is hidden.

Meat-eaters are distanced from the slaughter-house, the users of paper are remote from the felling of trees, scientists in search of the truth are far removed from the effects of the destructive technologies they make possible and road-builders do not even suspect that they are instrumental in destroying tribal cultures. Such hidden links need to be exposed in the process of informal education to sharpen the sensibilities of the generations to follow. The role of the media and the intrusion of war and violence into the homes of Americans was a very powerful factor in the American withdrawal from Vietnam.

The change of perspective initiated by people's movements would start at the cultural and societal levels and then proceed to the level of the state. When people's action acquires an optimum mass, societies and cultures would start to opt out of state projects of 'total' and 'permanent' war. This would deny the wielders of state power the use of collective violence as a primary instrument for solving external and internal problems. Such action will catalyse the disintegration of the global military order. In fact, opting out of the violence-system would necessarily entail retraction from the global economic order, the technological order and the global cultural order. Equally, if not more important, it would also mean the simultaneous dissolution of oppressive domestic orders. Both would be replaced with an ecological concept of existence in which the well-being of one constituent element – nature, society, culture, knowledge-system, ethnicity – enhances the well-being of all other elements.

Notes

1. R. L. Sivard, *World Military and Social Expenditures 1983* (Washington, DC: World Priorities, 1983), p. 2.

2. M. Howard, *The Causes of Wars* (London: Counterpoint/Unwin, 1983), pp. 23–35.

3. R. L. Luckham, 'Militarisation: The New International Anarchy', *Third World Quarterly* 6(2), April 1984, pp. 351–73.

4. For an excellent analysis of the US approach to national security and territorial integrity see B. Buzan, *People, States and Fear: The National Security Problem in International Relations* (Brighton: Wheatsheaf Books, 1983), pp. 156–72.

5. General D. Graham, *High Frontier: a New National Strategy* (Washington, DC: Heritage Foundation, 1982).

6. *World Armaments and Disarmament: SIPRI Yearbook 1985* (London: Taylor and Francis, 1985).

7. M. Kaldor, *Baroque Arsenal* (London: Andre Deutsch, 1982?)

8. F. C. Spinney, *Defence Facts of Life* (London: Westview Press, 1985), pp. 17–24.

9. N. R. Augustine, 'One Plane, One Tank, One Ship: Trend for the Future?', *Defence Management Journal*, April 1975, p. 34.

17

Transforming the International Order: Options for Latin America

José A. Silva Michelena

Introduction

The transformation of the operation of the international order results from simultaneous and multiple forces. At the beginning of the 1970s, political economists placed a great deal of emphasis on what came to be known as the new international economic order (NIEO). The world's economic crisis was perceived by Third World social scientists and politicians as an opportunity for Third World countries to reinsert themselves in the world-economy on terms more favourable than in the past. The opportunity was considered as favourable because of the practically universal abolition of colonialism, the new sense of national self-reliance and the significant development of productive forces in Third World countries as compared with the recent past.

Within this framework the so-called North–South dialogue was launched. A few years later, however, it was clear that central countries would make no concessions except those beneficial to their own economies and in accordance with tendencies in the world-economy. A case in point was industrial redeployment. Today, the North–South dialogue is dead and South–South co-operation is too modest to be a significant tendency.

Politically, there were also hopes that the climate of détente would provide sufficient space for manoeuvre to Third World governments and semi-peripheral states, so that they could experiment with new forms of government. Collective self-reliance and various 'new roads' to socialism appeared on the world political scene. But today it is clear that both the political and the economic space for manoeuvre by the Third World and semi-peripheral countries of the South has been significantly reduced.

In this chapter, after a brief overview of the main Third World schools of thought on the nature of the present and past international orders and on opportunities for their transformation, an attempt will be made to show the main forces currently transforming the international order. Specific alternatives for Latin America will be discussed at the end.

Theoretical background

Until the 1950s, in Latin America as in other Third World continents, the transformation of the world was viewed basically through two theoretical perspectives, both of European origin. On the one hand, academic social science was clearly dominated by what came to be known as the theory of modernization. On the other hand, critical social science was mostly inspired by the Leninist theory of imperialism.

The theory of modernization was widely accepted in Third World academic circles because it was a fresh synthesis of a long tradition of thought in sociology, anthropology and economics (Marshall, Durkheim, Tönnies, Weber, Redfield). Moreover, this synthesis of social thought appeared at a moment when African and Asian countries were being decolonized and new nations built. Liberation movements emerged everywhere.

The theory of modernization contrasted with the rather simplistic view prevailing in the immediate post-war era in academic and policy-making circles in the United States. It was believed then that these revolutionary movements were mainly the product of the Machiavellian influence of the Soviet Union, which relentlessly sought to expand communism; hence the main policy objective was to 'contain' such expansion by military opposition.

The theory of modernization implied a profound revision of the historical evolution of the world. It not only reinforced the idea that development would spread from Europe and the United States to backward or traditional countries, but most significantly also postulated that social and political movements which were seeking to transform the established order were the result of conditions of backwardness, misery and the disruption of values, which prevailed among the majority in traditional countries, contrasting with the affluent modernity of urban minorities and power groups.

International aid programmes were inspired by this theory. These programmes greatly influenced government planning in the Third World. It was thought that the transition of a traditional society to a modern one, i.e. resembling the US or Europe, would be achieved by foreign investment and accompanying technological transfer. The emergence of modern middle classes would soon bring political changes, which in turn would facilitate the modernization of both the agrarian structure and industry. International commerce would benefit from further specialization in raw materials, to reinforce the comparative advantages of these countries.

This conception of world order and international change prevailed in Latin America until the early 1960s (Germani, 1962). In other Third World regions it remained dominant for a few years longer. Moreover, since the late 1940s, a group of economists working for the UN Economic Commission for Latin America (ECLA), under the leadership of Raul Prebisch, were already questioning the basic premises of the economic theory of modernization. In particular they questioned the theory of international trade.

Raul Prebisch, a pioneer in the analysis of Latin American underdevelopment, explained that long-term weaknesses in the price of raw materials invalidated the positive results which were supposedly derived from comparative advantages. After analytically dividing the world into a developed Centre and an underdeveloped Periphery, Prebisch demonstrated not only that there has been no technological transfer from the centre to the periphery, but that, on the contrary, productivity growth in underdeveloped countries was being rechanelled toward the centre, through the mechanism of 'deterioration in the terms of trade'. (Munoz, 1985: 229)

A new strategy, which came to be known as developmentalist, was suggested by ECLA: domestically oriented growth through import-substituting industrialization, diversification of exports with manufactured products, agrarian reform, modernization of the state to make it more consonant with its new interventionist role, and institutional reforms at an international level to favour peripheral countries (Prebisch, 1963; CEPAL, 1969).

Many Latin American governments, sometimes encouraged by programmes such as the Alliance for Progress, incorporated ECLA's strategy in their development plans. However, in face of the continued failure of such plans and the persistence of underdevelopment a new interpretation of the centre–periphery relation emerged in the mid-1960s which came to be known as the 'theory of dependency'. This interpretation broke away from the notion that development spreads from the centre to the periphery. It also rejected the Keynesian–Parsonian paradigm which was at the base of both modernization and developmentalist theory. Instead it proposed a historico-structural interpretation of the capitalist world order. This theory was inspired by the Marxist-Leninist theory of imperialism, but went beyond its Eurocentrism. Underdevelopment of the periphery is seen, in part, as a consequence of the development of the centre, within the context of the expansion of capitalism throughout the world. It was emphasized that, as peripheral economies were incorporated into the capitalist system, their economic structures became heterogeneous and organically linked to the international economy in such a way that, through mechanisms like the deteriorations of the terms of trade, unequal exchange and super-exploitation of the labour-force, they contributed to the development of the centre while themselves becoming underdeveloped (Cardoso and Faletto, 1971; Frank, 1972; Marini 1973).

In recent times what has been emphasized is the increasing trans-nationalization of the productive apparatus and domestic markets and the role of national and international class alliances. Nation-states did not disappear from the analysis, but were complemented with class analysis. Moreover, analysis of the transformation of the world included considerations on both changes in the capitalist and in the socialist camps.

Dependentist theory greatly influenced analysis in other Third World continents (Amin, 1975), and also in certain academic circles in the United States and Europe (Cardoso, 1976). But this wide influence in the intellectual sphere contrasted sharply with the meagre impact it had at government levels, undoubtedly a sign of ideological dependency and self-imposed restrictions by the dominant local elites. Recently, dependency theory has been criticized from different points of view, but no clear theoretical alternative has yet emerged.

Meanwhile disenchantment with 'real socialisms' ran almost parallel to the bitter contentions of consumer society. The prolonged economic crisis of the world economy since the late 1960s has disenchanted the last 'true believers' in development. If it is true that, as mentioned in the introduction, it gave rise to hopes for a new international order, it is equally true that the continued failure of the North–South dialogue soon revealed that more than 'joint' approaches like those proposed by the Brandt Commission, the RIO Project or the Club of Rome to attaining a more just international order were needed.

Instead, at the centre, old economic theories were revived. The adoption of neoliberal policies by the United Kingdom and the United States was followed everywhere in the capitalist world. In Latin America, a new wave of dictatorships quickly adopted such ideas. As is well known, if at the beginning these countries as well as some democracies that also followed neoliberal ideas, experienced a certain economic growth, it is also true that this soon failed, leaving these countries in a deep and prolonged recession and literally mortgaged to the international banking community.

In face of this complex and confused panorama, Third World social science (or that elsewhere) has produced no new theoretical approaches to resolve the crisis. This is not to say, however, that important theoretical advances have not been made. There are indeed very fine and important contributions by Third World scientists, but they have yet to be integrated into a coherent theoretical body (Prebisch, 1981; Silva Michelena, 1976). Understandably, governments try to revive neoliberal or developmentalist policies without much success. In other words, during the profound crisis which the world-economy is undergoing there is an equally profound crisis of the social theory of the transformation of the world. In the following pages an attempt to understand the main forces behind such a transformation is made.

The impact of transnationalization

Since the end of the 1960s, the world-economy has been through a crisis likely to last for a few more years. The causes of the crisis are profoundly rooted in the present world-mode of economic accumulation and there are reasons to think that conditions for its transformation are not yet ripe enough. Since the crisis started, periods of recovery, like the present one (1983–5) have been brief. As has been pointed out recently (Martner, 1985: 1–11), forecasts by international organizations for the period 1985–2000 are not optimistic with respect to a sustained recovery of the industrialized economies which would also contribute to a thrust in the economies of Third World countries. Martner cites the conclusions of the *World Development Report* of the World Bank, studies made by the Social and Economic Affairs Department of the United Nations as well as studies by the United Nations Commission for Trade and Development (UNCTAD). All three agree that, at best, there will be slow growth, unless serious progress is made in transforming dominant tendencies in the world-mode of economic accumulation.

As has been pointed out some years ago (Frank, 1974: 2), the crisis can only be overcome in a more or less permanent way if a new model of accumulation emerges. It is true that reliance on cheap energy has been substantially changed, but other axes of the same model, like consumerism and militarization remain very much based on past sources of development. In truth, a new model can only come into being if technological break-throughs occur of the kind which open up new and wide opportunites for accumulation on a world scale.

Some authors (Perez, 1983; Herrera, 1984) have argued that micro-electronics may be one such technological break-through, still only in its infancy. Biotechnology, exploration of the sea-bed and new sources of energy are also frequently mentioned as possible sources of accumulation for the world-economy. However, the fact is that nobody can predict when these new sources will be able to initiate another long wave of prosperity.

With respect to the new international division of labour, it seems that transnationalization of the world-economy remains the most general tendency; in other words, transnational corporations (TNCs) seem to be playing an ever more important role in both developed and underdeveloped economies.

In the developed economies, TNCs are playing the most important role in the transformation of the social division of labour. The key consequences of this transformation seem to be different for the various centres. Thus, for the United States, the main negative consequence appears to be the slow growth in productivity as compared with Europe and Japan. For Europe, the main problem seems instead to be growing unemployment and for Japan the dependence of its economy on expanding foreign markets (see Thurow, 1985). According to the same author, this may result in a growing tendency for the major world-economies to isolate themselves, as a means of solving these problems.

Transnationalization, however, conspires against such a scenario. As their name indicates, transnational corporations operate at a world scale, while states can only effectively act at a national level. This manifests itself in the various difficulties experienced (even in a setting such as the EEC) by states to control multinational monopolies, financial flows, fiscal and monetary policies.

The impact of transnationalization in Third World economies is quite clear: external and internal macro-economic disequilibria, growing external debt, disintegration of domestic productive activities and further integration of national economies into the international circuit of accumulation, nutritional insecurity, urban and rural famine and the irrational use of natural resources. As already mentioned, a new and more favourable insertion into the world's economic order is becoming less and less likely.

The situation obviously varies according to the degree of trans-nationalization of national economies. But there is a problem that seems to burden equally all underdeveloped economies: external debt.

Over the past fifteen years (since the early 1970s), Third World debt to the international banking community increased very rapidly to reach the alarming total of near US$800 billion in 1986. Latin American debt accounts for about half, but some countries in Africa and Asia also have the doubtful honour of being on the list of the most highly indebted countries of the Third World.

Elsewhere, I have discussed why they became so highly indebted (Silva Michelena, 1985). To put it in a nutshell, I argue that Third World indebtedness was due to a combination of factors, among which the most important are the prolonged and pronounced recession at the centre, a variety of errors by both international financial institutions and Third World governments and, above all, the trend towards increasing trans-nationalization of Third World economies. This generated accumulation mechanisms which inevitably resulted in balance-of-payments and fiscal deficits. Increased military spending added fuel to the fire, for a substantial proportion of both balance-of-payments and fiscal deficits may be attributed to it. To cope with these problems Third World governments resorted to external borrowing from international sources overeager to lend at low interest rates.

With the possible exception of four Asian export-led economies, all underdeveloped economies, regardless of their particular model of accumulation, seem to be at the brink of debt. Governments have no leeway to define strategies to get out of this situation, because they apparently have no choice but to apply the politically risky austerity policies of the International Monetary Fund (IMF). This situation considerably worsened between 1981 and 1984 when rising interest rates unexpectedly obliged Third World countries to face the dilemma of not paying their debt (as proposed by Fidel Castro), or starving their populations to death by following the IMF recommendations. The fact is that the economies that Third World countries were making, which entailed great sacrifices by their populations, were swallowed up by rising interest rates. Since 1984 interest rates have come down somewhat, but still the most indebted countries must devote a third or more of their export incomes to service their debt.

This problem is also potentially dangerous for the financial security of central countries and for the peace and security of the whole world. But the negative effects on Third World populations are real and urgent. As examples we can mention the Draconian policies from which Mexicans and Filipinos are suffering because of the debt problem; families in

Nigeria, Zaire or Venezuela which hitherto barely subsisted, can cope no longer. Thus, it is not surprising that delinquency and personal insecurity in the capital cities of most underdeveloped countries are reaching alarming proportions. Discontent is everywhere and open protests are multiplying throughout the world, as is demonstrated by massive street demonstrations in Argentina, Egypt, Sierra Leone, Liberia, Indonesia and Colombia. General strikes and states of emergency have occurred in Bolivia and Peru; governments have been challenged in Morocco, Tunisia, the Dominican Republic and Haiti; in Brazil hungry masses have looted supermarkets and silos; in Chile, in the midst of the fight against dictatorship, hunger marches have alternated with political protests. There are many examples of popular protests by the masses against the set of policies imposed by the IMF which have already left hundreds of dead, thousands of wounded or imprisoned persons and which are forcing Third World states to become more and more repressive. In short, this multiplication of conflicts is menacing world peace, particularly if due account is taken of the new and tense political situation in the world.

Reduced space for political manoeuvring
Since the end of President Carter's administration, the policy of détente, of peaceful coexistence, began to deteriorate until it ended in a cold war (Halliday, 1983). Today, this new situation dominates the world's political panorama and determines changes in the global strategic scheme. It should be recognized that, since 1985, there have been events pointing to the conclusion that there may be a gradual easing of this tense situation, for instance, the resumption of the Geneva talks and the summit conference of November 1985 in Geneva. Yet the fact is that such initiatives have had no practical effects beyond fostering the illusion that nuclear holocaust is a bit further away than before.

The main consequences of this new period of confrontation between the two great powers for the rest of the world, is a greater control of dissidence within each bloc, an attempt to strengthen alliances and military pacts and, for the Third World, a reduction of the political space for manoeuvring of each country. This means that political and social experiments are not likely to be tolerated.

Such repression has been necessary in the capitalist camp to diminish the wave of revolutions which began in the 1970s and, in the socialist camp, to cope with the anxieties caused by direct Soviet intervention in Afghanistan and the prolonged confrontation between Vietnam and Kampuchea. In other words, an attempt is being made by the hegemonic powers to keep order in their respective zones of influence. As a result underdeveloped countries have suffered an important loss in the degrees of freedom they had attained to define autonomous policies oriented towards the transformation of their societies and the achievement of a more favourable situation in the world's economic order.

Among the factors which led towards the new Cold War was the realization by US leaders of the progressive weakening of US military, political and ideological influence *vis-à-vis* the USSR, and of economic deterioration *vis-à-vis* Europe and Japan. This so-called crisis of hegemony led the Reagan administration to overreact, in the sense of defining a policy that would recover for the United States its former position of absolute hegemony in the world scene. It implied the abandonment of the policy of defence of human rights and of action through the Trilateral Commission, which characterized the Carter administration, to concentrate on an overall policy based on force, militarism, political and economic pressures and direct intervention in the internal affairs of countries belonging to its sphere of influence. This is demonstrated by the nuclear redeployment imposed in European countries in spite of the massive opposition of their populations and, above all, by the insistence on pursuing the Strategic Defence Initiative which is apparently changing the entire post-war strategic scheme.

Clearly, peripheral countries have no real leverage to change this tendency. This has recently been demonstrated by the scant attention paid by the great powers to the results of the summit meeting of Argentina, Greece, India, Mexico, Sweden and Tanzania, held in New Delhi in January 1985, to foster peace and disarmament.

It is important to mention that, in the new strategic scheme being put into effect by the Reagan administration, there is a plan to cope with revolutionary movements in the Third World. One of the military elements of this strategy is the Rapid Deployment Force which is designed to place in any part of the world, rapidly and without warning, a combat force strong enough to put down any insurgency. However, as demonstrated in Nicaragua, this may be preceded by political and economic intervention.

Nevertheless, it is significant that at the beginning of 1986, when this text was written, there were some signs that the United States may be introducing important changes into its policy towards the Third World, in the sense of relying less on dictatorships to keep these countries in order and more on helping new democratic movements to reach power. The overthrow of Duvalier in Haiti, and the events in the Philippines may be examples of these changes. To be sure, the new democratic movements must demonstrate their allegiance to Washington before receiving any kind of backing.

Long-term trends

We have already mentioned that one long-term trend in the transformation of the international order is towards an increasing isolationism of the United States, Europe, Japan and the socialist bloc. This fragmentation of the world-market may come about because no country is really capable or willing to pay the price of managing the world-system, and because the particular problems powers are now facing apparently find no real solution within the present world-economy. For the Third World, such a scenario would probably mean, for each area, the severing of ties with the rest of the South and, perhaps, with other powerful zones of influence. However, if competition among the powers sharpens, then perhaps there may be more space for manoeuvring for the Third World.

A long-term vision of the trends transforming the international order may reflect a totally different perspective, one version being presented by Wallerstein (1985). He points out that, as in many other periods of history, the end of an expansive phase of the world-economy has given way to a new and prolonged recessive phase. This implies, as was the case in similar historical phases, that the reorganization of the world not only affects economic relations but also systems of interstate relations and the cultural-ideological configuration.

He argues that such a transformation may be the formation of a new axis between the United States, Japan and China. This new axis would seek to establish selective co-operation with semi-peripheral states of the South. This of course would imply a certain redistribution of surpluses, thanks to the significant increase in capital accumulation that this alternative implies. Moreover, the cost of such redistribution would be more than compensated for by the decrease of political exploitation in the South.

The formation of such an axis would imply the formation of another axis between the USSR, Western and Eastern Europe, for they would otherwise feel surrounded by an increasingly hostile world.

Wallerstein argues that, since both the United States and the USSR have to face growing internal dissidence and disorders, they would probably pay less attention to Europe: hence the tendency towards the reunification of Europe would be accentuated.

Wallerstein builds a series of considerations around these two main hypotheses. Perhaps it is worth mentioning here that such reorganization of the world order would provide new opportunities for the process of capital accumulation, but along with it 'a considerable proportion of the world population would continue to be scandalously exploited and who knows if worse than ever' (Wallerstein, 1985: 23).

However, such a process may be what is needed for a truly radical ideological and cultural change which might result in the overthrow of nineteenth-century social ideologies. Such an intellectual revolution may be what is needed to reassess the strategic options of world anti-systemic movements, to get them out of the historical cul-de-sac in which they have found themselves since 1945.

Another vision of the world's future comes from A.G. Frank, a scholar who has worked in the US, Latin America and is now based in Europe. According to his perspective, Western Europe faces several challenges: firstly post-war US hegemony; secondly obstacles to the formulation of a truly European policy in response to the present crisis, and thirdly the present economic crisis.

Since Eastern Europe faces the same challenges, except for the first which there concerns Soviet hegemony, it could be said that

> the European challenge then is also to forge a truly all- or Pan-European response based on increased and improved East–West (and North–South) European economic, strategic, political and cultural relations to promote political peace and economic progress in Europe and the world. (Frank, 1986: 2)

Frank argues that the prospects for closer East–West European relations are bright, because there is a 'renewed recognition of the need for and desirability of increased trade and other peaceful relations within Europe' (Frank, 1986: 2), both West and East. A larger Europe, through a criss-cross network of bilateral relations 'can be a means of overcoming or at least bypassing some of the obstacles to integration within a smaller Western Fortress Europe – and such a reemergence of pan-European relations can be a major step towards defusing the growing threat of nuclear war' (Frank, 1986: 4).

Such expansion of the EEC would provide a basis for a major international and national political realignment and an alternative regional or economic strategy for each bloc. In concrete terms, this means a *rapprochement* between the EEC and the CMEA, and stronger ties with both the Middle East and Africa.

According to this view, all the present allies of Western and Eastern Europe would have reasons to agree to such a realignment. The US would find itself freer to draw its economic and political attention away from Europe and the Atlantic and to turn them to the Pacific. The USSR would have a reduced economic and military burden, besides the prospect of a weaker, or perhaps broken NATO, which would mean the fulfilment of a long-cherished objective.

According to Frank, such political and economic realignments would not eliminate East European and Third World dependence, but at least they would offer greater hope for world peace, a greater possibility of economic growth in Western Europe, wider opportunities for liberalization in Eastern Europe, and increased political bargaining power and room for manoevre for socialist and nationalist liberation movements in the Third World.

Another perspective is offered by Robin Luckham, a European scholar who uses a different methodological approach. He considers a number of different scenarios, or loose cognitive maps, 'for reshaping the international order that have emerged in recent discussions' (Luckham, 1985: 83).

Luckham considers four proposals for restoring some form of the international status quo, and two alternative paradigms. The first set includes the trilateralist scenario which summarises the ideas and policies advanced in the reports of the Trilateral Commission in the 1970s. In brief, this proposal sought to restructure the international order on the basis of managed capitalism by the US, Western Europe and Japan. Policy for the Third World sought political order and respect for human rights, although in the end less liberal policies prevailed.

The 'monetarist-militarist' scenario is a consequence of the recession of the late 1970s and the deterioration of East–West détente. It was introduced as a new policy by the US and Great Britain. 'The most distinctive characteristic has been the combination of liberal economics and muscular geopolitics' (Luckham, 1985: 85).

'Gaullist' scenarios, says Luckham, have shaped French policy since General de Gaulle's presidency to Mitterrand's. They are based on state power and national capitalism and on six interrelated priorities, ranging from an 'independent' defence and nuclear deterrent to cultivation of political alliances in the Third World through aid policy and well-publicized support for the NIEO, as well as a direct military presence in regions of French (European) influence (Luckham, 1985: 85). There are advocates of this view throughout Western Europe, but the political viability of these scenarios is far from established because of European obstacles.

The scenario of 'socialism as it actually exists' is an extrapolation of the USSR's international behaviour. Great power and bloc objectives are given priority over the construction of socialism and support for states of socialist orientation in the Third World.

The first alternative scenarios is the 'Brandt–Palme–Thorsson' scenario which proposes gradual change instituted by the more progressive members of the global policy-making elite. The specific propositions are set out in the well-known reports of the respective commissions, so there is no need to summarize them here.

The second alternative scenario is called by Luckham the 'global transformation' scenario. Some of its features are: planned recovery and transformation of the North through co-ordination of economic policies and the rehabilitation of the European welfare state; a nuclear freeze, deep military expenditure cuts and planned conversion to civilian uses; step-by-step disengagement from NATO; structural transformation of Third World economies, non-alignment and demilitarization, releasing resources for development.

To conclude this section, it is important to note that, of all four visions of the world's future presented, only Luckham's is somewhat optimistic about the Third World. Let us now turn to the consideration of the alternatives open to Latin America, keeping in mind the international framework.

Future alternatives for Latin America

International political and economic trends certainly have a great deal of influence on the alternatives open to any particular country, but the viability of any project is set by the extent to which significant social and political movements adopt them as concrete projects of their own. For this reason, in the pages that follow, an attempt to summarize different proposals put forward in Latin America by significant social and political forces is made. Some of these proposals have been tried in the past, but continue to be backed by certain significant social forces waiting for the opportunity of a comeback. Others are mere intellectual constructs, but they may be considered as messages with a future. Since we will be generalizing for the whole of Latin America, the proposals inevitably acquire an abstract character. However, we hope that the loss in concreteness will be compensated for by a better understanding of each alternative.

The neoliberal proposal

This is usually backed by internal forces linked to transnational corporations, conservative politicians and the authoritarian military. It has recently been defeated in Argentina, Uruguay and Brazil, but it still appears to be a latent alternative. Even in countries with more or less long democratic traditions like Costa Rica, Mexico and Venezuela, there are strong sectors favouring this alternative, which is also backed by the Reagan administration. A worsening of the new Cold War, and a consolidation of new US hegemony tend to favour this alternative in the short run.

The proposal is formulated within the context of a reordering of the world capitalist system under the hegemony of the United States. The supporters of this proposal usually argue that factors blocking a further capitalist development are: (a) excessive democracy and the consequent deterioration of government legitimacy; (b) state gigantism and its effect on both a chronic fiscal deficit and inflation; (c) excessive growth of labour unions and their participation in the formulation of public policies; and (d) excessive nationalism. With respect to international perspectives, this proposal argues in favour of a greater integration with the United States economy in a global system of mutual complementarity.

Liberal democracy

For countries which recently became democratic, such as Argentina, Uruguay and Brazil, the main objective would be the consolidation of a restricted democratic regime. For countries such as Costa Rica, Mexico, Colombia and Venezuela, which have a certain democratic tradition, the main objective would be to achieve a better redistribution of wealth. This proposal is backed by the various elites: the entrepreneurs, the labour union leaders, the techno-bureaucracy, the main social democratic parties, the church and the armed forces. A social pact among these elites would guarantee both democratic stability and an appropriate management of conflicts of interest. Negotiation and consensus are general principles orienting politics. The implication is a restricted participation of the popular sector, which will be practically reduced to participating in national, state or municipal elections.

Given the present dimensions of the debt problem, the main policy concern of sectors favouring this alternative today is to pay debts through tacit or open agreements with the IMF. They favour bilateral negotiations, although they are willing to participate in international meetings such as the Quito Conference (January 1984) or the Cartagena Consensus. There is a growing resistance among the advocates of this alternative to blindly following the IMF's recommended policies. However, resistance is as yet more rhetorical than practical. In short, there is a lack of an alternative economic programme.

Projects of social transformation
The advocates of these proposals share the idea that a self-reliant Latin America for the year 2000 depends a great deal on the type of transformations that may take place now. These transformations require new social actors in order to express popular interests different from those of the currently dominant sectors. These new actors should have a profound democratic vocation and be capable of generating a new hegemony within each state. This proposal would benefit from international trends such as those envisaged by Wallerstein.

Within this general characterization in Latin America it is possible to identify three main versions: deepening liberal democracy, popular regional transformation, and socialism.

Deepening liberal democracy. This alternative radically questions the idea that economic growth is the main objective of development. It advances a new conception of development according to which the main purpose of productive growth is the improvement of the quality of life, reordering the logical order of needs and distributing resources geared to satisfy the new order of priorities.

Politically this implies a power coalition clearly favourable to meet the needs of the popular sectors. Hence, measures to avoid a reconcentration of power must be taken. Elite corporatism must be replaced by an effective participation of the popular masses, in an organized way, in decisions concerning the economy. Decentralization is essential to guarantee effective participation. It also implies a change in the social relations of production. A third form of ownership has been suggested, i.e. co-management and co-operatives.

Finally, basic structural transformation should facilitate the rearticulation of Latin America in the world-economy, substituting markets, reorienting exports and selectivity of imports, all in order to attain a greater economic autonomy.

Popular regional transformation. This is basically structured along the same lines as the previous alternative, but adapted to the particular conditions of Caribbean and Central American states. Thus, more emphasis is given to real regional integration, to cope with the fact that most Central American and Caribbean countries are mini-states. This integration should recognize the existence of such differing situations as those of Puerto Rico, Panama or Cuba (Gorostiaga, 1985).

Socialism. The existence of Cuba makes socialism a real alternative for Latin America. Advocates of this alternative constitute significant social and political forces in various countries, but they are more important in Peru, Nicaragua and El Salvador. In the rest of Latin America the overwhelming bloc constituted by social and Christian democracy forms a new ideological and political hegemony which, for the time being, seems to have diverted the appeal of the masses from socialism.

Disenchantment with socialism is due to a complex set of phenomena: the failure of guerrilla movements in the early 1960s, the realization that 'real socialism' has been unable to find a way of effectively guaranteeing civil and political liberties, and a pragmatic assessment of the costs involved for a socialist experiment in a climate of cold war and interventionism by the United States.

Finally, there is a certain widespread optimism due to the fact that in the past ten years Latin America has changed from having predominantly dictatorial regimes to predominantly democratic ones. This may not have a great deal of influence on the global strategic scheme, but it certainly provides a stimulus for democratic movements all over the Third World. There may not be a direct linkage between the Latin American democratization process and, for instance, the overthrow of Marcos in the Philippines, but these events certainly provide fresh air for democratic movements elsewhere. If democratization of the Third World becomes a steady tendency, then there may be fresh hopes for greater South–South co-ordination and interchange. This may, perhaps, be the first step towards a truly new international order.

References

Amin, Samir (1975) *Acumulacion a Escala Mundial.* Mexico: Siglo XXI.

Cardoso, F. H. (1976) 'El consumo de la teoria de la dependencia en Estados Unidos'. Caracas: CENDES, mimeo.

Cardoso, F. H. and Faletto, E. (1971) *Dependencia y Desarrollo en America Latina.* Buenos Aires: Siglo XXI.

CEPAL (1969) *El Pensamiento de la CEPAL.* Santiago de Chile: CEPAL.

Frank, A. G. (1972) *Capitalismo y Subdesarrollo en America Latina.* Buenos Aires: Ediciones Signos.

Frank, A. G. (1974) 'World Crisis and Latin American International Options', paper presented to the symposium on Latin America in the International System, The Royal Institute of International Affairs, London, 1 May.

Frank A. G. (1986) 'The Challenge for Peace and Progress', paper presented at the IPRA Conference, University of Sussex, Brighton.

Germani, Gino (1962) *Politica y Sociedad en una época en Transicion.* Buenos Aires: EUDEBA.

Gorostiaga, Xabier (1985) 'Condicionantes para una Alternativa Regional a la Crisis Centroamericana', in Heraldo Munoz (ed.) *Crisis y Desarrollo Alternativo en Latinoamérica.* Santiago de Chile: Aconcagua.

Halliday, Fred (1983) *The Making of the Second Cold War.* London: Verso Editions and NLB.

Herrera, Amilcar (1984) 'The New Technological Wave and the Developing Countries'. Brazil: UNICAP, mimeo.

Luckham, Robin (1985) 'Anarchy or Transformation? Scenarios for Change', *IDS Bulletin*. University of Sussex.

Marini, Ruy Mauro (1973) *Dialectica de la Dependencia*. Mexico DF: Ediciones ERA.

Martner, Gonzalo (1985) 'La insercion de América Latina en la Economia Mundial – Una Vision del Futuro'. Caracas: PROFAL–UNITAR, June, pp. 1–11.

Munoz, Heraldo (1985) 'Vias al desarrollo despues de la Crisis y el Neoliberalismo', in Heraldo Munoz (ed.) *Crisis y Desarrollo en Latinoamérica*. Santiago de Chile: Editorial Aconcagua.

Perez, Carlota (1983) 'Structural Change and the Assimilation of New Technologies in the Economic and Social System: a Contribution to Current Debate on Kondratiev Cycles', paper presented at the international seminar on Innovation, Design and Long Cycles in Economic Development at the Department of Design Research, Royal College of Art, London, 13–15 April.

Prebisch, Raul (1963) *Hacia una Dinamica del Desarrollo Latinoaméricano*. Mexico: Fondo de Cultura Economica.

Prebisch, Raul (1981) *El Capitalismo Periferico, Crisis y Transformacion*. Mexico: Fondo de Cultura Economica.

Silva Michelena, José A. (1976) *Politica y Bloques de Poder. Crisis en el Systema Mundial*. Mexico: Siglo XXI.

Silva Michelena, José A. (1985) 'Los intereses estratégicos globales y la problematica de la seguridad en el orden internacional: América Latina y Europa', in EURAL, *La Vulnerabilidad Externa de América Latina y Europa*. Buenos Aires: GEL.

Thurow, Lester (1985) 'The World at a Turning Point', paper presented at the seminar on Crisis and State Regulation: Policy Dilemmas for Latin America and Europe. Buenos Aires: EURAL, 14–16 October.

Wallerstein, Immanuel (1985) 'European Unity and its Implications for the Interstate System', paper presented at the seminar on The Role of Europe in the Peace and Security of Other Regions. Austria: UNU, Schlaining Castle, 2–4 May.

18

Violence in the Third World

Soedjatmoko

'Violence is a sign of institutional failure and system overload', writes Nazli Choucri (1986). These conditions are by no means unique to the Third World, but it remains a fact that the vast majority of wars and war-like incidents that have taken place since the Second World War have been fought in the Third World. Furthermore, the daily turmoil and frictions of life under circumstances of economic struggle and rapid social change give rise to violence among groups and individuals within Third World societies.

Despite their great diversity, the countries of the Third World have some characteristics in common, apart from their location in Africa, Asia or Latin America, that make possible some generalizations about violence as they experience it. In the first place, most developing countries share the experience of colonial domination, though the nature and duration of it vary tremendously among them. Most of them are poor. Perhaps even more important, most are engulfed in a process of very profound social and economic transformation which, though a necessary condition for development, is in itself a source of instability.

The roots of violence
For many of the countries of the Third World, one can begin the search for the roots of violence with the circumstances of decolonization. For those countries that gained their independence by armed struggle, the fight for independence gave a legitimacy to the use of violence that still clings to it in many settings. A further legacy of colonial rule is the forced cohabitation within a single state of antagonistic groups that are artificially bound together within the borders established by the colonizers. In many instances quarrels that were submerged but not resolved during the colonial period have re-emerged and, often, burst into violent conflict after independence.

Poverty is not necessarily a cause of violent conflict – though many argue that it is in itself a form of violence. It can be seen as such when it is the product of maldistribution of resources and denial of opportunity, and exists in the midst of plenty or even excess. Under these conditions, poverty is usually the result of social and economic relations that can only be maintained by the threat or the use of violence. One major feature of recent decades has been the growing self-assertiveness of poor and traditionally powerless groups. In some cases, groups of people have managed to move up the economic ladder, though many have met with violent resistance on the way. However, it is not poverty but the attempt to break out of poverty that generates violence both as a tactic and as a response.

Heightened aspirations and a refusal to accept a miserable lot have also contributed to massive population movements, within and across national boundaries. Violent clashes with established residents are a common result of migration. For example, in the Indian state of Assam, many lives have been lost in attacks by the Assamese on illegal immigrants from Bangladesh. In Honduras, the migration of Salvadorans in the early 1960s not only produced local clashes, but led to a build-up of tensions that culminated in war between the two states. Even in cases where migration is received peacefully or the initial violence simmers down, the long-term basis may be laid for communal tensions that erupt into violence at later stages – as has been the case throughout South and South-East Asia as well as in many parts of Africa.

The process of development itself is always a source of turbulence and often a source of violence. Developmental success inevitably brings about structural change, upsetting traditional hierarchies and often generating violent reaction. The failures of development lead to even greater strains on the social fabric. The global recession of the early 1980s, the debt burdens of many of the developing countries, the prospect of slow and uneven growth for many years to come, the drawing down of the financial and ecological capital of whole nations have created intolerable strains. In many parts of the Third World, communities are on the verge of breakdown. Societies are beginning to come apart at the seams as the despair, frustration and rage of the 'have nots' clashes with the fear, reluctance or intransigence of the 'haves' and erupts into religious, ethnic, tribal, racial and class violence.

The dislocations caused by rapid and extensive change make countries vulnerable to conflict arising from both internal and external sources. Adjustment to the developments of the late twentieth century is threatening enough to the equanimity of any society without the further challenge of trying to compress centuries of technological change and nation-building into the span of a few decades.

It is important to keep in mind, however, that the process of social transformation is by no means confined to the Third World. All countries are in some measure caught up in sweeping value-changes that respond to new technologies and modes of organization, and to a pace and scale of change that is unprecedented in human experience. It is not only in the Third World that the re-examination of old and newer values has led to challenges to the state, for example. The function, purpose, character and structure of the state encounter challenges from neoconservatives and religious fundamentalists in the United States, from 'green' parties in Europe, from minority nationalities in the Soviet Union, as well as from numerous social and political movements in the Third World.

The fragility of young states in the face of internal turbulence and external pressure leads many governments to attempt to centralize power and to rely upon the armed forces to maintain stability. The ease with which this tendency slides into a cycle of militarization, repression and internal conflict is all too familiar to students of Third World political development.

Many of today's violent conflicts are products of the inability to manage change. Others have their roots in contradictory perceptions of and beliefs about change. The complexity of the interlinkages among problems creates in many minds a longing for simple, reductionist explanations, whose foundations in reality are so insecure that they have no capacity for toleration of other approaches.

No region has quite mastered the dislocations of the twentieth century, with its dizzying growth of populations and massive movements of people, its instant communications, alienating technologies, shrunken spaces and horrifying destructive power – and so all remain vulnerable to conflict. The Third World is not unique in this. It would be difficult, for example, to draw a clear distinction between the violence in Northern Ireland and many of the ongoing conflicts in the Third World. None the less, three of the widely shared qualities that have been mentioned – colonialism, poverty and accelerated change – do give the Third World some distinctive preconditions for violence.

There is also a psychological sense of belonging to the Third World, which arises from the recognition that the international system is dominated by and directed for the primary benefit of countries that exclude the Third World from decision-making and a fair share of the benefits of interaction. The resulting sense of vulnerability and exclusion – and the often angry sense of injustice that accompanies it – gives the countries of the Third World some sense of solidarity despite their differences and leads them into conflict with the North. This kind of conflict has not often been pursued through armed conflict between states, but it undoubtedly feeds the atmosphere of confrontation that leads to isolated acts of violence. And isolated acts can all too quickly fall into a pattern of mutual escalation of violence, with states entering into conflict as patrons, sponsors or perpetrators of terrorist incidents, punitive responses, campaigns of destabilization and overt or covert interventions. Uncontrolled, indiscriminate and self-perpetuating cycles of violence are thus set in motion.

One further source of violence in the Third World should be mentioned: with the achievement of functional nuclear parity between the superpowers, and the virtually uncontested recognition of spheres of influence dominated by one or the other in the North, the Third World has become the only 'safe' battleground for the contest between East and West. Neither superpower is yet willing to run a serious risk of direct nuclear confrontation, which is implied by any armed conflict between them in the industrialized world. Thus the Third World has become a theatre, in both the military and the dramatic sense, of East–West competition. Of course this competition is not a factor in all violent conflicts in or among developing countries, but it has prolonged and intensified many of those in which it is not a prominent cause. Inevitably, it adds to the complexity of South–South or North–South confrontations.

The sources of violence in the Third World are thus an admixture of internal pressures resulting from rapid change and external pressures resulting from the clash of outside interests. Efforts to minimize and control violence must recognize that these two aspects require rather different approaches. The effort to minimize internal violence must focus on ways of increasing the resilience of societies; the effort to minimize external violence must focus on restraint in the definition of and response to threat.

Violence and social change

One might characterize the kinds of violence within Third World societies as violence that reacts to change, violence that attempts to force change, violence that reacts to the lack of change without any positive programme, and violence that attempts to prevent change. Many communal clashes are examples of the first type, as one segment of a community sees another getting ahead and perceives this movement to be at its own expense. Revolutionary movements and liberation movements are examples of the second type. Common urban criminality typifies the third type, which is nourished by the hopelessness and despair generated by widespread unemployment and economic stagnation. Criminality often engenders from the state authoritarian reactions that are equally lawless, in the name of law and order. The fourth type of violence is typified by repressive regimes that violate the human rights of their citizens and subject them to arbitrary arrest, disappearance, torture and execution for the sake of preserving an existing order.

A prevalent aspect of the fourth type of internal violence is militarization, though militarization has origins that are broader than domestic tensions alone. Militarization establishes a niche for violence within a society. When it is combined with lack of discipline in the armed forces (as it has been recently in Uganda, Sri Lanka and Lebanon), it holds civil society by the throat. The rationale for militarization, that it is needed to preserve security, is turned on its head, as the armed forces become the primary source of insecurity for substantial segments of the population.

Political systems may respond to the build-up of potentially explosive social tensions in one of several ways. They may learn to tolerate a high level of violence in ordinary political life, reacting with indifference to killings and destruction as long as they do not threaten the political system as such. In India, for example, intercaste, interclass and intercommunal violence is a fact of civic life. Only rarely does it become a problem for the continuity of a regime.

A second possible response is for the political system clearly to favour one group within the polity over others (often under pressure from the dominant group) and place the resources of the system at its disposal. The result is polarization and an escalation of tensions, as has been the case in Sri Lanka in the 1980s.

A third kind of response is a serious programme of gradual change that brings all contending groups into the system and mediates among them, moderating the impatience of the ascending groups and the defensive reactions of those whose relative position is descending. The Malaysian experiment in bringing the Malay majority into the economic mainstream, though not without violence, is perhaps one such attempt, which was engineered as a response to racial violence in the late 1960s.

The first two of these alternatives are violent responses. Under the first, the violence is sporadic, dispersed and systemic. In cases of the second, violence becomes concentrated in a struggle for control of the system. Only the third response makes possible the peaceful management of social tensions, but it is extremely difficult to implement.

National governments are not in full control of the processes of change. Their ability to direct the course of events in their countries is being eroded from two directions at once: from below by subnational groups which have lost faith in the government's commitment to represent their interests, and from above by transnational processes and institutions. The nation-state is on the defensive, which in many cases has prompted governments to respond to internal challenges with repression, and to external pressures with a refusal to co-operate in common endeavours. The pursuit of national security has come to place excessive reliance on the use of force, to the neglect of the economic, social and political factors that determine a nation's vulnerability in large part.

Given the incapability of governments to control the effects of change, it is important to consider what other kinds of institutions and modes of organization might help to enhance adjustment. Learning to manage conflict without resort to violence is a process in which the whole society must participate. It poses a particular challenge to the emerging nations. In many of them, the development of civil society was arrested, even destroyed, by colonialism. Indigenous forms of participation, indigenous vehicles of consensus and conflict-resolution and indigenous sources of legitimacy have only rarely survived or been restored; indeed, they have often been further suppressed by the modernizing bureaucratic state.

It is often simply impossible to know, through any ordered, rational investigation, which institutions or practices may prove to be the most effective. History tells of the rise of spontaneous, unexpected currents that have altered the course of history in a given area – such as the Gandhian movement in India, for example. The present time is characterized by profound shifts in the values held by significant groups of people. These shifts, which are both a result and a source of social change, occur simultaneously in disparate and sometimes conflicting directions. Some look back to a revival of traditional values, while others look to other cultural traditions, or attempt to define an entirely new configuration of values. Often, there is no agreement within a society on which values should take precedence; nor is there any toleration of different views. The problem of resolving conflict becomes much more difficult when one is no longer operating within a single world-view, but rather dealing with different systems that do not accept each other's legitimacy.

Under present conditions in the Third World, violence is very difficult to bring under control once it starts. Weapons are too easily available; the polity is too fragmented; sections of the population, especially among the young, are too alienated from the existing system; rival groups become too easily and quickly polarized. The emphasis therefore must be on prevention of violence, which in turn depends on strengthening other forms of political expression and communication.

Communication must, of course, be two-way, and must be able to proceed through multiple channels. A dialogue between the government and the political opposition is not enough; ways must also be found to reach out to and to hear from those who do not have access to the usual channels of expression. Representation is not simply a matter of political structures: the schools, churches, community groups, and even the security forces must also be representative. Otherwise, they are likely to be perceived as the tools of only one among many contending groups and thus lose their legitimacy in the eyes of society as a whole.

Much is made of the role of private-sector institutions in the health of the economy these days. A case at least as strong can be made for the role of private groups in the health of the polity as well. Private think-tanks are often better positioned than government-sponsored ones to analyse social issues from an independent stance, and to devise socially creative options for dealing with them. Traditional conflict-resolution mechanisms which operate at the local level often can tap springs of compromise that elude the government official or the formal judicial structures.

The cohesiveness of a society does not depend exclusively, or even primarily, on its laws. Cohesion depends much more on the existence of a general social consensus that the institutions of society are reasonably fair, just and accessible. Without this basic consensus, the rule of law becomes entirely dependent on enforcement, with the police and the army functioning as an occupying force within their own countries. The consent of the governed is not just a moral desideratum but a practical necessity for a non-violent society.

A society that has achieved a workable consensus is not necessarily a society without conflict. It is questionable whether such a society exists anywhere – it certainly does not exist in the developing countries that are caught up in the tumultuous processes of economic development and nation-building. The crucial question for these Third World societies is how to reduce the human cost of the necessary and in many cases desirable changes they are experiencing. How can they reconcile the need for change with the need for order and the need for justice? The dynamic equilibrium among these three defines the space for freedom and the realization of both collective and individual aspirations.

Resilience and restraint

Social resilience is the quality that permits people and institutions to interact with each other in each of the three dimensions without their conflicts erupting into violence. Resilience allows a people to accept change without losing their own cultural identity. Resilience permits faith in a system of justice to be maintained even in the face of flaws in the system; a single travesty or even a series of them will not bring about rejection of the system as a whole. The concept of resilience is quite different from that of stability. Stability under oppressive conditions means the perpetuation of violence. The interaction of resilience and order creates a capacity for adaptation without chaos. The lack of resilience in any of the three dimensions creates the conditions for violence. Change without resilience leads to alienation and loss of identity; a system of justice without resilience turns predictable human failures into catalysts for polarization; order without resilience leads to oppression and a corresponding resistance.

Building social resilience is not a task only for the state, though the state can play an important role. But the quality of resilience lies in the much broader sphere of civic culture. A collective commitment to the public good, to managing conflict without violence, depends as much on community groups, non-governmental organizations, religious institutions involving both clergy and laity, volunteer groups, political parties, educational institutions, the media and so forth – all of which have the responsibility and the capability for nurturing a sense of civic responsibility.

The spontaneous actions of inspired individuals also can be extremely important at times when the resilience of a society is stretched to the breaking point. In the aftermath of the 1985 Mexican earthquake, the unorganized actions of citizens were far more effective in the early stages than official relief efforts both in rescuing and sustaining people, and in preventing the development of an atmosphere in which looting and violence could have become widespread. Similarly, citizens intervened spontaneously in New Delhi after the assassination of Prime Minister Gandhi in 1985 to interrupt the attacks on members of the Sikh minority. There are many such examples, and they underscore the importance of a public philosophy in which the citizens bear a sense of responsibility for the collective good.

Existing social institutions must become the vehicles for creating and expressing this sense of responsibility, but it may also be necessary to create new kinds of institutions at the national level to cultivate the habit of thinking collectively but pluralistically about the public good. Political culture is nurtured by a broad approach to public-affairs education, including a multiplicity of forums, journals and research institutions engaged in a continuous process of dialogue and reflection across the divisions within the nation. For example, the concept of the national defence college could and should be broadened in scope, purpose and composition to provide a setting in which leaders from the military, the civil service, the private sector, the non-governmental sector, and the political cadres could be trained in thinking about the overall national interest. National security issues should be high on the agenda of any such institution; they should never be regarded as the exclusive concern of the military. Pluralism in the selection of students and staff would be essential, so that the political opposition also becomes familiar with the sources of social resilience and the dangers to it.

If resilience is a key concept in coping with the strains that lead to domestic violence within societies, restraint is one of the strategic concepts in minimizing violence imposed or inflamed by external forces.

Restraint has two major dimensions, one internal to the decision-making structures of Third World countries, and one to be exercised by external powers. The first of these applies chiefly to the ways in which actors in the developing countries express and pursue the very real disputes among themselves. All have a stake in the peaceful resolution of conflicts, limits on the production and importation of arms, and the vigorous application and extension of humanitarian law.

Above all, it is in the interest of the developing countries to wean themselves from external military support and involvement, for two compelling reasons. One is that external involvement almost always increases the scale and destructiveness of violent conflicts, by providing weapons that multiply the number of casualties (especially, in recent decades, civilian casualties) and do considerable damage to the social and economic infrastructure of the area of conflict.

When one party to a dispute turns to outsiders for support, its adversaries are encouraged to do the same, thereby subjecting the country or region to the expression of rivalries and antagonisms in which it has no direct stake. External military aid is often the trigger for region-wide arms races, which drain the resources and heighten the tension-level of the countries involved. The external patron may discourage client governments or factions from entering into negotiations or seriously pursuing negotiations that do get started. It may prefer to continue an armed conflict that costs it relatively little but is an effective source of discomfiture to its rivals.

The second compelling reason to forego external assistance is that such assistance undermines the autonomy of the recipient to such an extent that even the winner of a battle for control of a state may end up with a Pyrrhic victory. Measured against the loss of political independence and the danger of re-subjugation to the interests of external powers, the political or ideological goals of the combatants must be reassessed. Furthermore, the acceptance of external aid often entails a serious sacrifice of legitimacy, as the American-backed regimes in South Vietnam, the Soviet-backed regimes in Afghanistan, and the Vietnamese-backed regime in Kampuchea have discovered to their own and their patron's frustration.

For the sake of limiting the destructiveness and the duration of violent conflicts, as well as to protect claims to legitimacy, restraint in seeking external military assistance is a serious consideration for all parties to armed conflict in the Third World. But such a regime of self-restraint is unlikely to hold up without a symmetrical restraint on the part of the external powers themselves. In increasing numbers of armed conflicts in the Third World, the external intervenor is not one of the superpowers nor one of the former colonial powers but rather one of the more powerful Third World states – such as India, Libya, Vietnam and Tanzania, to name just a few. Therefore, any code of conduct that might be devised to discourage interference in armed conflicts will have to be negotiated on an inclusive basis, though regional organizations are often promising venues for initiating such discussions.

Restraint on the part of potential interventionist states has a powerful potential for limiting the scope of armed conflict in the Third World, given that few developing countries have sophisticated arms industries of their own. Only Brazil, China, India, Israel, South Africa and Taiwan have significant arms manufacturing capacity. Few other developing countries even approach self-sufficiency. Although the arms imports of the Third World countries as a whole increased dramatically in the 1960s and 1970s, they have been constrained by the global recession and the collapse of commodity prices. Many states are thus increasingly dependent upon military aid or credit.

A more demanding form of restraint on the part of external parties requires a narrow interpretation of the kinds of political developments that constitute threats to their national interests. Demanding as this is, however, it is not the same as insisting that states subordinate their national interests to higher principles such as respect for self-determination – for this, the realist must admit, is not likely to be accepted by powerful states in the near future.

Restraint in defining one's legitimate national security interests requires making a distinction between developments that are threatening and those that are merely distasteful. The accession to power of a leftist regime in Nicaragua is certainly profoundly distasteful to the current US administration, as was the prospect of a non-Marxist regime in Afghanistan to the Soviet Union, but it is difficult to convince most of the community of nations that either constitutes a genuine threat to the security of the superpower in the region.

Governments and non-governmental actors are motivated to observe restraints either because they recognize a moral imperative shored up by the approbation of the international community, or because they calculate the utilitarian value of reciprocal restraint on the part of adversaries. Any state that chooses to ignore restraints must calculate that its willingness to do so will inevitably encourage others to do the same; its calculations of self-interest must weigh the short-term advantages that might be gained in a particular conflict against the cost of achieving its objectives in an environment made more dangerous and difficult by a generalized lack of restraint.

The primary obstacle to restraint is desperation, and in that the Third World abounds. To reduce the sources of armed conflict there, as in the North, will call upon the deepest reserves of political innovation that governments and other political actors can command. The task is obviously not one for the Third World alone, given how closely its turbulence is tied to that of the international system as a whole.

Non-violence as a practical alternative

The record of violent struggle in achieving objectives is in recent years a dismal one: witness the intense and spreading destruction in the Middle East, the stalemate in the Gulf War, the growing intransigence of the South African government in the face of armed attacks. In the latter case, non-violent demonstrations have exerted more effective pressure for change, both domestically and internationally, than violence – violent resistance has in fact given the government an excuse for greater use of violence itself.

Non-violence is not just an ideal; it is also a tactic or even a strategy. Its effectiveness as a strategy of the outgunned has been repeatedly demonstrated – most recently in the Philippines where the heavily armed Marcos government was unable to resist the massive demonstration of popular support for the opposition led by Corazon Aquino. Also, it should not be forgotten that for all its violent rhetoric and the subsequent record of violence, the Iranian revolution was a non-violent revolution – a revolution of the popular demonstration, the sermon, the cassette, all leading up to a massive withdrawal of support for the Shah's government.

It may be that the practical appeal rather than the moral appeal of non-violent struggle may provide the impetus for reducing violence in the Third World. Non-violence is often described as the weapon of the weak. But this is true only in the sense of comparative arsenals. Confronting a tank with only one's body requires greater courage and entails greater risk than confronting it with another tank. Non-violent struggle is not easy; it is not risk-free; and it does not always work. But the physical and psychological and moral costs of violence are so great that an alternative form of political struggle deserves to be given the most serious consideration and trial.

There is little doubt that violence will be a constant companion to life in the Third World for the foreseeable future. There is little that the developing countries can do to extricate themselves single-handedly from the geopolitical competition of the world-system dominated by the superpowers. This fact gives the Third World a vital stake in the strengthening of collective, multilateral institutions of conflict resolution at the global and regional levels. Internal violence is also likely to persist. Within many developing societies, the disparities are so great, the injustices so gross, and the privileged so fearful of and resistant to change that violence will be turned to as a last resort. The irony that history has taught us so often is that the use of violence, however justified, may demolish the very goals and ideals that were sought, and create the mirror image of the injustice it sought to destroy.

Author's note

The author would like to thank Kathleen Newland for her valuable assistance in writing this chapter. The views expressed are those of the author and do not necessarily represent those of the United Nations University.

References

Al-Mashat, Abdul-Monem M. (1985) *National Security in the Third World*. Boulder: Westview Press.

Chege, Michael (1985) 'Conflict in the Horn of Africa', paper presented in Addis Ababa at the United Nations University's seminar on Peace, Development and Regional Security in Africa, January.

Choucri, Nazli (1986) 'Demographics and Conflict', *Bulletin of the Atomic Scientists* 42(4): 24–5.

Gavshon, Arthur (1984) *Crisis in Africa: Battleground of East and West*. Boulder: Westview Press.

Hansen, Emmanuel (1985) 'Peace and Regional Security in Africa: a State of the Art Report', paper presented in Addis Ababa at the United Nations University's seminar on Peace, Development and Regional Security in Africa, January.

Leiken, Robert S. (ed.) (1985) *Central America: Anatomy of Conflict*. New York: Pergamon Press.

Macfarlane, Neil (1985) 'Intervention and Regional Security', Adelphi Paper No. 196. London: The International Institute for Strategic Studies.

Porter, Bruce D. (1984) *The USSR in Third World Conflicts: Soviet Arms and Diplomacy in Local Wars 1945–1980*. Cambridge, New York, Melbourne: Cambridge University Press.

Snitwongse, Kusuma and Joo-Jock, Lim (1986) 'Security and Development in the Asean Region', a paper prepared for the United Nations University Project on Security and Development.

Thomas, Gerry S. (1984) *Mercenary Troops in Modern Africa*. Boulder: Westview Press.

Treverton, Gregory F. (1977) 'Latin America in World Politics: the Next Decade', Adelphi Paper No. 137. London: The International Institute for Strategic Studies.

PART VI

Transcending Violence

19

Peace Movements in Industrial Societies: Genesis, Evolution, Impact

Nigel Young

Introduction

Up until recently the peace movement has largely been defined as a phenomenon developing in the Western (and usually Christian) countries, in the industrial democracies and the English-speaking world. Although this is now changing, this chapter focuses on industrial societies – mainly Europe and North America. The history of peace movements, as with so many other social movements, is one of discontinuities and divisions. From the late 1880s until 1914 and from the 1920s until the mid-1930s, one can talk of a mass peace movement certainly in Europe and the USA: one can again in the 1960s and in the 1980s. The situation of the Western peace movement, even as it reached its first peak of support between 1890 and 1910, reflected prior origins and the development of a range of peace groups and organizations, just as the contemporary peace movement does. By the 1890s a number of major peace traditions had emerged, each with their own clear organizational expressions, some of them dating back to the early nineteenth century or before. Intellectual trends of the period (anarchism, socialism, liberalism, internationalism, etc.) all affected the peace movements and their various organizational groupings. In turn many new constituencies were mobilized around such ideas by the peace movement. In this sense one can define a core continuity of the peace movement for over a century in industrialized societies.

The history of anti-war sentiment or peace ideas is much older than even the first secular peace groups in Europe (*c.* 1815), but the first modern popular mass movements against war emerged in the late nineteenth century. Many peace sects and traditions (almost all religious) had had peace and the renunciation of war as a principle or goal, and other groups have opposed specific wars and conscriptions. The Society of Friends, or Quakers, despite their often small numbers, had a strong influence on the sustenance and growth of the peace movement through more than 300 years in the English-speaking countries and beyond. The long delayed but deeply rooted reaction to the accelerating arms race in the early twentieth century was interrupted by the cataclysm of the First World War. But a major spread of mass anti-war feeling in the armies of 1916–20 reflected a rejection of mass warfare represented by those important groups which emerged during and immediately after the First World War.

During the more recent past throughout the world peace movements have begun to grow strong again, especially in most European countries. They have mainly focused on the nuclear arms race and have emphasized the threat of the mass destruction of civilian populations by nuclear war. But even earlier there was the widespread impact of the almost universal introduction of compulsory male conscription by 1915, on different social groups in different countries, and indeed on the peace and anti-war movement itself.

Nevertheless, in what sense can one talk of 'the peace movement' as a continuous or unitary social phenomenon? Clearly there have been moments of popular activity on specific issues or broad programmes in which various strands and traditions, immensely diverse in character and often contradictory in their stance, have joined in broad coalitions with the politically mobilized from the mainstream of public life, in the great periods of anti-war feeling (1890–1914, 1916–21, 1930–9, 1957–63, 1965–70 (Vietnam), 1979–85). Some sought to abolish war as such ('pacifism' or 'pacificism'). Some opposed particular wars (such as the Boer War) on liberal, anti-imperialist or socialist grounds. Some aspired to limit or prevent war by negotiated disarmament, international law and peace treaties (the establishment of the International Court). Some opposed particular dimensions of armaments and war (such as conscription, compulsory military service, which had been spreading throughout industrial Europe). In some cases (e.g. the various socialist movements) anti-war movements were fused with movements concerned with removing the war-making society or institutions as they perceived them (i.e. capitalism and the system of nation-states). These and a number of later peace movements had a positive as well as negative concept of peace; they wished to create a non-violent or more just, equitable and harmonious society, and they linked with Utopian and communitarian movements.

One must conclude that peace and anti-war movements are broad, amorphous and sometimes ephemeral social phenomena containing specific organized peace traditions and expressed in often small but prophetic organizational groups which provide ideas, initiatives and motivation for the wider peace movement. It is this that I shall summarize in what follows.

The modern peace movement emerges
In the wake of the carnage of the Napoleonic Wars, the secular ideas of the *Aufklarung* – the development of modern ideological formulae – began to play a more dominant role. The necessity for social and human change, the view that the problem of war was linked to problems of economic injustice and political repression, to the selfishness of narrow

elites, of powerful ruling groups and national and imperial, as well as racial, chauvinism. This surfaced in the struggle against the causes of war as well as the opposition to expansionist national capitalism, slavery and serfdom – including compulsory military service – even the monopoly of legitimized, centralized, and territorialized violence in the modern state (or 'nation-state'). The latent dilemmas of violent social change were answered in part by Utopian and communitarian views of social change without violence or at least without resort to arms. From now on the peace movement would be divided over the ethics and issues of 'just wars', whether by progressive states or progressive oppositional groups.

Time and time again in the nineteenth and twentieth centuries this pattern would be repeated: the peace movement would divide over whether a war was 'just' or 'progressive', whether the evil to be overcome was any greater than the injustice and violence of the war or violence apparently needed to achieve it, and whether military service – the 'democratization of the means of violence' (by conscription) – might itself be a progressive phenomenon, or lead to radical change.

One can term these nineteenth-century groups 'modern' not because they were secular (they overlapped with religious non-conformity) but because they sought to organize public opinion in society either to create new institutions (like the Interparliamentary Union (IPU) and the Red Cross and the Postal Union) which would have a bearing on peace, or to pressure existing politicians and structures to change their ways or introduce new policies or institutions. Although reformists, they inevitably paved the way for the new socialist-oriented peace and anti-militarist concern which aimed to mobilize peoples to create a new warless world society, even if it meant the violent overthrow of the old order. As the public had become more involved in war – through conscription and the killing of civilians and through new communications – so was a vast reservoir of discontent drawn into religious and political activity against war, especially by certain intellectual currents in socialism. But these non-conformist inspirational roots did not produce a single or uniform socialist response to war and conscription. For example, socialists were deeply divided over the progressive character of conscription and the justification of progressive war. Anti-conscription, which was often linked to the liberal issues of civil rights or the liberty of the individual, also coincided with religious non-conformity (witness against war and conscientious objection) and with socialist war-resistance, especially organized by leftist labour unions (e.g. the Confédération Générale du Travail (CGT) in France).

The search for the means of preventing war, either through the reformed behaviour of states – peace plans, treaties and proposals, negotiations or international law and arbitration between all groups and peoples – was a search that was to develop in the 1890s with a great surge of support for such initiatives as mediation and a world court. With this broader basis in organized popular opinion and political pressure, a public opinion on war began to coalesce and to matter; the idea of a 'workers' strike against war' was heard for the first time; the first peace societies emerged, stressing a search for war-prevention through internationalist organization. Moreover, a transnational loyalty beyond states and national borders which characterized most religions had special meaning for the so-called 'peace' or pacifist churches, and the rise of popular socialist internationalism.

In the middle and later years of the nineteenth century, the liberal vision in its British version was probably the predominant tendency in the peace movement. It was largely middle class (and potentially individualistically anti-conscriptionist), and overwhelmingly male. Its key belief was in the gradual elimination of 'reactionary' and protectionist states – the creation of a global order of free trade, international law and communications – as well as through negotiations, treaties, peace conferences at the governmental and non-governmental level to create the beginnings of a 'world order'. The fact that their ideas coincided with European expansion, the export of nationalism, the spread of colonialism and global imperialism, was not altogether accidental. But it sustained great hopes for a league or union of all nations through its ideals, and the Hague Conferences (e.g. in 1899 and 1907) were seen as a step to that. The Swedish Peace and Arbitration Society (founded in 1883) had enough influence to help prevent a war between Norway and Sweden in 1905, and laid the basis for Swedish neutrality.

Liberal internationalism has often been termed 'pacificism' since it aims to avert war but never renounces its use, or participation in it, as absolute pacifists do. This distinction did not become clear until 1914 when the peace movement shattered – it split between its 'pacifist' and 'pacificist' wings. The latter (more numerous) segment were willing to support the war in most cases. The liberal internationalists (exemplified by the International Peace Bureau of 1892) were associated with the great peace conferences at the Hague. They agitated for a League of Nations (after 1920 supporting it through the League of Nations Unions). They also stressed civilian democratic control of war (via the Union of Democratic Control in Britain) with protection of civil liberties, as against military autocracy.

But the major obstacles to the liberal internationalist dream were the actual geopolitical developments which preceded the First World War. In the period before 1914, socialist anti-militarists tried to link their socialist critique to the idea of practical war-prevention: if the organized producers, now numbering tens of millions in Europe, could strike in unison against war across national frontiers, then the militarists and nationalists, generals, emperors, tsars and capitalist-backed governments would be immobilized by mass non-co-operation. Anti-militarist strikes took place before and after 1914 and the dream of an international general strike of workers of all countries against war did not die with the August mobilizations and indeed led on to other political action before and during the war and after.

By no means all socialists were anti-conscriptionist or internationalist (or even anti-militarist). All the debates and proclamations of the Second International came to nothing in 1914, despite the rhetoric of the anti-war Stuttgart Resolution (1904). This socialist peace tradition can be seen as having at least two major dimensions – 'socialist war-resistance' (as typified by the CGT in France) and 'socialist internationalism' with a third, 'communist internationalism', taking over some of that tradition after 1917.

But part of the cause of the peace movement's failure of 1914 was due to socialist internationalism's inability to act in a practical transnational way. Unlike socialist war-resistance, it was less rooted in popular movements and local communities; it was a movement of intellectuals, party leaders and organizers. Moreover, it was more closely linked to the sentiments of national parties and union leaders. It took the nation-state for granted and was largely wedded to advance within that framework. In a number of European countries – and a number of armies – the idea grew that peace would have to be made by turning the attack onto these ruling groups responsible for war ('peace through revolution'). In some armies (French and British) massive mutinies occurred, and in the Russian and German armies by 1917 the mood went beyond that to revolutionary discontent and mass desertion. The national mobilizations of August 1914 and the military consolidation of the Russian state after 1918 made socialist militarism a key factor in world politics. The events of 1914 and 1917–21 inevitably led to a major rupture in the socialist peace tradition.

Even before 1900 a new transnational women's peace movement had begun to assert an identity of its own, creating groups and bringing together Marxist, socialist, anarchist and liberal women, feminists and non-feminists, those involved in the suffrage movement and those from Christian backgrounds, all unified by an idea of a distinctive role for women on the issue of peace and an expression of female unity across national boundaries (and across the Atlantic), even in wartime. The wartime meeting in the Hague (1915) of over 1000 women (some from the USA) which founded the Women's International League for Peace and Freedom (WILPF) was symptomatic of this new transnational anti-militarist movement.

The secular pacifism of the war years passed on in the 1920s in movements like the No More War Movement in Britain. Meanwhile liberal internationalism regrouped in the League of Nations Union in Britain and the German Peace Society. A number of key international peace organizations (WILPF, the International Fellowship of Reconciliation and War Resisters' International) emerged after 1915. A new form of integral pacifism was born that was largely secular (and often socialist) in character. It drew on all the previous traditions and was more radical than pre-1914 pacifism, linking international war-resistance, anti-conscriptionism and civil libertarianism with schemes of social change.

The new non-violent direct-action techniques of Gandhi were advocated rather than the violent class-war scenarios of many socialist anti-militarists. In many countries, branches of the War Resisters' International were formed which expressed this radical synthesis, both socialist and anti-conscriptionist, forged during the war and now related to minority strands (conscientious objection, feminism and libertarianism).

A fundamental divide had opened up after 1918. One tendency was to organize public opinion to reform the world-system of nation-states, either through a League of Nations or hegemony by an enlightened power or powers. The other tendency was to stress increasing claims against that global system – that is, the extension of the rights of conscience, resistance to conscription, civil disobedience and anti-militarist direct action (radical non-violence and transnational and subcultural identification) associated with extra-parliamentarist strategies of social change.

In the short term both these tendencies in the peace movement were doomed to failure given the context of national rivalries and the new spread of political autocracy. Indeed the peace movements in this period achieved few manifest victories. The establishment of the League, the creation of a new socialist state, the Kellogg Pact, the widespread acceptance of peace propaganda – none of these arrested the drift towards militarization and the Second World War.

The latent effectiveness of the peace movement in preventing militarist excess is impossible to measure. All that can be claimed is that the peace movement evolved new perspectives from the disaster of 1914, maintained a moral critique of war, accumulated new peace traditions and acquired (but only temporarily) a new mass basis. It failed to halt the arms race after 1930, as it had failed after 1900. It failed in most of its other stated goals as well and several key peace traditions suffered dramatic discontinuities. Sectarian elements – the 'prophetic minorities' – were sometimes the source of major splits in peace-movement coalitions, and an explanation of failure. After 1917, socialist internationalism tended to merge either with social democracy, liberal internationalism and the League, or else identified with socialist militarism and the geopolitical interests of the Soviet Union after 1920.

A new internationalism, that of the Comintern, dominated by the Russian state, occupied the vacuum left by the Second International, and played a leading role in the mass peace fronts emerging in the later 1920s and in the 1930s. With the domination of the pro-Russian communist parties and the rise of fascism in Italy and Germany, the independent socialist anti-militarist tradition became a minority one. 'Cominternationalism' practised 'effective 'entryism' in the peace movements of the 1920s and 1930s, but switched to anti-fascist rather than peace activity. However, it established national peace committees (later linked to the World Peace Council) which played significant roles.

By 1932, the peace movements in Italy, Germany and Russia had already been crushed or had disappeared, though in the USA, Britain, the Netherlands and to some extent in France and Scandinavia mass peace movements still thrived. In the wake of the First World War, a new movement based on revulsion at the nature of the conflict resulted in mass concern in the 1920s. It retained a base only in those countries with a semblance of democracy and was focused after 1930 on the renewed arms race and the rise of fascism.

The period after the rise of the fascist movements and the cataclysm of the warfare of the 1930s until 1945 led to another profound disjuncture in the peace movement. Peace organizations and ideas remained, but not a peace movement. Indeed, this period from the protests against civilian bombing in the 1940s until the rising tide of concern in the mid-1950s almost a decade later is the longest single caesura in 200 years of the peace movement in industrial society. It can be best explained by the partial legitimation of war in the face of fascism East and West, and by extension in defending liberties against autocracy by force of arms. In the period before and after the First World War it is plausible to argue that the silent majority was sceptical of war as an instrument of politics and that the nation-states in almost every society were viewed as quasi-legitimate. Ironically the democratization of a number of states and the establishment of socialism in one country led to a more widespread legitimation of war by socialism and liberalism through expanding communications and literacy. The anti-fascist fronts of the 1930s produced the groundwork for the 'just war' theory which rationalized the Second World War. The silent majorities before and after 1945 supported the war alliances. The 'unjust' stereotype of war derived from 1918 was replaced by a grudging acceptance of the big battalions, and apostasy from pacifisms and anti-militarism lasted beyond 1945. This is the only way in which one can explain the delayed reaction to nuclear weapons (in Japan there are some specific circumstances). The state-system itself shared in the general legitimation of the peace of the victors, despite the division into rival political blocs and the new arms race. This acceptance of a 'just nuclear peace' was paralleled by the shift of liberation movements to anti-colonial war in Asia and Africa.

By the late 1950s, when the (again belated) upsurge of public opinion against nuclear arms, which had just manifested itself in Japan, grew in Europe, North America, Australasia and elsewhere, most of the old peace traditions still survived, though it can be argued that 'nuclear pacifism' (e.g. the British Campaign for Nuclear Disarmament (CND)) represented in itself a new type which reflected the drastically altered character of war and weaponry, and which has been revived since 1979 in new forms, and with possibly new traditions

During the post-1945 period, the lack of a movement against the growing atomic arsenal of the United States provided a vacuum into which after 1950 the World Peace Council stepped with its Stockholm Peace Appeal, a movement which gained a genuine mass support despite its aligned origins, because of the US monopoly of the genocidal weapons.

From the 1950s, rising radiation levels throughout the world, caused by nuclear testing, especially in the Pacific, by several countries, led to a global outcry in industrial countries.

Events, movements and ideas outside the white, Western and industrial countries became more significant. Gandhi's movement to liberate India came to fruition in 1947 through an overwhelming non-violent social movement that linked itself explicitly to peace. The first use of atomic weapons took place on an Asian country, Japan, whose earlier peace movement had been shattered by fascist militarism. A new peace movement arose, partly inspired by the witness of the atomic victims, the *Hibakusha*. In many countries the cause of peace became again identified with the cause of social justice, the ending of racial and colonial oppression, and many societies tried to follow India's example by using non-violent means. The repression of Indochinese independence led to a global anti-war reaction. Nuclear testing in the Pacific was responded to by transnational voyages for peace. There were international protests in the French Sahara. The movement of non-aligned states – involving mostly less developed countries – emerged after the Bandung conference with great prospects. Liberation movements in Algeria, Cuba and Indochina began to shift the locus of the peace movement to a more global plane. Certainly the emerging peace movements of the northern hemisphere began to find new echoes and counterparts in the South and the movements of Asia. Human or civil rights also came to be seen as integral to peace, as in the US movement for black social justice associated with Martin Luther King, and its massive use of non-violent action.

By 1965, US involvement in Indochina and the repression of the non-violent movements there forged a new international coalition. In relation to draft resistance, the most dramatic transnationalist movement against a specific, and barbarous, 'conventional' war was the movement against the war in Vietnam (1964–74). The continuity of a broad women's anti-militarist tradition only became clear in the later 1970s through its independent role in the new peace movement with, for example, the transnational marches and peace camps of the period. It contributes to the new peace movement an emphasis on radical destructuring, new forms and models of participation, and an emphasis on spontaneity. It is now closely identified with the environmentalist and anti-nuclear power-lobby – and of course to feminism itself. It tends to be both globalist in orientation and with strong community roots.

Communist internationalism declined in importance after the mid-1950s after practising effective 'entryism' in some mass peace and anti-nuclear movements and highlighting and opposing specific US or Western actions. The national peace committees (i.e. those linked to the World Peace Council) have only played key roles in a few countries, but since 1979 their significance has declined, except in France and Eastern Europe, and even there they are now challenged. A new possibility for organizing opinion effectively against the arms race and to prevent nuclear war has emerged. It is a more transnational and massive protest than anything in the 1960s, and it also involves a broader political coalition with new elements contributed during the period of the Vietnam War and by the women's movement and the ecological and anti-nuclear power movements. These gave a regional and cross-border, as well as international, dimension to the protest, together with new forms of political organization, less reliance on formal structure and leadership, and a greater political awareness of the need for autonomy, in a movement largely alienated from the state.

The churches were also more centrally involved than they had been in the nuclear disarmament campaigns twenty years earlier; following the example of the Dutch churches, both congregations and religious leaders, East and West, took considerably more radical stances. One result of the second awakening of public feeling against nuclear weapons – as in the 1958–63 period – was a renewed revival of critical reappraisal of the role of war and military change in socialism – and even hints of a re-emergence, after sixty years, of a unique socialist anti-militarist tradition. During the years of dormancy, especially since the 1930s, the tensions between socialism and pacifism have multiplied, but now a reopening of dialogue – foreshadowed in the 1960s – between radical pacifists and varieties of revolutionary socialists seems to be recurring. The absurdity of nuclear war and nuclear weaponry and the serious problems of militarized national revolutions are the main facts which make such a reappraisal inevitable.

Several elements are particularly important in understanding the re-emergence of widespread militant opposition to nuclear weapons in Europe after sixteen years: the revival of unilateralism as an idea, the prior strength and organizational experience of the anti-nuclear power movement, the subsequent acceptance of direct action, and the participatory grass-roots character of the new movement, rooted in local communities. The second, third and fourth elements were not as dominant in the anti-nuclear weapons campaigns of the late 1950s when the movement was much more sponsored and created from the 'top down', where direct action was more controversial, and where opposition to civil nuclear energy was lacking. In relation to this it is worth distinguishing between movements that have been essentially objects of mobilization by political elites and those which have been subjects. What might explain the difference between the mass peace movements of the 1930s or 1950s and those of the pre-1914 and post-1958 periods is that the latter were much more subjects of their own activity. In the contemporary peace movement, manipulation is a less dominant feature and synthesis emerges from the 'bottom up'.

This is not to say that tensions do not exist (especially in European Nuclear Disarmament (END) between the visionary, progammatic approach of the intellectual leadership and the down-to-earth pragmatism of the grass roots), but the gap between the mobilizers and the mobilized has closed in comparison with many earlier movements and may explain the successful activation of millions in Europe as against the relatively superficial activation of concern in the USA and Japan in the same period. The bottom-up 'subject' movements are not immune from co-optation or manipulation, but they are less vulnerable. Beneath the visible, superficial mass mobilization may lurk the potential for localized 'subject activism' as may be the case in the USA (and in Russia and Eastern Europe, though in differing contexts).

Civil disobedience has been a much less divisive issue than it was in 1960–1. The overwhelming consensus now accepts the need for massive, direct non-violent action and training for it as necessary. This shift in opinion is partly because of the civil disobedience campaigns of 1959–63 and the direct action taken against Polaris and US bases and partly, in the 1970s, because of action taken against nuclear power-plants. Civil disobedience has also won new respect because of admiration for the symbolic witness of the strongly feminist peace camps.

One novel element since 1980 has emerged as a significant social and political factor. Similar movements have arisen both in aligned and non-aligned countries, both East and West, and significant movements have also arisen in other parts of the world (e.g. North America, the Pacific and Australia). To many observers these appear to be quite new movements.

Conclusion

As stated in the introduction, it is arguable that there is no such thing as a single peace movement but a variety of peace traditions: religious pacifism; liberal internationalism; the women's peace movement; anti-conscriptionism; conscientious objection; socialist anti-militarism; socialist internationalism; the peace fronts associated with the Comintern; radical, secular pacifism; anarcho-pacifism; Gandhian non-violent revolution; the unilateralist nuclear pacifism of the nuclear disarmament movement; the transnational anti-war new left of the 1960s; the ecologically inspired movements of the 1970s and 1980s (the greens). Each has made a contribution, sometimes in coalition, sometimes as separate sects or subgroups. Yet at times a peace movement has arisen that is more than the sum-total of these traditions or the organizations that represent these traditions; at such times it has attracted a mass base. When the mass base falls away, however, there is a tendency (e.g. in 1914, 1930, 1963, 1970) for sectarianism and fragmentation to occur and the traditions are maintained by small groups – prophetic minorities – until the next surge of mass support.

In Europe in 1914 and the USA in 1917 (as in 1939 and 1942), the prophetic minorities remained even after war-mobilization: political sects and religious groups have sustained anti-war or anti-militarist positions even when these have lacked any real popular support; but certain traditions, such as the feminist peace movement of the early twentieth century, or the libertarian socialist, anti-militarist tradition of the same period have been discontinuous.

The revival of the peace issue within the churches in recent times exemplifies the way in which the ethic of Christian pacifism (which underwent such grievous testing in the early 1940s, and was indeed abandoned by many of its staunchest adherents) may reappear on the political stage in revitalized forms in new situations.

One other factor to be borne in mind is that the number of these strands has increased since the nineteenth century, adding on the one hand to the extensiveness of the peace movement's programme and, on the other, to the internal contradictions within its coalitions over strategy, goals and methods. Many previous such movements have declined because of their failure to achieve certain stated specific objectives; for example, peace movements prior to both the First and Second World Wars and the nuclear disarmament movements of 1957–63. Even the surge of global protests, especially in the USA and Europe, during the Vietnam War had ambiguous results.

The new peace movement in Europe rests on a political plateau at present, but it offers new ways of looking at the role of popular, non-governmental initiatives in relation to disarmament and their impact. This chapter has suggested that, like previous peace movements, it may well ebb. That in no way lessens the impact it has had on states or societies and on the political culture of the globe.

The American peace movement (e.g. the Nuclear-Freeze Campaign), which has focused on the MX missile, the Strategic Defense Initiative, on 'first strike' (or 'first use') and on deployment in Europe, has helped to alter the rhetoric of the political elites in ways that are complementary to the European movement's efforts. Moreover, the US movement is also concerned to prevent further Vietnam-type interventions in Latin America.

A new dimension to the nuclear disarmament movement is an emphasis on transnational linkage and non-alignment. Campaigns for a nuclear-free Europe or a nuclear-free zone or zones in Europe (e.g. Nordic, Balkan, Central European) attempt to link the national groups into a common third force crossing national boundaries and bridging East and West; hence its slogans 'No Cruise, No SS20s' (or 'an end to NATO and the Warsaw Pact'), and a 'nuclear-free zone from Poland to Portugal' (or 'from the Atlantic to the Urals'). Linked to these there is no doubt that the potentiality for popular pressure for peace in the East exists outside the official peace committees. Thus, the European nuclear movement has a distinctly independent and cross-national character (more reminiscent of pre-1917 internationalism), but its great danger remains that it too will be Eurocentric, a movement of leaders, parties and intelligentsia rather than of community, grass-roots impulses, and that it will remain dominated by small groups of Western intellectual and political elites. The strategy remains *implicit*, not explicit. Transnational linkages remain small, symbolic, weak, spasmodic and often elitist or confused. The relations of these linkages with any sort of disarmament process is inchoate. It is questionable whether the new nuclear disarmament movement in Europe *is* more than the sum of its parts (i.e. all the 'national' peace campaigns are still struggling for disarmament policies in each national context).

To talk of a 'new' peace movement is only to say that this one is a coalition of new and old elements. It includes those movements mentioned above as well as communist internationalists, independent Marxists, anarchists and groups largely new to the anti-nuclear weapons campaign – community groups, feminists and the anti-nuclear power groups. To these one must add a new generation of activists, many of them young and new to protests or resistance politics, and many active in the women's peace camps and movements. It is clear that the new professional, technical class is highly involved, and to some there are parallels with the emerging labour movement of the nineteenth century.

These demands have been linked to a grass-roots upsurge of protest and pressure since 1979. The idea of a Europe free of the nuclear giants now has great unifying appeal. The potential for linking different national movements across frontiers exists in an entirely new way because, since 1963, the world has seen the Vietnam War, the experiences of the new left (e.g. of 1968), the Russian activity in Czechoslovakia, and later the repression of Solidarity in Poland. The nuclear-free-zone idea is no longer a concept remote from popular understandings and movements, and transnationalism is much more solidly based, as the women's peace marches across Europe and various international gatherings have demonstrated. Such ideas are echoed in the growing movements for a nuclear-free Pacific and the successes in Australia and above all New Zealand.

An indication of the broad constituency of the new movement was the mobilization of women from many different social contexts and milieux: the new peace movement in Europe is complex and varied. Certainly it is better informed, more plural, probably larger, clearly ready to move towards a more political and militant strategy, than was the peace movement of the 1960s. It appears that non-violence is taken a great deal more seriously, both in relation to its own actions and as a potential alternative, localized form of resistance to aggression, than by previous movements. One of the limitations of many such previous peace campaigns has been their obsession with changes in their own governments (states) or in other states. They have tended to align with national political parties, national frameworks, the interstate-system or with 'peaceful' states, whether they are non-aligned, neutralist countries or the Soviet Union.

However, in contrast to the 1950s and 1960s, a multitude of local peace groups, women's peace programmes, local peace-action groups, peace camps, anti-Cruise missile campaigns, European disarmament groups, and other groups have arisen in each locality which are clearly non-aligned between East and West. They broaden the national movements to an internationalist (and European) approach and open up dialogue between 'unilateralists' and 'multilateralists' around the ideas of reciprocal initiatives and regional nuclear-free zones. European transnationalism has also created a special role for the non-aligned or neutral peoples to play, at the governmental and non-governmental levels, as a third force beyond the blocs. As a result, the official centre of gravity of conventional wisdom has moved towards the peace movement's platform: in a small way this is shown in Europe by the dramatic move in moderate public opinion.

Time has shown, however, that such shifts can be short-lived, and opinion is volatile. The greatest achievement of the present movement would be if it could establish a more permanent and widespread presence in global society much as the labour movement has done. An agenda and a set of institutions which despite recurrent defeats and co-optations will not disappear until the problems it arose to deal with are eliminated.

While no twentieth-century state of any size has shown any serious inclination to substantially demilitarize itself, it is clear that the increasing pressure on state policies and public attitudes has significantly shifted them on such issues as certain wars (e.g. Vietnam) and types of weapons (e.g. nuclear) or specific actions (bomb-testing) and on conscription. The threat of the breakdown of nuclear deterrence into a global nuclear war gives humanity one last chance to sustain a movement for species-survival which can emphasize those aspects of society (communal and trans-national, co-operative and non-violent) which can save it. The peace movement has failed for much of its history to harness even those emerging social tendencies which favour it (e.g. communal and trans-national growth). But the contemporary movement contains these elements within its present social character, and has the potentiality to become a permanent and global movement for peace.

Note on background sources

The information used in this survey is drawn from many sources. There are relatively few scholarly overviews of the peace movement, though in recent years academic journals and collections have carried an increasing number of case studies. On the history of the peace movement, the most significant individual scholarly input has been that of Peter Brock in his five volumes on the history of pacifism (in the broad sense) from 1815 to 1960 in Europe and North America.

The Garland collection of over 360 titles reprinted and edited by Blanche Cook, Charles Chatfield and Sandi Cooper is a major source of primary historical research on the peace movement with useful introductions.

Brock's book on *Twentieth Century Pacifism* (New York: Van Nostrand, Reinhold, 1970) covers most of the traditions mentioned in this survey with exceptions of socialist and communist peace movements which should be initially studied through one of the various histories of socialist internationalism. For the contemporary movement, there is little that is truly comprehensive, though the works by G. Sharp (*The Politics of Nonviolent Action*, Boston: Porter Sargent, 1973) on non-violence campaigns and R. Cooney and

H. Michalowski (*The Power of the People*, Philadelphia: New Society Publishers, 1986) on the USA are comprehensive in what they try to do. My own work on the sociology and history of peace movements has been published in a number of books and journals, including the *Bulletin of Peace Proposals*. Mention should also be made of C. Chatfield (*Peace Movements in America*, New York: Schocken, 1973) and R. Overy *How Effective are Peace Movements?*, Montreal: Harvest House, 1982). All of the above contain bibliographies and/or references.

20
Learning Peace

Elise Boulding

Introduction

What does it mean to talk about 'learning peace'? It is now generally accepted in learning theory that we can only learn something that we know already. That means the existing cognitive structures have to be compatible with the new information, and an experience-base has to exist for connecting the new information with what is already known. When new information is to be introduced which is incompatible with existing cognitive structures, or contradicts previous experience, then groundwork has to be very carefully laid in order that the new information can be assimilated.

One problem that peace education faces is that cognitive structures in the 'target audiences' for peace education are usually organized to support win–lose thinking, a we–they attitude towards any potential adversary. These attitudes are buttressed by a social experience of competitive struggles to win in every setting from the classroom and playground to the economic and political arenas. To shift from zero-sum to positive-sum game-thinking, and from a drive to dominate to a drive to co-operate, requires more than imparting information about new approaches. It requires the construction of new mental maps about reality, and a re-experiencing of that reality by the learners in ways that are intuitively convincing to them.

Much of peace education leaves cognitive structures and everyday experience untouched. While peace education as an acknowledged educational effort involving the preparation of curriculum materials has existed for over a century,[1] nations have gone to war repeatedly during that century, and today live in the dread of a nuclear war that to many seems inevitable.

It is now becoming clear that peace education has not resulted in *learning peace*. The longing for peace remains, but is unconnected to how people think the world really works. Yet there are promising developments in peace education that involve precisely experiential learning, and offer hope for the development of a less combative, more problem-oriented approach to international conflict on the part of adversary nations in our time. There are possibilities, not so much for transcending violence as for transforming, or re-forming violent behaviour towards actions that will produce genuinely attractive social outcomes for the participants in conflict. This chapter will consider some of these developments.

Finding the peace that already exists

One of the most important recent developments in the peace-research field has been the recognition that negotiation and conflict resolution are ubiquitous processes, going on all the time in daily life. Anselm Strauss's study of negotiation[2] has demonstrated that the ordinary business of life, whether being carried out in families, neighbourhoods, the civic arena, the world of business and industry, in schools, hospitals and welfare agencies or in politics, involves a process of continuous negotiation. The social order depends on this negotiation activity being carried out in the ordinary course of human affairs. Any two or more interacting human beings, in order to carry out a task that requires some degree of collaboration, must negotiate about differences in definitions of the situation and in perspectives on how the task can best be carried out. This is because each individual has a unique pattern of wants, needs, perceptions and aspirations unlike that of any other individual. The consequence is that conflict of interest, in however small a degree, exists whenever human beings come together. What Strauss points out is that this does not result in a war of each against all, but rather results in thousands of mini-negotiations in order to arrive at mutually acceptable ways of proceeding. It applies in the management of the family toothpaste and in handling a typewriter shortage in a business office.

Because so many of these negotiations are trivial, they are not thought of as negotiations. When someone becomes intransigent on a particular small issue it immediately becomes obvious how important the give-and-take of negotiation is. Some people are better at it than others, but everyone does it, hundreds of times each day.

This is the 'peace' that already exists: the peace of the negotiated social order. When the informal process of negotiation breaks down, then new behaviours are drawn on to deal with the conflict. What is important is the *fact* of the conflict of wants, interests, needs underlying all human interaction, and the realization that there are many ways to deal with these continually occurring differences. Because the word 'conflict' has a somewhat perjorative meaning, there is a reluctance to recognize how much peace-making we do every day. When asked to do a word-association with 'conflict', most people would probably come up with 'win'. Yet mostly we don't try to win. We just negotiate a mutually acceptable solution. Why? Because at a subconscious level we know that continuing goodwill is important for ongoing relationships. We negotiate as insurance against bad outcomes the next time a difference arises with our co-worker – which may be very soon!

One important part of peace-learning, then, is to recognize what we already do as peace-making, and to recognize the ubiquity of conflict. This paves the way for understanding that in a conflict situation there is a choice of behaviours for dealing with the conflict. Conflict management may be thought of as a continuum from total destruction of the other to complete integration with the other.

FIGURE 1
The conflict continuum

As can be seen in the Figure, limited war, deterrence and threat are all on the violence side of the continuum. Arbitration, mediation and negotiation are in the middle region, and various forms of co-operation and alliance are found near the integration end of the continuum. Our culture glorifies the violence end of the continuum. However, most of our behaviour in both public and private life falls in the middle region, with a good sprinkling of integrative behaviour to meet our deeper needs for well-being and a sense of belonging to a larger whole. When we turn to dealing with adversaries at the international level, however, the thinking of the general public and its leaders immediately shifts to the threat side of the continuum. This is the schizophrenia of nationalism.

We are already skilled at this out-of-hand rejection of behaviours which occurs the minute the behavioural context becomes international. This is what peace-learning has to deal with. The Hague Peace Conferences at the turn of the century laid down the processes by which nations might gradually substitute diplomacy for war, and the League of Nations and the United Nations have struggled to move nations from war and the threat of war to negotiation. The knowledge, skills, channels of communication are all there. The confidence to apply them is lacking. 'You can't trust the _____s' is the excuse each time, although we negotiate continually with people we mistrust within our own society. Pillar's study of the processes of war termination[3] shows how reluctant nations are to *appear* to be negotiating, and what a high price that reluctance exacts from all parties.

In fact, leaders and publics alike don't feel they have a choice. Threats and deterrence are the only behaviours they feel are available to them short of submission to the enemy. Yet all nations have to make peace eventually. A reaction to the horrors of nuclear peace has brought a new type of activity into being, the activity of highly trained professionals in law, medicine, the natural and social sciences, education and organizational development, all in the pursuit of alternative solutions to international conflict that will preclude war.[4]

While Europe and North America have the greatest concentration of such groups, they are all more or less transnational, and have members on all continents. It is these groups which are introducing new dimensions to peace-learning. Each from their own profession is working on a new cognitive mapping of international conflict, utilizing what they know as scientists and professionals about how physical and social phenomena transpire. They are knowledgeable about the conflict continuum, and are applying their skills to moving international political behaviour from the threat to the negotiation part of the continuum. The educators continue, as they have done for so long, to develop new curriculi to educate students about alternatives. They have more to work with now than formerly, precisely because of the work of their colleagues in the sciences. They are able to present a broader and more coherent view of the interlocking nature of local–global conflict systems, and of the interrelatedness of the environment, social and economic justice, human health and well-being with the types of security policy nations choose.

The new thinking about local–global linkages (the new slogan, widely used among both professionals and peace activists, is 'think globally–act locally') makes possible an experiential approach to peace-learning. Relating to personal experiences was the second condition stated at the beginning of this chapter, in addition to preparing new cognitive maps of reality, for new learning to take place. Creating a new experience-base is happening at two levels.

At one level there is a great proliferation of local groups concerned with the interrelated issues of peace, the environment, social justice issues and human rights. In a country like the US which has nearly 6000 such local groups,[5] more than half of them are strictly local in that they have no national or international affiliations, yet they are publicly identifiable. In the Third World traditional local groups primarily oriented to more place-oriented issues increasingly coexist with and are being affected by new local movements which combine traditional concerns with environmental and peace and non-violence issues. Examples are the Sarvodaya movement in several Asian countries, the Lokayan movement in India, the new co-operative consumer movement in Malaysia, the Council of Indigenous Peoples (representing indigenous peoples from all continents; now recognized as a non-governmental organization (NGO) by the United Nations) and some new peace-environment-development groups forming in Africa. Latin America, with its network of peace and human rights groups stretching from Central America to Chile, has a high degree of local group activity which includes a focus on larger social issues.[6]

The significance of these groups is that they deal with global security issues in their own communities with the tools at hand, on a physical and social terrain which is familiar to them. They are working on a manageable scale, getting feedback from the results of their actions. One particularly powerful aspect of some of these localist movements is the declaration of a given community or region as a zone of peace, or nuclear-free zone. Such a declaration combines a strongly internationalist political statement with a concrete local programme for improving the quality of community life. At last count there were 2840 nuclear-free cities, counties and towns in seventeen countries,[7] with many Third World countries involved in getting their regions declared nuclear-free.

At another level, experiential programmes in dealing creatively with conflict and severe social problems are beginning to be developed for children. They are found in some of the world's trouble spots such as Northern Ireland,[8] in communities in Israel where Arab and Israeli children go to school together[9] and in India in areas where communal violence threatens. They are found in African schools in Unesco projects to gain new perspectives on Africa's history and concrete ideas on what children can do about Africa's future.[10] They are found in Europe and North America in new organizations and publications for children, and in new types of experiential curriculum projects.[11]

The programmes and activities described above all move away from abstract ideological declarations about how to approach security and peace, and move to the level of daily perception and experience, in a framework which enables people to see the connections between what they know and how the world could work more peacefully.

Cultural mirrors and peace-learning

A society learns about itself from looking in the mirrors its culture holds up to it. In contemporary societies these mirrors are to a considerable extent the mass media. Since the mass media are the most highly developed in the West, the mirror held up for societies in all parts of the world is a peculiar distorting mirror made in the West. As detailed in the MacBride Commission report on the World Information Order,[12] much of what is shown in the mirror is Western stereotyping of other cultures, and much of it involves depiction of violence. The Consumer's Association of Penang, Malaysia, found in a recent study that Malaysian children 'were exposed to four killings, saw 24 guns, heard 14 gunshots and "witnessed" 38 physical blows on an average day',[13] mostly from US series such as *Dallas, Superman and Kojak*. In addition to the fictional violence is of course the very real violence of local warfare and guerrilla activity taking place in many parts of the world. The violence that exists is considerably magnified by a journalistic bias towards reporting stories of violence more fully and frequently than stories of peaceful conflict-resolving activity.

The US media are more violence-saturated than those of other Western countries, and are also the media distributed the most widely around the world. The contrast between the cultural glorification of violence in certain forms of art, music, television and literature as well as in newspaper reporting – all for passive spectator audiences – and the socially sensitive grass-roots activism described earlier, is very great. If we weigh this grass-roots activism in with the initially discussed reality that the great bulk of human transactions on any given day are peaceful negotiations of potentially conflictual situations, we can see that the cultural mirror reflects back a very unreal and distorted version of the actual social order. The cultural images are very persuasive, so people are easily convinced that societies are hopelessly violent by nature.

Another important task of peace-learning, then, is to learn to look with a critical eye at these distorted cultural images. Looking beyond the images to the reality of human behaviour does not mean to create illusions in another direction, of false peaceableness, but to become more familiar with the actual range of human responses, and to learn to evaluate and choose according to how socially productive different behaviours are. More first-hand experience with reality is the best antidote to false cultural images.

While experiential education and grass-roots activism move in the right direction, one educational innovation moves in the opposite direction: the rapid increase in the use of the computer for classroom teaching. Computers per se are not to be condemned. They are an important new tool (but only a tool) for dealing with complex interactions, large-scale information systems, and open information flows on a planetary basis. Used rightly, they will enhance all other human capacities. But this right use will only happen if children are given computer training along with the memory training developed in societies with an oral tradition, and the literacy training developed with the invention of printing. Each skill or discipline – memory, reading and computer literacy – is an indispensable skill along with the disciplines of fantasy, meditation, reflection and craft skills, for the full development of human potential. Each enhances perception of the world, and enriches the capacity to act creatively.

What is to be feared is that children will become deskilled, knowing only about abstract symbolic representations of the world through computer symbols, and no longer having direct experience of that world. Imagine a world in which children no longer had the manual craft skills to handle the natural environment, to see, hear and smell and love it; were no longer able to store accounts of other times and places, other beauty, in the memory; no longer took pleasure in the written record. Between television and the computer, there are already such children today, who only know the world through electronic images and symbols. They can be easily manipulated into violence because they have no basis for reality-testing.

Peace-learning then requires full development of each human capacity, and most particularly the capacity to learn directly from nature itself, still the greatest teacher of all.

Readiness for peace-learning

We have so far emphasized the contradictions between the actual everyday experience of negotiation and conflict resolution and the images of violence reflected back from society's cultural mirror. That theme of contradictions will be continued in an exploration of certain ways of thinking, certain capacities for imagining and fantasizing, which have historically been present in all societies and which continue to be present in our own society. There seems to be a human capacity to visualize 'The Other' as different and better than the experienced present which appears in archetypal form in all civilizational traditions, through visions of the Elysian Fields, the Isles of the Blessed, Zion, Valhalla, Paradise. Under the pressure of acute social conflict and upheaval, the archetypal vision is transformed into concrete imagery that answers to specific social needs and dissatisfactions. This concrete imagery takes the form of various kinds of Utopias, from Plato's *Republic*, produced in response to the upheavals of the Peloponnesian War, to the monastic desert communes established by Christians in Egypt and Syria in the first few centuries of the Christian era in order to escape the corruption of urban life. The twentieth-century versions of these Utopias are legion. They may be found to a degree in the new towns like Brasilia, in the village experiments such as the *ujamaa* in Tanzania, in state-level experiments with socialism, as in Sweden, and with communism, as in the Soviet Union and other Eastern European states, or in small intentional communities like Koinonia or Twin Oaks in the southern part of the US, or the kibbutzim in Israel. They are even found in the small protest encampments of the women's peace movement near military installations, such as Greenham Common in England or Seneca Falls in the US. The desire to design and build 'The Other and Better' seems to be as basic a feature of the human spirit as the impulse to envision it in the first place.[14]

It is important to realize that nuclear fears have not destroyed either capacity – the capacity to envision or the capacity to design and build. These capacities are an important part of the readiness for peace-learning. They can be tapped in everyone, although there are cultural obstacles to be overcome in getting people in touch with their own imagination. One of the myths of the culture of militarism and violence is that war and preparations for war are realistic, and that peace and peace-making are hopelessly unrealistic. Yet Fred Polak in his important book on 'imaging' the future, written just at the close of the Second World War,[15] showed how throughout history societies have been guided and drawn forward by their prevailing images of the future. What human beings vision as possible and desirable is what they work for, both at the individual and the societal level.

It takes time to persuade people today to look past their fears of nuclear holocaust, to put aside their conviction that it is silly to try to imagine the best that could be because it is not 'realistic', and begin again the work of visioning a desirable future as their forebears in every age have done. As another kind of experiment in peace-learning, I have worked with colleagues over the past several years to develop workshops which provide an opportunity for people to imagine what a world without weapons would be like. What is most interesting about these workshops is that once people have generated imagery about a future without weapons they *learn* from their own imagery, and seem able to go forward in working for disarmament and peace with new ideas, new energies.

Imaging a peaceful world as peace-learning
What is it that happens in an imaging workshop?[16] First of all, the participants accept the idea of a discontinuity, a breach in time. This concept is not only a poetic flight of fancy, but an absolute necessity if one is to free the imagination to do its work. If one tries to work towards the future from the present, the known realities cling like tendrils to every new idea, smothering it with awareness of what won't work because of the way things are. This is particularly true in the case of visualizing a weapon-free world, because the world is so highly armed at present that it is almost impossible, standing in the mid-1980s, to imagine that things could be different. The breach in time enables the mind to overleap those local impossibilities that loom so large in the present. There, in the new time-space, the mind can look around and see and hear with the inward eye and ear how things are in a world that we know, by declaration (there must be a willing suspension of disbelief), has no weapons. A thirty-year leap into the future is mandated to allow enough elapsed time for some social change to take place. No more than thirty years, so the participants can connect with the world they imagine as one they might experience in their own lifetime.

The type of imaging that takes place after this leap into the future is called *focused imaging*. It involves a very different use of the mind than is encouraged in any formal educational setting. Therefore time needs to be spent helping participants recover a fantasizing capacity which they had in childhood but which may have fallen into disuse. Focused imaging is a combination of free-floating fantasy (a type of mental play) and daydreaming and a kind of conscious night-time dreaming which is called 'lucid dreaming'. It is *intentional*. That is, the participant engages with a group of colleagues in a purposive use of the imagination on behalf of normatively defined social goals. There is a powerful contradiction between the invitation to enter into the free-flowing inner world of mental imagery with its evanescent material which can hardly be handled like potter's clay, and the instruction to *see* a community in which previously stated goals have been realized. Yet people find their way through that impossibility. The imaging is first done individually, and then shared in small groups.

There are no instructions about what to see. After a warm-up exercise of recalling childhood scenes, the person steps into a 'future present moment' and looks about. The raw material for the imagery which begins to form comes from many sources. The participants are told that everything each of them has ever experienced, seen, heard, tasted, touched, thought, felt, from their time in the womb to the present, is encoded in some manner in their being. This record of total life experience is not available to the conscious analytic mind except in fragments at certain moments. In fantasy, however, that whole repository is opened up and contributes in ways we do not consciously design to that which is fantasized. Some people see the equivalent of a movie unreeling in their heads. Others see disconnected image fragments, and still others do not 'see' but generate their sense of what is happening in this future world in other modalities. Participants are asked to look for specifics about how people live, work, transmit knowledge, govern themselves (from locality to planet), solve problems, handle conflict.

Whether participants 'see' a rural or urban setting, they generally picture a localized world with many transnational networks, in which nature–technology contradictions have been solved, a world in which life is less compartmentalized and less age-graded, in which everyone has a high degree of communication skills (including computer skills) and one in which skills in conflict resolution have a high value. Various ingenious social institutions not known in the 1980s are pictured as dealing with conflict. A lack of tension and lots of smiling is almost always reported. It is a world the participant *enjoys* being in.

After the fantasy material has been reported and discussed, people shift to the analytic mode and ask 'how' questions of the imagery. How does this world actually work? What has to be in place in this future society in order for what was seen to be possible? Only after details of this world have been crafted as far as possible in the time available (the workshop can take one to three days) does the most important work of all take place: imagining a history, backwards from the future, that brought such a world into being. The imagined history generates new ideas for social action in the present, which is the real purpose of the workshop. This is what is meant by the statement that this form of imagining involves peace-learning. By tapping capacities not ordinarily used, people are able to link their analytic and intuitive faculties in ways that produce perceptions of new possibilities, and an accompanying course of action. Over and over again, we find that people are *empowered* by their own imagery.

While the workshops were originally held for people in the peace movement, they are now carried out for all kinds of groups including military personnel, physical and social scientists, diplomats and policy-makers. Not everyone comes away with new insights. Strong resistance to the approach can inhibit learning. But most participants of whatever background do become involved, and feel they have 'learned' something, though they have in fact been their own teachers.

Community-support systems and peace-learning
No one learns in a social vacuum. All the other factors discussed in this

chapter – cognitive readiness, experiential learning, overcoming misleading cultural feedback, and releasing intuition and imagination – can only take place effectively if there is a supporting community, an active reference group, which can nurture the individual's groping for new understandings and new behaviours. The great variety of professional and grass-roots groups using their own knowledge and experience to work for the replacement of military technologies by peaceful problem-solving approaches to conflict have already been discussed. The mutual support they provide for ongoing activity is as important as any piece of work being done at any given moment.

These groups are forming a whole new set of global structures which will become increasingly important as the nation-state moves toward obsolescence. While about half of such groups see themselves as autonomous local groups, the other half are consciously linked to like-minded others through international non-governmental associations. INGOs, as they are called, are citizen interest groups which cross national borders, bringing together persons with common civic, professional, scientific, cultural, economic or welfare interests to pursue urgent concerns which cannot be handled within national borders alone. The phenomenon may be dated from the first world peace congress in Brussels in 1848. By the time of the Paris World's Fair of 1900 there were 122 such INGOs. Now there are thousands. Chambers of commerce, Rotary Clubs, girl and boy scouts, YW and YMCAs, church denominational councils, associations of farmers, teachers, doctors, physicists and athletes all form national sections of INGOs and provide specific global identities for their members.

It is the global identity I wish to emphasize here, for this is what gives a new dimension to the peace-learning which will make the construction of a peaceable social order possible. Each person who becomes seriously active in an INGO goes through a process of acquiring a human identity which is global in its inclusiveness, and subtly changes the character of the responses that person makes in their local community. There is a new context for action, a new set of responsibilities, and a new set of supporting groups, most of whom will never be met face to face, but only known through the numerous communication channels developed by INGOs. Nevertheless, there is a sense of belonging, an awareness that if one travelled there would be friends to take one in wherever there were other local groups of this INGO. Whether through newsletters, meetings or computer networks, INGO members receive a steady stream of messages about the world which are different from the messages they hear locally.

INGO members have a loyalty to their common purposes – scientific, cultural or human welfare – across national borders that is not easily swayed by the belligerencies of their respective national governments, though under stress some INGO members retreat from their transnational loyalties. INGOs struggling with disarmament issues, whether as scientists or citizen-activists, have developed a particularly intense commitment to 'world interest' as contrasted with 'national interest'. Of course they continue to care about the welfare of their own country, just as they continue to care about the welfare of their own family. But they use different criteria in assessing welfare and security. It's not, what's good for my country, but what's good for the world, my country included.

What are the characteristics of INGOs that enhance peace-learning, apart from the fact that they are a support and identity group for their members on a world scale?[17] They have a historical memory, which governments do not have. This is particularly important in the case of INGOs devoted to peace, the environment, social justice and human rights. They know where governments are in an ongoing process, and can sometimes help keep the international community from slipping backwards when states forget what they have already accomplished and agreed to. They are a continuing and persistent lobby for constructive international policies, in national and world forums. The entire nuclear-free-zone concept, which was embodied in successive treaties including the 1959 Antarctica Treaty, the 1967 Outer Space Treaty, the 1967 Treaty of Tlatlolco and the 1971 Seabed Treaty was developed and lobbied through the international system by INGOs. Non-military innovations in the world-security arena are INGO innovations. They don't come from national governments.

INGOs, then, provide a context for peace-learning, and actively engage in teaching nation-states how to manage their affairs peaceably. In a formal sense they are politically powerless, and they are certainly 'poor', operating on very small budgets. But unlike nation-states which are hemmed in by their own secrecy laws, they pool information and continually build up new knowledge through collaborative structures which generate the innovations the international community so urgently needs. The International Council of Scientific Unions, particularly its study groups on nuclear-winter and global climate warming, have probably done more for world security on a shoestring budget than all the national security budgets of the world combined.

Concluding reflections

We have seen that there is a strange and powerful contradiction between the experience and opportunities for learning new perspectives and behaviours related to peace-making which exist in the world today because of the communication networks available, and the cultural self-image of contemporary societies as violent and war-prone. There are tremendous resources for peace-learning, in the daily experience of negotiation and community experiments with peace-making, in the new applications being made by scientists and professionals of their own expertise to problems of conflict resolution and peace, and particularly in the human imagination as individuals and groups draw on the unique envisioning capacities of the mind in a historically venerable tradition of picturing desired futures of humankind. International non-governmental communities of individuals sharing similar concerns and skills provide a web of networks which can nurture this new peace-learning.

The as-yet unsolved problem is how to create a better match between the peace-learning which is actually taking place, and how society sees its own peace-making capacities. An analysis of the political and economic forces that contribute to that continued distortion of self-image lies outside the province of this chapter. Part of the answer to dealing with that distortion is probably to introduce learning processes into settings where they do not now exist, particularly in government. For the rest, continually affirming, expanding and making visible the peace-learning which is taking place all the time may finally move us over the watershed from violence to non-violence, from a militarized world-society to a peaceable one.

Notes

1. Documentation of this will be found in *Peace and War; A Guide to Bibliographies* by Berenice Carroll, Clinton Fink and Jane Mohraz (Oxford: ABC-Clio, 1983).

2. *Negotiations – Varieties, Contexts, Processes and Social Order* by Anselm Strauss (San Francisco: Jossey-Bass, 1978).

3. *Negotiating Peace; War Termination as a Bargaining Process* by Paul Pillar (Princeton: Princeton University Press, 1983).

4. For a description of this process, see 'Peace Movement, USA' by Elise Boulding, *International Peace Research Newsletter* 21(3), 1983.

5. Statistics on the peace movement in the US will be found in *Peace Resource Book*, from the Institute for Defense and Disarmament Studies, by Elizabeth Bernstein, Robert Elias, Randall Forsberg, Matthew Goodman, Deborah Mapes and Peter Steven (Cambridge: Ballinger, 1986).

6. For reports on these activities see *IFDA Dossier*, a bimonthly published by the International Foundation for Development Alternatives, Nyon, Switzerland.

7. Up-to-date information on nuclear-free zones is published regularly in the *New Abolitionist, Newsletter of Nuclear Free America* (Baltimore).

8. For example, *Northern Ireland: Studies in Conflict* by Lynn Shivers (Philadelphia: New Society Publishers, 1985).

9. See for example the *Newsletter of the International Center for Peace in the Middle East* (167 Hahashmonaim St., Tel Aviv 67011, Israel).

10. An example of such a project is found in the story entitled 'The Pain of the Past' about Thiers 1 Primary School in Dakar, Senegal; published in *Development Forum* XIV(1), 1986, p. 5.

11. See the following: *Sharing Space* from the Children's Creative Response to Conflict Program, Fellowship of Reconciliation (Box 271, Nyack, NY 10960); *Peacemaking for Children: A Peace Talks Magazine* for, by and with children (Milwaukee Peace Education Resources Center, 2437 N. Grant Blvd, Milwaukee, WI 53210); and publications of Global Education Associates (552 Park Ave., East Orange, NJ 07017).

12. *Many Voices, One World*, edited by Sean MacBride (Paris: Unesco, 1980).

13. This study is reported in 'Treacherous Tube' by Teh Poh Ai in *Development Forum* XIV(1), 1986, p. 14.

14. Utopism is more fully discussed in 'Utopism: Problems and Issues in Planning for a Peaceful Society' by Elise Boulding, for the Commission for a Just World Peace, International Year Peace Project (World Policy Institute, New York; publication in 1987).

15. *The Image of the Future* by Fred Polak (Dutch original, 1955; two-volume translation by Elise Boulding, Oceana Press, 1961; one-volume abridgement by Elise Boulding, San Francisco: Jossey-Bass/Elseview, 1972).

16. This process is further described in 'Social Imagination and the Crisis of Human Futures: A North American Perspective' by Elise Boulding in *Forum for Correspondence and Contact* 13(2), February 1983. (Also in 'Image and Action in Peace Building', *Journal of Social Issues*, in press.)

17. The role of INGOs in peace-development and peace-learning is further described in 'Nongovernmental Organizations' by Elise Boulding in the 40th anniversary issue of the *Bulletin of Atomic Scientists*, August 1985, pp. 94–6.

21

Peace and the World as Inter-civilizational Interaction

Johan Galtung

Occidental cosmology: peace and development

The problem to be explored in this chapter is the following: given some postulates about the deep structure or 'cosmology' of various civilizations, and more particularly about the organization of space, time, knowledge, person-nature, person-person and person-transperson relations in these civilizations,[1] what are we to expect in terms of the theories, and practice, of peace and development? From the very beginning a methodological remark is needed. This exercise is not a deductive exercise with a well-known outcome. We know, for instance, what occidental theories and empirical practice look like, so it might be tempting to try to deduce them from first principles. Rather than deduction with long, logical chains, however, what we are engaged in here is articulation: spelling out what those basic postulates mean in two areas, *in casu* peace and development. In this context, 'peace' stands for the reduction/elimination of direct violence and 'development' for the reduction/elimination of structural violence.[2] But they also may be seen as two sides of the same coin.

Thus, starting with 'peace' and with 'space': an occidental world order for peace and security would have to be centred, even rooted, in the West in order to be seen as normal and natural by *homo occidentalis*. A peaceful order cannot possibly have its centre elsewhere. In that case a secondary role would have been given to the West, which would not only not be in the interest of the West but would also be contradictory to the very idea of world order, hence of peace and security: a world with its centre in the West and a vast non-Western periphery waiting to be stimulated, converted, influenced, to be civilized.[3]

From this point on there are evidently two possibilities, depending on whether one is operating with a division of space in two parts, centre and periphery, or three parts, centre, periphery and 'evil'. The first conceptualization of space is compatible with the universalism of organizations like the League of Nations and the United Nations, with built-in executive power from Western countries, constructed around Western theories and practice, for instance, in connection with international law (the Hague system).[4] And the second concept, correspondingly, gives rise to a system of treaties and alliances centred on the major Western power, for the time being the United States (e.g. NATO, TIAR, SEATO, CENTO, ANZUS, AMPO and so on). All of these organizations tie the periphery to the centre in an alliance against the evil of 'international communism'. A reflection of this is then found in the system built around the major power in the Eastern part of the Occident: the Soviet Union and the Warsaw Treaty Organization, against 'imperialism'.

The principle of evil has been organized around two axes in history as seen from the West: one national and one ideological. The nations singled out as candidates for this important position in Western constructions of the world are above all the 'barbarians and savages' – the Jews, the Turks and the Russians and the corresponding ideologies paganism, Judaism, Islamism and communism, even 'atheistic communism', with imperialism as the Eastern version. Thus, the evil has been located in the non-Occident, on the one hand, and competitive religions and ideologies within the Occident on the other. The amount of violence exercised in the name of peace and security against these 'evil forces' in history in incredible: Jews killing Christians (Christ), Jews killing Muslims, Muslims killing Jews, Muslims killing Christians, Christians killing Muslims, Christians killing Jews (the Holocaust).[5] The stage is now set for the secular follow-up: liberalism-capitalism versus Marxism-socialism.[6]

When it comes to 'time' one would expect an occidental peace and security order compatible with the idea of progress, and also an idea of crisis that might lead either to *dem ewigen Frieden* (eternal peace) or to total disaster; in other words, an apocalyptic vision. I think it can be said that reliance on military means in general, and offensive military means in particular, either for retaliatory deterrence or simply for aggressive attacks in order to get at the evil at its roots, are compatible with both ideas. On the one hand, there is painstaking work to build alliances and a perfect balance of power; on the other hand, playing with fire. The point is that to the majority within the species referred to here as *homo occidentalis*, the warning so often given by all kinds of peace movements through the ages – that armament policies are dangerous and not only destructive but also self-destructive – is no longer newsworthy. On the contrary, such policies may be accepted precisely because they are seen as normal and natural, compatible with the general idea of progress, with crisis, even apocalypse. Disarmament, if it should ever take place, not to mention a 'disarmament race' as a process, would run against the natural course of affairs and probably be counteracted. Peace should come like a conversion, a sudden transformation, brought about by hard work, crisis, perhaps even by providential grace. And who is in need of conversion? The evil, of course, not the occidental centre.

The occidental theory of knowledge comes in here: a couple of simple ideas on the top, and a lot of highly concrete, more or less logical satellites at the bottom of the thought-system. The ideas are well known and also very old: *si vis pacem, para bellum* – if you want peace, prepare yourself for war – and 'attack is the best defence'. Believed in by occidentals for centuries, or millennia, with some important variations through time, they are essentially examples of how the Western theory of knowledge is based on a widespread faith in such ideas that attain axiomatic character, never to be falsified, not even falsifiable. Moreover, if war breaks out in spite of all the work done to deter evil, that is only taken as proof that we live in a dangerous world. And in that world, 'balance' comes to mean 'superiority', which, when pursued by opposing parties, closes the circle of conflict and arms races. To object that the 'peace through strength' theory is simplistic misses the point: it should be simplistic.

Obviously, warfare is compatible with the biblical four classes of society, with a godly principle on top, then humankind divided into two parts, men and women, and nature at the bottom. To possess overwhelming force and intelligence is a manifestation of omnipotence and omniscience; godly characteristics, and not only of occidental gods. But how can warfare be compatible with benevolence or good, a third major characteristic of god? War itself is malevolent for everybody. So benevolence in war can only manifest itself through the assumption that war is being fought for a higher principle, something far above the untold suffering on the battlefield and afterwards. And such principles indeed exist: the 'Triumph of the Lord' would be the religious version; the 'Fight for Freedom', for the 'Glory of the Nation' would be the ideological version. From such principles theories of the just war, the *justus bellum*, easily emerge, in the name of some occidental religion or ideology (e.g. Judaism/ Christianity/Islamism or liberalism/Marxism).

At the same time military organization is deeply vertical, except in the transitory non-hierarchical form of the guerrilla which is usually disbanded after use. It is also individualistic in the sense that there are great chances of rising high in these hierarchies through risk-taking and acts of heroism. War loosens rigid class structures and provides new opportunities as a reward for sacrifice, if sometimes only posthumously. But women have been denied this opportunity. They are on the margin of the system, and they also serve as victims of that particular anti-woman violence known as rape. They contribute by bearing babies, by acting as nurses, repairing the men for more war, and by taking over those productive tasks left undone by the males who have gone off to fight. And these are not the males of a professional warrior caste only, but in principle the entire male population (except individual objectors). In fact, the more universal the conscription, the more ideology has to enter as a motivating force.[7] Since conscription is imposed by the nation-state, nationalism will be the motivating ideology used by the state for war in a world construed as an interstate-system. Paradoxically, the more human rights the nation-state grants, the more human duties it can exact from the population (e.g. in the form of taxes and military service).[8]

To this picture, then, one need only add the image of war as a devastation and rape of nature, as a total lack of consideration which demonstrates the ascendancy of human beings over the lower levels of life and the environment in general.[9]

Consequently, anybody who in one way or another fights against the war-establishment and the military approach to peace and security should realize that this fight is at the level of deep ideology and deep structure, at the level of cosmology. It is not merely a question of an ideological debate and struggle like that between the ideological right and left in domestic occidental politics. Much more is at stake: the whole military approach is an almost perfect articulation of cosmological assumptions and for that reason is deeply rooted in occidentalism itself. Preparation for war, and war itself fit only too well into the general code. A change in attitude is very unlikely to occur unless that cosmology is challenged and to some extent altered. And that is more easily said than done. In the last 2500 years of Western history it probably only happened twice: during the transitions from the Roman Empire (in the West) to the Middle Ages and from the Middle Ages to the modern period.[10]

Unfortunately, a similar comment could be made about the occidental theory and practice of development. Although one may dislike it, one should realize that to *homo occidentalis* 'development = economic growth' and that this is not a random choice among many possible views of development. It is simply the truth in the sense of being normal and natural and so is compatible with occidental cosmology and for that reason is not a subject of serious debate. The language of discourse is already set by the cosmology, largely within the economic-growth approach – just as is done for peace within the balance-of-power approach.

Let us focus on time and space together. It goes without saying that 'development' is a special case of the more general 'idea of progress'. But it also goes without saying that however this special case is precisely defined, it will have to be done in such a way that the West consists of the 'more developed countries' (MDCs) and the non-West consists of the 'less developed countries' (LDCs) or, as they are sometimes described, 'the underdeveloped', or 'undeveloped' countries. There has to be centre and a periphery, both of them 'developing' since there is a universal dynamism in these matters. Also there is the promise of progress for everybody who accepts the basic parts of the Western code.[11] In this, however, there is a contradiction: if the non-West is developing and the West only stays developed, one day the non-West might well catch up with the West.

But this is precisely where the other aspect of the Western time cosmology comes in: the 'idea of crisis'. Yes, there may be a crisis: the LDCs may catch up! From this follow two clear possibilities: either that the developed countries will have to continue to develop along the same lines as before or along some new line, or that the non-West will take over and force the West out of its dominant position. I think it is precisely this frightening possibility – to some extent realized in the world today because of the rapid development of Japan and neighbouring countries – that confirms development theory as normal and natural, because of the strong identification of the West with crisis. It is a tantalizing challenge, like facing death and avoiding it. A non-Western centre as defined by development is anti-cosmological, a kind of crime against nature. The West has to be the model, not the non-West.

When it comes to the associated theory of knowledge, we are in a situation similar to the one connected with peace and security. Simple axioms, such as 'economic growth' and 'labour productivity' are on top of a thought-system guaranteeing development for all as the logical consequence of a mathematical economic theory. The bottom line is very promising – progress. There are variations of this theme, different schools of thought when it comes to the construction of theory, different assumptions, but the basic idea remains the same. The process devastates nature, but environmental degradation has become a familiar part of contemporary reality. It is compatible with verticality and individualism, with women being given an inferior position (reproduction rather than production) and with great opportunities, like in the military, for rapid personal mobility through risk-taking, even sacrifice. Entrepreneurs and other types of players on the 'market' are essential for this type of development.

There is also a god-like principle, the secular successor to striving in your daily work for the glory of god: individual well-being, not in the sense of a welfare state, but in the sense of a high standard of individual material life – comfort. Material living standards play very much the same role as freedom in connection with the pursuit of peace: it is the overriding goal that justifies the negative consequences of the actions engaged in, such as ecological degradation, human misery and alienation, repression, war. As for security and freedom, it can be argued that such well-being is something concrete that people pursue, not something abstract like 'peace' and 'development'. But that is at the individual level. At the national level, growth and productivity become goals in their own right because they are collective conditions for satisfying individual needs for security, freedom and well-being as these are understood in the Occident.[12] The basic point is the absence of 'system' thinking at the social and world levels. Peace and development are 'system' characteristics, not dependent on individual persons and nations. But epistemological atomism is central to the Occident.

There are cases of success. Military ascendancy has created a space in which some type of security and freedom can be wrought in the centre, although of course this is at the expense of the periphery, not to mention of the 'evil' forces. And the same is the case for material living standards. Our present world shows considerable well-being at the centre; there is less, though, at the periphery since the whole exercise is tied to patterns of exploitation, particularly through unequal exchange relations between the centre and the periphery, which then has to be construed as instrumental to development. Of course, there may also be high material living standards among the evil forces. They are regarded as 'evil' because they have their own way of trying to get to that goal, and in so doing neither recognize the West as the centre, nor the West as a model. However, in practice they tend to do both, which delights the Western centre because it sees itself confirmed through such heretic practices ('heretic' from the point of view of the centre's ideology, that is).

So in practice we end up with the four worlds that I think are useful in understanding peace and development across the globe.[13] The First World, the centre, defines 'development' and sees itself as a model; the Second, socialist World is 'evil' because it claims to have an alternative approach; the Third World is the periphery and continues to remain the periphery; and the Fourth World in East and South-East Asia was once like the Third World but is now threatening to overtake the First World. Hence there are problems, of course, just as there are for the pursuit of peace, but all these problems are already implicit in the occidental cosmology or implicit model, and they are not necessarily totally unwelcome since they spell crisis.

In consequence we have exactly the development theory and practice we deserve. Anyone who disagrees will have to understand that the struggle for 'another kind of peace' or for 'another kind of development' is not only a struggle for another ideology or, as it is often put, a struggle between right and left. In fact, when another kind of peace or development is launched from the left, for instance, within the Marxist frame of reference, it will tend in practice to turn out very much like what has been indicated above, with some minor modifications.[14] This is because there has not been sufficient awareness of the cosmological aspect of the problem. The struggle for another kind of development, like the struggle for another kind of peace, has to be conducted as a challenge to, even a transformation of, occidental cosmology, of all those deeply held beliefs that help to define peace in terms of arms and development in terms of money.

Peace and the world as inter-civilizational interaction

So far I have tried to explore the implications of the code or cosmology of occidental civilization in general, and the Western part of it in particular, for peace and development, theory as well as practice. Ideally I should now bring in a number of other civilizations and do exactly the same exercise for each one of them, bringing in all six aspects of the code, space, time and so on. However, that exercise, important as it is, lies outside the scope of the chapter.[15]

A more limited exercise shall be undertaken here, making use of only one aspect of the civilizational codes: the construction of space. After all, it is in the world-space that peace and war take place so it is a major aspect, although the other five also play a considerable role and will be alluded to, more or less systematically.

The civilizations to be considered are the occidental civilization in the expansion mode (explored in the preceding section), occidental civilization in the contraction mode (a more modest version of occidental civilization, corresponding to the Middle Ages), Hindu civilization, Buddhist civilization, Sinic (Chinese) civilization, Nipponic (Japanese) civilization, and then, in addition to these six, what will be simply referred to as indigenous civilization. Needless to say, there is no unity to indigenous civilization except perhaps, in a crucial sense which is the only one that will be made use of here.

The assumptions about the construction of space are then as follows:

Occidental civilization, expansion mode: the world is divided into three parts, an occidental centre, a periphery waiting to become occidentalized, and a recalcitrant, marginal, outer periphery of evil.

Occidental civilization, contraction mode: the world is divided into many parts, each of them a centre in its own right – in other words a multi-centric world.

Hindu civilization: the world is seen as one big unit, inspired by the fundamental unity of man. Basically this concept is Hindu, although Hinduism in its full richness has only been comprehended in India; elsewhere only aspects of it have been articulated.

Buddhist civilization: there is a basic unity-of-man assumption, but also a multi-centric construction of space, each centre being restricted to its own area of concern rather than controlling others.

Sinic civilization: the world is first divided into two parts, the centre in China and non-China, or the barbarian part, which is then divided into four, northern barbarians (the worst), eastern barbarians, southern barbarians (probably the best) and western barbarians.

Nipponic civilization: the world is divided into three parts, a centre which is Japan, a periphery consisting of the countries in the Fourth World, the world to the south-east, roughly speaking the Great East Asia Co-Prosperity Sphere (*daitōā kyoeiken*), and an outer periphery, the rest of the world, which is considered a resource for raw materials and other production factors, and as a vast market.

Indigenous civilization: the world is here again seen as multi-centric, with more or less explicit knowledge of the other centres. In this multi-centric construction there may also be elements of any one of the other configurations just mentioned.

Before we proceed, let us simplify a little by combining the occidental contraction mode, the Buddhist and the indigenous civilizations, because they all operate with the same basic configuration of space. They are not truly world-encompassing in comparison with the other four civilizations which give some structure to the world as a whole. Rather, they see the world as divided into many parts which basically relate only to themselves without assuming that others are a peripheral part of oneself, are necessarily antagonistic to oneself, or are something to be used by oneself. The elements of such ideas may exist, but not as basic and long-lasting conceptualizations. So we shall combine the three as civilisations with multi-centric constructions of space and relatively small centres.[16]

That leaves us with a total of five civilizations to consider, and the matrix now to be explored can be found in the Figure. The main diagonal has been emphasized; it marks the intra-civilizational encounters. They have been numbered in the order in which they will be explored, as have the combinations above the main diagonal which yield a total of fifteen bilateral relations. The case may be made that the matrix is not symmetrical, that a bilateral relation can always be seen from both sides, which is of course correct. But the nuances to be gleaned from such considerations are of minor significance in this context and so there are only fifteen tasks to be done. Let us start with intra-civilizational relations.

(1) This combination is probably considered as 'normal' in the international relations of the West, in the general theory of international relations and in the international relations theory of the United States in particular because of the strong assumption that the United States is the most 'normal' country in the world.[17] Expansionism is taken for granted for all states; empty space is filled and occupied space is conquered until the costs outrun the benefits – at that point a more-or-less stable border can be drawn if it is adequately protected through balance-of-power mechanisms. I have argued above that the system does not tend to be stable, that the offensive arms used for deterrence through the threat of retaliation engender arms races and that arms races sooner or later end with wars.[18] It is difficult to calculate what percentage of human belligerent activity is found in the first combination, but it must be considerable.

(2) We are here dealing with quite different logic. Ideally speaking, each one of the centres regards the rest as simply other parts of a multi-centric world, and continue to exist according to the doctrine of 'live and let live'. In practice, however, there was warfare in the Middle Ages, although much of it was ritualistic; and towards the end of the Middle Ages expansionism set in (even though one may argue that by then we were already in another civilization). Similarly there are Buddhist kingdoms with considerable belligerent activity (e.g. Burma and Thailand), and among the indigenous people expansionism and even imperialism are not unknown (e.g. the Inca, Aztec and Zulu empires). But it can also be argued that these are aberrations and in any case trifling compared with the first constellation. Probably much more can be learnt about a peaceful world from the promise of (2) than from the well-proven failure of (1). Yet it is one of the prerogatives of occidental civilization in expansion to forget its belligerent history and to believe itself to be the centre of any peaceful order that the world can attain.

(3) There is only one relatively cohesive Hindu civilization – India – and only one world, so it is difficult to see this as an inter-civilizational relation. In modern times the parts of the Hindu world, inside or outside India, cannot be said to have engaged in any consistent warfare against

FIGURE

Inter-civilizational relations: space

	Occidental, in expansion	Occidental, in contraction; Buddhist indigenous	Hindu	Sinic	Nipponic
Occidental, in expansion	(1) war	(6) absorption, extermination	(7) penetration	(8) penetration, war, defence	(9) war
Occidental, in contraction; Buddhist indigenous		(2) live and let live (by and large)	(10) tolerance, expulsion	(11) tolerance, expulsion	(12) absorption
Hindu			(3) horizontal tolerance, vertical violence	(13) vacuum	(14) distance, but danger
Sinic				(4) only one	(15) war, defence
Nipponic					(5) only one

each other. There is nothing there reminiscent of the First and Second World Wars in the Occident, nor of the preparation for the next world war between the United States and the Soviet Union. It may be objected that this is because most Hindu lands have been under foreign domination until recently (i.e. British rule and Mogul rule before that) and that this has had a pacifying effect. But this argument is not quite convincing. Rather, it looks as if India, as an inter-state system bringing together a number of nations speaking languages as different as those found in Europe and in about the same numbers, has been much more successful in achieving peace than Europe. Of course, there are conflicts, but there is nothing like a division of the Indian union into two alliances with a handful of neutral, non-aligned states in-between. What conflict there is takes the form of sporadic direct violence and heavily institutionalized structural violence, linked to the caste system.[19]

(4) There is only one China so the problem has not arisen. But China has maintained a high level of cohesion for the last 2200 years – a considerable achievement even if it has been marred by a warlordism that has not quite plumbed the depths of warlordism in Europe.[20] As in India, the remarkable fact is the stability of the system.

(5) There is only one Japan and it is remarkably cohesive today, although that cohesiveness is only about a century old. Some aspects of relations before then might indicate what would happen if there were more than one Japan in the world-system. Two Japans, each of them economically, militarily and politically expansionist, trying to capture the other as a resource or at least as a periphery, might create an intolerable situation. It would be similar to combination (1) with occidental, expansionist countries trying to make peripheries out of competing centres which they have chosen to regard as evil.

That concludes the first exercise in intra-civilizational relations. The key danger zone is very clear: occidental civilization in the expansion mode. One reason why is that the nation-states, which is itself a product, a construction coming out of that civilization, is a marvellous instrument for the type of relations already embedded in that particular civilizational code. Expansionist in its inclination, identifying expansion with progress, heading for a crisis of its own construction, inspired by simplistic theories about how to expand, inconsiderate to nature, eager to expand its periphery by conquering other peoples, thereby elevating its own kind, wholesale, into the centre, and driven either by occidental gods (e.g. Yahweh, God the Father, Allah) or by such secular versions as nationalism; all of this somehow cohering as one great implementation of occidental cosmology. Since the Occident has been relatively successful in bringing this construction to the periphery through colonialism and then, even more significantly, through deep neo-colonialism, there is little doubt that much of this characterizes the world in general. The Occident exports its self-destructive inclination.

At the other end of the spectrum is another danger zone – Japan. The danger stems from the same civilizational characteristics: of feeling they are a chosen people (in the Occident this is particularly pronounced in the Jews, with their dream of the promised land, and also in such countries as Germany, South Africa, the Soviet Union and the United States). Moreover, the Japanese tend to regard other parts of the world as a periphery or as a resource. It is not surprising that a major war of this century, the Pacific War, should have been between Japan and the United States.

In between, then, are the other three categories. In my view they are considerably less dangerous for three very different reasons. In the Chinese and Hindu cases there are no competitors. But there is more to it than that. In the Chinese case barbarians might not even be worth fighting because they are inferior – all the Chinese have to do is to maintain a credible deterrent through highly defensive defence measures. In the Hindu case, war may not be worthwhile since Hinduism is already at the centre of the religious universe, the richest of all religions found in human society. And the others, as I have mentioned, with all their differences, might have 'live and let live' as a basic doctrine.

Let us now pursue these ideas further, looking at inter-civilizational relations.

(6) This is, of course, the long history of occidental penetration into what it considers to be its periphery, both in the Greco-Roman period and in the modern period, the age of Western imperialism. Some of this activity may be taken to prove that the balance-of-power theory cannot be that wrong: most of the indigenous peoples were and are simply too weak to stand up against the occidental onslaught, and consequently end up peripheralized and/or exterminated, as happened in large parts of the Americas. However, simple logic informs us that from the possible validity of the statement that an imbalance of power does not lead to peace (in any conceivable interpretation of that word), it does not necessarily follow that balance of power does lead to peace.

It should be noticed that the other two categories here, occidental civilization in contraction and Buddhist civilization, present us with alternative versions. The manorial and feudal constructions typical of the Middle Ages have been absorbed into the equally typical construction of occidentalism in the expansion mode in the modern period of the nation-states. What can be said, however, is that the process has taken a remarkably long time, and is certainly not yet completed. There may not have been much military resistance, but there was considerable resistance on cultural, economic and political levels.[21] And the same applies to Buddhist civilization; perhaps precisely because of its non-violent doctrine it was not beaten, and because of its ability to withdraw into the *saṅgha* (i.e. into monastic communities, into its pagodas and other temples), Buddhism has shown remarkable resistance to cultural, economic and political absorption. In other words, we are dealing here with more refined inter-civilizational relations. However, it certainly helped that the expanding Occident neither saw the Occident in contraction nor Buddhist civilization as evil; 'savages' sometimes were seen as evil (or at least they were seen to belong to a neighbouring category to evil: the 'primitive').

(7) One of the chosen people in the Occident, in this case the British, conquered India and left behind indelible imprints before being forced to withdraw in 1947, to a large extent by Gandhian non-violence. The Indians, however, absorbed from the conquerors what they wanted, assimilating it into that incredibly rich culture of theirs. The British were as marked by India as the Indians were by Britain. Britain conquered India, but India to a large extent absorbed the British. In fact India may even do this again, serving as a receptacle of the cultures of conquering civilizations and turning out even richer than before. Which is stronger, the civilization that forces others onto the periphery, or the civilization that encompasses others and absorbs them into its own universe? Here we have two distinctly different ways in which civilizations relate to each other: on the one hand, military conquest, economic penetration, cultural imprinting and the imposition of political institutions, and on the other, absorption and enhancement.

(8) This combination is different. When Westerners came to China (and the United States belonged to the West from this point of view), they filled the slot of Western Barbarians; they behaved accordingly, and were perceived accordingly. In no sense does this mean that the Chinese cannot learn from barbarians what they want to learn, as they certainly did from the Northern Barbarians, the Russians. But whereas Indian civilization can absorp and encompass with its almost incredible tolerance, Sinic civilization was greatly wounded by the attack, retaliated and even exorcised (during the Cultural Revolution) the foreign devils. We are here dealing with an asymmetrical relation: the Occident wants to penetrate, even to expand; the Chinese (and their neighbours, the Vietnamese) behave according to the old French adage:

> Cet animal est très méchant;
> quand on l'attaque, il se défend.

The Chinese do not expand outside their traditional domain, which includes Tibet; Westerners seem to regard the world as their domain.

(9) This relation is considerably more symmetrical. China is not out to peripheralize other parts of the world, as Japan is, although it may be argued that for the outer periphery this is only true in the economic sense. It is the inner periphery that is treated in a way relatively similar to the way Western imperialism has tried to treat almost the whole world. The possibility of conflict here is obvious, and it has certainly not been removed by declaring Japan a part not only of the Occident but of the Western Occident. This declaration has little basis in fact, and even if it did, intra-occidental relations in the expansionist mode are not known

historically as being the most peaceful. Rather, these relations are typical of countries with geopolitical designs – the big powers in the Occident when in the expansionist mode (this idea is already built into the definition of a big power) as well as Japan.

(10) In relation to this another aspect of Hindu civilization is brought out very clearly. As I have mentioned, Hindu civilization has exhibited almost incredible tolerance to small occidental groups such as Jews, Christians and Parsees,[22] and even to large occidental groups such as Muslims, for long periods at a time, provided that the different communities do not offend each other religiously. Relations with that important intermediate religious community, the Sikhs have also until recently been marked by much the same tolerance.[23] But this has not always been the case with the indigenous peoples, which indicates that there is in Hindu civilization a dividing line between 'higher' and 'lower' cultures, probably similar to the dividing line between high castes, low castes and the caste-less. As to the latter, this is where Hindu violence shows up, directed downwards rather than outwards, as structural violence rather than direct violence. Buddhism was, like Gandhism, a basic challenge of this aspect of Hindu civilization, and had to be expelled. To put it another way, Hindu civilization is tolerant as long as the caste structure is either left untouched or can be reproduced within a social change, even when change is imposed from the outside. A brahmin remains a brahmin even if his god changes from 'Ram' (the Hindu word for god) to RAM (the computer jargon for random-access memory) and he himself is transformed from priest into computer specialist.

(11) In general it may be said that Sinic civilization is tolerant of small pockets of non-Han people so long as they do not constitute a basic threat. Occidental civilization in the expansion mode, when faced with strangers, wants to peripheralize, absorb, change and 'develop' them, while Sinic civilization is probably more likely to regard them as barbarians but to leave them in peace. The Cultural Revolution was an exception to this rule. Attacks were made on pockets of occidentalism, Buddhists and their temples, and also on indigenous peoples. It may be argued that this was an atypical period, and also that it is relatively easy to comprehend in the light of the long period of Western domination initiated by the opium wars.

(12) The same type of tolerance is not found in Japan. Japan may of course be visited, but to live in Japan, even to settle, presupposes a willingness to become Japanese, at least in such external manifestations as changing one's name to a Japanese name. This will then become one's official name, but even then one will have to sit at the bottom end of the table (as opposed to the visitor who might be very politely seated at the top end, a practice that is usually interpreted as a sign of reverence when it may actually be a sign of distance). And thus it is that Buddhism has become 'Japanized' and, particularly in the form of Zen Buddhism, has become a part of the expansionist nature of Nipponic cosmology.

In the same vein, indigenous peoples have been absorbed and Japanized, to the point of virtual disappearance (e.g. the Ainu).

(13) Two great civilizations, two large groups of humankind – in fact the two largest – even neighbours, and yet so little connection between them. To the Chinese, the Indians are among the Southern Barbarians, yet they are not regarded as dangerous (except when they cross a line drawn in the Himalaya mountains in the autumn of 1962, the MacMahon Line). The Indians are aware of the Chinese, but as the Chinese have not conquered India there is not much basis for contact. Fortunately, neither of these nations is expansionist, for if India had had occidental expansionist ambitions and China had had a Nipponic cosmology we might have had major wars in the Himalayas. It is also interesting to note that this, at least so far, has held true in this century, even though both countries have been equipped with that instrument of occidental expansionism, the nation-state with many of its trimmings, including a large army. But then, why should the Chinese conquer barbarians and the Indians conquer something that is already part of them?

(14) The basic point that has prevented Japan from conquering India is probably a simple geographical circumstance: India is a long way from Japan; and yet Japan did try to invade India (Imphal campaign of 1944), even though *daitōā* did not include India. Had Japan been a border country, logistical difficulties would have been overcome, many high-caste Indians would by now have developed patterns of Japanese efficiency and many Japanese would have been absorbed, even transformed, by the Indian mystique. In a sense India is fortunate: there are two other big countries in Asia, one of them close and non-aggressive, the other one quite aggressive but not close.

(15) But China was not that fortunate. For the Chinese, the Japanese were the Eastern Barbarians, and they behaved accordingly from 1931 and particularly 1937 on. Moreover, the Japanese attack on China was a case of pure, unadulterated aggression with no hint of a defensive purpose. It was similar, although on a smaller scale, to Nazi Germany's attack on the Soviet Union. But even if the Germans had little basis for assuming that the Soviet Union would expand militarily into German territory, they might say that designs for social transformation in a socialist/communist direction were being made in Moscow at the time which would certainly have affected Germany. Japan did not even have this pretext. Whether aggressiveness towards China is still present in Japan, in latent form, it is too early to judge. After all, Japan has only been beaten once, and that wasn't very long ago.[24]

Let us now look at the Figure again and try to summarize what has been said. Exclamation marks have been placed where danger is to be expected, among other reasons because it has been observed in those relations in the past. It will be noted that the exclamation marks all refer to two of the five civilizational categories; occidental in expansion, and Nipponic. There is only one relation without major wars. The

Hindu-Nipponic combination has not been marked as a danger zone but, for the reason of distance rather than innate non-aggressiveness on the side of Japan towards India, there was no real war (but the Japanese did attack India and would have advanced considerably if the war in general had not turned against them). Moreover, the only reason why Japan is not seen as dangerous to itself is also negative: there is only one Japan (hence no warning sign).

It should also be noted that the danger zones are of two different kinds. For the strong civilization, danger zones spell war. Such civilizations struggle to peripheralize each other, or to use each other as resources, or to demarcate the world as a periphery which is forbidden to the other powers in the centre. And then there is a second kind of danger zone. This consists of penetration, sometimes accompanied by absorption and extermination, that is inflicted on the militarily weaker civilization. These may have two defensive strategies, though: to hit back through a system of entirely defensive defence, and/or to retreat, to refuse to be absorbed, and to try to outlive the conquest. This may or may not be successful. At any rate it presupposes a long time perspective, patience, maybe also a conscious policy of non-violence – three characteristics that are absent from occidental expansionist civilization (and, although less so, from Nipponic expansionist civilization).[25]

And thus it is that the centre of the table, in six of the fifteen cells, exhibits a remarkable number of relatively positive relations. Upon further scrutiny more violence can be detected, but not the large-scale violence seen in the eight cells on the margin of the table.

Conclusion: 'what do we do about it?'

Assuming that there is some validity to this type of analysis of the deep structure of the international politics of peace (and also of development, although it has only been spelled out in the first section), the question of course arises; what can we do about it? Is it possible to remove civilizations? Is it possible to change them? These are legitimate questions, worth speculating on.

The candidates for removal would certainly be occidental civilization in the expansionist mode and Nipponic civilization. Of course, this may have the consequence that the remaining three civilizations (actually there are five since three were combined into one group) might acquire some of the characteristics of the expansionist civilizations that have been removed. A group dynamic may be operating here in which civilizations are playing roles relative to each other, and the world is also a system where the attitudes and behaviour of one civilization are determined not only by its own inner code, but also by the attitudes and behaviour of other civilizations. Yet this may work both ways; with the expansionists removed there may be less expansionism to imitate, less nation-state-building to do. Also 'modernization', with its concomitant, a heavy military-bureaucratic-corporate-intelligentsia complex, would be less influential.

A more important consideration is that these civilizations can not be removed. Precisely because of their characteristics they are at the top of the world community of civilizations rather than at the bottom, having themselves conquered many more peaceful civilizations. Had these 'bullies' been at the bottom, and been relatively small, they might have been given the same treatment as is meted out to delinquents: they would have been arraigned into court, a sentence would have been passed and adequate institutionalization would have followed. The process would probably have been better for individual than for general prevention, just as in the theory of punishment of crime in general.

But we are not in that situation. All the big nuclear powers are in this category (India and China are nuclear but not dangerous according to this analysis), and the superpowers are there. The most important industrial nations are also included in the concept. They are not easily removed. Hence we are left with the second question: can civilizations be changed?

The answer to this question is by no means clear, but the question seems to me to be about the most important that can be formulated in peace studies. We know that civilizations do change, in the sense that the deeper aspects, the code, what is here called cosmology, can be said to change (as I have indicated in the first section of this chapter). But this was change caused by a number of historical circumstances, not by voluntary design. We have today no such recipe, or one might even say therapy, for excessively belligerent civilizations to intervene deliberately and bring about the desirable change.

All we can do is to point out that much of this belligerence is rooted in the civilization itself. Change can come about, but probably only by going to the roots. The superficiality of believing that 'a transfer of the ownership of the means of production from private to public hands will liberate humankind from the scourge of war' becomes evident in the light of this type of exploration. Whether in public or private hands, the means of production can still be used for expansionist, occidental aims if this is in the code people in that civilization tend to enact.

Hence, what we need is an analysis that uses civilizations rather than states or economic systems as units. And this should be done in the spirit of seeking solutions rather than making condemnations. Evidently the present analysis does not live up to that goal, but this chapter is certainly not going to be the last word on this vital subject.

Notes

1. See Johan Galtung, Erik Rudeng and Tore Heiestad, 'On the Last 2500 Years in Western History and Some Remarks on the Coming 500', in Peter Burke (ed.), *The New Cambridge Modern History*, Companion Volume XIII (Cambridge: Cambridge University Press, 1979), pp. 318–61, for an elaboration of these concepts and an effort to use them diachronically in Western history.

2. Johan Galtung, 'Violence, Peace and Peace Research', *Essays in Peace Research*, Vol. I (Copenhagen: Ejlers, 1975), pp. 109–39.

3. This idea is developed further in Johan Galtung, 'Social Cosmology and the Concept of Peace', *Essays in Peace Research*, Vol. V (Copenhagen: Ejlers, 1980), pp. 415–36.

4. See Chad Alger, *The United Nations in a Historical Perspective: What We Have Learned About Peace Building* (Tokyo: UNU, 1985).

5. The problem here, it seems, is not merely monotheism but the idea of being in possession of the single valid faith for the whole universe, in other words, singularism *cum* universalism.

6. For an exploration of how this theme is used in order to maintain a conflict, see Johan Galtung, *There Are Alternatives* (Nottingham: Spokesman, 1984), ch. 2.1.

7. For a fine exploration of this theme, see J. E. C. Fuller, *The Conduct of War 1789–1961* (London: Eyre Methuen, 1972), ch. II, 'The Rebirth of Unlimited War'.

8. In other words, I am thinking of the obvious small print on the back of any human rights declaration, the human duties to those who are the presumed guarantors of the rights, the state (meaning the government).

9. See A. H. Westing, *Warfare in a Fragile World* (London: Taylor and Francis, 1980) and Johan Galtung, *Environment, Development and Military Activity* (Oslo: Universitetsforlaget, 1982).

10. This is one of the basic themes explored in Galtung, Rudeng and Heiestad, op. cit.

11. Of course, there is more than one Western code, and the point made is as valid for Marxism/socialism as for liberalism/conservatism/capitalism.

12. See Johan Galtung, 'The Basic Needs Approach', in K. Lederer (ed.), *Human Needs*, (Konigstein: Anton Hain, 1980), pp. 55–125.

13. They are: the world north-west (capitalist), the world north-east (socialist), the world south-west (Third World) and the world south-east (Japan, China and other countries in East and South-East Asia).

14. For one very interesting exploration of this theme, see R. N. Batra, *The Downfall of Capitalism and Communism* (London: Macmillan, 1972), especially chs 8 and 9.

15. This is a part of a large-scale research project on social cosmology and civilization theory.

16. I know perfectly well that this is doing violence to a diversity too rich to accommodate within the present scheme, but I see no other possibility in the present context.

17. And that all other countries, by implication, are aberrations from that norm. For some preliminary explorations of this theme, see Johan Galtung, 'The United States in Indo-China: The Paradigm for a Generation', in *Essays in Peace Research*, Vol. V (Copenhagen: Ejlers, 1980), ch. 8, pp. 219–28.

18. This is a basic theme in Galtung, *There Are Alternatives*, op. cit., ch. 3.2.

19. An unfinished research project that somebody should take up: India as an international system, with a systematic comparison of India with Europe. About the same size in population and territory, yet India is doing so much better with the same order of magnitude of nations, *inter*-nationally, and so much worse *intra*-nationally. They both have a universal religion so it is at least very tempting to relate some of this difference to the tolerance of Hinduism as opposed to Christianity where other teachings are concerned, yet Intolerance to the point of massive structural violence inside the system. I am indebted to K. P. Misra for giving me good opportunities to do some preliminary work on this during my stay as Visiting Professor at the School of International Studies of the Jawaharlal Nehru University in 1971.

20. For an excellent introduction to Chinese history from this angle, see A. Cotterell and D. Morgan, *China, an Integrated Study* (London: Harrap, 1975).

21. Few persons have explored this theme so well as the late Stein Rokkan, e.g. in 'Dimensions of State Formation and Nation-Building: A Possible Paradigm for Research

on Variations Within Europe', in Charles Tilly (ed.), *The Formation of National States in Europe* (Princeton: Princeton University Press, 1976) and his 'Territories, Centers, and Peripheries: Toward a Geoethnic-Geoeconomic-Geopolitical Model of Differentiation Within Western Europe', in Jean Gottmand (ed.), *Centre and Periphery. Spatial Variations in Politics* (Beverly Hills, London: Sage Publications, 1980). I have also found Charles Tilly's 'Stein Rokkan's Conceptual Map of Europe' (University of Michigan, February 1981) very useful.

22. See the chapter on Hinduism in Huston Smith, *The Religion of Man* (New York: Harper and Row, 1958).

23. With the trauma inflicted on that religious community by an act of sacrilege, the invasion of the Golden Temple in Amritsar in 1984, the situation has certainly changed, and probably for generations, even centuries. Imagine a Muslim act of sabotage in St Peter's in Rome!

24. Not exactly this idea, but the potential for renewed violence must have been a basic consideration inspiring the Japanese historian Ienaga Saburo to write his book *The Pacific War 1931–1945* (New York: Pantheon, 1975). (See particularly pp. 135–9, 154–5, 188–9, 200–1.)

25. And yet with all obvious and not so obvious shortcomings, there is also the soft undertone of occidental civilization witnessed, for instance, in the acts of non-violence in the Philippines in 1986, in the civil rights struggle in the United States, etc.

Index

Academy of Science (USSR), 99
accumulation of wealth, 246
affective attitude, 23
affect-led behaviour, 5, 6
Afghanistan, 56, 298
aggression, animal, 19–29
agriculture, 255, 261
aid, foreign, 113, 276, 297–8; *see also*
    arms trade/arms aid
Alcock, N., 245
Allende, Salvador, 248
alliances, 75–6, 222
American Revolution, 57
anarchy, international, 109, 110, 123,
    128
anthropology, 32–45
anti-war movements, 105, 106, 200,
    272, 303–16
    and churches, 303, 311, 313
    and 'just war' dilemma, 309
    grass-roots movements, 310,
        311–312, 314, 320–1
    history of, 303–9
    international non-governmental
        organizations (INGOs), 326–7
    rise of modern movement, 309–11
    transnationalism of, 313–15
    women's, 307, 310, 312, 314
anxiety, 24–5
Aquino, Corazon, 299
Ardrey, R., 247
Arendt, Hannah, 80
Argentina, 226, 232
arms manufacture, 223–4, 225, 227–9
arms race, 7, 10, 210–11
    and 'balance of power' concept,
        147–8
    and erosion of democracy, 151
    and instability, 169–71
    and military industrial complexes,
        150–1
    and 'missile gap' debates, 150
    and 'security', 100–1
    and self-fulfilling assumptions, 167–9
    attempts to de-escalate, 175–6
    combined with negotiations, 144–5
    mathematical models of, 164–7
    pre-1914, 75

technological imperatives in, 176–7,
    265–71
see also weapons
arms trade/arms aid, 153–4, 223,
    224–5, 226–9, 297–8
Aron, Raymond, 210
artefacts, human, 50–1
arts, 54–5
Ashley, Richard K., 89–90
Ashoka, Emperor, 264, 265
Association of South East Asian States
    (ASEAN), 122
assumptions, self-fulfilling, 167–9
Austen, Jane, 54
autonomy of systems, 181–2
Aztecs, 35–6

'balance'/'balance-of-power', concept of,
    128–9, 158, 340
    interpreted as superiority, 146–7
Barbusse, Henri, 180
Barkun, Michael, 38
Baruch, Bernard, 147
Benedict, Ruth, 32
Bergesen, Albert, 87
bipolarity in international politics, 7,
    11–12; *see also* East-West conflict
Bloch, Ernst, 22
Book of Mencius, 260
Boulding, Kenneth, 187
Bradley, P. N., 255
'Brandt-Palme-Thorsson' scenario, 285
Brazil, 36, 40, 221, 226
Bremer, Stuart A., 191
Brown, D. J. J., 43
Brown, Roger, 19–20, 21
Buddhist civilization, 336, 337, 340–1,
    342
Bull, Hedley, 123
Bunge, W., 255–6
Burnham, Philip, 39

Campaign for Nuclear Disarmament
    (CND), 309
Canada, 214
capability, concept of, 207, 209
capitalism, 24, 26, 74, 87, 88
    and world economy, 241–3, 246

Index compiled by Peva Keane